ECO-EFFICIENCY IN INDUSTRY AND SCIENCE

VOLUME 33

More information about this series at http://www.springer.com/series/5887

Ki-Hoon Lee · Stefan Schaltegger
Editors

Accounting for Sustainability: Asia Pacific Perspectives

Springer

Editors
Ki-Hoon Lee
Griffith Business School
Griffith University
Brisbane, Australia

Stefan Schaltegger
Centre for Sustainability Management
Leuphana University of Lüneburg
Lüneburg, Germany

ISSN 1389-6970
Eco-Efficiency in Industry and Science
ISBN 978-3-319-70898-0 ISBN 978-3-319-70899-7 (eBook)
https://doi.org/10.1007/978-3-319-70899-7

Library of Congress Control Number: 2017964499

Printed on acid-free paper

This Springer imprint is published by Springer Nature
The registered company is Springer International Publishing AG
The registered company address is: Gewerbestrasse 11, 6330 Cham, Switzerland

Foreword

Corporate sustainability is today's watchword, and leaders of different countries and corporations throughout the world would do well to bear this in mind when implementing their day-to-day business decisions and operations. Corporate sustainability represents a market shift, and environmental issues such as climate change will alter the market environment. Companies will find that their raw material and energy costs will go up as governments set policies to reduce greenhouse gas emissions. In addition, consumers are becoming more aware of energy consumption, and investors are starting to screen the investment potential of renewables. These shifts in the market will create winners and losers, and companies should act to embrace corporate sustainability issues in order to transform their companies to assist in moving toward sustainable development. The journey to corporate sustainability or sustainable development isn't one that can be traversed over a matter of several years, or even over several decades, but the ideas that underlie it have evolved to the point where we can fully grasp and employ them to transform both business and society.

The book, *Accounting for Sustainability: Asia Pacific Perspectives*, edited by Ki-Hoon Lee and Stefan Schaltegger, is a timely publication in the sense that it conceptualizes the principles of sustainability accounting and corporate sustainability in sectors, countries, and perspectives within the Asia Pacific region, hence demonstrating that even in times of economic turbulence, more and more businesses are embracing these principles. The editors of this book well understand the importance of multi-perspectives and the huge diversity in the Asia Pacific region and the challenges to integrate these perspectives into corporate sustainability management and sustainability accounting practices. Importantly, this book identifies the multifaceted contexts, approaches, and values of sustainability accounting inherent in achieving corporate sustainability in the Asia Pacific region.

This book provides academic and practical advice grounded in cases and examples drawn from a wide array of empirical research and businesses in the context of the Asia Pacific region. Much can be gained by recognizing the contributions that a diversity of perspectives relating to this area can make, providing new ideas and innovative approaches to sustainability accounting, and supporting corporate sustainability management. Professor Lee and Professor Schaltegger lead the development in this field and engage the issues at the frontier of corporate sustainability today. I congratulate them for their notable achievement.

Strategic Planning Division
Hyundai Steel Company,
Seoul, South Korea

Sang-Gyu Kim

Contents

Contributors

Rashid Ameer IPU New Zealand Tertiary Institute, Palmerston North, New Zealand

Wichai Chattinnawat Department of Industrial Engineering, Chiang Mai University, Chiang Mai, Thailand

Joel Corona ORISE post-doctoral research fellow, participating at U.S. EPA Office of Water, Washington, DC, USA

Den Thi Thu Nguyen Graduate School of International Social Sciences, Yokohama National University, Yokohama, Japan

Anthony Dvarskas Stony Brook University, Stony Brook, NY, USA

John Finisdore African Centre for Technology Studies (ACTS), Albert Luthuli Centre for Responsible Leadership – University of Pretoria (ALCRL – UP) and Synegriz, Johannesburg, South Africa

A.D. Nuwan Gunarathne University of Sri Jayewardenepura, Nugegoda, Sri Lanka

Griffith University, Brisbane, Australia

David M. Herold Griffith Business School, Griffith University, Brisbane, Australia

Joël Houdet African Centre for Technology Studies (ACTS), Albert Luthuli Centre for Responsible Leadership – University of Pretoria (ALCRL – UP) and Synegriz, Johannesburg, South Africa

Sadako Inoue University of Marketing and Distribution Sciences, Kobe, Japan

Parichat Jindapanpisan Department of Industrial Engineering, Chiang Mai University, Chiang Mai, Thailand

Amanpreet Kaur Centre for Sustainability Governance (CSG), School of Commerce, University of South Australia Business School, Adelaide, SA, Australia

Il-Woon Kim The University of Akron, Akron, OH, USA

Fawzi Laswad Massey University, Palmerston North, New Zealand

Ki-Hoon Lee Griffith Business School, Griffith University, Brisbane, Australia

Simone Maynard Simone Maynard Consulting, Brisbane, QLD, Australia

Nirmala Nath Massey University, Palmerston North, New Zealand

Kensuke Ogata Osaka City University, Osaka, Japan

Radiah Othman Massey University, Palmerston North, New Zealand

Wei Qian Centre for Sustainability Governance (CSG), School of Commerce, University of South Australia Business School, Adelaide, SA, Australia

Charles Rhodes U.S. EPA Office of Water, Washington, DC, USA

Stefan Schaltegger Centre for Sustainability Management (CSM), Leuphana University Lüneburg, Lüneburg, Germany

Samanthi Senaratne University of Sri Jayewardenepura, Nugegoda, Sri Lanka

Riana Sitawati Dharmaputra Economics Institute, Semarang, Indonesia

Warangkana Suriya Department of Industrial Engineering, Chiang Mai University, Chiang Mai, Thailand

Atsuki Ueda Senshu University, Tokyo, Japan

Lanita Winata Griffith Business School, Griffith University, Gold Coast, Australia

Hiroyuki Yagi Yokohama National University, Yokohama, Japan

Keun-Hyo Yook Busan University of Foreign Studies, Busan, South Korea

About the Editors

Ki-Hoon Lee is professor of business sustainability and sustainable enterprise at Griffith Business School, Australia, where he leads corporate sustainability management research and teaches corporate sustainability and strategy courses at MBA and master's levels. One of his recent books *Business Value and Sustainability* is published by Palgrave (London) in September 2016. He is the chairman of the Environmental and Sustainability Management Accounting Network (EMAN) in the Asia Pacific.

Stefan Schaltegger is professor of management and head of the Centre for Sustainability Management (CSM) and MBA program in sustainability management at Leuphana University Lüneburg, Germany. He is the chairman of Environmental Management Accounting Network (EMAN) Europe and Global.

Abbreviations

A4S	Accounting for Sustainability Project
AAT	Association of Accounting Technicians of Sri Lanka
ACCA	Association of Chartered Certified Accountants UK
AD	Anno Domini
ADB	Asian Development Bank
AMDAL	Analisis mengenai dampak lingkungan/analysis of environmental impact
ANGER	Australian National Greenhouse and Energy Reporting
ANOVA	Analysis of variance
APO	Asian Productivity Organization
ASEAN	Association of Southeast Asian Nations
ASX	Australian Securities Exchange
BC	Before Christ
BTA	Buddhist temple accounting
CASL	Institute of Chartered Accountants of Sri Lanka
CB-SEM	Covariance-based structural equation modeling
CBSL	Central Bank of Sri Lanka
CDSB	Climate Disclosure Standards Board
CEO	Chief executive officer
CFO	Chief financial officer
CICES	Common International Classification of Ecosystem Services
CIMA	Chartered Institute of Management Accountants UK
CMA	Institute of Certified Management Accountants of Sri Lanka
CO2	Carbon dioxide emissions
CPD	Continuous professional development
CRD	Corporate Reporting Dialogue
CSR	Corporate social responsibility
DA	Department of Accounting
DIMO	Diesel and Motor Engineering PLC
Dow	Dow Chemical Company
EBIT	Earnings before interest and tax

ECC	Environmental conservation costs
EMA	Environmental and sustainability management accounting
EPL	Employment protection legislation strictness
ERB	Environmental Reporting Bill
ERP	Enterprise resource planning
ES	Ecosystem services
ESG	Environment, social, and governance
ETS	Emission trading schemes
EU	European Union
FAO	Financing and accounting outsourcing
FEGS-CS	Final Ecosystem Goods and Services Classification System
FES	Final ecosystem services
FR	Financial reporting
FTI	Federation of Thai Industries
G4	Sustainability Reporting Guidelines ver.4
GDP	Global domestic product
GM	General managers
GNP	Global national product
GRI	Global Reporting Initiative
GSSB	Global Sustainability Standards Board
HSP	Hotel sustainable performance
HTMT	Heterotrait-monotrait ratio
IASB	International Accounting Standards Board
IDV	Individualism-collectivism
IES	International Education Standard
IFAC	International Federation of Accountants
IFC	International Finance Corporation
IHRA	Indonesian Hotel and Restaurant Association
IIRC	International Integrated Reporting Council
IoDSA	King Code of Governance Principles for South Africa
IPAL	Instalasi pembuangan air limbah/wastewater disposal installation
IR	Integrated reporting
ISIC	International Standard Industrial Classification
ISO	International Organization for Standardization
IT	Information technology
LTO	Short-/long-term orientation
MA	Millennium Ecosystem Assessment
MAES	Assessment of ecosystems and their services
MAPS	Megatrend analysis and portfolio strategy
MAS	Masculinity/femininity
MEFA	Material and energy flow accounting
MEMA	Monetary environmental and sustainability management accounting
METI	Ministry of Economy, Technology and Industry
MFCA	Material flow cost accounting
MOE	Ministry of Education

MSC	Marine Stewardship Council
NAICS	North American Industry Classification System
NESCS	National Ecosystem Services Classification System
NGO	Nongovernmental organization
NPO	Nonprofit organization
NTFPs	Non-timber forest products
NZ	New Zealand
OECD	Organisation for Economic Co-operation and Development
PABs	Professional accounting bodies
PDCA	Plan-do-check-act
PDI	Power distance index
PEMA	Physical environmental management accounting
PLS	Partial least squares
PSO	Public sector organizations
R&D	Research and development
ROA	Return on assets
SASB	Sustainability Accounting Standards Board
SBSC	Sustainability balanced scorecard
SCC	Social contribution costs
SDGs	Sustainable Development Goals
SEC	Securities and Exchange Commission
SEEA	System of Environmental-Economic Accounting
SEEA-EEA	SEEA Experimental Ecosystem Accounting
SEM	Structural equation modeling
SG&A	Selling, general, and administrative
SIS	Stakeholder information strategy
SME	Small and medium enterprise
SR	Sustainability reporting
SSP	Strategy-structure-performance
SSPA	Supplement for public agencies
SVS	Stakeholder involvement strategy
TEEB	The Economics of Ecosystems and Biodiversity
TNC	The Nature Conservancy
TPI	Thailand Productivity Institute
TQM	Total quality management
USA/US	United States
UAV	Uncertainty avoidance
UGC	University Grants Commission
UK	United Kingdom
UN	United Nations
UNFCCC	United Nations Framework Convention on Climate Change
UNICEF	United Nations Children's Fund
USJ	University of Sri Jayewardenepura
VND	Vietnam dong
WBCSD	World Business Council for Sustainable Development

WCED	World Commission on Environment and Development
WEF	World Economic Forum
WIP	Work in process
XRB	External Reporting Board

List of Figures

List of Tables

Chapter 1
Asia Pacific Perspectives on Accounting for Sustainability: An Introduction

Ki-Hoon Lee and Stefan Schaltegger

Keywords Accounting for sustainability · Sustainability accounting · Asia pacific

1.1 Why Accounting for Sustainability in the Asia Pacific Context?

The interplay between "accounting" and "sustainability" or "sustainable development" has spurred a long-standing debate among academics and practitioners alike for decades. During the last 25 years, networks like the Environmental and Sustainability Management Accounting Network (EMAN) and the Centre for Social and Environmental Accounting Research (CSEAR) have played a central role in building research capacity and promoting this research field. Within this topic, the number of publications and researchers has increased, and corporate and practitioner interest is growing continually, but key challenges are also increasing. On a global scale, most global environmental and social sustainability indicators show a negative trend, reflecting the ever-worsening state of our planet (e.g., IPCC 2014; WWF 2016; Sachs et al. 2017).

Scientific research in various fields such as climate, biodiversity, and marine biology has provided ample evidence about the collective *negative* environmental and social impacts of human and business activities. Notably, due to strong economic development and continuing population growth, in conjunction with drastic

K.-H. Lee (✉)
Griffith Business School, Griffith University, Brisbane, Australia
e-mail: ki-hoon.lee@griffith.edu.au

S. Schaltegger
Centre for Sustainability Management (CSM), Leuphana University Lüneburg, Lüneburg, Germany
e-mail: schaltegger@uni.leuphana.de

K.-H. Lee, S. Schaltegger (eds.), *Accounting for Sustainability: Asia Pacific Perspectives*, Eco-Efficiency in Industry and Science 33,
https://doi.org/10.1007/978-3-319-70899-7_1

increases in overconsumption, the demands for natural resources, especially increasing demands for fossil-fuel-based energy, are rapidly expanding in the Asia Pacific region (Lee and Min 2014). The heavy reliance on fossil fuels has degraded the ecosystem and the air quality, has reduced the supply of clean water, and has created significant health problems and social upheavals. The impacts of climate change and the depletion of natural resources are becoming visible in various ways in the Asia Pacific region (Lee 2014). Despite the popularity and development of environmental, social, and sustainability accounting during the past three decades (e.g., Bebbington and Larrinaga 2014; Schaltegger et al. 2013b), scholars note that there is still very limited academic and practical investigation in the context of Asia (Lee et al. 2017; Herzig et al. 2012).

While it is without doubt difficult to define and measure what sustainable development means in an organizational context in practice (e.g., Gray and Milne 2004), this book aims to discuss this challenge for the Asia Pacific region. In an Asian context in particular, the contributors to this book investigate "why" and "how" companies and industries use accounting tools and approaches to improve corporate sustainability management, with a focus on local and regional contextual and dynamic issues.

Many companies in the Asia Pacific region are already facing serious resource constraints linked to water scarcity, loss of biodiversity, soil erosion, etc., and various sustainability challenges contribute to increasing material costs, energy costs, and commodity prices. Currently, the Asia Pacific region is consuming more resources than its ecosystems can replenish, threatening the sustainability of the region (Lee 2014). In the famous Brundtland Report (WCED 1987), sustainable development has been broadly defined as development which meets the needs of the present without compromising the ability of future generations to meet their own needs. At a firm level, corporate sustainability has multifaceted meanings and implications, including corporate social responsibility, corporate environmental management, and corporate sustainability management. More importantly, corporate sustainability is *contextual* and *dynamic*. It is thus important to closely understand and develop corporate sustainability management and accounting in the cultural, economic, social, and ecological contexts within the Asia Pacific region. Companies in this region are increasingly challenged to integrate social and ecological issues as economically as possible and to contribute to the sustainable development of their economies and their societies (Schaltegger and Burritt 2005; Lee and Vachon 2016). The Asia Pacific region covers a huge geographical area and is highly diverse. Obviously the challenges of environmental, social, and economic sustainability issues are global, but they require local action and local implementation. Due to the contextual differences and dynamics in institutions, regulations, social and cultural values, and diversities, there is no single sustainability solution which can fit all nations, industries, companies, and actors in the region. In the research for, and practice of, developing accounting for sustainability, we must acknowledge the Asia Pacific area's specific regional and local contextual differences and diversities, and we must understand how to embrace global sustainability challenges locally.

1.2 Competing Views on Sustainability Accounting

As corporate leaders and decision makers become more aware of an array of sustainability challenges, the companies they control have sought a range of accounting and assurance practices to identify and manage sustainability-related risks and opportunities (Bebbington et al. 2014; Schaltegger and Burritt 2010; Lee et al. 2017). Over the past four decades, sustainability accounting has evolved, so that ways in which accounting tools and systems can contribute to the support of corporate sustainability management have become better understood (Burritt and Schaltegger 2010; Unerman and Chapman 2014). Two widely recognized schools of thought have developed, reflecting two different perspectives on how accounting and sustainability are related: the critical view which focuses on transparency and reporting, creating accountability for misconduct, and the pragmatic perspective which emphasizes those management decisions that support and improve the sustainability performance of companies. Most researchers in the field agree that conventional accounting is an important driver of unscrupulous and declining global developments and that corporate misconduct is a key driver of a lack in sustainability (e.g., Maunders and Burritt 1991). Differences, however, exist in understanding of what role the development of accounting and reporting approaches could be in the context of sustainable development.

The "critical perspective school" emphasizes the limits of the usefulness of accounting in general for the purpose of recording information and contributing to sustainable development at a firm level. Sustainability is a societal vision, and thus in this view cannot be pursued or achieved by companies, as the problems are too complex and too large for any organization (e.g., Gray 2010). While social and environmental accounting and reporting are seen as being important areas, their purpose could be only to create transparency about the key problems companies cause. Sustainability should not be used by companies as a term, as it blurs the debate rather than representing what companies can achieve. The critical perspective considers that sustainability accounting plays a very limited role in supporting corporate sustainability and will disappear in the future (e.g., Milne and Gray 2013). The important empirical contributions of critical scholars highlight the failures of companies to achieve high sustainability aims and propose that environmental disclosure is used as a substitute for poor performance (e.g., Cho et al. 2012).

The "pragmatic school" is more management and solution oriented and focuses on how possible solutions could be developed and implemented in corporate practice. It adopts a pragmatic approach, linking sustainability accounting and corporate management practice (Baker and Schaltegger 2015), including inter- and transdisciplinary approaches and projects (Schaltegger et al. 2013a). The pragmatic perspective views sustainability accounting from a management information perspective, providing a set of tools which support corporate managers when taking sustainability into consideration (Burritt et al. 2002). This perspective highlights the role of management accounting in improving corporate sustainability performance (Burritt and Schaltegger 2010). Pragmatic scholars' key empirical analyses show examples (e.g., Herzig et al. 2012; Lee 2012; Gunarathne and Lee 2015) and performance improvements which have been achieved through the implementation of innovative accounting and reporting practices (e.g., Hörisch et al. 2015; Lee 2017; Qian and Schaltegger 2017).

Both schools of thoughts have demonstrated that measuring and reporting sustainability issues remain a challenge because of information uncertainty; the innovation needed to overcome tensions between economic, environmental, and social goals; and the large influence of external and organizational factors (Passetti et al. 2014). Given the pressing sustainability problems, a solution-oriented perspective and better interplay between these two schools of thought are sorely needed. While the critical perspective highlights problems and reasons for current failures, the pragmatic perspective develops approaches which need to be tested and further developed to find effective solutions.

1.3 Asia Pacific Views and Definitions of Sustainability Accounting

To begin our journey in exploring Asia Pacific perspectives on accounting for sustainability, we asked all of the authors who are contributing to this book to send us their views on "sustainability accounting" or "accounting for sustainability." Table 1.1 shows that scopes, ranges, foci, and approaches vary. Some authors use the Brundtland Report's broad definition of sustainable development to explain their approach to sustainability accounting, some refer to conventional accounting, and others take a pragmatic perspective on accounting for sustainability.

The different views about what sustainable development is or could be and how it relates to sustainability accounting reveal some key difficulties in this area: the huge diversity, the spread of different goals subsumed under "sustainability," and the challenge to integrate the perspectives.

1.4 Motivations for This Book: *Accounting for Sustainability: Asia Pacific Perspectives*

Despite the long-standing development of sustainability accounting in management and accounting research and practice, no clear and general answer exists as to "why" and "how" sustainability accounting is applied in the Asia Pacific region. A general answer may in fact be impossible, as the Asia Pacific region is characterized by huge geographical, historical, cultural, environmental, and social diversity. As no single sustainability management and accounting approach exists that fits all companies, it becomes essential to understand contingencies and contextual influences as to why and how companies apply sustainability accounting in different cultural,

Table 1.1 Views and definitions of sustainability accounting or accounting for sustainability

Authors	Definitions and/or descriptions of sustainability accounting or accounting for sustainability
Author(s) 1	Put simply, sustainability accounting is the language of sustainable businesses
Author(s) 2	Accounting for sustainability provides a platform for organizations to reflect their thinking and actions on social, economic, and environmental challenges. This makes accounting professionals responsive to the long-term sustainability of a business and its relationship to the stakeholders and the supply chain
Author(s) 3	Corporate sustainability accounting is a process to identify, measure, integrate, and report economic, environmental, and social information of an entity for the purpose of internal management decision making and discharging accountability to external stakeholders
Author(s) 4	The self-regulating mechanism aims to report the fulfillment of organizational activities, and their impacts on society and the environment, and to disclose the direction and totality of all business planning
Author(s) 5	Sustainability accounting transforms the rather abstract principle of "sustainable development," which refers to a "development that satisfies the needs of the present without compromising the ability of future generations to satisfy theirs," into a structured and measurable and thus quantifiable approach
Author(s) 6	Sustainability accounting is a system of measurement and reporting for the preservation of the physical resources and the stewardship of the natural resources such as water and air. This system should incorporate a cost-benefit analysis including social, economic, and financial factors
Author(s) 7	Sustainability accounting is the provision and analysis of sustainability-related financial and nonfinancial information to the stakeholders. This information relates to organizations' actions and reactions in monitoring their use of the financial, natural, and social capital
Author(s) 8	Accounting for sustainability is an indispensable infrastructure which promotes harmonized development between economy, environment, and society globally, as one system
Author(s) 9	Sustainability is the means for humans to prosper within the natural resource limitations of the global environment, allowing that future generations may also prosper. In striving to make complex human systems sustainable, we will need clear definitions, metrics, and targets – so sustainability accounting will be useful as an early step in this effort and will contribute further as we refine our accounting measures and management targets over time

Note: We list authors anonymously to avoid any unnecessary national effects or biases to readers

industrial, and geographical settings. This book *Accounting for Sustainability: Asia Pacific Perspectives* therefore intends to open the discussion of "pragmatic perspectives" in sustainability accounting to support corporate decision makers in improving corporate sustainability management practices at organizational and industry levels in the Asia Pacific region.

To improve our understanding and knowledge about accounting for sustainability in the Asia Pacific region, it is important to examine a range of corporate and organizational practices related to sustainability accounting. It is also important that we understand the roles of management accounting in supporting corporate sustainability management in the Asia Pacific region. The book therefore raises a range of questions including: How do regional and national characteristics, in particular institutional or cultural contexts, influence the approaches and practices of sustainability accounting for companies operating in the Asia Pacific region? How and to what extent does (national) culture affect sustainability accounting practices in the Asia Pacific region? How does sustainability accounting support measures of corporate sustainability performance in different Asia Pacific regions? How and why do companies adopt and use sustainability accounting for corporate sustainability management implementation, and how do they respond to sustainability issues in different Asia Pacific countries? What is the relationship between social and environmental performance and economic performance in the Asia Pacific region? When adopting and implementing corporate sustainability management, what role does sustainability accounting play in supporting corporate decision making? What are the risks of, and opportunities for, sustainability reporting in the Asia Pacific region? Particularly for developing and newly industrialized countries where the improvement of the economic welfare situation has been emphasized for the last decades, the question arises, how can corporate sustainability management practices be improved and what role can sustainability accounting play?

This book is structured in 4 parts and 12 chapters. Part I, "National Culture and Sustainability Accounting in the Asia Pacific Region," identifies and addresses regional and national contexts affecting the adoption and implementation of sustainability accounting. Part II, "Environmental and Sustainability Performance Measurement and Management," collects empirical cases and evidence on managements' use of environmental and sustainability performance measures. The collected cases and empirical studies demonstrate innovative sustainability accounting approaches to reduce the negative impacts of companies and to improve sustainability performances. Part III, "Environmental Management Accounting: Material Flows, Cost Accounting, and Business Cases," provides corporate cases of material flow cost accounting and corporate environmental management systems and how they contribute to environmental protection and social improvements. Part IV, "Sustainability Reporting: Challenges and Approaches," reflects the current debate on sustainability reporting, in particular the functional practices between the International Integrated Reporting Council (IIRC) and the Global Reporting Initiative (GRI).

This book seeks to initiate and motivate further solution-oriented, pragmatic research in sustainability accounting and corporate sustainability management in order to better understand how accounting can more effectively contribute to sustainable development. This book aims to provide insights into new approaches to enhance corporate sustainability management and corporate practices in sustainability accounting in the Asia Pacific region.

References

Baker M, Schaltegger S (2015) Pragmatism and new directions in social and environmental accountability research. Account Audit Account J 28(2):263–294

Bebbington J, Larrinaga C (2014) Accounting and sustainable development: an exploration. Account Organ Soc 39:395–413

Bebbington J, Unerman J, O'Dwyer B (eds) (2014) Sustainability accounting and accountability, 2nd edn. Routledge, Abingdon

Burritt R, Schaltegger S (2010) Sustainability accounting and reporting: fad or trend? Account Audit Account J 23(7):829–846

Burritt R, Hahn T, Schaltegger S (2002) Towards a comprehensive framework for environmental management accounting. Links between business actors and environmental management accounting tools. Aust Account Rev 12(2):39–50

Cho C, Guidry R, Hageman A, Patten D (2012) Do actions speak louder than words? An empirical investigation of corporate environmental reputation. Account Organ Soc 37(1):14–25

Gray R (2010) Is accounting for sustainability actually accounting for sustainability … and how would we know? An exploration of narratives of organisations and the planet. Account Organ Soc 35(1):47–62

Gray R, Milne M (2004) Towards reporting on the triple bottom line: mirages, methods and myths. In: Henriques A (ed) Triple bottom line: does it all add up? Assessing the sustainability of business and CSR. Earthscan, London, pp 70–80

Gunarathne N, Lee K-H (2015) Environmental Management Accounting (EMA) for environmental management and organizational change: an eco-control approach. J Account Organ Chang 11(3):362–383

Herzig C, Viere T, Schaltegger S, Burritt R (2012) Environmental management accounting. Cases of south-east Asian companies. Routledge, Abingdon

Hörisch J, Ortas E, Schaltegger S, Alvarez I (2015) Environmental effects of sustainability management tools: an empirical analysis of large companies. Ecol Econ 120(December):241–249

IPCC (2014) Climate change 2014: mitigation of climate change. In: Intergovernmental Panel on Climate Change (ed) Fifth assessment report: Intergovernmental Panel on Climate Change

Lee K-H (2012) Carbon accounting for supply chain management in the automobile industry. J Clean Prod 36:83–93

Lee K-H (2014) Globalization, green management and climate change in the Asia-Pacific economy. J Asia Pac Bus 15(2):101–104

Lee K-H (2017) Does size matter? Evaluating corporate environmental disclosure in the Australian Mining and Metal Industry: a combined approach of quantity and quality measurement. Bus Strateg Environ 26(2):209–223

Lee K-H, Min B (2014) Globalization and carbon constrained global economy: a fad or a trend? J Asia Pac Bus 15(2):105–121

Lee K-H, Vachon S (2016) Business value and sustainability. Palgrave, London

Lee K-H, Park B, Song H, Yook K (2017) The value relevance of environmental audits: evidence from Japan. Bus Strateg Environ 26(5):609–625

Maunders KT, Burritt RL (1991) Accounting and ecological crisis. Account Audit Account J 4(3):9–26

Milne MJ, Gray R (2013) W(h)ither ecology? The triple bottom line, the global reporting initiative, and corporate sustainability reporting. J Bus Ethics 118(1):13–29

Passetti E, Cinquini L, Marelli A, Tenucci A (2014) Sustainability accounting in action: lights and shadows in the Italian context. Br Account Rev 46(3):295–308

Qian W, Schaltegger S (2017) Revisiting carbon disclosure and performance: legitimacy and management views. Br Account Rev 49(4):365–379

Sachs J, Schmidt-Traub G, Kroll C, Durand-Delacre D, Teksoz K (2017) SDG index and dashboards report 2017. Bertelsmann Stiftung and Sustainable Development Solutions Network, New York

Schaltegger S, Burritt R (2005) Corporate sustainability. In: Folmer H, Tietenberg T (eds) The international yearbook of environmental and resource economics. Edward Elgar, Cheltenham, pp 185–232

Schaltegger S, Burritt R (2010) Sustainability accounting for companies: catchphrase or decision support for business leaders? J World Bus 45(4):375–384

Schaltegger S, Beckmann M, Hansen E (2013a) Transdisciplinarity in corporate sustainability. Mapping the field. Bus Strateg Environ 22(4):219–229

Schaltegger S, Gibassier D, Zvezdov D (2013b) Is environmental management accounting a discipline? A bibliometric literature review. Meditari Account Res 21(1):4–31

Unerman J, Chapman C (2014) Academic contributions to enhancing accounting for sustainable development. Account Organ Soc 39:385–394

World Commission on Environment and Development (1987) Our common future. Oxford University Press, Oxford

World Wildlife Fund (2016) Living planet report 2016. WWF International, Gland

Part I
National Culture and Sustainability Accounting in the Asia Pacific Region

Chapter 2
Cultural Relevance in Environmental and Sustainability Management Accounting (EMA) in the Asia-Pacific Region: A Link Between Cultural Values and Accounting Values Towards EMA Values

Ki-Hoon Lee and David M. Herold

Abstract Despite the increasing popularity of environmental and sustainability management accounting (EMA) in corporate sustainability management, researchers in the sustainability accounting and sustainability management field neglect the importance and the relevance of national culture and its effect on the level of implementation of sustainability accounting and management practices. Yet, to our knowledge, there is no recent study of how national culture affects corporate environmental and sustainability management accounting practices in the different nations where they operate. In order to provide new insights into the link between national culture and EMA practice, we adopt Gray's (1988) Abacus 24(1):1–15 theory of cultural relevance in national accounting systems. In brief, Gray proposed a framework to explain how national culture affects national accounting system using Hofstede's (1986) The cultural context of accounting: accounting and culture. Paper presented to annual conference of the American Accounting Association, New York culture dimensions. An understanding of the national culture and its effect on the adoption and implementation of EMA can help us to improve the relevance of EMA practice and implementation in different countries. Based on Gray's (1988) Abacus 24(1):1–15 framework, we develop the link between national cultural values and EMA values. As original contributions to sustainability accounting, we propose four EMA value dimensions (symbolic versus action, reactionary versus responsible, voluntary versus transparent, and integration versus differentiation).

Keywords Cultural relevance · Accounting values · Corporate sustainability · Sustainability accounting · Environmental and sustainability management accounting · Asia Pacific region

K.-H. Lee (✉) · D.M. Herold
Griffith Business School, Griffith University, Brisbane, Australia
e-mail: ki-hoon.lee@griffith.edu.au; d.herold@griffith.edu.au

K.-H. Lee, S. Schaltegger (eds.), *Accounting for Sustainability: Asia Pacific Perspectives*, Eco-Efficiency in Industry and Science 33,
https://doi.org/10.1007/978-3-319-70899-7_2

2.1 Introduction

Environmental sustainability, together with the adoption of sustainability performance measurement systems, is strongly related to sustainable development, which is defined by the World Commission on Environment and Development (1987, p. 8) as "development that meets the needs of the present without compromising the ability of future generations to meet their own needs". The Asia-Pacific region is characterised by diverse climate, ecosystem and social-historical conditions (Hofstede 2007). It contains more than 60% of the global population, accounts for one-third of global GDP and is a growing emitter of greenhouse gases (Lee 2014). One of the major drivers of this development is the rapid industrialisation occurring in Asian countries, and the related global resource extraction, which has a reputation for damaging the natural environment, particularly in China and India (Owen and Kemp 2012). Asia has the highest absolute rate of resource extraction, and has increased its global share from 40% in 1980 to 60% in 2011. In contrast, the countries of Oceania, dominated by Australia, account only for 3% of extraction worldwide (SERI/WU 2014). These combined effects of globalisation and climate change threaten the environment and ecosystem throughout the region. Since a decrease in the usage of fossil resources in the Asia-Pacific is rather unlikely, sustainable development is increasingly becoming a strategic priority for both countries and individual companies (KPMG 2014; Yasunari et al. 2013; Lee 2017).

Over the last two decades, environmental and sustainability management accounting (EMA) has developed significantly as a managerial decision-support tool when organisations develop environmental and/or sustainability management strategies (Schaltegger et al. 2013). EMA is viewed as a body of accounting practices that acts as the interface between environmental and sustainability management strategies, and management accounting (Bennett et al. 2002). It provides physical and monetary information regarding various environmental aspects for both internal and external decision-makers. This leads to two types of EMA systems: physical EMA (PEMA) and monetary EMA (MEMA) systems (Burritt et al. 2002b). EMA encompasses a wide array of accounting tools and techniques used for internal decision-making, such as accounting for energy, material flow cost accounting, environmental capital budgeting, life-cycle analysis, carbon accounting and waste accounting. These EMA tools are increasingly being adapted for use by specific organisations.

Despite the increasing popularity of EMA in corporate sustainability management, researchers in the sustainability accounting and sustainability management field have tended to neglect the importance and the relevance of national culture and its effect on the level of implementation in sustainability accounting and management practices. National culture is considered to be a powerful institutional factor that affects the national accounting system as well as accounting value at both the individual and organisational levels. The link between culture and accounting values has been elaborated by Gray (1988), who applied Hofstede's (1986) cultural dimensions and values into accounting culture and values. Although Gray's (1988) work was at the conceptual level, many scholars in the accounting discipline have adopted or tested it to explore cultural relevance and accounting systems in particular contexts.

Over the last two decades, two predominant areas in which the influence of culture on accounting has been studied are financial reporting and management control systems. For example, Chanchani and MacGregor (1999) provide a summary of the literature on culture and financial reporting under a chronology of pre-Gray (1988) literature, Gray (1988) literature, and post-Gray (1988) literature. Using an extensive literature review, Harrison and McKinnon (1999) examined the impact of culture on management control systems. They found several omitted cultural dimensions and differential intensity of cultural norms and values. To test the influence of culture on accountants' application of financial reporting rules, Tsakumis (2007) applied Gray's framework and its hypotheses in Greece and the United States, but found no support for Gray's hypotheses. More recently, Salter et al. (2013) tested Gray's framework with a focus on accounting conservatism using panel data analysis, and found that accounting conservatism is greater in countries with more conservative and accounting values. Although critiques of Hofstede have appeared periodically in the accounting literature (e.g. Baskerville 2003; Doupnik and Tsakumis 2004; Salter et al. 2013), these have not curtailed the attractiveness of his cultural dimensions and applications.

Since the influence of the work of Hofstede (1983, 1986) as well as that of Gray (1988) has impacted accounting research, we adopt this work to advance our understanding and knowledge in order to explore the relationship between culture and EMA value. In this chapter, we focus on EMA to explore the links between cultural relevance and accounting value in the Asia Pacific region.

This chapter is organised as follows. First, we introduce corporate sustainability management and EMA in Asia-Pacific and discuss its challenges. Then we review relevant literature on national culture and EMA to develop a theoretical foundation and related propositions. We discuss EMA values from cultural values perspective in the following section. We end with a conclusion and directions on future research.

2.2 Corporate Sustainability Management and EMA in Asia-Pacific

The adoption of sustainability management practices to reduce the ecological footprints of companies is a starting point for tackling sustainability challenges. These practices become visible through technical solutions, the publication of corporate sustainability reports and the integration of sustainability performance measures – in short, the application of EMA tools. More importantly, companies should consider why and how these sustainability performance measurements, approaches and tools will be adopted, and to what extent EMA will be integrated into their operations. Sustainability accounting has its roots in traditional accounting practices: management accounting involves internal organisational practices that assist in the management of an organisation and financial reporting provides a financial account of organisational performance (Lodhia and Hess 2014).

Traditional financial accounting has been criticised heavily for not facilitating an understanding of corporate sustainability and environmental impacts. Thus sustainability accounting can be regarded as an extension of, or modification to, traditional financial or management accounting (Gray 1992; Lamberton 2005). The main role of sustainability accounting would be to develop or further modify traditional accounting principles to help management foster the sustainable development of a company. However, different conclusions are drawn from the discussion that exists about the adoption of corporate sustainability practices and about the best way to implement these practices. For this reason, the role of accounting for sustainability is interpreted in various ways by corporate management, and is reflected in the different implementation approaches of companies.

2.2.1 The Framework and Tools of EMA

EMA can be regarded as the generation and analysis of monetary and physical information in order to support internal environmental management processes (Schaltegger and Burritt 2000; Burritt and Schaltegger 2010). It is complementary to the conventional financial and management accounting approach, with the aim being to develop a broad set of approaches and principles that provide insight into the physical flows and costs that assist in the identification and allocation of environment and sustainability-related costs (Frost and Wilmshurst 2000). While sustainability accounting generally is discussed in a broader sense, Burritt et al. (2002b) developed a multidimensional framework of EMA with specific environmental measurements, approaches and tools, which they relate to different dimensions. In particular, their framework considers the distinctions between four dimensions (see Fig. 2.1):

1. *Physical versus monetary classifications (MEMA versus PEMA).* Monetary environmental management accounting (MEMA) reflects the environmental impact affecting the company, measured in monetary value, while physical environmental management accounting (PEMA) reflects the impact of an organisation's activity on the environmental systems, measured in physical value.
2. *Past and future timeframes.* These timeframes focus on signals or the meaning behind EMA tools, which can be divided into the measurement of past-oriented transactions or a prediction of the impact of possible future transactions.
3. *Short- and long-term planning periods.* This dimension highlights the length of planning periods and distinguishes between long-term strategic planning to solve environmental issues and short-term transactions – for example, a reaction from management to satisfy shareholders.
4. *Ad hoc versus routine information-gathering.* This further distinguishes routinely generated information (general accounting systems that routinely produce information for management) and ad hoc information (specific accounting tools that produce information on a 'needs' basis for particular decisions).

		Environmental Management Accounting (EMA)			
		Monetary Environmental Management Accounting (MEMA)		Physical Environmental Management Accounting (PEMA)	
		Short Term Focus	Long Term Focus	Short Term Focus	Long Term Focus
Past Oriented	Routinely generated information	Environmental cost accounting	Environmentally induced capital expenditure and revenues	Material and energy flow accounting	Environmental (or natural) capital impact accounting
Past Oriented	Ad hoc information	Ex post assessment of relevant environmental costing decisions	Environmental life cycle (and target) costing & Post investment assessment of individual projects	Ex post assessment of short term environmental impacts (e.g. of a site product)	Life cycle inventories - Post investment assessment of physical environmental investment appraisal
Future Oriented	Routinely generated information	Monetary environmental operational budgeting (flows) & Monetary environmental capital budgeting (stocks)	Environmental ling term financial planning	Physical environmental budgeting (flows and stocks)	Long term physical environmental planning
Future Oriented	Ad hoc information	Relevant environmental costing	Monetary environmental project investment appraisal & Environmental life cycle budgeting and target pricing	Relevant environmental impacts	Physical environmental investment appraisal & Life cycle analysis of specific project

Fig. 2.1 EMA tools and dimensions (Source: Burritt et al. 2002b, p. 43)

The EMA dimensions and the respective tools are important, as they provide a platform from which to allocate specific measurements tools and approaches to management and cultural behaviour. Moreover, according to Burritt and colleagues (2002a), EMA can be regarded to consist of two parts: (a) an external component, which is the formal reporting of sustainability and environmental issues, and (b) specific internal measurement tools through the framework of EMA, which can be linked to particular management approaches.

2.2.2 *Implementation of EMA: Differences and Challenges*

As part of EMA, Schaltegger and Burritt (2010) argue that sustainability accounting can also be divided into an internal and an external component. The internal component represents the management of sustainability issues, often referred to as sustainability management, while the external component represents the formal reporting of these issues, referred to as sustainability reporting. It is within these broad parameters that the practice of sustainability accounting has been analysed in the academic literature.

The underlying rationale for adopting a corporate sustainability approach is arguably legitimacy. Sustainability accounting and reporting can be regarded as the organisational response to the management and reporting of a company's social and environmental issues to legitimise actions by the business through a social contract (Hrasky 2011). Schaltegger and Burritt (2010) list six specific reasons for the adoption of sustainability accounting, three of which are related directly to legitimacy to gain the 'licence to operate', including greenwashing, industry pressure, and legislative and stakeholder pressure. Greenwashing is described as a tool to support communicative activities without being involved in substantial sustainability activities, while industry and stakeholder pressure can be described as a reaction to immediate concerns from shareholders. The remaining three reasons – corporate responsibility, sustainability as a business case and self-regulation – require proactive involvement. Corporate responsibility needs accountable information and sustainability accounting can help to achieve accountability. Moreover, sustainability can also help to justify a business case, and could result in cost savings or incremental revenue (a win–win situation in terms of environmental/social and financial sustainability). The last proactive reason is self-regulation, where a company commits itself to fulfil certain requirements to avoid further mandatory regulations.

These different reasons for adopting EMA lead to different degrees of implementation. Kim et al. (2007) and Hrasky (2011) discuss the different accounting approaches from a legitimacy perspective, and distinguish between a symbolic management approach and a behavioural or action-oriented approach. A symbolic management approach may be characterised by rhetoric statements without any meaningful outcome, while behavioural management requires substantial implementation and execution of accounting measures. These two extremes also apply to EMA activities, as symbolic EMA can be used for corporate 'greenwashing', while a strategic implementation of EMA tools can be regarded as behavioural management. Schaltegger and Burritt (2015) further describe the behavioural management approach and divide corporate action for sustainability into a reactionary and a responsible approach. A company's reactionary approach is characterised by a short-term view and sees sustainability engagement and accounting outside the core business and as a cost-driver. A responsible behaviour in EMA, however, is characterised by an implementation of the right EMA tools to manage and control sustainable development (Schaltegger and Burritt 2015).

The degree of implementation is also characterised by the voluntary nature of EMA practices within companies. Companies have the freedom to follow sustainability guidelines that best fit their interests, or even to choose to ignore any EMA practices. In other words, companies that adopt a purely voluntary approach represent an extreme end of the scale, in contrast to a fully accountable and transparent EMA perspective. According to Herzig and Schaltegger (2011), a fully accountable and transparent perspective is characterised by a strategic approach under the condition of the actual implementation of relevant EMA tools. These tools are used to collect relevant internal EMA information in order to inform internal and external stakeholders with comprehensible and comparable data.

To further explain the degree of implementation of EMA activities, Linnenluecke and Griffiths (2010) offer a distinction between companies that have fully integrated sustainability values and those where sustainability values are not shared by all units and members in the organisation. The 'integration' perspective is characterised by a consensus among employees around the set of shared sustainability values promoted by top management. A further condition for a full integration is that all units are involved and all members share or embrace similar attitudes towards corporate sustainability and the adoption of EMA tools. The opposite of the 'integration' perspective is the 'differentiation' perspective, which is characterised by different attitudes and values throughout the company. According to Linnenluecke and Griffiths (2010), the reason why the sustainability values are not fully disseminated throughout the entire company can range from physical distance to demographic differences, and from non-involvement by top management to individual resistance to organisational change.

These degrees of implementation reflect the broad principles of EMA. However, these principles do not reflect or describe actual EMA tools that can be used to measure sustainability and environmental performance of processes or services. The EMA framework provides a variety of tools and approaches to measure corporate sustainability performance. We argue that the degree of EMA implementation and the adoption of specific EMA tools are affected by the cultural values within an organisation. A successful implementation of corporate sustainability and accounting can be regarded as largely dependent on the national culture, which in turn affects whether, how or the extent to which EMA measurements are implemented (Jarnagin and Slocum 2007; Linnenluecke and Griffiths 2010). In order to further explore the relationship between culture and EMA systems in an Asia Pacific context, it is necessary to identify the mechanism by which values at the cultural level are linked to values at the EMA level, as EMA values are likely to have a direct influence on the adoption of EMA practices.

2.3 National Culture, Accounting Values and EMA in Asia Pacific

2.3.1 National Culture and Accounting Values

The influences of culture are omnipresent, and are related to national contexts, including the institutional environment. Thus national cultural contexts influence organisations and corporate management, and their assumptions, organisational structures and activities (Van der Laan Smith et al. 2005). In addition, culture is also considered to be a powerful factor that affects a country's accounting system, and how individuals perceive and use accounting information (Doupnik and Tsakumis 2004). According to Hofstede (1986), the differences in accounting practices between countries are related mainly to cultural rather than technical issues. Similarly, Radebaugh (2014) and Gray (1988) argue that organisational cultural behaviour can be regarded as a factor that influences a country's or a company's accounting system and its objectives, as well as its standards and practices. From a sustainability perspective, the adoption of corporate sustainability management can also be regarded as largely dependent on the values of an organisational culture (Linnenluecke and Griffiths 2010; Lee and Herold 2016). Arguments like these have led to the notion that the culture of a country influences its choice of sustainability accounting techniques. Against this background, we can assume that the adoption of different EMA frameworks and tools is also related to the different cultural dimensions.

National culture is a complex and multi-dimensional construct that has been studied systematically by Hofstede (1983), who created a model of underlying cultural value dimensions. Based on this model, Gray (1988) developed a framework to explain how national culture affects national accounting systems (see Fig. 2.2). In brief, Gray (1988) argues that shared cultural values within a country lead to shared accounting values, which in turn influence the nature of a nation's accounting system.

In his development of the relationship between culture and accounting values, Gray (1988) identifies four accounting values – authority, enforcement, measurement and disclosure – and describes how they manifest themselves in four attributes of a national accounting system. Specifically, Gray (1988) suggests that the accounting values that are most relevant to the authority for accounting systems and their enforcement are professionalism and uniformity, as these are concerned with regu-

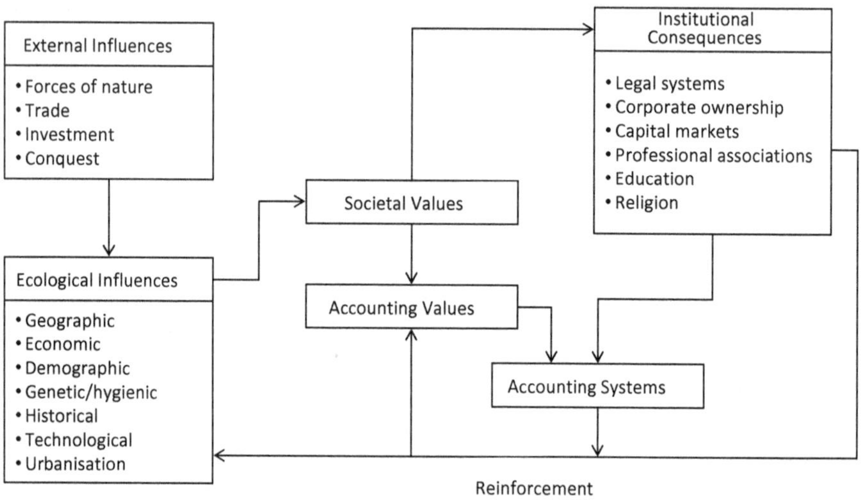

Fig. 2.2 Societal values and accounting values (Source: Gray 1988, p. 7)

lation and the extent of enforcement or conformity. The accounting value that is most relevant to accounting measurement practices is conservatism, and the value that is most relevant to the disclosure of information is secrecy. These four specific accounting values describe only one extreme position, but organisations can also have an opposite point of view, and take a completely contrary position to these values. Accordingly, these values allow for a broad range of interpretations; thus the degree of implementation of these accounting values can be used to define a country's accounting subculture. Gray (1988) distinguishes the four accounting values as being conflicts between the following dichotomies:

1 *Professionalism versus statutory control.* This is a preference for the exercise of individual professional judgement and the maintenance of professional self-regulation as opposed to compliance with prescriptive legal requirements and statutory control.
2 *Uniformity versus flexibility.* This is a preference for the enforcement of uniform accounting practices between companies and for the consistent use of such practices over time, as opposed to flexibility in accordance with the perceived circumstances of individual companies.
3 *Conservatism versus optimism.* This is a preference for a cautious approach to measurement so as to cope with uncertainty of future events as opposed to a more optimistic, laissez-faire, risk-taking approach.
4 *Secrecy versus transparency.* This is a preference for confidentiality and the restriction of disclosure of information about the business only to those who are closely involved with its management and financing as opposed to a more transparent, open and publicly accountable approach.

As shown in Table 2.1, Gray (1988) links the accounting values to the cultural values, and introduces four hypotheses to describe the relationship between the cultural dimensions and the accounting values:

1 The higher a country ranks in terms of individualism and the lower it ranks in terms of uncertainty avoidance and power distance, the more likely it is to rank highly in terms of professionalism.

Table 2.1 The relationship between Gray's accounting value dimensions and Hofstede's cultural value dimensions

	Cultural dimensions			
Accounting values	Power distance	Individualism	Masculinity	Uncertainty avoidance
Professionalism	–	+	?	–
Uniformity	+	–	?	+
Conservatism	?	–	–	+
Secrecy	+	–	–	+

'+' indicates a direct relationship between the variables, '–' indicates an inverse relationship, and '?' indicates that the relationship is indeterminate (Source: Adopted from Baydoun and Willett 1995)

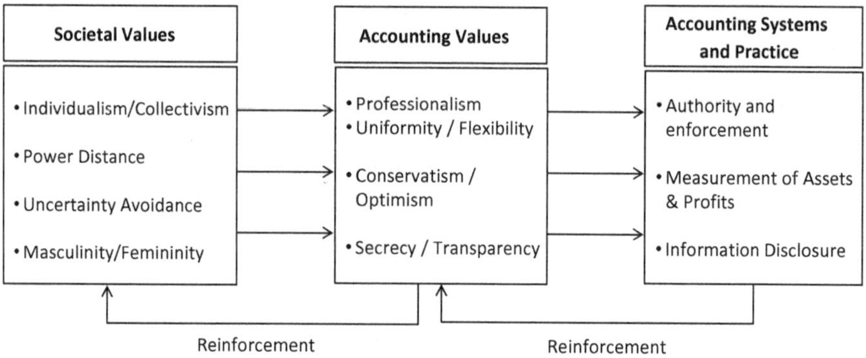

Fig. 2.3 Accounting dimensions, measurement and disclosure (Source: Adapted from Radebaugh and Gray 1993)

2 The higher a country ranks in terms of uncertainty avoidance and power distance and the lower it ranks in terms of individualism, the more likely it is to rank highly in terms of uniformity.
3 The higher a country ranks in terms of uncertainty avoidance and the lower it ranks in terms of individualism and masculinity, the more likely it is to rank highly in terms of conservatism.
4 The higher a country ranks in terms of uncertainty avoidance and power distance and the lower it ranks in terms of individualism and masculinity, the more likely it is to rank highly in terms of secrecy.

As shown in Fig. 2.3, Radebaugh and Gray (1993) further develop the framework to link cultural values (societal values), accounting values, and accounting systems and practices. In particular, they provide specific accounting practices, such as measurement of assets and profits, and information disclosure.

In order to test Gray's proposition, some scholars conducted empirical studies. Baydoun and Willett (1995) applied Gray's framework in a Lebanese context to examine accounting measurement and disclosure. They argue that Gray's accounting values are defined in terms of preferences for particular courses of action rather than in terms of apparent attributes of financial statements. When they tested technical aspects of accounting practice, they found that Gray's framework was aimed at an accounting system for developed nations, and was not relevant to developing countries like Lebanon. More recently, Doupnik and Tsakumis (2004) provided a critical literature review of empirical studies testing Gray's propositions, and found that most empirical studies focused on 'secrecy' and the rest of the propositions (professionalism, uniformity and conservatism) remained largely unexplored. They conclude that there is only limited evidence to prove (or disprove) Gray's propositions. Alternatively, they suggest focusing on conservatism, which affects the recognition and measurement of items in financial statements. With a focus on conservatism accounting value, Salter et al. (2013) tested Gray's proposition with panel data composing 341 country-year observations from 22 countries between

1989 and 2006. They found that accounting conservatism was greater in countries with more conservative societal and accounting values. The femininity of the Hofstede value was another significant finding for measures of conservatism.

Although cultural relevance has increasing importance in accounting practices, to our best knowledge, no study has built a research framework to explore the accounting value of EMA. In order to establish the accounting value dimensions of EMA in terms of the Hofstede cultural dimensions, this study set out to explore each dimension of Hofstede's cultural dimensions from an EMA perspective.

2.3.2 *EMA and Hofstede's Cultural Values in Asia Pacific*

In research investigating the relationship between culture and EMA, culture can be considered the independent variable. Thus, to be useful in accounting research, and subsequently in sustainability accounting research, the concept of culture needs to be broken down into specific elements that can be used to establish linkages between specific cultural values and specific values of EMA.

The cultural framework most widely used in accounting research is that of Hofstede (1983). His framework deconstructs national culture into cultural value dimensions and provides quantitative measures of those dimensions by country. As such, these quantitative measures lend themselves to use as independent variables in statistical analyses.

Hofstede (1983) identified five underlying cultural values: power distance (PDI), individualism–collectivism (IDV), short/long-term orientation (LTO), masculinity/femininity (MAS) and uncertainty avoidance (UAV). These five values were used to categorise 'culture areas' – that is, lists of countries that could be categorised on the basis of cultural characteristics. From an Asian management perspective, we need to pay particular attention to cultural categorisation. Asia is not at all an homogeneous entity; rather, it is a diverse, multicultural society. Within Asia, management is heterogeneous, with different processes adopted, depending on whether we focus on China, India, Japan or Malaysia (Hofstede 2007).

To understand the cultural influences on corporate sustainability management and the adoption of EMA practices, the five dimensions are described in more detail below, with a focus on the differences in Asian management practices and their relationship to sustainability management.

2.3.2.1 Power Distance (PDI)

According to Hofstede et al. (1997), power distance refers to the extent to which the less powerful members of institutions and organisations within a country expect and accept that power is distributed unequally. In high power distance countries, there is considerable dependence of subordinates on their superiors. From an Asian cultures perspective, Malaysia, the Philippines and Indonesia score relatively high on power distance while Japan and Taiwan are in the middle of the scale. Hofstede (2001) notes strong parallels between his notion of high power distance and paternalism. Paternalism is a system by which superiors provide favours to subordinates in return for their loyalty. Decisions are not made on the basis of merit, but rather on the basis of a balance of favours to subordinates and loyalty to superiors.

Thus a large power distance culture may lead to uncontrolled power for authorities and/or management executives. For example, management that holds uncontrolled power may have a greater temptation to use official power for unofficial personal gain – for example, side payments. Moreover, a system characterised by high levels of power distance may lead to a weaker capacity for debate and weaker corporate management responsiveness to environmental sustainability problems (Katz et al. 2001). Interestingly, power distance weakens with economic growth and rising prosperity. With increasing economic wealth, power holders more often need to justify themselves, as can be observed in countries like Korea and Indonesia. Consequently, the most consistently significant and positive relationships with the adoption of environmental sustainability were found for low power distance (e.g. Beekun et al. 2008; Scholtens and Dam 2007; Williams and Zinkin 2008).

2.3.2.2 Individualism–Collectivism (IDV)

The individualism–collectivism dimension refers to the extent to which the decisions about a person's life are determined by the individual or by the in-group – a person's circle of family, friends or peers (Kim et al. 1990). Collectivism stands for a society in which people are integrated into strong, cohesive in-groups from birth onwards; throughout their lifetime, these groups continue to protect them in exchange for unquestioning loyalty. Individualism stands for a society in which the ties between individuals are loose: everyone is expected to look after themselves and their immediate family only.

'Western' related countries in the Asia Pacific score above average on individualism, with Australia the most individualistic. In contrast, Asian countries all score below average on individualism and high on collectivism, with China, Indonesia and Korea relatively more and India and Japan relatively less collectivist. The in-group to which people relate in most cases is the extended family, but in Japan the employer fulfils part of the in-group role. A relationship between economic wealth and cultural individualism can also be observed (Hofstede 2007). Not only do wealthier countries score as relatively more individualistic, but countries that have become wealthier have also become more individualistic, a process we have observed in recent years in the economically successful countries of Asia, such as Japan, Korea and Thailand. For example, the elderly are now less automatically taken care of by their families than they used to be.

From a management perspective, the individualism–collectivism dimension has implications for the management style and adoption of environmental sustainability appropriate within a culture. The concept of "management" itself was developed in Britain and the United States; it is thus based on individualist society, and all theories of management that were developed subsequently portray these individualist roots. According to Katz et al. (2001), environmental activity and the pressure to adopt environmental sustainability practices appear to be much more widespread and diverse in individualistic cultures than in collectivistic cultures. As a result, a high individualistic society should have a greater social and institutional capacity to respond to environmental problems.

2.3.2.3 Short/Long-Term Orientation (LTO)

The long-term orientation dimension refers to a forward-looking perspective rather than an historical perspective. Long-term orientation means valuing, for example, persistence and thrift. A short-term orientation means valuing "face" and respect for tradition. This dimension places many Asian countries in contrast to the rest of the world, in the sense that the Asian countries score high on long-term orientation and the others high on medium- or short-term orientation. The top long-term scorers are China, Hong Kong, Taiwan, Japan and Korea. Medium-term oriented Asian countries include India, Thailand and Bangladesh. Asian countries on the short-term side include the Philippines and Pakistan.

The main reason for the emergence and the introduction of the long-term orientation dimension, driven by Hofstede and Bond (1988), was to capture Asian cultures and values. Based on the assumption that questions specifically relevant to Asian minds might not even have been asked, a specific survey with deliberate Chinese culture bias was developed, and subsequently revealed this dimension. As a result, the long-term orientation dimension is strongly related to Confucian values because, both at the positive and at the negative poles, it is closely connected to the teachings of Confucius: it opposes future-oriented, dynamic values in favour of present- and past-oriented static Confucian values. However, these values contain values other than a long-term orientation, and Hofstede and Bond (1988) refer to Confucius's teachings as 'practical ethics'. Distinctive principles of Confucianism are family and hierarchy: while the former represents a basic social construct and can be linked to a social orientation for society as a whole, the latter can be linked to power distance. Consequently, while the dynamic and family-oriented values indicate openness to change, a strong hierarchy could be regarded as a barrier to debate and implementation of institutional change – for example, the adoption of environmental and sustainability practices.

2.3.2.4 Masculinity/Femininity (MAS)

Masculinity/femininity refers, among other things, to a focus on "material success" as opposed to a concern with the "quality of life" (Hofstede et al. 1997, p. 82). For example, if there is a trade-off between high pay and leisure time, the masculine society prefers higher pay and the feminine society prefers more leisure time. Hofstede's discussion directly links masculinity to the preference for material wealth, and argues that masculinity creates a preference for economic growth over environmental conservation.

From a management accounting perspective, Gray (1988) researched the relationship between national culture and accounting classification, and argues that low masculinity is likely to lead to an increase in transparency. Consequently, the pursuit of material success, represented by high masculinity, would result in lower levels of environmental sustainability engagement. In contrast, a low-masculinity or a high-femininity culture indicates a focus on relationships, cooperation and higher responsiveness to environmental problems (Husted 2005).

2.3.2.5 Uncertainty Avoidance (UAV)

Hofstede et al. (1997, p. 113) define uncertainty avoidance as "the extent to which members of a culture feel threatened by uncertainty or unknown situations". This dimension reflects the degree to which a culture tolerates ambiguity and constitutes a response to anxiety about the future. High uncertainty avoidance cultures tend to reject citizen protest and accept citizen dependence on the government, while low uncertainty avoidant cultures foster citizen empowerment and protest. Citizen empowerment and environmental debate are essential requirements for a country's institutional capacity for environmental sustainability (Pezzoli 1997).

Moreover, a high score on the dimension of uncertainty avoidance indicates a lack of will for transparency to "avoid conflict and competition and to preserve security" (Gray 1988, p. 12). High uncertainty avoidance is also related to aversion to entrepreneurial risk, which leads to lower entrepreneurial activity (Geletkanycz 1997). Consequently, a culture with high uncertainty avoidance is related to a weaker market orientation and may neglect institutional change, including the adoption of environmental and sustainability practices.

These five cultural dimensions identify core values that attempt to explain the general similarities and differences in cultures, and provide explicit constructs from which accountants can benefit when considering the impact of culture on accounting or sustainability accounting practices. Hofstede (1983, 1991) provides quantitative measures for each of these five cultural dimensions over 50 countries. Hofstede (1991, p. 25) indicates that these values "represent relative, not absolute positions of countries: they are measures of differences only". As our focus is on the Asia-Pacific region, the relative scores for the selected Asia Pacific countries on Hofstede's cultural dimension are presented in Table 2.2.

This chapter uses the Asia Pacific cultural value dimensions to operationalise the concept of culture to investigate its effect on EMA values and tools in implementation. As mentioned earlier, Gray (1988) proposed four accounting values with a link to Hofstede's (1983) cultural values. We adopt Gray's approach to investigate EMA values and implementation with regard to Hofstede's (1983) cultural values. As this chapter closely follows the framework and structure of Gray (1988), the next section discusses this framework, and provides a detailed overview of its accounting values and Gray's propositions for how the accounting values are linked to cultural values.

Table 2.2 Hofstede's cultural values in the Asia Pacific region

Country	Power distance	Individualism	Uncertainty avoidance	Masculinity	Long term orientation
Australia	36	90	51	61	21
China	80	20	30	66	87
Hong Kong	68	25	29	57	61
India	77	48	40	56	51
Indonesia	78	14	48	46	62
Japan	54	46	92	95	88
Malaysia	100	26	36	50	41
New Zealand	22	79	49	58	33
Pakistan	55	14	70	50	50
Philippines	94	32	44	64	27
Singapore	74	20	8	48	72
South Korea	60	18	85	39	100
Taiwan	58	17	69	45	93
Thailand	64	20	64	34	32
Vietnam	70	20	30	40	57

The scale runs from 0 to 100 with 50 as a mid-level. The rule of thumb is that if a score is under 50 the culture scores relatively LOW on that scale and if any score is over 50 the culture scores HIGH on that scale. In the case of 'Individualism' – the LOW side (under 50) is considered 'Collectivist' and above 50 considered 'Individualist'. A country with a score of 43 would be collectivist but less collectivist than someone with 28 who is moving down toward the 0 mark

2.4 Development of EMA Values

Based on Gray's (1988) framework, we develop four EMA value dimensions from the EMA literature. These EMA values are based on certain principles and values, but allow for a broad range of interpretations within the respective value dimension. Second, we introduce four propositions to describe the relationship between the cultural dimensions in the Asia Pacific and the EMA values. We argue that the systematic differences in the EMA values indicate a preference for specific EMA approaches or tools.

The following four EMA values are derived from a review of sustainability and environmental accounting literature and practice, and cover four crucial values within EMA:

1. *Symbolic versus action-oriented EMA.* This is a preference for a self-seeking or legitimacy-seeking behaviour, mainly through the disclosure of sustainability reports without meaningful data as opposed to actual action by management for the implementation and incorporation of sustainability and environmental accounting to measure true progress (Hrasky 2011; Kim et al. 2007).
2. *Reactionary versus responsible.* This is a preference for reactive, short-term solutions, or action with no actual change of an existing business as opposed to a proactive, long-term solution that uses EMA to change existing structures and

create strategic competitive advantages through innovative products or services (Schaltegger and Burritt 2015; Carroll 1991; Gray 1992).

3. *Voluntary versus transparent EMA*. This is a preference for setting the company's 'own' standards with the possibility of manipulating data for greenwashing purposes as opposed to setting up an accounting system that, at a minimum, fulfils all relevant international standards and provides information to internal and external stakeholders for comparison (Hahn et al. 2015; Kolk 2008; Herzig and Schaltegger 2011).
4. *Integration versus differentiation.* This is a preference for an organisation that values sustainability and environmental accounting as well as integrates and disseminates these values throughout the entire organisation. Such values are shared by all members in the organisation, as opposed to resistance to change from organisational members or a lack of commitment from top management to make EMA a priority (Linnenluecke and Griffiths 2010; Schaltegger and Hörisch 2015).

We argue that these values can be considered relevant to EMA, and we focus on these values above with a reference to the current literature and as an attempt to explain corporate EMA behaviour in a national context. The next section describes the main arguments of the EMA values and relates them to cultural values, which leads to four propositions regarding EMA values.

2.4.1 Symbolic Versus Action-Oriented EMA

This EMA value dimension can be considered significant, as it represents the *rationale* behind EMA. Companies and their accountants can choose from a range of EMA tools to provide information about the extent of the company's environmental and sustainability management activities. The extent of the company's activities and the rationale behind EMA can only range between symbolic behaviour and relevant corporate action (Gotsi and Wilson 2001). Symbolic behaviour may be rhetorical statements designed to create an impression of sustainable or environmental responsibility, which are not necessarily accompanied by corporate action (Hrasky 2011; Kim et al. 2007). Symbolic behaviour can also be related to reputation management, which Schaltegger and Burritt (2015) describe as a company's focus on societal, political and media attention. In a symbolic or reputational approach, sustainability activities and the sustainability department are closely linked to the PR department to gain the support of the company's most immediate audiences (Hrasky 2011). Hence symbolic management can be regarded as self-interested or narcissistic behaviour, with an emphasis on maintaining, building and repairing the corporate image as well as extensive sustainability reporting with more or less substantiated claims of sustainability achievements (Schaltegger and Burritt 2015). In contrast, relevant corporate action can be described as instrumental actions taken by a company to achieve sustainable accomplishments (e.g. reduce its carbon footprint) (Hrasky 2011). Hence action-oriented sustainability accounting focuses on accounting practices rather than reporting (Zvezdov 2013). In other words, relevant corporate action is the actual implementation of processes and techniques in order to make a substantial sustainable or environmental impact.

To what extent, then, can a *symbolic and action-oriented approach* be linked to cultural dimensions? It is argued here that symbolic and action-oriented behaviour can be linked most closely with the long-term orientation, uncertainty avoidance and power distance dimensions. A preference for symbolic behaviour is consistent with a low long-term orientation because the focus of activity is the corporate image rather than substantial sustainability activities. This leads to a heightened risk that perception and reality will diverge, and symbolic greenwashing behaviour will be uncovered over time (Schaltegger and Burritt 2015). Consequently, a close relationship with weak uncertainty avoidance also seems likely, following from a concern with security and a perceived need to adopt a stable and predictable future environment. There would also seem to be a link – albeit less strong – between symbolic management and a large power distance culture, as high levels of power distance may lead to a weaker corporate responsiveness to environmental problems (Katz et al. 2001).

Based on our discussion, we propose the following:

Proposition 1 The higher a country ranks in terms of power distance, and the lower it ranks in terms of long-term orientation and uncertainty avoidance, the more likely it is to rank highly in terms of symbolic behaviour.

2.4.2 Reactionary Versus Responsible EMA

This EMA value dimension can be regarded as significant, as it represents the *ethical intention* behind the activities of EMA. The scope of the ethical intention of EMA can be distinguished between two extremes: *reactionary* behaviour and *responsible* behaviour. Reactionary corporate behaviour represents the view that sustainability and environmental accounting measures and tools should only be implemented to defend and protect the existing practices (Schaltegger and Burritt 2015). This views environmental and sustainability activities mainly as an additional cost driver, without creating any economic benefits, which can be regarded as adopting a philanthropic or 'profit-sacrificing' perspective (Carroll 1991; Lee et al. 2016). In other words, a reactionary behaviour treats any EMA activity and measures as 'outside' the core business, with the aim of continuing the existing business as in the past – hence EMA is only used for defensive activities (Schaltegger and Burritt 2015).

In contrast, responsible EMA behaviour represents an approach to implementing the right EMA tools and instruments to achieve substantial sustainability and environmental improvements. The ultimate goal may set up an accounting system that, as described by Gray (1992), provides a calculation of what incremental cost must be borne by a company if the corporate activities were not to leave the planet worse of, or "what it would cost at the end of the accounting period to return the planet and biosphere to the point it was at the beginning of the accounting period" (Gray 1992,

p. 419). To achieve this goal, companies may adopt specific sustainability management tools and implement rigorously international industry standards to go beyond regulatory requirements (Schaltegger and Hörisch 2015). Although the responsible perspective may lead to a costly investment in order to introduce and implement EMA tools, these proactive initiatives result in reduced costs in the long term through efficiency gains, growth in sales and reputation, or improved operations, products and services (Schaltegger and Burritt 2015).

To what extent, then, can the *reactionary* or *responsible* approach be linked to cultural dimensions? It is argued that a reactionary and responsible approach can be linked most closely to the uncertainty avoidance, masculine-feminine and the long-term orientation dimensions. A preference for a responsible approach can be linked to a preference for strong uncertainty following a concern to comply with the rules, follow rigid codes of behaviour and, most importantly, the search for ultimate, absolute truths and values (Gray 1988). Responsible behaviour is also consistent with preference for femininity – the opposite of masculinity – and indicates an emphasis on the quality of life, the environment and a socially oriented society (Van der Laan Smith et al. 2005). There would also be an apparent link between long-term orientation and responsible behaviour. The investment and the implementation of EMA tools make sense only in the long run, while reactive activities are short-term by nature.

Based on our discussion, we propose that:

Proposition 2 The higher a country ranks in terms of uncertainty avoidance and long-term orientation, and the lower it ranks in terms of masculinity, the more likely it is to rank highly in terms of responsible behaviour.

2.4.3 Voluntariness Versus Transparency

This EMA value dimension can be regarded as significant, as it represents the degree of *accountability* of EMA. Gray (1988) used a comparable accounting value dimension – secrecy vs transparency – to describe the influence of management and a company's accountants over the quantity of information. While Gray's accounting value of *transparency* can be regarded to have a similar function in EMA, the value 'secrecy' does not apply to EMA. EMA represents a mainly *voluntary* organisational practice within companies (Hahn et al. 2015; Kolk 2008). Because of the mainly voluntary nature of EMA, management can choose which tools or guidelines to apply in order to measure sustainability and environmental performance. If EMA is voluntary, it may lead to a higher information asymmetry between management and stakeholders. As the control about the information in a pure voluntary environment lies with the company's management, companies may not be willing to provide all available information about their performance to stakeholders (Sarkis et al. 2011). Hence, if a company follows a purely voluntary EMA approach, it can be extremely difficult to gain an insight into the company's activities, let alone the firm's actual achievements, which leads to an overall lack of comprehensibility (Kolk et al. 2008).

In contrast, the value dimension *transparency* indicates full accountability – that is, a strategic design of internal information systems to collect sustainability or environmental accounting information to calculate the key performance indicators, and the respective external communication through sustainability reporting (Herzig and Schaltegger 2011). Moreover, an indicator of transparent EMA is the adoption of technical international and industry procedures, and following official international guidelines (e.g. GRI Sustainability Reporting Guideline) to make the information not only accountable, but also comparable.

To what extent, then, can a *voluntary* and a *transparent* approach be linked to cultural dimensions? It is argued here that a voluntary and a transparent approach can be linked to the uncertainty avoidance, power distance and individualism-collectivism dimensions. Similar to Gray's (1988) argument for 'secrecy', we argue that a preference for voluntariness is consistent with strong uncertainty avoidance, following from a need to control or manipulate information to avoid conflict and competition and to preserve security. Voluntariness can also be linked to high power distance, as high power distance may lead to a restriction of information within companies to preserve power inequalities. In contrast, transparency is also consistent with a preference for collectivism, as opposed to individualism, with its respect for group norms and the respective guidelines and standards, as well as for auditing and verification processes.

Based on our discussion, we propose that:

Proposition 3 The higher a country ranks in terms of collectivism, and the lower it ranks in terms of uncertainty avoidance and power distance, the more likely it is to rank highly in terms of transparency.

2.4.4 Integration Versus Differentiation

This EMA value dimension can be regarded as significant as it represents how deep a corporate sustainability strategy and its values are embedded and *disseminated* in the organisation. The *integration* perspective also represents as strategic perspective, and assumes that corporate sustainability values and principles exhibited by top management will be widely shared and held by all organisational members and that changes in the values of top management will translate into changes in actual practice throughout the organisation (Linnenluecke and Griffiths 2010). A full integration perspective also implies that sustainability values and accounting measures are implemented and executed in the daily operations in organisational units (Schaltegger and Hörisch 2015). Thus, through the integration of sustainability values in all units, a highly sustainability-driven organisational culture may develop which unites corporate members and fosters a sense of identity and commitment to common corporate environmental goals and aspirations.

In contrast, the *differentiation* perspective assumes that the adoption of sustainability tools and values promoted by top-management are not equally implemented in all units within the organisation. In this case, units might have an own agenda and not follow the consistent and unified sustainability accounting tools. Instead, these units implement different sustainability performance-measurement approaches or tools that are not aligned with the overall company's sustainability strategy or only adopt EMA tools on an ad-hoc basis to solve an immediate issue or to manage a business case (Schaltegger and Burritt 2010). Moreover, a differentiation perspective could also emerge if top management is only partly engaged in sustainability concerns and sustainability is not a priority, or not embedded in the corporate strategy.

To what extent, then, can the *integration* and *differentiation* approach be linked to cultural dimensions? It is argued here that an integration and a differentiation approach can be linked to power distance, individualism-collectivism and masculine-feminine dimensions. A preference for differentiation is consistent with low power distance, which can be interpreted as a high degree of resistance to organisational change and strong hierarchical levels (Jermier et al. 1991). This value dimension is also consistent with a preference for individualism, as opposed to collectivism, as differentiation is more linked to status and prestige in an organisational role (Martin 2002). There would also be a link between differentiation and high masculinity, in that differentiation emphasis the assertiveness of an organisation's member (Orij 2010).

Based on our discussion, we propose that:

Proposition 4 The higher a country ranks in terms of power distance and collectivism, and the lower it ranks in terms of masculinity, the more likely it is to rank highly in terms of integration.

2.5 The Relationship Between Cultural Values and EMA Values

Having formulated propositions relating cultural values to EMA values, it is evident that the most important cultural values are uncertainty avoidance and power distance, followed by long-term orientation, individualism and masculinity. Furthermore, the propositions can be used to visually present the relative association between cultural values in the Asia Pacific countries and the four EMA values (see Figs. 2.4 and 2.5 below).

We argue that a useful distinction can be made between the *rationale* of and the *ethical intention* behind EMA. The rationale dimension explains the 'why' behind the EMA implementation, which is characterised by either symbolic or action-oriented behaviour. The ethical intention dimension indicates the 'how', and the extent to which an EMA action is applied, which is characterised by either reactionary action or responsible action. EMA values most relevant to the rationale and to the ethical intention dimension would seem to be described best as an overall trend to a more symbolic and reactionary approach within the Asia Pacific, led by the Philippines (see Fig. 2.4). The Philippines has a very low score in long-term orientation and a low preference for avoiding uncertainty – hence the Philippines' focus on achieving quick results and undertaking hard work only when necessary

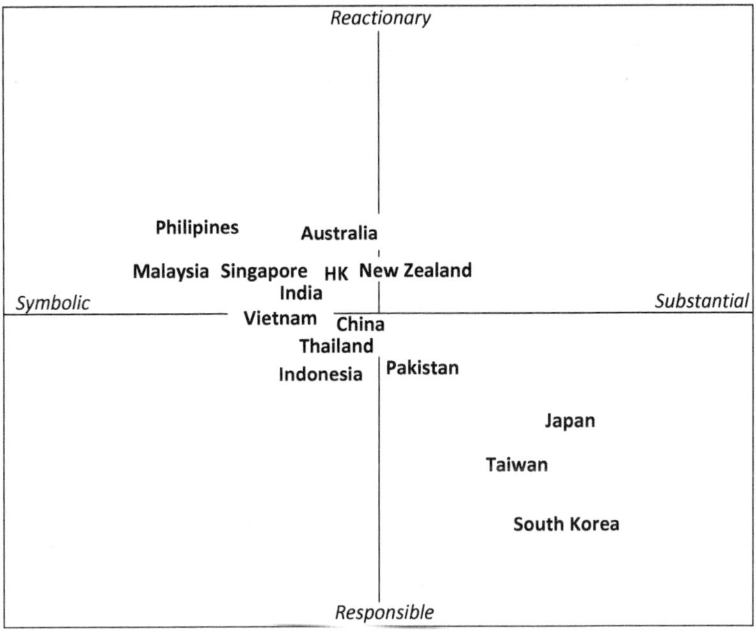

Fig. 2.4 EMA values – rationale and ethical intention

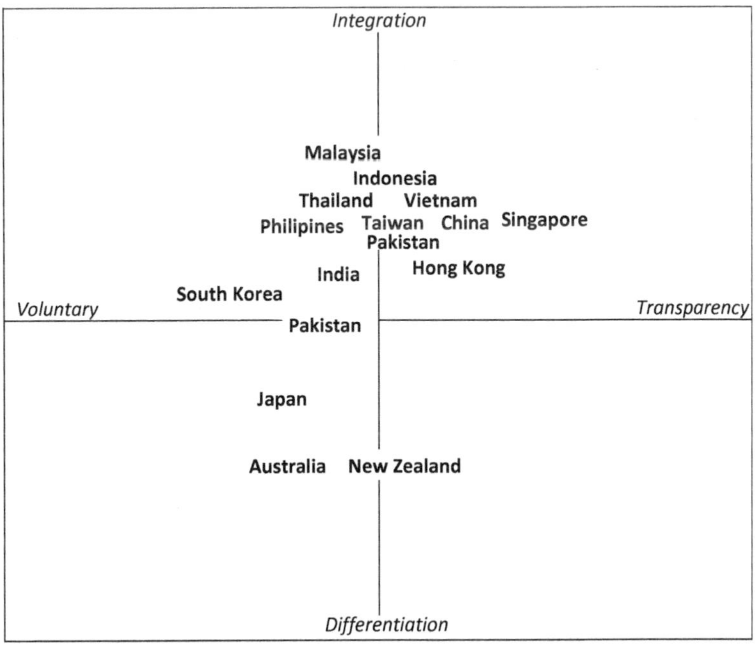

Fig. 2.5 EMA values: accountability and dissemination

(Hofstede 2015). However, the exceptions to this trend are South Korea, Taiwan and Japan, which show a clear preference for an action-oriented and responsible EMA approach. As a leading example for responsible and action-oriented behaviour, South Korea is not only one of the most uncertainty-avoiding countries in the world, but also one of the most pragmatic, long-term perspective societies, with a focus on the durability of companies and a strong inner drive to work hard (Hofstede 2015).

How can we link those findings of the relation between country-based cultural values and EMA values to relevant EMA approaches and tools? We argue that the findings of the EMA value dimensions can be related to specific EMA tools. It seems that companies in countries with an action-oriented and responsible approach, such as Taiwan, Japan and South Korea, apply EMA to actual change structures as well as implement and measure EMA activities. It can be assumed that an action-oriented and responsible behaviour is consistent with a long-term focus on providing regular and routinely generated information for future business cases or transactions. According to Burritt et al. (2002b), these assumptions would correlate with a monetary and physical environmental project investment appraisal as a tool, as well as an environmental life-cycle analysis or budgeting for specific projects or business cases. In contrast, countries with a symbolic and a reactionary approach use EMA for external reporting purposes rather than for actual accounting measurement processes. It can be assumed that reactionary behaviour is consistent with a short-term focus on providing ad-hoc information regarding a past activity. This assumption would then correlate with the EMA tool of an ex-post assessment of relevant environmental costing decisions or of short-term environmental impacts (Burritt et al. 2002b). Moreover, it can be assumed that a symbolic behaviour is consistent with past-oriented and short-term activities, where information is routinely generated, which would correlate with environmental cost accounting or a material flow analysis (Burritt et al. 2002b). This information could be used to demonstrate sustainability engagement to external stakeholders and satisfy immediate requests.

Another useful distinction can be made between the *accountability* of EMA on the one hand, and the *dissemination* of EMA and sustainability values on the other. That is, the accountability dimension can help to explain to what extent and 'for what purpose' companies introduce or implement EMA, which is characterised by either voluntary or a transparent approach. The dissemination dimension indicates how deeply the sustainability strategy and EMA values are embedded and accepted within the organisation; this is characterised either by an organisation with fully integrated EMA values (the integration perspective) or by an organisation with different values or EMA approaches (the differentiation perspective).

The EMA values most relevant to accountability and dissemination would seem to be described best by an overall trend to integrative and transparent behaviour, led by Singapore (see Fig. 2.5). Singapore has a more feminine approach and scores high on power distance; hence Singapore eventually embraces consensus, and abides by rules (Hofstede 2015). More interestingly, Singapore's mindset allows for a more pragmatic approach to business, as stated by Hofstede (2015, p. 2): "Westerners believe that if A is right, B must be wrong, whereas people from East and Southeast Asian countries see both A and B combined produce something superior." The exceptions to this trend are Japan, Australia and New Zealand, which are characterised by a high differentiation perspective and a rather voluntary approach to EMA. Australians and New Zealanders score low on power distance and high on individualism, which indicates that hierarchy is only established for convenience and employees are expected to be self-reliant – hence the acceptance of EMA is strongly related to unique employee behaviour (Hofstede 2015). Compared with Australia and New Zealand, Japan scores higher on power distance, which indicates a preference for hierarchy. However, Japan is not as hierarchical as most other Asian cultures, which can help explain the gap in EMA values compared with the other Asian countries.

How can we link those findings regarding the relationship between country-based cultural values and EMA values with relevant EMA approaches and tools? It seems that companies in countries with an integrated and transparent approach, such as Singapore, Vietnam or Indonesia, use EMA to inform internal and external stakeholders about the usefulness and values of EMA activities, and see EMA as an opportunity to include all relevant parties on their EMA journey. It can be assumed that an integrated and transparent approach is consistent with a long-term focus to provide ad-hoc and routinely generated information for past and future activities. According to Burritt et al. (2002b), these assumptions would correlate with the tools of environmental capital accounting or environmental long-term financial planning. To be fully transparent, companies in these countries might also use environmental life-cycle costing or life-cycle inventories to inform employees about current EMA activities. In contrast, countries such as Australia, Japan or New Zealand, with a voluntary and differentiation approach, use EMA only for ad-hoc decisions and own business case calculations. It can be assumed that a voluntary behaviour in combination with a differentiation approach is consistent with a short-term focus to provide ad-hoc information for a future activity. This assumption would then correlate with the EMA tool of an evaluation of relevant environmental impacts or costings – an ex-post assessment of relevant environmental costing decisions or an ex-post assessment of short-term environmental impacts (Burritt et al. 2002b).

2.6 Conclusion and Implications for Future Directions

While prior research has shown that the development of environmental and sustainability management accounting is influenced by external factors, the importance of cultural influences in this context has largely been neglected in the current accounting literature. Using Gray's (1988) approach, we have proposed a framework for analysing the impact of culture on corporate environmental and sustainability management accounting practices in the Asia Pacific region. To our best knowledge, this is the first study to establish the relationship between cultural values and EMA values in the Asia Pacific.

The contribution of this chapter is threefold. First, based on the current literature, we defined four 'EMA values'. These addressed the rationale and ethical intention behind EMA, as well as the accountability of EMA and the dissemination of its values, each with a scope of interpretation. The *rationale* perspective is divided into a 'symbolic' versus 'action-oriented' approach, while the *ethical intention* perspective is divided into 'reactionary' versus 'responsible' behaviour. The *accountability* of EMA is divided into 'voluntary' versus 'transparent' EMA and the *dissemination* perspective follows an 'integration' versus 'differentiation' approach.

Second, we connected the 'EMA values' to Hofstede's country-based cultural values, and introduced four propositions, which led to a classification of countries based on certain cultural values and their degree of implementation in the context of the *rationale* and the *ethical intention* behind EMA on the one hand, and *accountability* and *dissemination* of EMA on the other.

Third, we analysed the country-based findings in the context of the EMA values and related them to specific EMA tools and measurement approaches. Certain cultural and EMA values can be viewed as similar to the EMA framework dimensions formulated by Burritt et al. (2002b). As a result, we were able to correlate country-based EMA values with specific EMA tools.

Since the development of this framework, EMA values and the outcomes of this study represent the first attempt to make these connections, we acknowledge some limitations of our study. For instance, EMA values are based on selected principles and values, and there are possibilities for other dimensions of cultures in EMA. Further research is needed to ensure that the framework and approach are generalisable to other contexts and cultural areas. In addition, we did not test our approach to empirical EMA measures and disclosure in practice. The generalisability of this study to other cultural dimensions or areas is worth investigating to determine the real impact of culture on the comparability of EMA practices.

While we acknowledge that this research is of an exploratory nature, and leaves room for interpretation, this chapter is offered as a contribution towards a theory of cultural influence on the development of EMA systems and practices internationally. We encourage academics, researchers and practitioners to test our propositions and assumptions for validity. Specifically, empirical research may be carried out to assess the extent to which there is in fact a match between (1) cultural values and EMA values, or (2) the countries' classification based on EMA values and the specific EMA tools. We hope that our study provides an understanding of cultural influences on EMA practices in order to further develop corporate sustainability management to address the challenge of sustainable development.

References

Baskerville R (2003) Hofstede never studied culture. Acc Org Soc 28:1–14

Baydoun N, Willett R (1995) Cultural relevance of Western Accounting Systems to developing countries. Abacus 31(1):67–92

Beekun RI, Hamdy R, Westerman JW, HassabElnaby HR (2008) An exploration of ethical decision-making processes in the United States and Egypt. J Bus Ethics 82(3):587–605

Bennett MJ, Bouma J, Walters T (2002) Environmental management accounting: informational and institutional developments. Kluwer, Dordrecht

Burritt R, Schaltegger S (2010) Sustainability accounting and reporting: fad or trend? Acc Audit Accountability 23(7):829–846
Burritt RL, Hahn T, Schaltegger S (2002a) An integrative framework of environmental management accounting – consolidating the different approaches of EMA into a common framework and terminology. In: Bennett MD, Bouma JJ, Wolters TJ (eds) Environmental management accounting: informational and institutional developments. Springer, Dordrecht, pp 21–35
Burritt RL, Hahn T, Schaltegger S (2002b) Towards a comprehensive framework for environmental management accounting: links between business actors and EMA tools. Aust Acc Rev 12(2):39–50
Carroll AB (1991) The pyramid of corporate social responsibility: toward the moral management of organizational stakeholders. Bus Horiz 34(4):39–48
Chanchani S, MacGregor A (1999) A synthesis of cultural studies in accounting. J Acc Lit 18:1–30
Doupnik TS, Tsakumis GT (2004) A critical review of tests of Gray's theory of cultural relevance and suggestions for future research. J Acc Lit 23:1–48
Frost GR, Wilmshurst TD (2000) The adoption of environment-related management accounting: an analysis of corporate environmental sensitivity. Acc Forum 24:344–365
Geletkanycz MA (1997) The salience of "culture's consequences": the effects of cultural values on top executive commitment to the status quo. Strateg Manag J 18(8):615–634
Gotsi M, Wilson AM (2001) Corporate reputation: seeking a definition. Corp Comm Int J 6(1):24–30
Gray SJ (1988) Towards a theory of cultural influence on the development of accounting systems internationally. Abacus 24(1):1–15
Gray R (1992) Accounting and environmentalism: an exploration of the challenge of gently accounting for accountability, transparency and sustainability. Acc Org Soc 17(5):399–425
Hahn R, Reimsbach D, Schiemann F (2015) Organizations, climate change, and transparency: reviewing the literature on carbon disclosure. Organ Environ 28(1):80–102
Harrison G, McKinnon J (1999) Cross-cultural research in management control systems design: a review of the current state. Acc Org Soc 24:483–506
Herzig C, Schaltegger S (2011) Corporate sustainability reporting. In: Godemann J, Michelsen G (eds) Sustainability communication. interdisciplinary perspectives and theoretical foundations. Springer, Dordrecht, pp 151–169
Hofstede GH (1983) The cultural relativity of organizational practices and theories. J Int Bus Stud 13:75–89
Hofstede GH (1986) The cultural context of accounting: accounting and culture. Paper presented to Annual Conference of the American Accounting Association, New York
Hofstede GH (1991) Cultures and organisations: software of the mind – intercultural cooperation and its importance for survival. McGraw-Hill, London
Hofstede GH (2001) Culture's consequences: comparing values, behaviors, institutions and organizations across nations. Sage, Thousand Oaks
Hofstede GH (2007) Asian management in the 21st century. Asia Pac J Manag 24(4):411–420
Hofstede GH (2015) The Hofstede Centre: strategy, culture, change. The Hofstede Centre, Helsinki
Hofstede G, Bond MH (1988) The Confucius connection: from cultural roots to economic growth. Org Dyn 16(4):5–21
Hofstede G, Hofstede GJ, Minkov M (1997) Cultures and organizations. McGraw Hill, New York
Hrasky S (2011) Carbon footprints and legitimation strategies: symbolism or action? Accounting. Audit Account J 25(1):174–198
Husted BW (2005) Culture and ecology: a cross-national study of the determinants of environmental sustainability. Manag Int Rev 45(3):349–371
Jarnagin C, Slocum J (2007) Creating corporate cultures through mythopoetic leadership. Org Dyn 36(3):288–302
Jermier JM, Slocum JW, Fry LW, Gaines J (1991) Organizational subcultures in a soft bureaucracy: resistance behind the myth and facade of an official culture. Organ Sci 2(2):170–194

Katz JP, Swanson DL, Nelson LK (2001) Culture-based expectations of corporate citizenship: a propositional framework and comparison of four cultures. Int J Organ Anal 9(2):149–171
Kim K, Park H, Suzuki N (1990) Reward allocations in the United States, Japan, and Korea: a comparison of individualistic and collectivistic cultures. Acad Manag J 33(1):188–198
Kim J, Bach SB, Clelland IJ (2007) Symbolic or behavioral management? Corporate reputation in high-emission industries. Corp Rep Rev 10(2):77–98
Kolk A (2008) Sustainability, accountability and corporate governance: exploring multinationals' reporting practices. Bus Strat Environ 17(1):1–15
Kolk A, Levy D, Pinkse J (2008) Corporate responses in an emerging climate regime: the institutionalization and commensuration of carbon disclosure. Eur Acc Rev 17(4):719–745
KPMG (2014) Corporate sustainability: a progress report. Available at: http://www.kpmg.com/Global/en/IssuesAndInsights/ArticlesPublications/Documents/corporate-sustainability-v2.pdf. Accessed 10 May 2016
Lamberton G (2005) Sustainability accounting: a brief history and conceptual framework. Acc Forum 29(1):7–26
Lee K-H (2014) Globalization, green management and climate change in the Asia-Pacific economy. J Asia-Pac Bus 15(2):101–104
Lee K-H, Herold DM (2016) Cultural relevance in corporate sustainability management: a comparison between Korea and Japan. Asian J Sustain Soc Resp 1:1–21
Lee K-H, Herold DM, Yu AL (2016) Small and medium enterprises and corporate social responsibility practice: a Swedish perspective. Corp Soc Resp Env Manag 23(2):88–99
Lee K-H (2017) Does size matter? Evaluating corporate environmental disclosure in the Australian mining and metal industry: a combined approach of quantity and quality measurement. Bus Strateg Environ 26(2):209–223
Linnenluecke MK, Griffiths A (2010) Corporate sustainability and organizational culture. J World Bus 45(4):357–366
Lodhia S, Hess N (2014) Sustainability accounting and reporting in the mining industry: current literature and directions for future research. J Clean Prod 84:43–50
Martin J (2002) Organizational culture: mapping the terrain corporate social responsibility and environmental management. Sage, Thousand Oaks
Orij R (2010) Corporate social disclosures in the context of national cultures and stakeholder theory. Acc Audit Account J 23(7):868–889
Owen JR, Kemp D (2012) Assets, capitals, and resources frameworks for corporate community development. Min Bus Soc 51(3):382–408
Pezzoli K (1997) Sustainable development: a transdisciplinary overview of the literature. J Environ Plan Manag 40(5):549–574
Radebaugh LH (2014) Environmental factors influencing the development of accounting objectives, standards and practices in Peru. Int J Acc Edu Res 11(1):39–56
Radebaugh LH, Gray S (1993) International accounting and multinational enterprises. Wiley, New York
Salter S, Kang T, Gotti G, Doupnik T (2013) The role of social values, accounting values and institutions in determining accounting conservatism. Manag Int Rev 53(4):607–632
Sarkis J, Zhu Q, Lai K (2011) An organizational theoretic review of green supply chain management literature. Int J Prod Econ 130(1):1–15
Schaltegger S, Burritt R (2000) Contemporary environmental accounting: issues, concepts and practice. Greenleaf Press, Sheffield
Schaltegger S, Burritt R (2010) Sustainability accounting for companies: catchphrase or decision support for business leaders? J World Bus 45(4):375–384
Schaltegger S, Burritt R (2015) Business cases and corporate engagement with sustainability: differentiating ethical motivations. J Bus Ethics. https://doi.org/10.1007/s10551-015-2938-0
Schaltegger S, Hörisch J (2015) In search of the dominant rationale in sustainability management: legitimacy or profit-seeking? J Bus Ethics. https://doi.org/10.1007/s10551-015-2854-3

Schaltegger S, Gibassier D, Zvezdov D (2013) Is environmental management accounting a discipline? A bibliometric literature review. Meditari Acc Res 21(1):4–31
Scholtens B, Dam L (2007) Cultural values and international differences in business ethics. J Bus Ethics 75(3):273–284
SERI/WU (2014) Global material flow database, sustainable Europe Research Institute/Vienna University of Economics and Business, Vienna
Tsakumis G (2007) The influence of culture on accountants' application of financial reporting rules. Abacus 43(1):27–48
Van der Laan Smith J, Adhikari A, Tondkar RH (2005) Exploring differences in social disclosures internationally: a stakeholder perspective. J Acc Pub Policy 24(2):123–151
Williams G, Zinkin J (2008) The effect of culture on consumers' willingness to punish irresponsible corporate behaviour: applying Hofstede's typology to the punishment aspect of corporate social responsibility. Bus Ethics 17(2):210–226
World Commission on Environment and Development (1987) Our common future. Oxford University Press, Oxford
Yasunari T, Niles D, Taniguchi M, Chen D (2013) Asia: proving ground for global sustainability. Curr Opin Environ Sustain 5(3):288–292
Zvezdov D (2013) Rolling out corporate sustainability accounting: a set of challenges. J Env Sust 2(2):19–28

Chapter 3
Country Readiness in Adopting Integrated Reporting: A Diamond Theory Approach from an Asian Pacific Economy

A.D. Nuwan Gunarathne and Samanthi Senaratne

Abstract Different countries have exhibited dissimilar levels of adoption of IR. Yet, we still do not know why some countries enjoy more competitive advantage than others in IR adoption. The chapter addresses this gap by selecting Sri Lanka, a country which exhibits a high rate of adopting IR, to explain the national competitive advantage in its readiness for IR adoption. The chapter draws on its theoretical framing of Porter's Diamond Theory. Ample availability of professional accountants, mounting stakeholder demands, a supportive accounting profession and intense competition among organizations aided by award schemes play a key role in propelling Sri Lanka towards a high adoption level of IR. Authors also identify the national culture of the country plays a key role in this process. In addition to its theoretical contributions, this chapter also sheds light on important implications for local and international institutions, policy makers, and various professions in identifying the requisite conditions for promoting new managerial tools and techniques such as IR or sustainability reporting (SR).

Keywords Accounting tools · Diamond theory · Integrated reporting · National competitive advantage · National culture · Sri Lanka

---

A.D.N. Gunarathne (✉)
University of Sri Jayewardenepura, Nugegoda, Sri Lanka

Griffith University, Brisbane, Australia
e-mail: nuwan@sjp.ac.lk; nuwan.gunarathne@griffithuni.edu.au

S. Senaratne
University of Sri Jayewardenepura, Nugegoda, Sri Lanka
e-mail: samanthisenaratne@sjp.ac.lk

K.-H. Lee, S. Schaltegger (eds.), *Accounting for Sustainability: Asia Pacific Perspectives*, Eco-Efficiency in Industry and Science 33,
https://doi.org/10.1007/978-3-319-70899-7_3

3.1 Introduction

Society's growing awareness of environmental, social and governance issues has transformed the way a business is conducted (Kolk and Van Tulder 2010; Seuring and Muller 2008). Due to the magnitude of corporate activities, businesses have a broader responsibility to meet the aspirations of all its stakeholders – both current and future generations. This extended view on corporate responsibility has led to an improvement in environment, social and governance (ESG) disclosures provided by companies. However, there were concerns as to whether the improvement in ESG disclosures of corporate entities reflects their integrated performance (Baron 2014; Lodhia 2015). These concerns have created a need to bring together the financial and ESG aspects of a company's performance in a single report to integrate ESG components into the company's strategy. This has led to the development of IR, which integrates SR more closely with financial reporting and governance reporting of an entity *(refer Appendix 1 to see how the three pillars of sustainability are linked to the six capitals in IR)*. By identifying different types of capitals IR, is focused on the value creation process of an entity (International Integrated Reporting Council, IIRC 2013). In the recent years, IR has been fast diffusing as a new managerial technology. Reflecting this trend there are now many studies that focus on various aspects related to the adoption of IR. However, these studies do not provide a systematic explanation of why countries display different rates of adoption. Since the available studies on IR have mainly focused on developed countries (Jensen and Berg 2012), our understanding is incomplete without a sufficient knowledge of emerging economies. In this context, this chapter focuses on how a South Asian Country in the Asia Pacific Region has successfully moved towards integrated reporting (IR), which enhances the way corporate entities think and report the story of their business.

The country selected for this purpose is Sri Lanka, which has a long history dating back to 543 BC (de Silva 2014). Sri Lanka is a country that has recognized the importance of sustainable development from ancient times embracing integrated thinking and accountability (Weeramantry 2002). The sophisticated irrigation systems constructed during the ancient kingdoms of Sri Lanka, which were even admired by the British who ruled the country from 1815 to 1948 as a remarkable achievement, were an embodiment of integrated thinking, sustainability and accountability (Bailey and Tennent as cited in de Silva 2014). Over the years, Sri Lanka has become a hub of accountants in Asia exporting its accountants to Australasia, Middle East and Africa (Senarathne and Gunarathne 2017). Moreover, according to the World Bank (2015) report on 'Observance of Standards and Codes on Accounting and Auditing', Sri Lanka has always shown a keen interest in the improvement of its accounting and auditing practices. Reflecting this interest, many Sri Lankan companies have embraced SR and IR on a voluntary basis though they have not yet been mandated in the country (World Bank 2015). Further, it indicates that these companies have implemented their policies, governance structures and monitoring mechanisms to comply with Global Reporting Initiative (GRI)

Guidelines on SR. This claim is also supported by the findings of studies of Dissanayake et al. (2016), Gunarathne and Alahakoon (2016) and Abeydeera et al. (2016b). As identified in the World Bank report, some Sri Lankan companies had started to provide an Integrated Report even before the International Integrated Reporting Council (IIRC) issued the Framework on IR with one company[1] joining its pilot project. Further, the adoption of IR in Sri Lanka is at the diffusion[2] stage and hence there will be many adopters in the future (Gunarathne and Senaratne 2017). These factors highlight that Sri Lanka is a unique case for exploring how it displays competitive advantage in adopting IR. This uniqueness is discussed in this chapter based on Porter's Diamond Framework, which has been extensively used in the management literature as a theory that explains the international competitiveness of countries. This theory is described in detailed in Sect. 3.3.

The required data was collected from multiple sources, which include discussions, participation in forums, experiences of the authors and available rich literature. The authors held discussions with the relevant officials of companies engaged in SR and/or IR, assurance providers on SR, and representatives of PABs. These discussions were used to identify the factors that have motivated Sri Lankan companies to engage in SR and IR, the systems that they have established in this respect and the challenges faced. Further, the authors participated in several workshops on SR and IR conducted in Sri Lanka and sometimes even as panelists. In addition, both authors have served as judges of Institute of Certified Management Accountants of Sri Lanka (CMA) Excellence in IR Awards held in 2015. One of the authors participated in the evaluation committee of Institute of Chartered Accountants of Sri Lanka (CASL) for its first ever IR awards held in 2014 and in the panel of judges of Association for Chartered Certified Accountants (ACCA) Sustainability Reporting Awards 2015. Moreover, the authors have also drawn insights in developing this chapter from their research studies carried out in Sri Lanka on SR and IR.

The subsequent sections of this chapter are organized as follows: Sect. 3.2 provides a review of extant literature on IR, while the subsequent section presents the Diamond Theory of Porter (1990). Section 3.4 presents the application of Porter's Diamond Theory in order to illustrate how and why Sri Lanka displays a high level of IR adoption rate. The last Section presents the conclusions and the contributions of the chapter to accounting practices.

[1] Diesel and Motor Engineering PLC (DIMO) is the Sri Lankan company that has taken part in the IIRC Pilot Project. DIMO has a long history dating back to 1939. It has evolved over the years as a corporate entity with a significant presence in the automotive industry and providing services in an array of engineering sectors.

[2] Diffusion is the process by which an innovation is spread or disseminated through a social system over time (Rogers 1983). As per the temporal trend of diffusion the cumulative adoption path is "S- shaped" with primary, diffusion, condensing and saturation phases. The diffusion stage has a rapidly increasing number of adopters. For more details see Bjørnenak (1997)

3.2 Integrated Reporting

In this section, the extant literature on IR is reviewed under three broad headings: emergence of IR; concept of IR; and state of IR around the world.

3.2.1 Emergence of IR

Corporate reporting has undergone a dramatic transformation over time with the broadening of the accountability of companies to diverse group of stakeholders inclusive of the environment and society at large. Post et al. (2002) in their book *Redefining Corporation* explain this extended accountability as follows:

> The modern corporation is the centre of a network of interdependent interests and constituents each contributing (voluntarily or involuntarily) to its performance, and each anticipating benefits (or at least no uncompensated harms) as a result of the corporation's activities (p. 8).

This has led corporate entities to report on areas such as governance, risk management and sustainability in addition to their financial performance (Eccles and Serafeim 2011; Gray et al. 2001; KPMG 2008; Owen 2006). As a result, new forms of reporting such as social and environmental reporting, triple bottom line reporting, and SR have been developed (Eccles and Krzus 2010) under the broad heading of social responsibility reporting, which has led to a substantial increase in non-financial reporting by corporate entities (Van Staden and Wild 2013).

Despite these efforts, concerns have been raised as to whether clear information on the strategy, governance, performance and prospects of a company is reported to its stakeholders (Van Staden and Wild 2013). This discussion grew with the mega corporate scandals in many parts of the world in recent times causing much economic and social turmoil. As a result, the need arose to develop a reporting model that could combine different strands of corporate reporting, namely, financial, governance, and sustainability, into a coherent whole to explain an organization's ability to create and sustain value (Eccles and Krzus 2010). This provided the impetus for the emergence of IR as a new area of policy and practice in corporate reporting reflecting 'integrated thinking', and how value is created and sustained within an organization. Simnett and Huggins (2015) argue that prior to the advent of IR, there was no reporting framework by which companies could communicate their value-creation story across different time frames to interested stakeholders. IR, a contemporary managerial technology,[3] drives organizational change towards more sustainable outcomes (Eccles and Krzus 2010).

---

[3] Managerial technologies are those tools, devices and knowledge that mediate between inputs and outputs (Abrahamson 1991). Since IR combines the inputs, outputs and outcomes of the business models of an organization in terms of various forms of capitals, it falls within the definition of a managerial technology.

The pioneering work towards IR was made by the Danish pharmaceutical company Novo Nordisk in 2002 and the King III Report prepared in 2009, officially named as *King Code of Governance Principles for South Africa* (IoDSA and King III 2009), under the leadership of Professor Mervyn King, who championed the cause of IR in South Africa. Novozymes, a Danish enzyme company, spun off from Novo Nordisk in 2000, produced the first corporate integrated report in 2002 and Novo Nordisk began IR shortly thereafter (Eccles and Krzus 2010). Since then, Novo Nordisk has become a leader in the quest to measure and report social, environmental and financial performance within a single document (de Villars et al. 2014). This was followed by several Danish, US and Brazilian companies issuing integrated reports during the period from 2004 to 2008 (Eccles and Saltzman 2011). Even though these companies varied in terms of industry and geographical diversity, their reasons for issuing integrated reports are similar and are linked with their commitment to sustainability, which is defined broadly in financial and ESG terms. These companies had identified that an integrated report was the best way to communicate to stakeholders how well a company was accomplishing these objectives; and recognized that IR is an important discipline for ensuring that a company had a sustainable strategy. On the other hand, King III urged organizations to commit to the principles of integrated thinking, promoting the concept that strategy, governance and sustainability are intimately intertwined. These principles were subsequently incorporated into the Johannesburg Stock Exchange, requiring the listed companies to file an integrated report or explain why they were not doing so.

However, IR rapidly gained prominence globally with the formation of IIRC in 2010[4] with its mission to create a globally accepted framework on IR bringing together financial and ESG information of organizations into a clear, concise, consistent and comparable format (IIRC 2013). The International <IR> Framework of IIRC, the first complete globally accepted framework on IR, was published in 2013. Since then over 100 organizations have become a part of the IIRC pilot program for reporters, whose aim is to provide an opportunity to discuss and challenge technical material, test its application, and share learning and experiences (IIRC 2014).

3.2.2 *The Concept of IR*

IR is a process that focuses on how an organization creates value in the short, medium and long term. Hence, it combines different strands of corporate reporting (e.g. financial reporting- FR), governance reporting and SR into a coherent whole that explains an organization's ability to create and sustain value. Thus, IR combines two traditions of corporate reporting – FR and SR. FR views a firm as a

[4] The formation of IIRC took place in 2010 with the initiation of Prince's Accounting for Sustainability Project (A4s) and Global Reporting Initiative (GRI). It was initially called the International Integrated Reporting Committee and its name was changed to the International Integrated Reporting Council in 2012.

"nexus of contracts" among boards, managers, employees, suppliers and other actors, whose core purpose is to maximize returns to investors (Jensen and Mackling 1976). Conversely, SR provides a broader concept of a firm as a community of interdependent stakeholders who come together to create value as a collectivity (Sison 2010). Combining these two views, IIRC (2011) describes IR as follows:

> Integrated Reporting brings together the material information about an organization's strategy, governance, performance and prospects in a way that reflects the commercial, social and environmental context within which it operates. It provides a clear and concise representation of how an organization demonstrates stewardship and how it creates value, now and in the future. Integrated Reporting combines the most material elements of information currently reported in separate reporting strands (financial, management commentary, governance and remuneration, and sustainability) in a coherent whole, and importantly:
>
> - Shows the connectivity between them; and
> - Explains how they affect the ability of an organization to create and sustain value in the short, medium and long term (p. 3).

However, developing an IR approach within a company requires 'integrated thinking' to identify the connectivity between different facets of a company that contribute to creating value and complexity in its value creation process. Eccles and Krzus (2010) developed integrated thinking in line with their concept of 'One Report', which has become synonymous with IR. They describe the concept of 'One Report' as producing a single report that combines the financial information of a company with its non-financial information (such as environmental, social and governance issues) showing their impact on each other. They also propose that 'One Report' can help to shift the focus of an organization from short-term financial goals to long-term business strategy that encourages commitment to corporate social responsibility and to a sustainable society as well.

Further, Stent and Dowler (2015) identify that integrated thinking, which is the process central to IR, is concerned with a higher level of thinking, decision making and reporting processes, in contrast to superficial compliance with mandatory requirements to produce corporate reports. He finds significant parallels between IIRC's concept of "integrated thinking" and the systems thinking paradigm. Hence, it is through this process of integrated thinking that a company is able to create and sustain value.

IIRC (2013) distinguishes between IR (the process) and an integrated report (the end product of the process). In the IIRC <IR> Framework, an integrated report provides concise communication about how an organization's strategy, governance, performance and prospects, in the context of its external environment, lead to the creation of value over the short, medium and long term. Hence, an integrated report should explain how an organization creates value. The value is not created by or within an organization alone. It is influenced by the external environment, is created through relationships with stakeholders and is dependent on various resources. Thus, the integrated report of a company is required to provide insights into the following aspects:

Table 3.1 Categories and description of six capitals

Category	Description
Financial	Pool of funds available for an organization to use in the production of goods or provision of services and obtained through financing modes such as equity, debt, grants, or funds generated through operations or investments
Manufactured	Manufactured physical objects that are available to an organization for use in the production of goods or the provision of services
Intellectual	Organizational, knowledge-based intangibles that provide competitive advantage. These include (a) intellectual property, such as patents, copyrights, software, rights and licenses and (b) organizational capital such as tacit knowledge, systems, procedures and protocols
Human	People's competencies, capabilities and experience, and their motivations to innovate
Social and relationship	Institutions and relationships within and between communities, groups of stakeholders and other networks, and ability to share information to enhance individual and collective well-being
Natural	All renewable and nonrenewable environmental resources (e.g. air, water, land, minerals and forest) and processes (e.g. bio-diversity, eco-system health) that provide goods or services that support the past, current or future prosperity of an organization

Source: The International <IR> Framework 2013

(a) The external environment that affects the company;
(b) The resources and the relationships used and affected by the company, which are referred to collectively as capitals under six categories: Financial, Manufactured, Intellectual, Human, Social and Relationship, and Natural (Refer Table 3.1).
(c) The way the company interacts with the external environment and the capitals to create value over the short, medium and long term.

The accounting profession considers that the movement towards IR potentially represents the most significant change to the corporate reporting seen in years (Deloitte 2012) and its benefits have been considered in the academic literature. Eccles and Krzus (2010) classify the benefits of IR under two classes: internal benefits and external market benefits, where the former refers to better allocation of internal resources, greater engagement with stakeholders and lower reputational risk whilst the latter refers to meeting the needs of investors who require ESG information, appearing on sustainability indices, and ensuring data vendors report accurate non-financial information of a company. Eccles and Armbrester (2011) extend these benefits to include a third class of benefits termed managing regulatory risk covering the preparation for global regulations on IR and responding to local stock exchange requirements to report on IR.

3.2.3 State of IR Around the World

Companies are at varying stages in their path towards integration of different facets of reporting in moving towards IR, as revealed in the survey of ACCA and Net Balance Foundation (2011) in ASX 50 companies. The study carried out by Jensen and Berg (2012) reveals that there are several country-level determinants of IR such as investor and employment protection laws, intensity of market coordination and ownership concentration, the level of economic, environmental and social development, degree of national corporate responsibility and the value system of the country of origin. However, more recent studies show that IR is gaining momentum as a reporting model. The survey carried out by KPMG in Japan reveals that the number of Japanese companies that have prepared integrated reports in 2014 has considerably increased (i.e. by 38%) compared to that of 2013 and 26% of these companies have made explicit reference to the IIRC Framework. Further, 42% of these companies have presented their business models with 41% of them making reference to capitals identified in the IIRC Framework (KPMG 2015). Nevertheless, there are impediments to adopting an IR reporting model. Stent and Dowler (2015), providing early evidence of the changes required for current corporate reporting in New Zealand in terms of the IR Framework requirements, observe a gap between IR requirements and current best practice reporting processes. The study finds that common deficiencies that contribute to this gap include failing to: integrate reporting processes and to provide for oversight of these processes; report against regional/industry benchmarks; and to report on uncertainties in the future outlook of the entities concerned.

On the other hand, several studies have addressed the potential of reporting practices employed by the early adopters of IR to promote the transition to sustainable business practices. Stubbs and Higgins (2014), who investigated the internal mechanism employed by early adopters of IR in Australia, find that these organizations have changed or claimed to have changed their processes and structures; they have not necessarily stimulated new innovations in disclosure mechanisms. Hence, this study suggests that currently IR represents rather a transition from SR than an innovation driving transformation in organizations. Higgins et al. (2014) examined the business organizations in Australia that were the first to adopt IR, drawing from institutional theory to explain how early adopters made sense of IR. They suggest that the institutionalization of IR is unfolding and that isomorphism is likely to follow. However, this study also shares the view that this process is unlikely to deliver a fundamental change to organizational operations. While most of these studies are limited to developed countries, in the Sri Lankan context, Gunarathne and Senaratne (2017) find that IR adoption is at a diffusion stage with the number of companies that have adopted IR increasing rapidly from two companies in 2011 to 32 by the end of 2014. Further, Gunarathne and Senaratne (2017) find that the early adopting companies of IR in Sri Lanka had also been engaged in SR in the past. These companies are characterized by their integrated business models, a progressive work culture and the supportive role extended by the top management for adopting managerial innovations. The study also finds a transitional approach to IR in these companies evolving through incremental changes to systems and processes that are already established in them in relation to SR. This reflects a similar pattern to that observed by Stubbs and Higgins (2014) in Australia.

Further, Brown and Dillard (2014) critically assess IR to broaden the dialogue on how accounting and reporting standards assist or hinder efforts to foster sustainable business practices. In their study, they criticize the IIRC proposals stating that they offer few critical insights into the current ways of thinking, acting and reporting. Thus, drawing on natural science and technology research, they present the ways in which IR can be rearticulated. Further, Simnett and Huggins (2015) provide insights and details of the process of adoption of IR with implications for adopters and assurance providers of integrated reports, standard setters and regulators. They argue that in the early stages of the International <IR> Framework, there is a need and desire for corporate decisions to be based on a high quality and appropriate evidence base. This indicates that any business case for either regulatory initiatives or individual entity decision-making should be informed by high-quality research. Hence, the studies on IR in general have provided insights into the thinking, policy and practices around IR in different countries posing many interesting issues for further investigation in future studies. In this context, this chapter attempts to address how an Asian Pacific country displays competitive advantage in adopting IR using Porter's Diamond Theory.

3.3 Porter's Diamond Theory

Porter's (1990) Diamond Theory suggests several important determinants of a nation's global competitiveness. This model cleverly integrates the important variables that determine a nation's competitiveness into one model while most of the other models are not comprehensive models (Moon et al. 1998). Porter's model has been widely used to analyze a country's competitive advantage, in general, or the global competitiveness of industries (Bellak and Weiss 1993; Cartwright 1993; Clancy et al. 2001; Curran 2000; Hodgetts 1993; Moon et al. 1998; Sardy and Fetscherin 2009; Sledge 2005; Zhaoa et al. 2011). According to Porter (1990), the ability to derive advantages in international trade and sustain them is not a cause, but an effect. Porter is of the view that a nation is most likely to be successful in industries when the national 'diamond' is the most favorable. The Diamond Theory has four broad interrelated attributes, namely, (a) factor conditions; (b) demand conditions, (c) related and supporting industries, and (d) firm strategy, structure, and rivalry (refer Fig. 3.1). He further suggests that government and chance events act as exogenous parameters of the model.

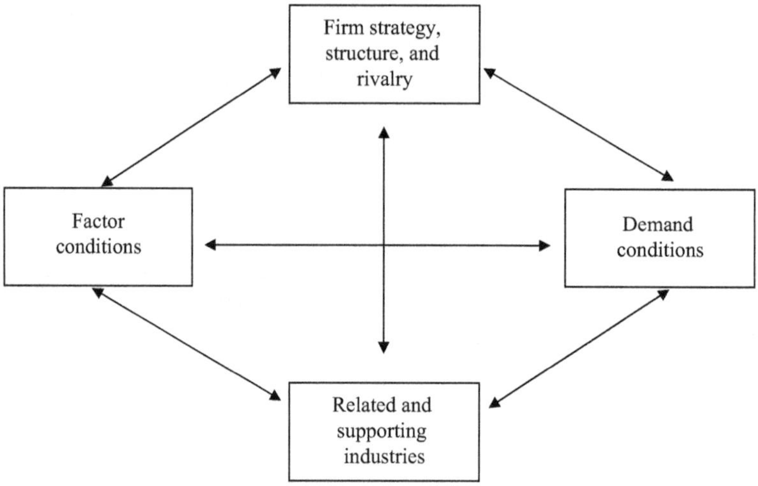

Fig. 3.1 Determinants of national competitive advantage (Source: Porter 1990, p. 72)

3.3.1 Factor Conditions

Every nation possesses factors of production – the inputs necessary for competing in any industry such as labor, land, natural resources and infrastructure. These factors can be grouped broadly into human resources, physical resources, knowledge resources (in universities, research institutes, databases, and trade associations), capital resources and infrastructure (transportation systems, communications systems). In suggesting a hierarchy of factors, Porter distinguishes between basic factors (natural resources, climate, location, unskilled labor and semi-skilled labor) and advanced factors (modern communications infrastructure, educated personnel, and research institutes). He is of the view that advanced factors are the most important for achieving higher order competitive advantage. They are scarce since their development needs sustained investments of both human and physical capital. In discussing the importance of factor creation, Porter opines:

> Nations succeed in industries where they are particularly good at creating, and most importantly, upgrading the needed factors. Thus, the nations will be competitive where they possess unusually high quality institutional mechanisms for specialized factor creation. (Porter 1990, p. 80)

3.3.2 Demand Conditions

Another important component of the model, namely, home demand conditions, shapes the rate and character of improvement and innovation by firms. Porter suggests that there are three broad attributes of home demand: nature of buyer needs of home demand, the size and patterns of growth of home demand (rate of growth of home demand, the presence of independent buyers and early home demand) and the mechanisms by which a nation's domestic preferences are transmitted to foreign markets through multinational local buyers (Porter 1990, p. 86). Nations can gain advantage when home buyers exert pressure on local firms to innovate faster and achieve more sophisticated advantages. In explaining the nature of buyer needs, Porter suggests that when domestic buyers are sophisticated and demanding and the needs of home buyers anticipate those of other nations, a nation's firms gain competitive advantage. In support of this view, Moon et al. (1998) hypothesize that a higher level of education among consumers, inter alia, could also increase demand sophistication.

3.3.3 Related and Supporting Industries

Home-based suppliers and related industries are another attribute of the diamond. The presence of internationally competitive supplier industries creates advantage for downstream industries by providing efficient, early and rapid access to cost-effective inputs and fostering the process of innovation and upgrading (Porter 1990). According to Moon et al. (1998), related and supporting industries are "those whereby firms coordinate or share activities in the value chain or those which involve products that are complementary to the firms of a given nation" (p. 143). The internationally successful related industries provide opportunities for information flow and technical interchange, share activities and forge alliances (Porter 1990)

3.3.4 Firm Strategy, Structure and Rivalry

Explaining another broad determinant of national competitive advantage, Porter suggests that the context in which firms are created, organized and managed and the nature of domestic rivalry play a significant role. Firms will succeed when the management practices are favored by the national environment. Also, Porter proposes that some important aspects such as attitudes towards authority, interpersonal interactions, social norms of individualistic or group behavior and professional standards influence the way in which firms are organized and managed. Porter suggests that these grow out of the education system, social of religious history, family structure and many other unique conditions of a nation. The nature of corporate governance and motivations of owners or managers who manage the firms can enhance the success of certain industries when these goals and motivations are aligned with the sources of competitive advantage. Porter expresses a strong preference for vigorous domestic rivalry for creating and sustaining competitive advantage (p. 117). In contrast to the popular argument of wasteful domestic competition, Porter is of the view that nurturing "national champions" can enhance national competitive advantage. He prefers domestic rivalry when improvements and innovations are recognized as the essential ingredients of competitive advantage. Domestic rivalry can take many forms such as price or even technology. Rivalry creates pressure on others to improve, signals others that advancements are possible, attracts new rivals to an industry and fosters government support. Sometimes, domestic rivalry by going beyond economic rationales can become emotional and even personal.

In explaining the exogenous parameters, Porter suggests that chance events, the occurrences that have little to do with the circumstances of a nation, and hence are outside the powers of firms and government, by influencing and being influenced by each of the four determinants, are also significant for determining national competitive advantage.

Despite its wide acceptability, the model is not without its critics. Moon et al. (1998) are of the view that Porter fails to incorporate the effects of multinational activities in the model and this has limited its predictive power (Grant 1991). Hence, a Double Diamond Theory (Rugman and D'Cruz 1993) has been suggested incorporating both domestic and foreign diamonds. Moreover, Moon et al. (1998) have also suggested a generalized Double Diamond Model to analyze small economies.

The next section of this chapter explains how the attributes of Porter's (1990) Diamond Theory can be used to explain the country readiness of Sri Lanka in adopting IR.

3.4 Application of Diamond Theory to Sri Lanka

This section illustrates how Sri Lanka displays a high level of readiness for IR adoption by using the four attributes, namely, (a) factor conditions, (b) demand conditions, (c) related and supporting industries, and (d) firm strategy, structure, and rivalry of Porter's (1990) Diamond Theory.

3.4.1 Factor Conditions

Sri Lanka is home to many advanced factors that could favorably impact the fast adoption of IR. Among them, its skilled labor force, which is a result of the country's significant investment in education from 1947, plays a major role (Ministry of Education, MOE 2013). Sri Lanka introduced free education from kindergarten to university in early 1947 (MOE 2013) and this has enabled it to maintain a very high primary and secondary education enrolment ratio (refer Table 3.2).

Due to these investments in human capital, the country enjoyed a literacy rate of 92.5% in 2013 (Department of Census and Statistics of Sri Lanka 2013), which is one of the highest in Asia. Moreover, the country produces approximately 29,000 graduates (both graduate and postgraduate) annually (University Grants Commission, UGC 2013) through its university system. In addition, there are many vocational training colleges, technological institutions, private universities, etc. that

Table 3.2 Selected education enrolment indicators in Sri Lanka

Indicator	% (out of total category)
Primary net enrolment ratio (5–9 years)	98.45
Secondary net enrolment ratio (10–14 years)	99.19
Age-specific enrolment ratio (5–14 years)	98.77

Source: Central Bank of Sri Lanka (CBSL) 2014, p. 77

offer both graduate and postgraduate level qualifications. While some of these courses focus on accounting and business management that are related to IR directly, others are from different disciplines. These figures, compared with the country's population of twenty million, become significant in facilitating the adoption of IR. As outlined in the Six Capital Model (refer Sect. 3.2), this diverse knowledge of functional areas facilitates integrated thinking and creating integrated business models within organizations. Since sustainability (or even accounting), in general, can be supported and/or practised by accountants as well as non-accountants (Bennett et al. 2013; Gunarathne et al. 2015; Montano et al. 2001; Schaltegger and Zvezdov 2015), this diverse skill base of the country provides a generally favorable condition for the adoption of IR.

In addition to this general skill base, Sri Lanka is home to three local PABs and two international PABs of UK origin (World Bank 2015). Sri Lanka's strong accounting profession has its roots dating back to British colonial rule in the country (Senaratne and Cooray 2012). Due to the long presence of the two UK- based accounting bodies, now the country boasts the highest UK-qualified accountants among countries outside the UK (SLASSCOM 2015). Table 3.3 shows the number of students and members of these PABs. Even though the PABs in Sri Lanka date back to British colonial times, the richness of its accounting practices can be traced back to the time of its ancient kingdoms (Liyanarachchi 2009, 2015). Liyanarachchi (2009) provides evidence of the accounting and auditing practices that prevailed in ancient Sri Lanka (from 815 to 1017 AD) showing how accounting was relied upon to maintain the reputation of a Buddhist monastery and that of its members, and thereby maintain goodwill among Buddhist monks, rulers, and people. Liyanarachchi (2015), which is an extension to Liyanarachchi (2009), shows that Buddhist Temple Accounting (BTA) emerged to address the societal need for accountability during that era reflecting the socio-economic needs that motivated them. Hence, concepts such as accounting and accountability have been deeply rooted in Sri Lankan society for a long period, providing a conducive background for the PABs to flourish during and after colonization.

In addition, there are 13 universities and several vocational training colleges that offer degrees and diplomas in accounting specialization (UGC 2013). Additionally, the students of engineering, physical sciences and agriculture also learn accounting and/or business management as part of their degree programs. This skill base, either specializing in accounting or being familiar with accounting/business management, provides an encouraging climate for adopting IR. This is evident in the fact that about 50% of students who earn higher education degrees are trained in technical and busi-

Table 3.3 Numbers of students and members of PABs in Sri Lanka

Name of the PAB	No. of students	No. of members	IFAC member status
CASL	44,007	4300	Full member
CMA	16,877	2253	Full member
AAT	40,118	4069	Associate member
CIMA	15,727	3163	Full member
ACCA	790	264	Full member

Source: World Bank (2015, p. 28)
CASL – Institute of Chartered Accountants of Sri Lanka
CMA – Institute of Certified Management Accountants of Sri Lanka
AAT – Association of Accounting Technicians of Sri Lanka
CIMA – Chartered Institute of Management Accountants UK
ACCA – Association of Chartered Certified Accountant UK

ness disciplines (AT Kearney 2012). The density of qualified accountants in the country has enabled Sri Lanka to be considered a vibrant business process outsourcing sector for financing and accounting outsourcing (FAO) (World Bank 2015) and to be ranked among the top 19 global centers of excellence for FAO (SLASSCOM 2015).

There have been remarkable infrastructural developments in Sri Lanka recently, particularly in information technology. Colombo, the commercial capital of the country, has been ranked among the top 20 outsourcing destinations in the Asia Pacific region (Tholons 2014). Moreover, AT Kearney (2012) recognized Sri Lanka as a hidden gem for IT, business process outsourcing and knowledge services outsourcing. Compared to other developing nations, the country has a high level of IT literacy as well. In addition to this high level of general IT literacy, the country places a high level of emphasis on the IT skill development of accountants by making it an integral component of the curriculum. Given below are some notable steps taken in this regard:

- The Department of Accounting (DA) of the University of Sri Jayewardenepura (USJ)[5] has focused on the development of IT skills among its graduates from the inception (i.e. from 1992); this emphasis is still sustained in its curriculum).
- The two local PABs, CASL and CMA, offer IT-based accounting course units during and after the professional course.
- CIMA has now converted its entire examination system into a computer-based system.

In addition to the high level of IT skills, the level of English is high in the country and is considered the language of the business community. Due to the impact of colonial rule from 1815 to 1948, (AT Kearney 2012; Jayewardene 2000), the country has placed a lot of emphasis on learning the English language from kindergarten to university level. The emphasis on English language skill development is also essential for accountants. For instance,

[5] DA, USJ introduced the first accounting degree program in the Sri Lankan University system in 1991.

- The medium of instruction is English in many of the academic accountancy degree programs such as USJ and University of Colombo.
- In CASL and, CMA only the first two stages are not conducted in English while ACCA and CIMA courses are conducted totally in English.
- CASL and CMA have separate English language skill development course units.
- DA of USJ, CASL and CMA have oral practical requirements in the English medium.

The high level of IT use and fluency in English also provide a very positive environment for the accountants to adopt IR easily by means of, but not limited to,

- Enabling them to easily access international resources including new developments on IR and practices of internationally pioneering companies using the internet.
- Enabling them to better understand the contents of IR and also to collaborate with foreign parties which could further strengthen its adoption.
- Supporting them to easily capture sophisticated Information Systems required for the adoption of IR.
- Enabling them to utilize the available systems and processes in organizations to facilitate models that support IR.

3.4.2 Demand Conditions

The buyers of IR are a wide set of stakeholders who will use the report for various purposes. There is a great need in Sri Lanka for corporate reporting that focuses not only on financial but also on non-financial performance. This demand stems from various stakeholders including business partners, government, customers, and even society at large.

Sri Lankan society is generally vigilant about the environmental and social implications of business activities. In recent years, ignorance of environmental and social ramifications, corruption, cronyism, nepotism and malpractices have been extensively criticized in the political and social arenas in Sri Lanka. This phenomenon was powerful enough to overthrow the former government of Sri Lanka at the 2015 election (Bandarage 2015). Thus, civil society continuously expects the government as well as organizations to act in an environmentally and socially friendly manner. There are many instances where failure to maintain the social license (Deegan 2000, 2002; Patten 1992), particularly due to ignorance of the impact of organizational activities on the environment and community, have led to a suspension of business activities or social chaos (Cho 2009). For example, water contamination issues such as in Rathupaswela[6] created significant social unrest in

[6]In 2013 the villagers in Rathupaswela had been protesting against a water crisis they faced for a long period. They were demanding that the Rubber Gloves Factory in the area be shut down claiming that the factory waste was polluting the groundwater in the area. When the army was deployed

civil society. Due to very high penetration levels of IT, civil society in Sri Lanka is very active in using the electronic media in general and social media in particular for a variety of purposes (Gunawardene 2015). For instance, any malpractice of the government, a corporation or a public institute is immediately published in the social media thus demonstrating the empowerment of the people in developing nations (Ali 2011). This creates pressure on companies to cautiously monitor their activities and performance and also report on them targeting the wider society in a bid to maintain or enhance its social license to operate.

Apart from these pressures, local and foreign buyers of products of Sri Lankan companies also demand better social and environmental performance together with good governance. Since the country has been following an export-oriented policy from 1978, it has become a preferred supplier of apparel, IT solutions, tea, etc. Hence, these organizations, which are mainly export-oriented, are compelled to follow integrated business practices and report on their performance (Fernando et al. 2015; Dissanayake et al. 2016) as part of a global supply chain.

3.4.3 Related and Supported Industries

From a related and supportive industry perspective, the availability of three local PABs and two foreign PABs bodies (refer Table 3.3) is another favorable condition. These PABs contribute to the adoption of IR in different ways as follows:

- Since these PABs are IFAC member bodies, they need to align their curricula and Continuous Professional Development (CPD) programs with the International Education Standards (IESs) of IFAC (IFAC 2014). This ensures that the members of these PABs are kept updated on the latest developments in the field of accounting (World Bank 2015).
- In order to remain relevant and also to differentiate between each other, these PABs (both local and foreign) that operate in Sri Lanka actively take many initiatives to popularize IR. These activities improve the awareness of members while providing training and guidance in IR which provides a favorable environment for adopting IR. Some of these notable activities are shown in Table 3.4 below:
- These PABs also hold competitions/award schemes on IR. They have become very effective in the speedy diffusion of IR in the Sri Lankan context (Gunarathne and Senaratne 2017). They are listed in Table 3.5 below. They promote awareness, identify issues, and provide guidelines and training opportunities. Through a combination of resources, preparers of integrated reports have access to a rich pool of resources to support high quality reports (World Bank 2015).

---

to disperse the protesters, 3 people (including 2 schoolboys) were killed and 36 civilians were injured. This spurred a wide social and political crisis in the country, making the government of that time highly unpopular. Due to the widespread social unrest, the Human Rights Commission of Sri Lanka (HRCSL) conducted an investigation and held the army responsible for the shooting (Maduwage 2015).

Table 3.4 Activities organized in Sri Lanka on IR

Activity	Organized by	Year
Conference on IR (Business Resilience through IR)	CMA	2015
Launch of "Preparer's Guide to Integrated Corporate Reporting"	CASL	2015
Roundtable discussion on IR	CASL	2013
CFO Forum on IR	CASL	2013
Seminar on IR	CASL	2013

Table 3.5 Competitions organized in Sri Lanka on IR

Competition	Organized by
Excellence in integrated reporting awards	CMA
Sustainability reporting awards	ACCA
Integrated reporting award presented at annual report competition	CASL
Sustainability reporting award presented at annual report competition	CASL

- These PABs not only promote IR but also set an example by preparing their annual reports as integrated reports. Almost all the PABs, both foreign and local, have prepared their latest annual reports as integrated reports. This provides guidance, motivation and models for the companies to prepare their integrated reports.

Not only PABs but also some universities in the country are very active in promoting IR and SR (Gunarathne and Alahakoon 2016). Among them, the DA of USJ has taken many initiatives in this regard including the following:

- Introduction of IR into the degree curricula.
- IR has now been included in the curricula of the following course units in bachelor's and master's levels:
  - ACC 3320: Financial Reporting
  - ACC 4322: Advanced Accounting Theory
  - ACC 4327: Sustainability Management Accounting
  - MPACC 1301: Contemporary Issues in Financial Reporting
- Guest lectures on IR to share industry experiences.
- Forums and conferences related to sustainability that also discuss IR, for example,
  - 2014 – Forum on Sustainability Management Accounting
  - 2015 – EMAN Global Conference
  - 2015 – Business Forum on Sustainability held in parallel with the EMAN Global Conference

While the first two activities focus on the students, who will be the future accountants, the last activity mainly focuses on the business community, academics and policy makers of the country who directly apply or promote the adoption of IR.

The availability of consulting firms and assurance providers also plays an important role in providing a conducive environment for the adoption of IR. The country has a well developed supportive industry that comprises:

- Annual report preparing companies;
- Consulting firms; and
- Assurance providers.

The authors see a nexus between players with related and supportive industry points of view. This nexus is depicted in Fig. 3.2.

The PABs, universities and consulting firms provide the necessary inputs and guidance to the preparers of integrated reports while the annual report preparing companies provide a facilitating role in the integrated report preparation process. The assurance provided by furnishing an external independent view improves the credibility of the information in the reports. In addition to providing inputs for the integrated report preparers, the PABs drive the adoption of IR through their competitions. Hence, the motivating impact of PABs is shown as a dotted line in the nexus.

3.4.4 *Firm Strategy, Structure and Rivalry*

The strategies and structures of Sri Lankan business firms also support the adoption of IR. The preparation of sustainability reports over a long period of time has led many Sri Lankan firms to adopt conducive strategies and structures to support the adoption of IR. As Senaratne et al. (2015) found, there are 105 listed companies that

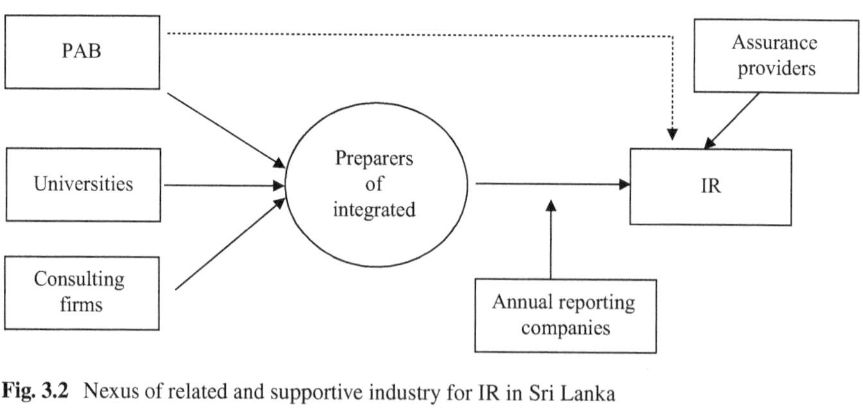

Fig. 3.2 Nexus of related and supportive industry for IR in Sri Lanka

Table 3.6 Competitors in IR award schemes

Competition	Organized by	No. of applicants
Sustainability reporting awards	ACCA – 2014	76
	ACCA – 2015	55
Excellent in integrated reporting awards	CMA	41
Integrated reporting award presented at annual report competition	CASL	29
Sustainability reporting award presented at annual report competition	CASL	29

prepare sustainability reports. Also, there are a few other non-listed firms that prepare sustainability reports. As identified by Stubbs and Higgins (2014), the companies that prepare sustainability reports find the adoption of IR to be a transition from sustainability reporting rather than a transformation. This view is further confirmed by Gunarathne and Senaratne (2017) in the Sri Lankan context. By practising sustainability reporting, these companies have built an integrated business model/thinking. For example, these companies have:

- Separate well established sustainability units/divisions;
- Persons responsible for sustainability such as sustainability champions whose job descriptions now include the work they have to carry out for sustainability;
- Availability of information systems that support sustainability information; and
- Sustainability thinking within the organizations and availability of mechanisms such as 14,000, and ISO 50001.

From a rivalry perspective, as mentioned in the related and supportive industry section, PABs hold many competitions (refer Table 3.6). The situation has therefore promoted competition among the business community to win awards. The number of applications received for the competitions provides evidence of the enthusiasm of the Sri Lankan business community to compete for awards.

Although the four attributes of Porter (1990) can be used to explain why Sri Lanka enjoys a competitive advantage in adopting IR, the authors strongly felt that the explanation is incomplete in this context. Hence, further deliberations and analysis led them to discover a missing attribute in adopting Porter's Diamond Theory. The next section explains this missing attribute.

3.5 The Missing Attribute: Impact of National Culture

In the Porter's Diamond Theory, too little attention has been given to the influence of national culture on the national competitive advantage (Bosch and Prooijen 1992). Bosch and Prooijen (1992) suggest that "the influence of national culture can be shown for every determinant of Porter's Diamond" and they go on to say "national culture is the base on which the national diamond rests" (p. 176). Echoing a similar view, the authors clearly noticed crucial role the Sri Lankan national culture plays in facilitating IR adoption and its effect on the four attributes of the Diamond Theory. The impact of national culture on accounting practices has been studied extensively and widely debated (Askary 2006; Askary et al. 2008; Gray 1988; Gray and Vint 1995; Lee and Herold 2016; Perera 1989). Many of these studies have referred to Hofstede's (1980) notable work on national culture. However, so far, we did not come across any study that attempts to integrate national culture to the Diamond Theory to explain the competitive advantage of a nation towards adopting accounting practices.

As outlined briefly in Sect. 3.1, the growing interest in IR in Sri Lanka is a manifestation of concepts such as accountability and sustainability, which are deeply rooted in Sri Lankan society from the time of the ancient kingdoms of the country (from 543 BC to 1815). The maintenance of an irrigation network spreading over the dry zone in the country during the Anuradhapura Kingdom, the first capital of Sri Lanka from 377 BC to 1017, is a classic example of the holistic view adopted in the development of the country by its kings. These irrigation systems consisting of tanks, canals and channels were made to conserve water during the rainy season and use it in paddy cultivation, which was the main livelihood of the people during that time and was remarkably attuned to coping with geological and geographical peculiarities of the location (de Silva 2014). Hence, these irrigation systems contributed to improving the agriculture sector of the economy and social conditions of the people while safeguarding the environment through the conservation of water. This also indicates the broad connotation given to accountability by the Sri Lankan kings focusing on all three dimensions of sustainability – economic, social and environmental. This thinking that has shaped the national culture of the country for many centuries still remains in Sri Lanka.

Though there is no unified national culture (de Silva 2014; Jayawardena 2000), Sinhalese-Buddhist culture is dominant and shared by the majority of Sri Lankans. The central doctrine of Buddha is the concept of "dependent origination" (known as *paticca-samuppada*), in which the conditionality of all physical and psychical phenomena can be observed (Payutto 1994; Wijeratne 2006). This is in contrast to theism, which advocates the idea of linear thinking and evolution of time and space. Since this way of thinking has been internalized in Sri Lankan society over many centuries, society, including the individuals and social institutions, believes in holistic and system thinking, which is very much akin to the integrated thinking in IR. Thus, the central idea of IR is not alien to Sri Lankan society. In support of our view, Lodhia (2015) shows how the ethical principles valuing the inter-connected nature of economic, environmental and social dimensions of an organization impact on creating integrated thinking on which IR is grounded on. While integrated thinking is a part of the Sri Lankan ethos, there are many other ways in which the Six Capital Model of IR is positively influenced by the concepts in Buddhism. For example, the Buddha's path to emancipation (*vimikka*) is laid down in the four Noble (*ariya*) Truths. The path to emancipation (known as *aria attangika-magga* or the noble eightfold path), which is the last noble truth, consists of *sila* (morality), *samadhi* (mental discipline) and *panna* (wisdom) (refer Appendix 2). For instance, the *sila* of the eightfold path is based on compassion and universal love towards all living and non-living beings, which essentially covers the human and natural capitals in the Six Capital Model of IR. The third *sila* – right livelihood – is to refrain from all ill-virtuous activities and the Sri Lankans regard right livelihood as very important when choosing an occupation or business. This highlights the importance of following governance (mainly self-governance) which is also an essential ingredient of IR. Moreover, Buddha emphasized the importance of investment in the *Sigalovada Sutta* (of *Digha-nikaya*), the importance of the environment in the *Thera-Theri Gatha* (*Kuddhika-nikaya*), and the duties of a layman towards different stakeholders including employees in the *Digha-nikaya* (Wijeratne 2006). *Though a detailed coverage of Buddhist way of thinking is not expected to be given in this chapter, the authors wish to stress that Buddhist thinking greatly facilitates the integrated thinking and concepts of IR in a number of ways.*

However, the authors do not believe that IR will necessarily be an absolute happening in Sri Lanka, mainly due to this cultural aspect. While providing a very favorable condition, Buddhist culture itself leads to a dilemma in regard to the adoption of IR. The Buddhists engage in virtuous and rightful activities as part of their religious observances and do not display an interest in reporting. Perhaps, frequent reporting of such activities, particularly CSR or sustainability, is deemed insincere, not genuine, and this managerial intent overrules the accounting aspect (Fernando 2014). Thus this poses a challenge for managers or corporations. Similarly Buddhists, through their middle path thinking, are self-contained in a mediocre life in which accumulation of material wealth is hardly valued (Nanayakkara 1988). This aspect, the authors think, may reduce the Sri Lankan managers' or accountants' desire to achieve excellence in IR. They might possibly settle for an indifferent attitude to IR, and thus may lose interest in keeping abreast of international developments in IR. The duality of the Buddhist culture offers a very conducive environment for the adoption of IR, coupled with the other four factors of national competitive advantage, while restraining the Sri Lankan business community or organizations from achieving great heights in IR. The authors believe that it is the interplay of these two opposing forces of Sri Lankan culture that will decide the future of IR in Sri Lanka.

On the other hand, recent empirical evidence shows that the corporate reporting practices in Sri Lanka are strongly influenced by global reporting guidelines such as GRI (refer Abeydeera et al. 2016b, b for more details). For example, Abeydeera et al. (2016b) find a disconnect between Buddhism as a prevalent institutional force in the local culture and corporate representations evident in SR practices in Sri Lanka particularly owing to later being highly institutionalized by global reporting frameworks such as GRI. Further Abeydeera et al. (2016a) argue that Buddhist values, which that typically shape managers' private moral positions on sustainability are not generally reflected in the organizations in which they work since the economic factors overshadow the activities of these organizations. Thoradeniya et al. (2015) find that Buddhism significantly affect values and beliefs of managers of Sri Lankan companies particularly of non-listed entities when they engage in SR practices. Though these studies are mainly focused on SR (not necessarily IR), we believe that the national culture alone does not influence the corporations (or managers) to engage in IR or SR practices. Only when these attributes of the Porter's Diamond Theory are present along with the favourable cultural environment, Sri Lanka is positioned on a strong situation to adopt IR practices than other countries. The recent growth in IR adoption by the corporations in Sri Lanka provides evidence to this.

3.6 Conclusions

The chapter explained why and how Sri Lanka, an emerging Asia Pacific island nation, displays a high rate of adoption of IR. By drawing on the theoretical framing of Porter's Diamond Theory, the chapter illustrated how attributes such as the availability of qualified professional accountants and the high level of general education, various stakeholder demands for better ESG reporting, a dynamic accounting profession together with supportive industries, intense competition among organizations and established structures and strategies for SR play a crucial role in facilitating the adoption of new accounting tools such as IR. More importantly, the authors suggest that the national culture, which is very much akin to integrated thinking and Six Capital Model, provides a favourable condition to follow integrated thinking that would eventually lead to IR.

By explaining country readiness of Sri Lanka in adopting IR, the chapter makes several important contributions to the existing body of knowledge of both IR and SR. First, it demonstrates the country context in an emerging Asia Pacific nation in adopting new emerging ESG reporting tools and techniques such as IR (de Villars et al. 2014). Through this, the chapter attempts to broaden the knowledge of IR, which is, so far, based on theoretical investigations and stand-alone case studies (Jensen and Berg 2012) limited mainly to developed countries. Second, the chapter extends Porter's (1990) Diamond Theory to analyze how a country enjoys competitive advantage in adopting new managerial or accounting technologies. This is a novel approach since the Diamond Theory has been largely used to explain the national competitive advantage of certain industries such as automobile, petrochemical, dairy, music, software, power or education or countries (for instance, see Clancy et al. 2001; Curran 2000; Hodgetts 1993; Sardy and Fetscherin 2009; Sledge 2005; Zhaoa et al. 2011). Third, the paper attempts to integrate the crucial role played by the national culture in promoting or restraining new managerial or accounting tools and techniques in Porter's Diamond Theory. Although the culture and accounting have been studied extensively in the past, we hardly found any research that investigates the impact of national culture on recently emerging accounting practices such as IR or SR, particularly in the emerging Asian Pacific economies.

Apart from these academic contributions, this chapter deals with some important implications for policy makers and various professions in identifying the requisite conditions for promoting new managerial tools and techniques such as IR and

SR. The Diamond Theory essentially provides an analytical framework for governments, regulators, policy makers and professional institutions to identify a situational analysis (such as SWOT). The global accounting players such as IFAC, GRI or IIRC or even other bodies such as the World Bank, UNICEF or UN can understand why some countries report a fast diffusion of new (accounting) concepts or tools while other countries are slow in adopting them. These local or international players thereby can identify the focus areas to concentrate on when promoting new managerial technologies.

Appendices

Appendix 1: Linking sustainability performance to six capitals

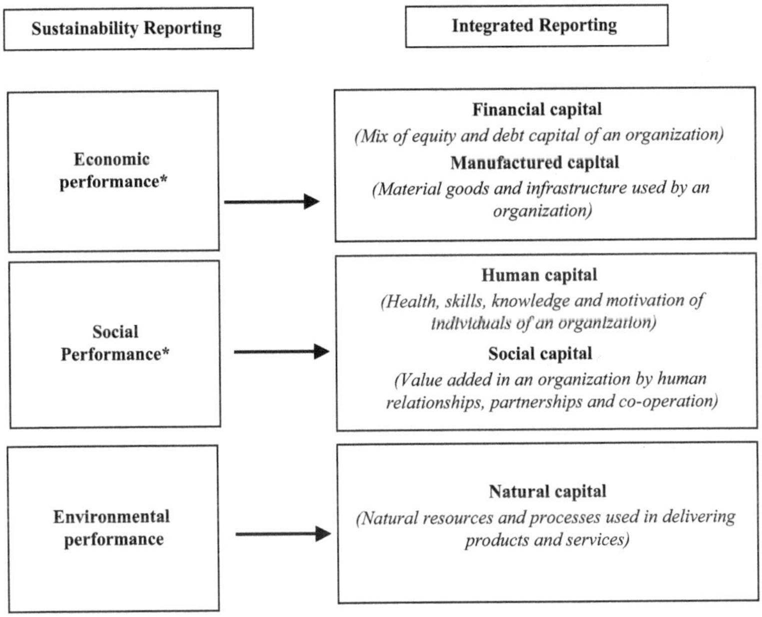

* Intellectual capital (i.e. organizational knowledge-based intangibles, including intellectual property and organizational capital) can be mainly related to economic and social performance. It should also be noted the relationships given above are not mutually exclusive and hence there can be many other linkages among sustainability performance aspects to six capitals

Appendix 2: Eightfold path of Buddha's way of emancipation

Division	Eightfold-path factors
Wisdom (*panna*)	1. Right view/understanding (*Samma-Ditthi*)
	2. Right intention (*Samma-Sankappa*)
Ethical conduct/morality (*sila*)	3. Right speech (*Samma-Vaca*)
	4. Right action (*Samma-Kammanta*)
	5. Right livelihood (*Samma-Ajiva*)
Concentration/mental discipline (*samadhi*)	6. Right effort (*Samma-Vayama*)
	7. Right mindfulness (*Samma-Sati*)
	8. Right concentration (*Samma-Samadhi*)

Source: Narada (2010)

References

Abeydeera S, Kearins K, Tregidga H (2016a) Does Buddhism enable a different sustainability ethic at work? J Corp Citizenship 6:109–130

Abeydeera S, Tregidga H, Kearins K (2016b) Sustainability reporting – more global than local? Meditari Acc Res 24(4):478–504

Abrahamson E (1991) Managerial fads and fashions: the diffusion and rejection of innovations. Acad Manag Rev 16(3):586–612

ACCA and Net Balance Foundation (2011) Adoption of integrated reporting by the ASX 50. Available via: http://www.accaglobal.com/content/dam/acca/global/PDF-technical/sustainability-reporting/tech-tp-air2.pdf. Accessed 17 Aug 2014

Ali AH (2011) The power of social media in developing nations: new tools for closing the global digital divide and beyond. Harvard Hum Rights J 24:185–219

Askary S (2006) Accounting professionalism – a cultural perspective of developing countries. Manag Audit J 21(1/2):102–111

Askary S, Yazdifar H, Askarany D (2008) Culture and accounting practices in Turkey. Int J Account Audit Perform Eval 5(1):66–88

AT Kearney (2012) Competitive benchmarking: Sri Lanka knowledge services. AT Kearney, Korea

Bandarage A (2015) Good governance in Sri Lanka. The world post. Available via: http://www.huffingtonpost.com/asoka-bandarage/good-governance-in-sri-lanka_b_7087768.html. Accessed 22 Nov 2015

Baron R (2014) The evolution of corporate reporting for integrated performance- background paper for the 30th round table on sustainable development. OECD, Paris

Bellak CJ, Weiss A (1993) A note on the Austrian "diamond". Manag Int Rev 33(2):109–118

Bennett M, Schaltegger S, Zvezdov D (2013) Exploring corporate practices in management accounting for sustainability. Institute for Chartered Accountants of England and Wales, London

Bjørnenak T (1997) Diffusion and accounting: the case of ABC in Norway. Manag Account Res 8(1):3–17

Bosch FAJ, Prooijen A (1992) The competitive advantage of European nations: the impact of national culture – a missing element in Porter's analysis? Eur Manag J 10(2):173–177

Brown J, Dillard J (2014) Integrated reporting: on the need for broadening out and opening up. Account Audit Account J 27(7):1120–1156

Cartwright WR (1993) Multiple linked diamonds and the international competitiveness of export-dependent industries: the New Zealand experience. Manag Int Rev 33(2):55–70
Central Bank of Sri Lanka (CBSL) (2014) Annual Report. CBSL, Colombo
Cho CH (2009) Legitimation strategies used in response to environmental disaster: a French case study of total SA's Erika and AZF incidents. Eur Account Rev 18(1):33–62
Clancy P, O'Malley E, O'Connell L, Egeraat CV (2001) Industry clusters in Ireland: an application of Porter's model of national competitive advantage to three sectors. Eur Plan Stud 9(1):7–28
Curran P (2000) Competition in UK higher education: competitive advantage in the research assessment exercise and Porter's diamond model. High Educ Q 54:386–410
De Silva KM (2014) A history of Sri Lanka. Vijitha Yapa, Colombo
De Villiers C, Rinaldi L, Unerman J (2014) Integrated reporting: insights, gaps and an agenda for future research. Account Audit Account J 27(7):1042–1067
Deegan C (2000) Financial accounting theory. McGraw Hill, Sydney
Deegan C (2002) The legitimizing effect of social and environmental disclosures: a theoretical foundation. Account Audit Account J 15(3):282–311
Deloitte (2012) Integrated reporting, navigating your way to a truly integrated report. 2nd ed. Available via: www.itweb.co.za. Accessed 23 Jan 2015
Department of Census and Statistics of Sri Lanka (2013) Sri Lanka labour force survey annual report – 2013. Department of Census and Statistics, Sri Lanka
Dissanayake D, Tilt C, Xydias-Lobo M (2016) Sustainability reporting by public listed companies in Sri Lanka. J Clean Prod 129:169–182
Eccles RG, Armbrester K (2011) Two disruptive ideas combined: integrated reporting in the cloud. IESE Insight 8(First Quarter–2011):13–20
Eccles RG, Krzus MP (2010) One report: integrated reporting for a sustainable strategy. Wiley, Hoboken
Eccles RG, Saltzman D (2011) Achieving sustainability through integrated reporting. Stanf Soc Innov Rev. Summer–2011:56–61
Eccles RG, Serafeim G (2011) Accelerating the adoption of integrated reporting. de Leo F, Vollbracht M CSR index 2011, Innovation Publishing, Zurich, 70–92
Fernando S (2014) Global and local influences on Corporate Social Responsibility (CSR) performance and disclosures; evidence from Sri Lankan corporate sector. Keynote address at the Faculty of Management Studies and Commerce (FMSC) Research Session, University of Sri Jayewardenepura, Sri Lanka, 5–27 Second Semester – 2014
Fernando S, Lawrence S, Kelly M, Arunachalam M (2015) CSR practices in Sri Lanka: an exploratory analysis. Soc Responsib J 11(4):868–892
Grant RM (1991) Porter's competitive advantage of nations: an assessment. Strateg Manag J 12(7):535–548
Gray SJ (1988) Towards a theory of cultural influence on the development of accounting systems internationally. Abacus 24(1):1–15
Gray SJ, Vint HM (1995) The impact of culture on accounting disclosures: some international evidence. Asia Pac J Acc 2(1):33–43
Gray R, Javard M, Power DM, Sinclair DC (2001) Social and environmental disclosure and corporate characteristics: a research note and extension. J Bus Finance Acc 28:327–356
Gunarathne N, Senaratne S (2017) Diffusion of integrated reporting in an emerging South Asian (SAARC) nation. Manag Audit J 32(4/5):524–548
Gunarathne N, Peiris S, Edirisooriya K, Jayasinghe R (2015) Environmental management accounting in Sri Lankan enterprises. Department of Accounting, University of Sri Jayewardenepura, Nugegoda
Gunawardene N (2015) Social media and general elections 2015. Daily mirror. Available via: http://www.dailymirror.lk/85811/social-media-and-general-elecations-2015. Accessed 23 Nov 2015

Gunarathne ADN, Alahakoon Y (2016) Environmental management accounting practices and their diffusion: the Sri Lankan experience. NSBM J Manag 2(1):1–26
Higgins C, Stubbs W, Love T (2014) Walking the talk(s): organisational narratives of integrated reporting. Account Audit Account J 27(7):1090–1119
Hodgetts RM (1993) Porter's diamond framework in a Mexican context. Manag Int Rev 33(2):41–54
Hofstede G (1980) Culture's consequences: international differences in work-related values. Sage Publications, Beverly Hills
IIRC (2013) The international <IR> framework. Available via: http://integratedreporting.org/wp-content/uploads/2013/12/13-12-08-THE-INTERNATIONAL-IR-FRAMEWORK-2-1.pdf. Accessed 10 Sept 2014
IIRC (2014) Pilot programme investor network. IIRC. Available via: http://integratedreporting.org/wp-content/uploads/2014/03/IIRC-Pilot-Programme-Investor-Network-backgrounder-March-2014.pdf. Accessed 23 Dec 2014
International Federation of Accountants (IFAC) (2014) Handbook of international education pronouncements. International Accounting Education Standards Board, IFAC, New York
International Integrated Reporting Council (IIRC) (2011) Towards integrated reporting, communicating value in the 21st century. IIRC, New York
IoDSA and King III (2009) King code of governance for South Africa 2009. Institute of Directors in Southern Africa and the King Committee on Governance. Available via: http://african.ipapercms.dk/IOD/KINGIII/kingiiireport/. Accessed 23 Feb 2014
Jayawardane VK (2000) Nobodies to somebodies: the rise of the colonial bourgeoisie in Sri Lanka. Social Scientist Association and Sanjiva Books, Colombo
Jensen JC, Berg N (2012) Determinants of traditional sustainability reporting versus integrated reporting, an institutionalist approach. Bus Strateg Environ 21:299–316
Jensen M, Meckling W (1976) Theory of the firm: managerial behaviour agency cost and ownership structure. J Financ Econ 3(4):305–360
Kolk A, Van Tulder R (2010) International business, corporate social responsibility and sustainable development. Int Bus Rev 19(2):119–125
KPMG (2008) International survey of corporate responsibility reporting. Available via: https://www.kpmg.com/EU/en/Documents/KPMG_International_survey_Corporate_responsibility_Survey_Reporting_2008.pdf. Accessed 20 Dec 2014
KPMG (2015) Survey of integrated reports in Japan 2014. Available via: https://www.kpmg.com/jp/ja/knowledge/article/integrated-reporting-article/documents/integrated-reporting-20150628e.pdf. Accessed 22 Nov 2015
Lee K-H, Herold DM (2016) Cultural relevance in corporate sustainability management: a comparison between Korea and Japan. Asian J Sustain Soc Responsib:1–21
Liyanarachchi GA (2009) Accounting in ancient Sri Lanka: some evidence of the accounting and auditing practices of Buddhist monasteries during 815–1017 AD. Account Hist 14(1–2):101–120
Liyanarachchi GA (2015) Antecedents of double-entry bookkeeping and Buddhist temple accounting. Account Hist 20(1):85–106
Lodhia S (2015) Exploring the transition to integrated reporting through a practice lens: an Australian customer owned bank perspective. J Bus Ethics 129:585–598
Maduwage S (2015) Water woes of Rathupaswala still continue. Daily mirror. Available via: http://www.dailymirror.lk/83401/water-woes-of-rathupaswala-still-continue. Accessed 10 Dec 2015
Ministry of Education (MOE) (2013) Education first – Sri Lanka. Policy and Planning Branch, Ministry of Education, Sri Lanka
Montano JLA, Donoso JA, Hassall T, Joyce J (2001) Vocational skills in the accounting professional profile: the Chartered Institute of Management Accountants (CIMA) employers' opinion. Acc Educ 10(3):299–313
Moon HC, Rugman AM, Verbeke A (1998) A generalized double diamond approach to the global competitiveness of Korea and Singapore. Int Bus Rev 7:135–150

Nanayakkara G (1988) Culture and management in Sri Lanka. Postgraduate Institute of Management, Sri Lanka
Narada (2010) The Buddha and his teaching, 3rd edn. Buddhist Publication Society, Kandy
Owen D (2006) Emerging issues in sustainability reporting. Bus Strateg Environ 15:217–218
Patten DM (1992) Intra-industry environmental disclosures in response to the Alaskan oil spill: a note on legitimacy theory. Acc Organ Soc 17(5):471–475
Payutto PA (1994) Dependent origination- Buddhist way of conditionality. Buddhamma Foundation, Thailand
Perera MHB (1989) Towards a framework to analyse the impact of culture on accounting. Int J Account 4(1):42–56
Porter ME (1990) The competitive advantage of nations. Free Press, New York
Post JE, Preston LE, Sachs S (2002) Redefining the corporation- stakeholder management and organizational wealth. Stanford University Press, Stanford
Rogers EM (1983) The diffusion of innovations, 3rd edn. Free Press, New York
Rugman AM, Cruz JRD (1993) The "double diamond" model of international competitiveness: the Canadian experience. Manag Int Rev 33(2):17–39
Sardy M, Fetscherin M (2009) A double diamond comparison of the automotive industry of China, India, and South Korea. Compet Forum 7(1):6–16
Schaltegger S, Zvezdov D (2015) Gatekeepers of sustainability information: exploring the roles of accountants. J Account Organ Chang 11(3):333–361
Senaratne S, Cooray S (2012) Dominance of professional accounting bodies and dependence of universities: the case of accounting education in Sri Lanka. In: Proceedings of the accounting and finance Australian and New Zealand AFAANZ annual conference-2012, Melbourne, no pagination July 2012
Senaratne S, Gunarathne N (2017) Excellence perspective for management education from a global accountants' hub in Asia. In: Baporikar N (ed) Management education for global leadership. IGI Global, Hershey, pp 158–180
Senaratne S, Gunarathne ADN, Herath R, Bandara C (2015) Diffusion of integrated reporting in an emerging economy. In: Proceedings of the Environmental and Sustainability Management Accounting Network (EMAN) global conference 2015. University of Sri Jayewardenepura, Colombo, 120–137, January 2015
Seuring S, Muller M (2008) From a literature review to a conceptual framework for sustainable supply chain management. J Clean Prod 16(15):1699–1710
Simnett R, Huggins AL (2015) Integrated reporting and assurance: where can research add value? Sustain Acc Manag Policy J 6(1):29–53
Sison AJG (2010) Corporate governance and ethics: an Aristotelian perspective. Edward Elgar Publishing, Cheltenham
SLASSCOM (2015) Sri Lankan IT/BPM industry 2014 review. SLASSCOM, Colombo
Sledge S (2005) Does Porter's diamond hold in the global automotive industry? Adv Compet Res – ACR 13(1):22–32
Stent W, Dowler T (2015) Early assessments of the gap between integrated reporting and current corporate reporting. Meditari Acc Res 23(1):92–117
Stubbs W, Higgins C (2014) Integrated reporting and internal mechanisms of change. Account Audit Account J 27(7):1068–1090
Tholons (2014) 2014 – tholons top 100 outsourcing destinations: regional overview. Available via: http://www.tholons.com/nl_pdf/Whitepaper_December_2013.pdf. Accessed 01 Dec 2015
Thoradeniya P, Lee J, Tan R, Ferreira A (2015) Sustainability reporting and the theory of planned behaviour. Account Audit Account J 28(7):1099–1137
University Grants Commission (UGC) (2013) Thirty fourth annual report- 2012. UGC, Sri Lanka
Van Staden C, Wild S (2013) Integrated reporting: an initial analysis of early reporters. In: Proceedings of the Massey University Accounting Research Seminar. Massey University, Auckland

Weeramantry CG (2002) Sustainable development: an ancient concept recently revived. Global judges symposium on sustainable development and the role of law. Johannesburg, South Africa, Available via: http://www.unep.org/delc/Portals/119/publications/Speeches/Weeramantry.pdf. Accessed 08 Dec 2015

Wijeratne AT (2006) A Buddhist's view on sustainability – a heretic's thoughts on the economy. Agra T. Wijeratne, Pannipitiya

World Bank (2015) Report on the observance of standards and codes, accounting and auditing – Sri Lanka. World Bank, Washington, DC

Zhaoa Z, Zhanga S, Zuo J (2011) A critical analysis of the photovoltaic power industry in China – from diamond model to gear model. Renew Sust Energ Rev 15(9):4963–4971

Chapter 4
Corporate Values and Corporate Social Responsibility Communication Strategies in a Small Economy

Rashid Ameer and Radiah Othman

Abstract This paper explores the influence that companies' values have on CSR communication. In particular, it focuses on the impact of these values on the CSR communication strategies, communication medium, and CSR information quality. This paper employs the corpus linguistics methods to explore CSR dimensions, with the analytical focus on the companies' postures. From pragmatic perspectives, the companies may adopt a strategy that best represent their relationship with the stakeholders. Hence, the CSR communication strategy may evolve from stakeholder information strategy to stakeholder response strategy to stakeholder involvement strategy. This evolution is consistent with deliberative democracy, which has a potential to affect corporations' actions concerning stakeholders' interests, and encourages constant improvement and transformation of institutional accountability in which the stakeholders can be fully engaged. Our empirical findings suggest that corporate values of social-centeredness and self-centeredness have a positive influence on the strength of CSR communication strategies. Furthermore, CSR communication strategies significantly influence the issuance of stand-alone CSR reports. Our findings also suggest that New Zealand companies use explanation and justification posture, which combines bolstering, differentiation, and transcendence, to legitimize business operations that link work, society, and environment. We found that New Zealand companies' value orientation may have been influenced by national socio-political systems. Our study establishes a link between corporate values and CSR communication strategy in communicating the impacts companies have on the society and the natural environment. The emphasis is on the language of CSR reports as a linguistic mediation of communication between corporations and stakeholders.

R. Ameer
IPU New Zealand Tertiary Institute, Palmerston North, New Zealand
e-mail: rameer@ipu.ac.nz

R. Othman (✉)
Massey University, Palmerston North, New Zealand
e-mail: r.othman@massey.ac.nz

K.-H. Lee, S. Schaltegger (eds.), *Accounting for Sustainability: Asia Pacific Perspectives*, Eco-Efficiency in Industry and Science 33,
https://doi.org/10.1007/978-3-319-70899-7_4

Keywords Communication strategy · Corporate identity · Values · CSR · New Zealand

4.1 Introduction

Much of the literature on the corporate social responsibility (CSR) has principally focused on the question: Can a company do well while doing good? A wide variety of factors not only impacts the mere decision itself on what the company is to engage in; precisely those factors will further constitute a major influence on whether a company's CSR strategy will eventually succeed or fail (Fifka 2013; Wood 2010; Banerjee 2008). Despite inconclusive evidence on this question, there is an unprecedented increase in the demand from companies to behave in a responsible manner and CSR engagement calls for more sophisticated CSR communication strategies than previously (Morsing and Schultz 2006, p. 323).

Our research is motivated by an apparent lack of empirical research of an interdisciplinary nature into CSR communication. Much of the empirical CSR literature has ignored the importance of corporate identity, values, and their influence on CSR communication strategy, CSR communication medium, and CSR communication quality. Indeed, Crane (2000, p. 32) pointed out that the positivist approach in the study of business ethics fails to get to grips with the issues of moral meaning. CSR often implies a personal moral designation for managers and a high level of managerial opportunism influences CSR communication that is uninteresting to stakeholders. Therefore, by aligning corporate values with stakeholders' expectations results in a CSR communication that not only fills the gaps in stakeholders' knowledge but also boosts corporate reputation for meeting perceived societal obligations. Ellen et al. (2006) report that CSR communication based on 'self-centered values' (strategic and egoistic) versus 'society centered values' (stakeholder-driven) produce different outcomes for society and firms. Individuals react to a company's CSR activities in multiple ways, not simply by buying more products but also by prompting other stakeholder behaviors, such as seeking employment with the company and investing in the company (Sen et al. 2006). Thus, the choice of CSR communication strategy and its intelligibility are two important outcomes that are relevant to companies and society in sustaining mutually beneficial relationships (Perron and Duffy 2012). From pragmatic perspectives, the companies may adopt a strategy that best represent their relationship with the stakeholders. Hence, the CSR communication strategy may evolve from stakeholder information strategy to stakeholder response strategy to stakeholder involvement strategy. This evolution is consistent with deliberative democracy (Baker and Schaltegger 2013, p. 14) which has a potential to affect corporations' actions concerning stakeholders' interests, and encourages constant improvement and transformation of institutional accountability in which the stakeholders can be fully engaged.

Based on a review of extant literature, we propose a new interdisciplinary conceptualization of CSR communication. It is interdisciplinary in nature as it frames CSR communication using the concepts of (i) organization values (van de Merwe and Puth 2014) and personal values (Rokeach 1973), (ii) organizational posturing and the positive (negative) evaluation of identity (Ware and Linkugel 1973), (iii) organizational stakeholder orientation (Morsing and Schultz 2006), and (iv) information quality. The primary objective of this paper is to examine the relationship between corporate values and CSR communication strategy, which we hypothesize would affect the choice of the organizations' commitment to using a particular CSR communication medium. We posit that corporate values depicted in the mission statements of the companies act as an anchor for the companies. These values in the mission statements specify not only a strategic intent of company but also its moral stance towards society. These values guide modes of conduct and end-state of existence for companies. A secondary objective is to examine the relationship between the organizations' CSR communication commitment and the quality of CSR communications in order to gauge the clarity and intelligibility of the resultant CSR communication.

Our approach is similar to a number of researchers who have proposed integrative frameworks that link moral, cultural, and organizational aspects to provide a more comprehensive perspective of the CSR phenomenon. For instance, an integrative framework developed by Du et al. (2010) links the CSR message construction to CSR channel and examines the impact the stakeholder-specific factors have on the effectiveness of CSR communication. We apply the conceptual framework in a small economy of New Zealand because in smaller economies companies' reputational capital is at high stake due to higher visibility of companies to stakeholders, in particular the media. We choose to examine CSR communication within the smaller economy of New Zealand for the following reasons: (i) KPMG's (2011) international survey on corporate responsibility reported that companies in New Zealand are 'starting behind' many of their counterparts in OECD countries; and (ii) the CSR concept is not a dominating management concept in New Zealand business but its importance has been growing rapidly in recent years (Eweje and Bentley 2006, p. 6). According to Orlitzky (2005, p. 37), two related factors might explain the reticence of New Zealand companies to adopt voluntary social and environmental programs. First, these initiatives are perhaps too costly, and second, the relatively small size of New Zealand companies is making these initiatives particularly unaffordable. According to Day (2012), limited research on CSR communication in New Zealand has omitted the impact corporate values have on CSR. Of particular importance is the need to tease out nuances, and the role of organizational values in CSR communication.

We acknowledge that the growing influence of integrated reporting could potentially have a larger impact on the CSR reporting medium, and this emerging reporting practice indeed offers opportunities to engage with stakeholders; however, we did not include integrative reporting in our analysis for the following reasons. First, in March 2016, Paul Druckman, CEO of the International Integrated Reporting Council (IIRC), was in New Zealand to share his insights on the benefits of integrated thinking and reporting. New Zealand is progressing quite slowly in adopting Integrated Reporting (IR). Second, the External Reporting Board (XRB), the national standard setter, is currently considering Integrated Reporting and the extent to which the XRB should encourage and/or require it in New Zealand. Changes had to be made to the New Zealand Financial Reporting Act 2013, which explicitly refer to <IR>, and are expected to be an enabler to adoption by New Zealand organizations (IIRC 2016a). Third, the principles-based approach of IR framework may provide the flexibility for companies in reporting their CSR activities and some degree of comparability in terms of CSR medium and information. We concur with Lueg et al. (2016, p. 31) that CSR reporting can support a company in implementing IR and improve its CSR communication, but IR requires a company to move beyond CSR and narrate how CSR contributes to a company's values, strategy, and achievements (KPMG 2010; PwC 2010). How the majority of New Zealand companies listed on the stock exchange are able to achieve this is yet to be seen. The results of this study provide a benchmark for New Zealand companies' performance in CSR communication and the strategies they undertook prior to IR.

Our main contribution is twofold: First, we build on the corporate reputation and impression management literature that speaks about the influence of corporate identity and values for understanding the quality of CSR communication. We use an interdisciplinary approach to problematize the CSR discourse and communication strategy in order to provide an understanding of ulterior corporate values that encourage managers to move from 'informing' to 'responding' and, later, to 'involving' stakeholders in their companies' CSR planning and performance reporting. This continuous improvement signifies deliberative democracy of stakeholder engagement pragmatism (Baker and Schaltegger 2013, p. 14). Indeed, Hemingway (2013, p. 80), motivates this idea further to suggest that managers interpret company strategy and match company resources and opportunities according to their own values. We posit that, a research emphasis on interpretation and meaning in a study of the role of personal values in the workplace would be highly appropriate to focus on the ways that people make sense of the world and share their experiences with others [stakeholders] via the medium of language.

Second, we use Structural Equation Modeling (SEM) to test the main hypotheses developed in this paper. It is more suitable for the predictive studies, which explore complex problems and where the previous theoretical background is scarce, and it is the only technique that allows modeling variables of a formative nature (Hulland 1999). Madueno et al. (2016) used the SEM approach to examine the relationship between CSR and competitive performance for SMEs. They found that CSR practices contribute to increasing competitive performance, both directly and indirectly.

Overall, this study contributes to the understanding of the CSR communication strategies pursued when dealing with stakeholders. Using SEM, our study establishes a link between corporate values and CSR communication strategy in communicating the impacts companies have on the society and the natural environment. The emphasis is on the language of CSR reports as a linguistic mediation of communication between corporations and stakeholders.

The rest of the paper is organized as follows: Sect. 4.2 provides a review of studies to develop research hypotheses. Section 4.3 describes the sample, data coding, and SEM methodology used in this paper. Section 4.4 provides results of thematic analysis of the mission statements, and the CSR texts followed by results of the estimated path relationships in the SEM and Sect. 4.5 concludes the paper.

4.2 Literature Review and Hypotheses Development

4.2.1 Corporate Identity and Values

For-profit companies are incentivized to behave in a socially and environmentally responsible manner because of either altruistic (intrinsic) or extrinsic (external) motives (Matten and Moon 2008; Carroll 1991). The former relates to brand reputation enhancement, market differentiation, and corporate identity and reputation building in varied social contexts, whereas the latter relates to strategic investment that is expected to yield higher financial returns in the future (Noland and Phillips 2010; He and Baruch 2009; Porter and Kramer 2006; Lantos 2001). Corporate identity is the core foundation of corporate reputation (van de Merwe and Puth 2014; Aust 2004). It has been described as the deepest commitment that characterizes an organization over time. Mission statements are widely seen as indispensable in helping a company form its identity, purpose, and direction. They are important instruments by which a company's essential values are conveyed to its stakeholders. A mission statement tucked securely into an annual report can provide a consistent message about all facets of a firm to the various publics concerned (Leuthesser and Kohli 1997, p. 59). Van de Merwe and Puth's (2014) view corporate identity as an organization's inherent character as what it stands for, and can be held accountable for, and which vision and values effectively make it unique and distinctive from other organizations. They assert that an organization, in its quest to attain a goal of sustainable economic growth, should include the need to behave in a transparent, ethical, and trustworthy manner as part of its inherent identity, character, and basic focus. This will ensure that core values resonate on an emotional level with their stakeholders and thus increase the probability that not only stakeholders but also others will like, admire, and possibly identify with it and its values (van der Merwe and Puth 2014).

According to Melewar (2008, p. 9), the texts are manifest expressions of corporate identity because they are well controlled and carefully prepared articulations of what the company is. A content analysis approach such as this is in accordance with the previous study by Verboven (2011, p. 419), who incorporated mission slogans and corporate taglines into his work. This approach addresses the public-facing corporate identity desired by many companies, which carries considerable content, and associative and connotative potential. We argue that self-concept and concern for the public image are the two main components of the mission statement that influence stakeholders' perceptions (refer to, e.g., Rhodes and Brown 2005).

The management of a corporate identity involves the dynamic interplay amongst the company's business strategy, the philosophy of its key executives, its corporate culture, and its organization design (Gray and Balmer 1998, p. 695). Corporate culture and organizational ethical climate affect how CSR aids reputational development. While there are multiple factors, both internal and external to the company, which may influence top management's general ethical values, the ethical climate provides "norms, criteria, and expectation of ethical conduct." According to Schaltegger and Burritt (2006, p. 17), it creates well-known distinction in social business climates between 'trust me,' 'show me,' and 'prove to me.' Thus, organizational values are an important part of an organization's CSR identity because moral judgments people make are determined by the values they hold. Organizational values can be argued as providing the basis for defining a company's role and responsibility in society.

In this paper we used Rokeach (1973), who identifies two distinctively different ways that the concept of value has been employed, (i) the values that a person has, and (ii) the values that an object has (the person is engaged in valuing, and the object is being valued). According to Rokeach (1973, p. 5) "a value is an enduring belief that a specific mode of conduct or end state of existence is personally or socially preferable to an opposite or converse mode of conduct or end-state of existence. A value system is an enduring organization of belief concerning preferable modes of conduct or end-states of existence along a continuum of relative importance." The values are not completely stable and may change within a person's lifetime; however, they are sufficiently stable to provide continuity to one's personal and social existence. A value (or belief about something desirable) involves certain knowledge regarding the means or ends that the person considers desirable. Rokeach (1973) stresses that a value is a preference as well as a conception of the desirable, and preferences are choices that people make when confronted by a set of alternatives, where the alternatives involve a particular mode of conduct or an end-state of existence or orientation. The important function of values is to provide standards that guide behavior. Values serve adjustive, ego-defensive, knowledge, and self-actualizing functions (Rokeach 1973, p. 25).

Rokeach's value system, which is developed on the basis of an extensive literature review followed by empirical studies, comprises 36 values in total (see Table 4.1). The values refer to either a mode of conduct, *instrumental values*, or an end-state of existence, *terminal values*. The instrumental values are sub-divided into *moral* values (interpersonal focus) and *competence values* (personal focus). Similarly, terminal values subdivide into personal (self-centered) values and *social* (society-centered) values. Instrumental values guide the behavioral aspects, making it possible to reach the end goals, which are the terminal values. All of Rokeach's terminal values apply in a corporate context except companionship and mature love, which is excluded from this study.

According to the corporate identity literature, a social value orientation creates a distinct identity in the hearts and minds of stakeholders (Schmeltz 2012, 2014; Cornelissen 2011; Albert and Whetten 1985; Markwick and Fill 1997; Lee et al. 2016). In a survey of consumer perceptions and evaluation of companies' engagement in, and communication about CSR, Schmeltz (2012) found that the respondents seem to favor competence-oriented instrumental values such as ambitious/hardworking, capable, and logical, whereas the moral oriented values that are more evidently linked to general understanding of CSR such as 'helpful,' 'responsible,'

Table 4.1 Rokeach value categorization

Instrumental values (desirable modes of conduct)		Terminal values (desirable end-states of existence)	
Competence-oriented	Morally oriented	Personally oriented	Socially oriented
Ambitious (hardworking, aspiring)	Broadminded (open-minded)	A comfortable life (a prosperous life)	The world at peace (free of war and conflict)
Capable (competent, effective)	Cheerful (lighthearted, joyful)	An exciting life (active life)	A world of beauty (of nature and the arts)
Clean (neat, tidy)	Courageous (standing up to your beliefs)	A sense of accomplishment (lasting contribution)	Equality (brotherhood and equal opportunity)
Imaginative (daring, creative)	Forgiving (willing to pardon others)	Family security (taking care of loved ones)	Freedom (independence, free choice)
Intellectual (intelligent, reflective)	Helpful (working for the welfare of others)	Happiness (contentedness)	National security (protection from attachments)
Logical (consistent, rational)	Honest (sincere, truthful)	Inner harmony (freedom from inner conflict)	
	Independent (self-reliant, self-sufficient)	Pleasure (an enjoyable life)	
	Loving (affectionate, tender)	Salvation (saved, eternal life)	
	Obedient (dutiful, respectful)	Self-respect (self-esteem)	
	Polite (courteous, well-mannered)	Social recognition (respect, admiration)	
	Responsible (dependable, reliable)	Wisdom (a mature understanding of life)	
	Self-controlled (restrained, self-disciplined)		

TP terminal personal, *TS* terminal social, *IC* instrumental-competence, *IM* instrumental-moral

and 'honest,' are not rated as high as we may expect of consumers. We propose that CSR communication is an outcome of a company's social value orientation. A company's 'self-centeredness' social orientation, indicated by its *competence-oriented instrumental values*, e.g., ambitious and capable, to address stakeholders' concerns about social and environmental issues, will have a positive influence on its CSR communication strategy. Similarly, a company's 'self-centeredness' social orientation, indicated by its *personally-oriented terminal values*, e.g., performing an act to feel a sense of accomplishment and to gain self-respect and social recognition for making a world of beauty, will have a positive influence on its CSR communication strategy. In contrast, we posit that a company's 'society-centeredness values' orientation, indicated by its *morally oriented-instrumental values*, e.g., being 'honest' and 'responsible' to address stakeholder concerns about social and environmental issues, will have a positive influence on its CSR communication. Similarly, a company's 'society-centeredness values' orientation, indicated by its *socially oriented terminal values*, e.g., concern for a world of beauty, equality, and social freedom, will have a positive influence on its CSR communication strategy. Therefore, we hypothesize that:

Self-centeredness

> *Hypothesis 1* The competence oriented instrumental values and personally oriented terminal values (self-centeredness) have a positive influence on CSR communication.

Society-centeredness

> *Hypothesis 2* The morally oriented instrumental values and socially oriented terminal values (society-centeredness) have a positive influence on CSR communication.

The company also uses different rhetoric to rebuild or minimize damages to organizational legitimacy and manage reputation. In the impression management literature, the concept of 'account' refers to an organization's CSR message. Most studies on the concept of 'account' emphasize the remedial function they serve (Braaten et al. 1993), which suggest that 'account' is an effective remedy for a specific single alleged offense (i.e., illegal dumping of industrial effluent and waste). An effective 'account' is one that the receivers find credible and through which the account-giver is forgiven or exonerated of blame, and avoids negative evaluation, penalties, and conflicts (Cody and McLaughlin 1990).

In this paper, we used four factors and four postures suggested by Ware and Linkugel (1973) to evaluate CSR discourse. We describe the four factors followed by four postures. *Denial*, *bolstering*, *differentiation*, and *transcendence* (hereafter referred to as WLP-Factors) are the four factors. The first factor is denial, which occurs when an organization denies alleged facts, sentiments, objects, or relationships. The second factor is bolstering, which refers to any rhetorical strategy that reinforces the existence of a fact, sentiment, object, or relationship. The organization attempts to identify itself with something viewed favorably by the audience. Both denial and bolstering are reformative communication strategies as these do not change the audience's meaning or affect for whatever is in question; they simply revise or amend the cognition of the audience. The third factor is differentiation, which serves the purpose of separating some fact, sentiment, object, or relationship from some larger context within which the audience presently views that attribute. Transcendence, in contrast, cognitively joins some fact, sentiment, object, or relationship with some larger context within which the audience does not presently view that attribute. Differentiation and transcendence are transformative strategies that involve a change in meaning.

Ware and Linkugel (1973) identify four postures available to the organizations: *absolution*, *vindication*, *explanation*, and *justification* (hereafter referred to as WLP-

Postures). Each of these postures involves the combination of one transformative factor with one reformative factor. The first posture is *absolution*, in which the organization seeks acquittal. This results from the combination of the differentiation and denial factors. The second posture is *vindication,* which involves denial and transcendence, and aims not only at the preservation of the accused's reputation but also at the recognition of his/her greater worth as a human being relative to the worth of his/her accusers. The third posture is an *explanation*, which combines bolstering and differentiation. In this posture, the speaker assumes that if the audience understands his/her motives, actions, beliefs, or whatever, they will be unable to condemn him/her. The fourth posture is *justification*, which occurs when bolstering and transcendence are joined. The justification asks not only for understanding but also for approval. The corporate CSR disclosures defending their corporate persona, which are grounded in ethical considerations, may be considered true examples of the apologetic genre (Dionisopoulos 1985, p. 5). We argue that inclusion of Ware and Linkugel (1973) with Rokeach value classification provides a robust and richer interpretation of the CSR discourse.

4.2.2 CSR Communication Strategies

The methods and channels of communication influence stakeholders in many different ways (Gray and Balmer 1998). According to Balmer and Gray (2000) communication serves three distinct phases, starting with primary communication, which should present a positive image of the company and set the stage for a strong reputation. Secondary communication should be designed to support and reinforce the primary communication. Later, tertiary communication should be positive and result in a superior reputation if the other two stages of corporate communication are properly conceived. The authors argue that senior managers could gain significant competitive advantage through this three-tiered communication approach. Crane and Glozer (2016, p. 10) categorized the purpose of CSR communication into six categories: stakeholder management, image enhancement, legitimacy and accountability, attitude and behavioral change, sensemaking and identity, and meaning creation. According to Pruzan (2001, p. 282), businesses have social orientations in the same way that individuals do. Managers' actions represent desired prosocial traits, which signify the social-end state of the corporations to stakeholders. The objective of CSR communication is to establish and maintain a favorable image in the eyes of stakeholders that the organization depends on (Cornelissen 2011; Hooghiemstra 2000).

Gioia and Chittipeddi (1991, p. 443) noted that the articulation of abstract corporate visions and values, and the dissemination of these to stakeholders, as championed by managers, represent the phenomenon of sensegiving. Applying the dynamic and socially constructed framing to the design, format, and CSR communication medium, the CSR message or disclosure is the phenomenon of sensegiving and sensemaking by stakeholders. Based on Grunig and Hunt's (1984) characterization of models of public relations, stakeholder theory (Freeman 1984; Friedman and Miles 2006), and sensemaking theory (Weick 1995; Morsing and Schultz 2006, p. 325) suggested a framework of CSR communication strategies that operationalizes how companies strategically engage in CSR communication vis-à-vis their stakeholders: stakeholder information strategy (*one-way*); stakeholder response strategy (*two-way asymmetric*); and stakeholder involvement strategy (*two-way symmetric*) (see Table 4.2).

In their view, in the case of a company that uses the *stakeholder information strategy* (hereafter the SIS), communication is basically viewed as 'telling, not listening,' and therefore SIS has the purpose of disseminating information

Table 4.2 Three CSR communication strategies

	SIS	SRS	SVS
Communication Ideal: (Grunig and Hunt 1984)	Public information, one-way communication	Two-way asymmetric communication	Two-way symmetric communication
Communication ideal: sensemaking and sensegiving:	Sensegiving	Sensemaking	Sensemaking
		↓	↕
		Sensegiving	Sensegiving – in iterative progressive processes
Stakeholders:	Request more information on corporate CSR efforts	Must be reassured that the company is ethical and socially responsible	Co-construct corporate CSR efforts
Stakeholder role:	Stakeholder influence: support or oppose	Stakeholders respond to corporate actions	Stakeholders are involved, and participate and suggest corporate actions
Identification of CSR focus:	Decided by top management	Decided by top management	Negotiated concurrently in interaction with stakeholders
		Investigated in feedback via opinion polls, dialogue, networks, and partnerships	
Strategic communication task:	Inform stakeholders about favorable corporate CSR decisions and actions	Demonstrate to stakeholders how the company integrates their concerns	Invite and establish a frequent, systematic, and pro-active dialogue with stakeholders, i.e., opinion makers, corporate critics, the media, etc.
Corporate communication department's task:	Design appealing concept message	Identify relevant stakeholders	Build relationships
Third party endorsement of CSR initiatives:	Unnecessary	Integrated element of surveys, rankings and opinion polls	Stakeholders are themselves involved in corporate CSR messages

Source: Morsing and Schultz (2006, p. 326)

focused on information, not necessarily with a persuasive intent but rather to inform the public as objectively as possible about the organization. A company must inform stakeholders about its good intentions, decisions, and actions to ensure positive stakeholder support. The top management, confident the company is doing the right thing, believes the company is doing the right thing, and believes the company just needs to inform the general public efficiently about what it is doing to build and maintain positive stakeholder support (Morsing and Schultz 2006, p. 327). It is outside the realm of this strategy to consider external stakeholders' views i.e., third party stakeholders should endorse corporate CSR initiatives. Trustworthy communication originates from the company itself. We argue that SIS is in some ways similar to Ware and Linkugel's (1973) *bolstering* posture and Rokeach's (1973) *competence-oriented* instrumental values and *morally oriented* instrumental values.

In contrast to SIS, an organization may use the *stakeholder response strategy* (hereafter the SRS). It is a two-way asymmetric model that assumes an imbalance from the effects of public relations in favor of the company, as the company does not change as a result of the public relations. Rather, the company attempts to changes public attitude and behavior. This is similar to the accommodation strategy by Wilson (1975) and Ware and Linkugel's (1973) vindication posture, whereby an organization denies (or accepts) that social issues exist and takes responsibility (or no responsibility) for problematic behavior. In this regard, differentiation or transcendence transformative strategies that involve a change in meaning of future CSR messages might be the pertinent solution for problems of organizational legitimacy. Since CSR communication is perceived as a feedback in terms of finding out what the public will accept and tolerate, it is an evaluative mode of measuring whether a particular communication initiative has improved stakeholders' understanding of the company and vice versa. It is a one-way method of supporting and reinforcing corporate actions and identity and relates to the concept of 'self-centeredness' as developed above.

Finally, with respect to companies that use the *stakeholder involvement strategy* (hereafter the SVS), ideally the company and its stakeholders will change as a result of engaging in a symmetric communication model, i.e. progressive iterations of sensemaking and sensegiving process. We argue that this strategy corresponds with Ware and Linkugel's (1973) transcendence transformative strategy for strategic CSR management. This approach also echoes the CSR communication role of enhancing democracy, i.e., through companies' engagement in deliberative forms of democracy through stakeholder dialogue (Crane and Glozer 2016). Pruzan (2001) remarked that to maintain a company's 'self-centeredness,' management needs to take upon itself the very important responsibility of facilitating ongoing dialogue, which is a continuous process of creating and coordinating shared values.

Therefore, we hypothesize that:

Hypothesis 3 The corporate values (self-centeredness and society-centeredness) positively influence each of the CSR communication strategies (SIS, SRS, SVS).

4.2.3 CSR Communication Medium

There are a variety of communication channels through which information about a company's CSR activities or record can be disseminated. A company can use its official documents, such as an annual corporate responsibility report, and dedicate a section of its official corporate website to CSR (Du et al. 2010, p. 13). Some argue that websites are superior to annual reports (refer to, e.g., Esrock and Leichty 1998; Wanderley et al. 2008), whereas others argue that a social report that is not regulated by standards or external guidelines risks becoming merely a marketing tool that fails to meet the requirements of stakeholders such as investors, lobbyists, and NGOs (Tschopp 2005). According to Melewar (2008, p. 9) the texts are manifest expressions of corporate values. Standalone CSR reports are on the rise, as indicated by KPMG International. According to the 2011 CSR survey, nearly 95% of the largest 250 companies in the world now provide a standalone CSR report. The fact that the firms are issuing the CSR reports when they are not mandatory is an indicator of their commitment, as it is normally difficult to gain access to information regarding a firm's commitment to solving social and environmental problems (Belal and Cooper 2011).

Therefore, we hypothesize that:

Hypothesis 4 There is a positive relationship between CSR communication and CSR medium of standalone CSR reports.

4.2.4 Quality of CSR Communication

Readability is one of the important qualities that affects CSR communication because it can influence the motivation of stakeholders to process CSR information. As Courtis (1995, p. 4) pointed out, "no matter what the presentation style, organization of content, color graphics, pictorial choice and overall length, the intelligence that must be communicated via this document [annual report] is that which will enable diligent reader to perform or confirm *ex ante* risk-return assessment of the company." CSR information or messages are conveyed through a choice of words that portray responsible and virtuous behavior (Ziek 2009; Maignan and Ralston 2002). However, verbal, visual, and structural manipulation is often employed to choose benchmarks that portray performance in the best possible light (Merkl-Davies and Brennan 2000). Although the purpose of the reporting is to influence the public's 'knowledge' or 'perception' of the reporting entity (Schneider et al. 2012), the largest challenge of communicating CSR is increasing the likelihood of the audience noticing, processing, and accepting CSR communication (Schmeltz 2012b, p. 36). Therefore, CSR communication should be factual and avoid the impression of bragging (Sen et al. 2009). Thus, specific examples of CSR programs and achievements, with accompanying facts, are preferable to general descriptions of principles (Berens and van Rekom 2008). We argue that a high readability score for a CSR text demonstrates a commitment to a communication strategy that makes the information provided in the CSR report readable and understandable, so that stakeholders do not have an impression of corporate obfuscation and bragging.

We hypothesize that:

Hypothesis 5 There is a positive relationship between CSR medium and quality of CSR disclosure.

4.3 Method

4.3.1 Data

We downloaded the annual reports, stand-alone CSR, and/or Corporate Sustainability reports of the constituents of the NZX50, which is the headline benchmark index for the New Zealand equity market. There is a possibility that same CSR information might be reproduced by a company on its website as well as the CSR or annual report. The NZX50 is a widely-used index by investment professionals, mainstream media, and the public. It is calculated by using a free float market capitalization method. This method ensures that the most liquid and investable companies represented in the New Zealand market are purposively chosen for the analysis over the period of 3 years from 2011 to 2013. The sample companies were representative of six main industrial sectors: Energy; Industrial; Financial; Telecommunication; Consumer Goods and Information Technology. Out of 50 companies, 18 companies did not provide such reports, meaning that our final sample consisted of 33 companies from 2011 to 2013.

4.3.2 Thematic Analysis

First, we used the Schmeltz (2014) approach to code the CSR texts and the texts that describe corporate values in the mission statements of the sample companies (see Table 4.3). We used the mission statements found in the annual report and/or on the webpages of companies for two reasons: (i) mission statements are widely viewed as necessary to convey corporate values to stakeholders, e.g., the purpose and direction of a firm, and (ii) a company's annual report or webpage is the most widely available and visible form of formal communication with stakeholders and is an effective way to convey the mission statement.

In Table 4.4, we provide results of coding mission statements according to instrumental competence (IC), instrumental (IM), terminal personal (TP), and terminal social (TS) values. We followed the Schmeltz (2014) approach for making an assessment of the relative importance of these four values expressed in the

Table 4.3 Content analysis of mission statements

Source of information	Preliminary coding	Selection of texts	Primary coding	Analysis	Final coding
Annual report/ webpage texts	Reading text on the websites	Texts explaining mission and vision	Coding according to Rokeach's (1973) value system	Rhetorical analysis at sentence level to assess the relative importance of values expressed in the text data	Prioritized lists of corporate values

Corporate communication components		Rokeach's value system
Vision (desired future state of the company)	Can be expressed via	Terminal values
Mission (purpose of the company aligned with stakeholder value)	Can be expressed via	Instrumental values
Corporate values comprising both the vision and mission (what do we want to achieve, and how will we go about it?)	Can be expressed via	A mix of instrumental and terminal values

Source: Schmeltz (2014, p. 7)

mission statement and the CSR texts, by categorizing them into primary, secondary, and tertiary values. Table 4.4 provides the results of this categorization and clearly shows that the most important values that are stressed the most linguistically are IC and IM, in particular IC values of 'ambitious,' 'capable,' and IM values of 'Responsible.' The TP and TS values are less stressed in the corporate mission statements than in the CSR texts. TP values are mostly stressed than TS values in the CSR texts.

Second, we operationalize the CSR communication strategies as follows: A company follows the SIS strategy if two-thirds of its CSR communication (in a standalone CSR report, the CSR section in its annual report, or a webpage) is informative, i.e., providing only certain types of *self-opinion* statements. A company follows the SRS strategy if two-thirds of its CSR communication (in a standalone CSR report, the CSR section in its annual report, or a webpage) provides information that suggests responsiveness to stakeholders' social and environmental concerns. Finally, a company follows the SVS strategy if two-thirds of its CSR communication (in the form of a standalone CSR report, the CSR section in its annual report, or a webpage) provides a more detailed level of information regarding its engagement with stakeholders in the attempt to find solutions to social and environmental issues. We used an independent coder to verify the coding results of both authors and highlighted the text where the authors had certain differences. All doubts were discussed with the third coder until a mutually satisfactory code could be assigned. Table 4.5 shows sample of CSR text taken from the reports for the categorization of companies as per their CSR communication strategies of SIS, SRS, and SVS respectively. Table 4.6 summarizes this categorization results.

Third, we used QDA Miner and WordStat software to code the CSR text into three CSR domains: Environment, Employees, and Society, and later used this coded data to identify the postures and factors exhibited by the companies in

Table 4.4 Result of coding the companies' mission statements

Sl. no	Stock code	Primary (main values)	Variable	Secondary (supporting values)	Variable	Tertiary (additional values)	Variable
1	AIR	Ambitious (IC)	CVP1				
		Responsible (IM)	CVP2				
2	ANZ	Equality (TS)	CVP4	Honest (IM), responsible (IM)	CVS1	A sense of accomplishment (TP)	CVT3
3	ARG	Capable (IC)	CVP3				
4	ATM	A comfortable life (TP), a sense of accomplishment (TP)	CVP1	Ambitious (IC)	CVS3		
5	CEN	Ambitious (IC)	CVP1	Responsible (IM)	CVS1	Capable (IC)	CVT2
				Honest (IM)		An exciting life (TP)	CVT3
						Intellectual (IC)	CVT2
6	CNU	Forgiving (IM)	CVP2	Responsible (IM), Honest (IM)	CVS1		
7	DNZ	Capable (IC)	CVP1	Ambitious (IC)	CVS3		
8	FBU	Honest (IM)	CVP2	Sustainability (TS)	CVS2		
		Responsible (IM)					
9	FPH	Capable (IC), ambitious (IC)	CVP1	Responsible (IM)	CVS1	Equality (TS)	CVT4
				Social recognition (TP)	CVS2	Honest (IM)	CVT1
10	FSF	Ambitious (IC), capable (IC)	CVP1	A sense of accomplishment (TP)	CVS2	Honest (IM)	CVT1
				Responsible (IM)	CVS1	Courageous (IM)	CVT1
11	GMT	Responsible (IM)	CVP2	Ambitious (IC)	CVS3	Imaginative (IC)	CVT2
				Courageous (IM)	CVS1	Honest (IM)	CVT1
						Equality (TS)	CVT4
						Self-respect (TP)	CVT3
12	HNZ	Honest (IM)	CVP2				
		Equality (TS)	CVP4				
13	KIP	Ambitious (IC), capable (IC)	CVP1				
14	KMD	Honest (IM)	CVP2	A sense of accomplishment (TP)	CVS2	Imaginative (IC)	CVT2

(continued)

Table 4.4 (continued)

Sl. no	Stock code	Primary (main values)	Variable	Secondary (supporting values)	Variable	Tertiary (additional values)	Variable
15	MET	Ambitious (IC)	CVP1	Imaginative (IC)	CVS3	A sense of accomplishment (TP)	CVT3
				Self-respect (TP)	CVS2	Honest (IM)	CVT1
16	MFT	Ambitious (IC)	CVP1	Honest (IM)	CVS1		
17	MHI	Ambitious (IC)	CVP1	Honest (IM)	CVS1	Courageous (IM)	CVT1
		Responsible (IM)	CVP2			Imaginative (IC)	CVT2
		Loving (IM)	CVP2			Freedom (TP)	CVT3
18	NPX	Capable (IC)	CVP1	Ambitious (IC)	CVS3	Equality (TS)	CVT4
				Courageous (IM)	CVS1		
19	NZO	Honest (IM)	CVP2				
		Equality (TS)	CVP4				
		Responsible (IM)	CVP2				
20	OGC	Ambitious (IC)	CVP1	Honest (IM)	CVS1		
		Social recognition (TP)	CVP2	Responsible (IM)			
21	POT	Ambitious (IC)	CVP1	Honest (IM)	CVS1		
22	PPL	Family security (TP)	CVP3	Responsible (IM)	CVS1		
23	SKC	Ambitious (IC)	CVP1				
24	SKT	Ambitious (IC)	CVP1				
25	STU	Honest (IM), Responsible (IM)	CVP2				
26	SUM	Self-respect (TP)	CVP3				
27	TEL	Ambitious (IC)	CVP1				
28	TME	Ambitious (IC)	CVP1	Courageous (IM)	CVS1	Honest (IM)	CVT1
				Responsible (IM)		Equality (TS)	CVT4
29	TPW	Ambitious (IC)	CVP1	Self-respect (TP)	CVS2		
				Honest (IM)	CVS1		
30	VCT	Courageous (IM)	CVP2	Honest (IM)	CVS1	Imaginative (IC)	CVT2
31	WBC	Ambitious (IC)	CVP1	Responsible (IM)	CVS1	Honest (IM)	CVT1
				Self-respect (TP)	CVS2	Courageous (IM)	CVT1
32	XRO	Ambitious (IC)	CVP1				

This table reports the results of the coding text of corporate mission statements and CSR text using Schmeltz (2014) approach. The prefix of P denotes the primary values, which were stressed most linguistically, S denotes secondary values with more supportive role and less frequency, T denotes tertiary values of lower importance and not frequently present, and numbers 1, 2, 3, and 4 represent Rokeach values of Instrumental-competence (IC), instrumental-moral (IM), terminal personal (TP), and terminal social (TS) respectively. For example, CVP1 denotes the corporate identity primary Instrumental-competence (IC) values, which were stressed most linguistically

Table 4.5 Sample of CSR text used for CSR communication strategies

SIS	
ARG	"Having the ability to harvest rainwater from the building allows us to reduce water consumption and control storm water runoff from the site"
CNU	"... This joint project is bringing better broadband to rural schools, health providers and tens of thousands of rural residents. It will also help rural businesses access the communications technology they need to drive business innovation and efficiencies"
FBU	"We have adopted a life cycle approach to the way we operate. We work so that the eco-system we depend on operates in a closed loop system. We aim to use sustainable resources with zero waste, use energy as efficiently as possible, borrow water then return it clean, eliminate pollutants from discharges to the environment, achieve a low carbon footprint and reuse or recycle by-products"
FPH	"At Fisher & Paykel healthcare, we recognize the importance of minimizing the impact of our operations on the environment. We have started our 3-year journey towards Certified Emissions Measurement and Reduction Scheme (CEMARS) certification. We now recycle approximately 90% of our waste, up from 50% the previous"
FSF	"... We support projects that are in line with our values of quality, safety, wellbeing, the environment, and fostering community spirit. Awards are granted for between NZ$500 and NZ$5000 and applications are considered twice a year"
GMT	"We are an active industry participant and work to advance the interests of all our stakeholders through membership of various groups, the most notable of which include The Property Council of New Zealand and the Green Building Council of New Zealand"
HNZ	"We have always been committed to local communities and New Zealand as a whole and that commitment will continue and grow in the future. HNZ's donation provided the funding for the programme and as a direct result, 24 people diagnosed with MS were able to develop firm plans to move forward and live their lives to their true potential"
MFT	"We have been recycling office and depot waste for 25 years in New Zealand. We store and use rainwater and recycle grey water for truck washing, ablutions and irrigation ... we have invested in excess of $750,000 in IT and computer equipment"
MHI	"Every year, MHI prides itself on giving back to the community by supporting the communities around our 252 stores globally. This year our sponsorship and donations of products, gift vouchers and cash amounted to $245,000"
RBD	"We continue to place great emphasis on making our stores safe for everyone working in them. Lost time injuries were down 26% on prior year to an all-time low..."
RYM	"We are also contributing to the community in other ways. We give a massive boost to the local economy every time we build a new village, both during the construction phase and in terms of employment, services and supplies once the village is open"
STC	"The project demonstrates our commitment to the Canterbury recovery and illustrates how our stronger organisation and greater focus benefits our customer..."
TPW	"In order to report on our progress in this regard we report economic, staff, environmental, customer and community related measures ... Our performance this year was comparable with previous years across the five areas we report on although not all targets were achieved"
VCT	"We take our safety message to the broader community and this year, we were recognised by the Electricity Engineers' Association (EEA) for the contribution we make to public safety"

(continued)

Table 4.5 (continued)

WHS	"…We have bought in additional expertise to help improve our energy efficiency, refining the continued roll-out of energy efficient T5 lighting via our store modernization and refit programmes, and ensuring our new store designs incorporates the most contemporary and efficient lighting and air-conditioning solutions…"
SRS	
ANZ	"…Our financing decisions take into account social and environmental impacts before and during customer relationships. These are monitored on a continuous basis through our 'Reputation Risk Radar'. Notable incidents and allegations inform regular Early Alert Review meetings, which consider social, environmental, governance and credit risks. Regular dialogue between our relationship managers and customers alert us to issues that may arise"
CEN	"…Our Native Fish Management Plan enhances both inanga spawning and inanga habitat. Each year we release three carefully timed flows from the Roxburgh Dam to coincide with the natural spring tides, which helps to lift the inanga up to the riverbank where they can lay their eggs before returning to the water … We originally applied for consents for the Waitahora wind farm in August 2008. When the commissioners declined the application in April 2009, we responded by reducing environmental effects further and addressing many of the concerns raised by the local residents"
KMD	"…We undertook a small number of materiality interviews with internal and external stakeholders... Stakeholders were selected based on their different functional expertise within the business to obtain a diversity of views … each stake holder was asked about the issues that they felt were most material to Kathmandu's sustainability impacts and performance. The analysis led to the identification of the top five material issues … These issues have helped to guide the disclosures in this report"
NPX	"…[T]here was an odour emission as a result of an unexpected reaction in a production vessel. The chemicals involved were typical of those used in textile treatment and paint production. An investigation was undertaken by the Company using independent experts and the recommended corrective actions have been implemented…"
OGC	"The second incident of non-compliance related to a blasting event that took place outside of the consented time. Under the previous consent, blasting was permitted between sunrise and sunset without stating the specific period. As a result, we applied for and were subsequently granted consent to more explicitly state the permissible hours for blasting activities
	"The stakeholder feedback process makes up a large part of our stakeholder management program. Formal and informal mechanisms are now provided at our operations for community consultation and comment regarding our programs and activities. We look forward to continued advancement of our reporting and sustainability programs as we work to strengthen our engagement with and understanding of our internal and external stakeholders"
SVS	
AIA	"… During 2011 and 2012 Auckland Airport consulted widely with all stakeholders on a successor to its first sustainability plan. This consultation process produced both a revised policy and set the business targets out to 2020 and inspirational goals out to 2030"

(continued)

Table 4.5 (continued)

KIP	"We continually strive for best practice and during the year undertook a review of our program, which included seeking input from our key stakeholders. The review assessed environmental, social and governance risks and opportunities. As a result, we have developed a new Sustainability and Responsible Investment Policy ... We now have sustainability objectives incorporated into performance targets for relevant executives"
MRP	"Relationships with local communities and with Waikato River iwi are crucial to the success of our business. MRP's environmental outcomes are developed in partnership with local regulators and communities whose natural resources are used to generate power ... We apply our knowledge, expertise and technology to manage resources sustainably"
TWR	"...Each manager spends up to a day entrenched on-the job talking with team members, understanding their challenges and looking for opportunities for improvement. Ideas are filtered through our Customer Insight team to assess and action"
WBC	"...This year we also sought specific stakeholder feedback to assist in the development of additional credit policy statements. During the year, we commissioned a series of independent stakeholder interviews, which assessed the effectiveness of these channels, tested emerging themes and confirmed the identification of current issues"

their CSR reports. Fourth, for determining the CSR information quality, we used the readability of CSR disclosure as a criterion. We used the Flesch readability formula, as a predictor of readability. The formula considers two important variables that affect the style of writing: sentence length and word length (Flesch 1960). This formula was chosen because first, it is one of the most widely used indicators in readability studies (Courtis 1986, 1998, 2004; Schroeder and Gibson 1990, 1992; Smith and Taffler 1992; Subramanian et al. 1993; Smith et al. 2006) and second, the formula generates a readability score on a scale that ranges from 0 to 100. The higher the point on the scale, the easier it is to read the text, whereas the lower the point on the scale, the greater the reading difficulty. In order to calculate the Flesch reading ease score, the review tool in Microsoft Word was used. Because Flesch reading ease is available in a computerized format, this method ensured that the analysis was more accurate than if it had been calculated manually. A number of studies have examined the association of readability scores with companies' financial performance (refer to, e.g., Courtis 1986; Smith and Taffler 1992; Subramanian et al. 1993; Rutherford 2003; Smith et al. 2006; Abu-Bakar and Ameer 2011).

4.3.3 Empirical Approach

We used SmartPLS 3.0 to test the hypotheses (Ringle et al. 2015). The Partial Least Square (PLS) approach is a soft modeling approach to Structural Equation Modeling (SEM), which focuses on the analysis of variance rather than covariance based Structural Equation Modeling (CB-SEM). This approach has been widely applied in the fields of environmental and social performance research (refer to Lin and Hsu

Table 4.6 NZX 50 companies' CSR communication strategies

Code	Name	CSR text location	CSR communication strategies		
			SIS	SRS	SVS
AIA	Auckland Airport Limited	Webpage			X
AMP	AMP Limited	Report			X
ANZ	Australia and New Zealand Banking Group	Report		X	
ARG	Argosy Property Limited	Webpage	X		
CEN	Contact Energy Limited	Report		X	
CNU	Chorus Limited	An. Report	X		
DNZ	DNZ Property Fund Limited	Webpage	X		
FBU	Fletcher Building Limited	Report	X		
FPH	Fisher and Paykel Healthcare Corporation Limited	An. Report	X		
FSF	Fonterra Shareholder's Fund	Webpage	X		
GMT	Goodman Property Trust	Webpage	X		
GPG	Guiness Peat Group Plc	An. Report	X		
HNZ	Heartland New Zealand Limited	An. Report	X		
KIP	Kiwi Income Property Trust	An. Report			X
KMD	Kathmandu Holdings Limited	Report		X	
MFT	MainFreight Limited	An. Report	X		
MHI	Michael Hill International Limited	An. Report	X		
MRP	Mighty River Power Limited	An. Report			X
NPX	Nuplex Industries Limited	An. Report		X	
OGC	OceanaGold Corporation	Report		X	
POT	Port of Tauranga Limited	Webpage	X		
RBD	Restaurant Brands New Zealand Limited	An. Report	X		
RYM	Ryman Healthcare Limited	An. Report	X		
SKC	Skycity Entertainment Group Limited	Webpage	X		
SKL	Skellerup Holdings Limited	An. Report	X		
STU	Steel and Tube Holdings Limited	An. Report	X		
TEL	Telecom Corporation of New Zealand Limited	An. Report			X
TME	Trade Me Group Limited	An. Report	X		
TPW	Trust Power Limited	An. Report	X		
TWR	Tower Limited	An. Report			X
VCT	Vector Limited	An. Report	X		
WBC	Westpac Banking Corporation	Report			X
WHS	The Warehouse Group	Report	X		
		Total	21	5	7

X donates availability of CSR text from the companies' annual report, Stand-alone CSR report (Report), and webpage

2015; Bhattacharyya and Cummings 2015), marketing (Henseler et al. 2009), organization, and business strategy research (Sosik et al. 2009; Hulland 1999). According to Wong (2013), PLS-SEM is a good alternative to CB-SEM when the sample size is small, the application has a little available theory, and the correct model specification cannot be ensured.

There are two sub-models in a SEM: the inner model and the outer model. The inner model specifies the relationships between the independent and dependent latent variables, whereas the outer model specifies the relationship between the latent variables and their observed indicators. In our PLS-SEM model, the inner model specifies the relationship between the CSR communication and CSR medium, whereas the outer model specifies the relationship between corporate identity values (hereafter self-centeredness and society-centeredness) by using the first order variables of instrumental-competence, instrumental moral, terminal personal, and terminal social. Since the main objective of this paper is to test the hypothesis between second order constructs such as corporate values and CSR communication, CSR communication and CSR medium, and CSR medium and CSR information quality, we focus primarily on the results of the analysis of these second-order constructs.

We used the bootstrapping in the SmartPLS, which is a nonparametric procedure that can be applied to test whether coefficients such as outer weights, outer loadings, and path coefficients are significant by estimating standard errors for the estimates. We chose the option of construct level changes wherein the signs of a group of coefficients e.g., all outer loadings of a specific latent variable in a bootstrapping subsample are compared with the signs of the original PLS path model estimation. If the majority of signs needs to be reversed in a bootstrap run to match the signs of the model estimation using the original sample, all signs are reversed in that bootstrap run. Otherwise, no signs are reversed. Table 4.7 shows the outer model, inner model, and the measurement/indicator variables used in the PLS-SEM model.

The corporate identity values and CSR communication strategy variables used in this study are formative indicators in nature. According to Hair et al. (2016), each formative indicator's VIF value should be lower than 5, therefore those variables that have VIF greater than 5 were excluded from the measurement model in the first stage. We used a number of criteria to ascertain the goodness of fit of the PLS-SEM model, these are: SRMR and the Heterotrait-Monotrait Ratio (HTMT). Henseler et al. (2014) introduce the SRMR as a goodness-of-fit measure for PLS-SEM that can be used to avoid model misspecification. A value less than 0.10 or of 0.08 is considered a good fit. In order to infer the discriminant validity of formative indicators, the HTMT ratio of formative indicators, should be below 1 (see Henseler et al. 2015).

Table 4.7 Measurement model

Corporate values -> CSR communication	
Measurement/indicator variables:	*Exogenous latent variables*
Corporate identity values construct:	*Social-centeredness*
Instrumental competence values (CVP1, CVS3, CVT2)	*Self-centeredness*
Instrumental moral values (CVP2, CVS1, CVT1)	
Terminal personal values (CVP3, CVS2, CVT3)	
Terminal social values (CVP4, CVS4, CVT4)	
CSR communication ->CSR communication strategy	
Measurement/indicator variables:	*Endogenous latent variable:*
Social-centeredness, Self-centeredness	*CSR communication*
SIS = Stakeholder information strategy	*CSR communication strategy*
SRS = Stakeholder response strategy	
SVS = Stakeholder involvement strategy	
CSR communication ->CSR medium	
Measurement/indicator variables:	*Endogenous latent variable:*
Social-centeredness, self-centeredness	*CSR Communication*
Standalone CSR report	*CSR medium*
CSR medium ->CSR information quality	
Measurement/indicator variables:	*Endogenous latent variable:*
Stand-alone CSR reports	*CSR medium*
High readability score values above the median value of RSCORE	*CSR information quality*

This table describes the hypothesized path relationship and measurement/indicator variables of their underlying constructs

4.4 Results and Discussion

4.4.1 Thematic Analysis Results

We applied a popular technique of a word cloud or text cloud developed from the corpus analysis to visually represent prominent themes in company mission statements that underlie their value orientation. This technique is an easy and visually appealing means of presenting the frequency of words in a text as a weighted list. The font size of the words represents the frequency of the keywords. High frequency keywords appear in a larger font size. It is evident that the keywords frequently used by New Zealand companies are *people*, *integrity*, and *respect* (refer to Fig. 4.1).

We found that most reports have a similar lexical and textual genre i.e., the same topics are covered, in some cases with the same terms, which suggests low lexical variation in the corpus of CSR reports. In terms of CSR disclosure, the community, environment, and work were prominent in the CSR reports by the New Zealand companies; however, at the same time, there are significant variations in scope and focus of CSR domains across the industries (see Fig. 4.2). For instance, policies and

Fig. 4.1 Word cloud – corporate values in mission statements

actions taken in regard to waste management, carbon, and carbon emissions targets were found in the CSR disclosures of the energy, consumer, finance, and telecom sectors. In contrast, conservation and water management issues (storm water and rainwater harvesting) were in the CSR disclosures of the companies in the energy and ports sectors, and the energy-saving efficient technologies, tools, and green buildings were prominent in the CSR disclosures of the companies in the property, Telecom, and transport sectors. These findings suggest that New Zealand companies might have interpreted and strategized resources and opportunities consistent with their own values (Hemingway 2013) but also consistent with their corporate identity (Leuthesser and Kohli 1997; van der Merwe and Puth 2014). We found that New Zealand companies were more or less altruistic in communicating their identity in vision and mission statements. The keywords that they used seemed to be focusing primarily on rules, norms, and compliance, which is an implicit orientation that is often associated with the European approach (Matten and Moon 2008). New Zealand is identified as a rule-based and transparent society with European roots (Hooker 2008). Thus, it is possible that national socio-political systems may have

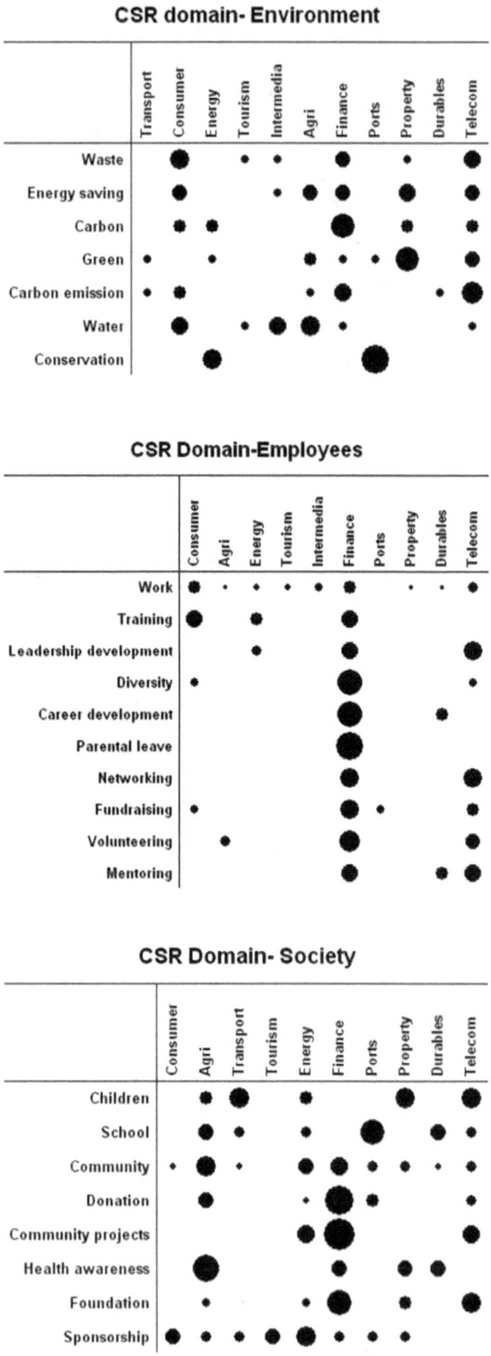

Fig. 4.2 CSR domains

influenced the companies' approach and engagement with CSR (Rhodes and Brown 2005; Schmeltz 2014; van de Merwe and Puth 2014).

Regarding the use of the four factors and postures in the CSR corpus of New Zealand companies, as suggested by Ware and Linkugel (1973), we found three factors, *bolster*, *differentiation,* and *transcendence* in their CSR corpus. Table 4.8 provides some examples relating to WLP-factors. Of particular note in this regard is the use of the words 'best' and 'top'; *transcendence* posture was used for description of their workplace, support for employees' training, leadership development, mentoring, and workers' involvement in volunteering and fundraising. 'Support' ($N = 208$) and 'help' ($N = 165$) *bolster posture* was used for descriptions of their involvement with community initiatives, local charities, schools, rehabilitation, and disadvantaged people/families. Interestingly, the word 'help' ($N = 55$), *differentiation* posture was often used to address social and environment issues, and the word 'understand' was being used for describing of the work and environment. Thus, these findings suggest that New Zealand companies might use explanation and justification postures to legitimize business operations that link work, society, and environment. In this regard, the companies assumed that if the audience understands its motives, actions, and beliefs they were unable to condemn and give approval.

4.4.2 PLS-SEM Estimation Results

We report the results for the hypothesized path relationships in Table 4.9 (also see Fig. 4.3). The formative constructs of corporate identity values i.e., self-centeredness and society-centeredness are well captured by their first order dimensions of instrumental-competence, instrumental-moral, terminal personal, and terminal social values, as their outer weights are above 0.2 and significant at 5% and 1% level of significance. For the composite construct of self-centeredness, the highest outer loading was on terminal personal values, while in the composite construct of society-centeredness, the highest outer loading was on instrumental-moral values. The empirical results show a significant positive path coefficient of 0.39 from self-centeredness to CSR communication as well as a significant path coefficient of 0.41 from social-centeredness to CSR communication. The R^2 value of 0.29 is above the minimum value of 10% (Falk and Miller 1992), which seems to suggest that corporate identity values can predict or explain at least 29% of CSR communication variance among the sample companies. The results support previous literature that both self-centeredness and society-centeredness influence CSR communication strategy (e.g., Schmeltz 2012, 2014). A company's value system may change over time, a move from self-centeredness to society-centeredness, and this may influence its preferable modes of conduct (Rokeach 1973) in terms of CSR communication strategy. Maon et al. (2010) suggest that a company starts out by seeing CSR as a restraint, then later on as a duty and obligation. As New Zealand companies are lagging behind in terms of corporate responsibility (KPMG 2011), it is possible that

Table 4.8 WLP-factors in CSR corpus

Factor	Text	Code	CSR categories
Transcendence	Our primary school years are the formative years of growth and development and we all want every Kiwi kid to have the **BEST** nutritional start	School	Society
	We have been finalists in the Kenexa **BEST** Workplaces survey for the last 2 years	Career development	Employees
	The global **'BEST** in class' engagement rating is 83%		
	AAPT is dedicated to minimizing waste and ensuring the **BEST** possible use of resources	Waste	Environment
	Voted as the **BEST** trading company in Australasia for carbon in 20112, WIB is consistently recognized as a leader in understanding the risks and opportunities around carbon and broader environmental challenges for business	Carbon emission	Environment
	This is just one element of our diversity and flexibility agenda where we are creating an environment to attract and retain the very **BEST** people	Diversity	Employees
Bolster	CREATE runs programs to assist young people transition from care into independence through the development of life skills encompassing job readiness, budgeting, accessing healthcare and housing **SUPPORT**, and cooking	Donation	Society
	We **SUPPORT** initiatives that encourage learning and the development of knowledge in science, technology, engineering, and healthcare	School	Society
	For the sixth year, we provided **SUPPORT** for the NZ VEX Robotics Competition, which seeks to increase student interest and involvement in science, technology, engineering, and mathematics	Donation	
	Together with Foodbank Australia, we're proud to **HELP** two million Australians who rely on food relief every year		
	Our donations of milk, cheese, spreads, and yogurts **HELP** make more than 88,000 nutritious meals every day		
Differentiation	It aims to improve the ability of staff to identify, **UNDERSTAND**, and resolve social and environmental issues	Work environment	Employees
	This will help us better **UNDERSTAND** how well we reflect our customer and community base and help us build deeper insights of how inclusive we are as an organization	Diversity	Employees
	For these reasons EarthCheck was a seen as the best fit for Auckland Airport. We **UNDERSTAND** sustainability requires a long-term view of our business, a long-term view that takes into consideration the needs of future generations today	Sustainability	Environment

Table 4.9 PLS-SEM estimation results

Path relationships	Coefficients original sample	Coefficients sample mean	Std error	t-value	Hypothesis
Self-centeredness -> CSR communication	0.287**	0.309**	0.183	1.571	H1-Supported
Social-centeredness -> CSR communication	0.451***	0.411***	0.145	3.096	H2-Supported
CSR communication -> SIS	0.663***	0.622***	0.277	2.396	H3-Supported
CSR communication -> SRS	0.239	0.196	0.361	0.331	
CSR communication ->SVS	0.860***	0.775***	0.138	4.921	H3-Supported
CSR communication -> CSR medium	0.446***		0.112	3.963	H4-Supported
CSR medium -> CSR information quality	0.09		0.149	0.572	H5-Not supported
Goodness of fit indicators					
	Original sample	**Sample mean**	**Std error**	**t-values**	
SRMR	0.097	0.107***	0.020	4.929	
Heterotrait-Montrait ratio (HTMR)					
CSR communication -> CSR medium	0.502	0.500***	0.081	6.204	
CSR medium -> CSR information quality	0.288	0.290***	0.011	2.614	
Coefficient of determination – R^2					
CSR communication	0.258	0.295***	0.085	3.049	
CSR medium	0.186	0.196**	0.081	2.290	
CSR information quality	0.009	0.014	0.043	0.419	

*, **, and *** show significance at level 10, 5 and 1%

the companies were at the initial stage of CSR cultural grasp phase and adopted the appropriate CSR strategies that harmonized with its value system.

This figure shows the p-values for each hypothesized path relationship using the bootstrapping procedure in the Smart-PLS.

The interplay between corporate identity and communication strategy was managed through a distinct CSR communication strategy (Gray and Balmer 1998), in our analysis, the outer loading for SIS and SVS were higher than SRS. Consistent with Schmeltz (2014), this finding seemed to suggest that the sample companies accommodated their stakeholders by listening to them, found out the stakeholders' expectations, and aligned the company's strategy accordingly. The aim is to be seen as favorable by the stakeholders (Hooghiemstra 2000; Cornelissen 2011) and could be a good start to what Perron and Duffy (2012) termed as "a sustaining mutually beneficial relationships." However, whether SRS strategy would produce different outcomes for society and firms (Ellen et al. 2006), as compared to SIS

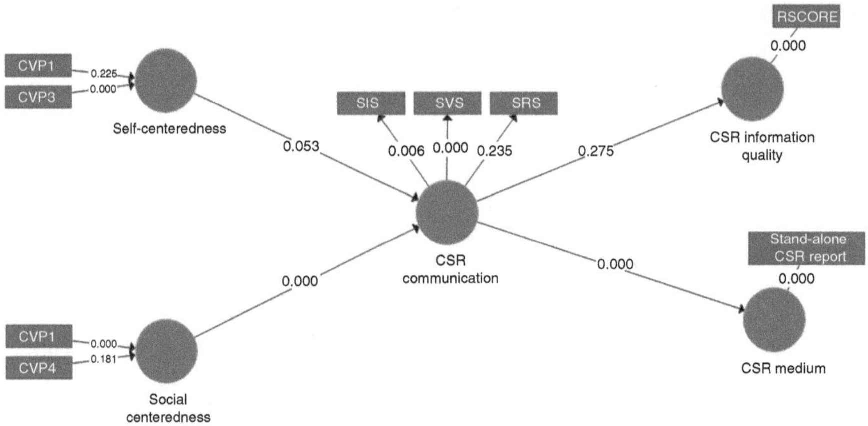

Fig. 4.3 Estimation results

and SVS, is beyond the scope of this paper. The inner model shows a significant positive path from the CSR communication strategy to the standalone CSR report of 0.44, thus H4 was also supported. Therefore, the communication strategy (SIS, SRS, SVS) that a company adopts may influence the choice of the communication medium it uses to communicate to the stakeholders (Morsing and Schultz 2006). The decision on the communication medium is important because it can influence the way the stakeholders perceive an organization's CSR commitment (Gray and Balmer 1998) and the texts included in the communication medium to echo the corporate values (Melewar 2008).

The path relationship between CSR medium and CSR information quality was not significant, thus H5 was not supported. This finding suggests that stand-alone CSR reports did not significantly influence the quality of information disclosed. This seems to suggest the notion of 'substance over form' was consistent with Courtis (1995), Maignan and Ralston (2002), Berens and van Rekom (2008), and Ziek (2009). Our findings suggest that the companies mostly prioritize instrumental values at the expense of terminal values in their mission statements, which is similar to findings of Schmeltz (2014) for a sample of companies. According to Schmeltz (2014, p. 15), it is reasonable for a company to focus on just a limited number of desirable end states, and then concentrate on the multiple ways of achieving them. Similarly, the terminal values present in the corporate mission statements are primary of personal, not social, nature.

4.5 Conclusion

In this study, we examined the relationship between two types of corporate values and three types of CSR communication strategies, and whether these different CSR communication strategies result in standalone CSR reports. In addition, we examined the relationship between CSR commitment, indicated by a standalone CSR report, and its influence on CSR information quality. Our findings suggest that New Zealand companies use explanation and justification posture, which combines bolstering, differentiation, and transcendence to legitimize business operations that link work, society, and environment. The companies assumed that if the audience understands its motives, actions, and beliefs they were unable to condemn and give approval. We found that New Zealand companies' value orientation may have been influenced by national socio-political systems.

Our results, using the SEM, showed that corporate values of social-centeredness and self-centeredness have a positive influence on the CSR communication strategies. Furthermore, CSR communication has a positive influence on three communication strategies, in particular, SIS seems to have been adopted widely by the New Zealand companies. CSR communication strategies have also significantly resulted in the issuance of stand-alone CSR reports. We did not find that standalone CSR reports influence the CSR information quality.

New Zealand is well known for its flexibility, lack of bureaucratic inertia, and willingness to innovate (Frame et al. 2003); these attributes should be conducive for rapid uptake of CSR. This study offers no judgment on the values of companies or their communication strategies. Various drivers for the adoption of CSR initiatives are reported in the literature. However, this study focuses on corporate values in order to show how different values influence the different means by which companies communicate with their stakeholders. Although outcomes from communication strategies can vary, the analysis conducted in this research measures outcome by the quality of the CSR communication.

Another obvious caveat for interpreting this study is that it examines CSR, a context-dependent phenomenon that affects a small sample of companies, which does not allow for broad generalizations. In addition, the measurement of values by means of single items, such as the terminal social or instrumental social might be questionable since individual differences may reflect variations in linguistic usage rather than variations in underlying constructs. Although we have used a four values operationalization rather than one, increasing the number might have added to ambiguity. However, it is plausible that the observed patterns in the configurations of corporate values may be analytically informative in relation to similar companies in similar contexts, and can offer useful insights into how to address matters of corporate identity and reputation.

We acknowledge that our results cannot be generalized to all companies listed on the New Zealand stock exchange. We do not specifically test the impact of industry affiliations on the CSR communication and this might provide an avenue for future research. Future longitudinal studies can be conducted to examine changes in corporate CSR communication strategies from sense-making to sense-giving (Weick 1995). There is a scarcity of research on the manner in which corporations respond to legitimacy-threatening events, particularly those challenging their corporate identity and values. The drivers for companies issuing stand-alone reports are also worth investigating.

Our findings suggest a link between CSR communication with communication strategies and the issuance of stand-alone CSR reports. Future research should examine the role of accountants in driving both, the CSR communication strategies and preparation of stand-alone CSR reports. Their role in the measurement and reporting CSR performance indicators, controlling and monitoring CSR-related expenditures may influence CSR communication strategic choices including the stand-alone CSR reports. Future research should also examine how the accountants align their fiduciary duties to the shareholders and how they internalize corporate values into a choice of accounting and reporting practices. In this way, the future work would expose how the accountants respond to complex information needs of various stakeholder groups. The drivers for companies issuing stand-alone reports are also worth investigating.

In jurisdictions where CSR reporting has been made mandatory, the accountants are expected to extend their role to emphasize CSR information for compliance purposes and exception reports where non-compliance occurs to make suggestions for future improvement. This new position reinforces the emerging roles that the accountants have in driving sustainability beyond the preparation and reporting of accounting and financial performance – from passive bean-counters to dynamic strategists. This extended role of accountants in driving CSR initiatives warrants future research. This study would inform an understanding of the complex challenges that the accountants might have to overcome in enacting or making sense of change.

References

Abu Bakar AS, Ameer R (2011) Readability of corporate social responsibility communication in Malaysia. Corp Soc Responsib Environ Manag 18:50–60. https://doi.org/10.1002/csr.240
Albert S, Whetten D (1985) Organizational identity. Res Organ Behav 7:263–295
Aust PJ (2004) Communicated values as indicators of organizational identity: a method for organizational assessment and its application in a case study. Commun Stud 55:515–534. https://doi.org/10.1080/10510970409388636
Baker M, Schaltegger S (2013) Pragmatism, truth and social accounting research, Paper presented at the Seventh Asia Pacific Interdisciplinary Research in Accounting (APIRA), Kobe 26–28 July. Retrieved from http://www.apira2013.org/proceedings/pdfs/K133.pdf (25 Dec 2016)
Balmer JMT, Gray ER (2000) Corporate identity and corporate communications. Ind Commer Train 32(7):256–261
Banerjee SB (2008) Corporate social responsibility: the good, the bad and the ugly. Crit Sociol 34(1):51–79
Belal AR, Cooper S (2011) The absence of corporate social responsibility reporting in Bangladesh. Crit Perspect Account 22:654–667. https://doi.org/10.1016/j.cpa.2010.06.020
Berens G, van Rekom J (2008) How specific should corporate communication be? The role of advertising language in establishing a corporate reputation for CSR. In: Melewar TC (ed) Facets of corporate identity, communication and reputation. Routledge, New York, pp 96–121
Bhattacharya A, Cummings L (2015) Measuring corporate environmental performance-stakeholder engagement evaluation. Bus Strat Environ:309–325. https://doi.org/10.1002/bse.1819
Braaten DO, Cody MJ, DeTienne KB (1993) Account episodes in organizations remedial work and impression management. Manag Commun Q 6(3):219–250
Carroll AB (1991) The pyramid of corporate social responsibility: toward the moral management of organizational stakeholders. Bus Horiz 39–48. https://doi.org/10.1016/0007-6813(91)90005-G
Cody MJ, McLaughlin ML (1990) Interpersonal accounting. In: Giles H, Robinson P (eds) Analyzing everyday explanation. A casebook of methods. Sage, London

Cornelissen J (2011) Corporate communication. A guide to theory and practice, 3rd edn. Sage, London

Courtis JK (1986) An investigation into annual report readability and corporate risk-return relationships. Account Bus Res J 16:285–294. https://doi.org/10.1080/00014788.1986.9729329

Courtis JK (1995) Readability of annual reports: Western versus Asian evidence. Account Audit Account J 8(2):4–17

Courtis JK (1998) Annual report readability variability: tests of the obfuscation hypothesis. Account Audit Account J 11:459–471. https://doi.org/10.1108/09513579810231457

Courtis JK (2004) Corporate report obfuscation: artefact or phenomenon? Br Account Rev 36:291–312. https://doi.org/10.1016/j.bar.2004.03.005

Crane A (2000) Marketing, morality and the natural environment. Routledge, London

Crane A, Glozer S (2016) Researching corporate social responsibility communication: themes, opportunities, and challenges. J Manag Stud 53:1223

Day K (2012) Social Social responsibility in New Zealand's offshore supply chains: what would it take to contribute towards improved labour conditions in China. Master of Arts in Political Science, Thesis, University of Canterbury, New Zealand

Dionisopoulos GN (1985) Generic description of corporate apologia. Paper presented at the Central States Speech Convention, Indianapolis, Indiana

Du S, Bhattacharya CB, Sen S (2010) Maximizing business returns to corporate social responsibility (CSR): the role of CSR communication. Int J Manag Rev 12:8–19. https://doi.org/10.1111/j.1468-2370.2009.00276.x

Ellen PS, Webb D, Mohr L (2006) Building corporate associations: consumer attributions for corporate socially responsible programs. J Acad Mark Sci 34:147–157. https://doi.org/10.1177/0092070305284976

Esrock SL, Leichty GB (1998) Social responsibility and corporate web pages: self-presentation or agenda setting? Public Relat Rev 24:305–319. https://doi.org/10.1016/S0363-8111(99)80142-8

Eweje G, Bentley T (2006) CSR and staff retention in New Zealand companies: a literature review. Department of Management and International Business No. 6, 2-16, Massey University, ISSN 1177–2611

Falk M (1992) A primer for soft modeling. The University of Akron Press, The University of Akron, Akron

Fifka MS (2013) Corporate responsibility reporting and its determinants in comparative perspective – a review of the empirical literature and a meta-analysis. Bus Strateg Environ 22:1–35. https://doi.org/10.1002/bse.729

Flesch R (1960) How to write, speak and think effectively. Harper and Row, New York

Frame B, Gordon R, Whitehouse I (2003) In: Shah R, Murphy D, McIntosh (eds) Something to in: creating trust in organisations: stories of transparency, accountability and governance. Greenleaf Publishing, Sheffield

Freeman R (1984) Strategic management: a stakeholder approach. Pitman, Boston

Friedman A, Miles S (2006) Stakeholders. Theory and practice. Oxford University Press, New York

Gioia DA, Chittipeddi K (1991) Sensemaking and sensegiving in strategic change initiation. Strateg Manag J 12:433–448. https://doi.org/10.1002/smj.4250120604

Gray ER, Balmer JMT (1998) Managing corporate image and corporate reputation. Long Range Plan 31(5):695–702

Grunig J, Hunt T (1984) Managing public relations. Wadsworth Publishing, Belmont

Hair JF, Hult TM, Ringle C, Sarstedt M (2016) A premier on partial least squares structural equation modeling (PLS-SEM). Sage, Thousand Oaks

He H, Baruch Y (2009) Organizational identity and legitimacy under major environmental changes: tales of two UK are building societies. Br J Manag 21:44–62

Hemingway CA (2013) Corporate social entrepreneurship. Cambridge University Press, Cambridge

Henseler J, Ringle C, Sinkovics R (2009) The use of partial least squares path modelling in international marketing. Adv Int Mark 20:277–320

Henseler J, Dijkstra TK, Sarstedt M, Ringle CM, Diamantopoulos A, Straub DW, Ketchen DJ, Hair JF, Hult GTM, Calantone RJ (2014) Common beliefs and reality about partial least squares: comments on Rönkkö & Evermann (2013). Org Res Method 17(2):182–209

Henseler J, Ringle CM, Sarstedt M (2015) A new criterion for assessing discriminant validity in variance-based structural equation modeling. J Acad Mark Sci 43(1):115–135

Hooghiemstra R (2000) Corporate communication and impression management – new perspectives why companies engage in corporate social reporting. J Bus Ethics 27:55–68. https://doi.org/10.1023/A:1006400707757

Hooker J (2008) Cultural differences in business communication. Available at: http://web.tepper.cmu.edu/jnh/businessCommunication.pdf (Retrieve 18 Dec 2016)

Hulland J (1999) Use of partial least squares (PLS) in strategic management research: a review of four recent studies. Strateg Manag J 20:195–204

IIRC (2016) Find out what is happening in your region. Available from http://integratedreporting.org/when-advocate-for-global-adoption/find-out-what-is-happening-in-your-region/. Retrieved on 13 December 2016.

KPMG (2010) Integrated reporting – closing the loop of strategy. KPMG, Amsterdam. http://www.integratedreportingsa.org/LinkClick.aspx?fileticket=mqrhIkTg5bs%3d&tabid=237

KPMG (2011) KPMG international survey of corporate responsibility reporting 2011. http://www.kpmg.com/Global/en/IssuesAndInsights/ArticlesPublications/corporate-responsibility/Documents/2011-survey.pdf. [12 Feb 2014]

Lantos G (2001) The boundaries of strategic corporate social responsibility. J Consum Mark 18:595–632. https://doi.org/10.1108/07363760110410281

Lee K-H, Herold DM, Yu A-L (2016) Small and medium enterprises and corporate social responsibility practice: a Swedish perspective. Corp Soc Responsib Environ Manag 23(2):88–99

Leuthesser L, Kohli C (1997) Corporate identity: the role of mission statements. Bus Horiz 40(3):59–66

Lin H, Hsu M (2015) Using social cognitive theory to investigate green consumer behavior. Bus Strateg Environ 24:326–343. https://doi.org/10.1002/bse.1820

Lueg K, Lueg R, Andersen K, Dancianu V (2016) Integrated reporting with CSR practices: a pragmatic constructivist case study in a Danish cultural setting. Corp Commun Int J 21(1):20–35

Madueno JH, Jorge MLM, Conesa IM, Martinex-Martinez D (2016) Relationship between corporate social responsibility and competitive performance in Spanish SMEs: empirical evidence from a stakeholders' perspective. Bus Res Q 19:55–72

Maignan I, Ralston DA (2002) Corporate social responsibility in Europe and the US: insights from businesses' self-presentations. J Int Bus Stud 33:497–514. https://doi.org/10.1057/palgrave.jibs.8491028

Maon F, Lindgreen A, Swaen V (2010) Organizational stages and cultural phases: a critical review and a consolidative model of corporate social responsibility. Int J Manag Rev 12(1):20–38

Markwick N, Fill C (1997) Towards a framework for managing corporate identity. Eur J Mark 31:396–409. https://doi.org/10.1108/03090569710167619

Matten D, Moon J (2008) "Implicit" and "explicit" CSR: a conceptual framework for a comparative understanding of corporate social responsibility. Acad Manag Rev 33:404–424. https://doi.org/10.5465/AMR.2008.31193458

Melewar T (2008) Facets of corporate identity, communication and reputation. Routledge, New York

Merkl-Davies D, Brennan N (2000) Discretionary disclosure strategies in corporate narratives: incremental information or impression management? J Account Lit 27:116–196

Morsing M, Schultz M (2006) Corporate social responsibility communication: stakeholder information, response and involvement strategies. Bus Ethics Eur Rev 15:323–338. https://doi.org/10.1111/j.1467-8608.2006.00460.x

Noland J, Phillips R (2010) Stakeholder engagement, discourse ethics and strategic management. Int J Manag Rev 12:39–49. https://doi.org/10.1111/j.1468-2370.2009.00279.x

Orlitzky M (2005) Social responsibility and financial performance: trade-off or virtuous circle? Univ Auckland Bus Rev Autumn 7:37–43

Perron GM, Duffy JFJ (2012) Environmental and business communities of practice: graduate students comparing community-relevant language. Bus Strateg Environ 21:170–182. https://doi.org/10.1002/bse.725

Porter M, Kramer M (2006) Strategy and society: the link between competitive advantage and corporate social responsibility. Harv Bus Rev 84:78–92

Pruzan P (2001) The question of organizational consciousness can organizations has values, virtues and visions? J Bus Ethics 29:271–284. https://doi.org/10.1023/A:1026577604845

PwC (2010) Integrated reporting – what does your reporting say about you? PwC, London. http://www.pwc.com/gx/en/services/audit-assurance/corporate-reporting/integrated-reporting/integrated-reporting.html

Rhodes C, Brown AD (2005) Narrative, organizations and research. Int J Manag Rev 7:167–188. https://doi.org/10.1111/j.1468-2370.2005.00112.x

Ringle CM, Wende S, Becker J-M (2015) SmartPLS 3. SmartPLS GmbH, Boenningstedt. http://www.smartpls.com. [29 August 2015]

Rokeach M (1973) The nature of human values. The Free Press, New York

Rutherford BA (2003) Obfuscation, textual complexity and the role of regulated narrative accounting disclosure in corporate governance. J Manag Gov 7:187–210. https://doi.org/10.1023/A:1023647615279

Schaltegger S, Burritt R (2006) Sustainability accounting and reporting: development, linkages and reflection. An introduction. In: Schaltegger S, Bennett M, Burritt R (eds) Sustainability accounting and reporting. Springer, Dordrecht

Schmeltz L (2012) Consumer-oriented CSR communication: focusing on ability or morality? Corp Commun Int J 17:29–49

Schmeltz L (2014) Identical or just compatible? The utility of corporate identity values in communicating corporate social responsibility. Int J Bus Commun 51:1–25

Schneider A, Samkin G, Pitu E (2012) Incorporating indigenous values in corporate social responsibility reports. J New Bus Ideas Trends 10:19–38

Schroeder N, Gibson C (1990) Readability of management's discussion and analysis. Account Horiz 4:78–87

Schroeder N, Gibson C (1992) Are summary annual reports successful? Account Horiz 6:28–37

Sen S, Bhattacharya C, Korschum D (2006) The role of corporate social responsibility in strengthening multiple stakeholder relationships: a field experiment. J Acad Mark Sci 34:158–166. https://doi.org/10.1177/0092070305284978

Sen S, Du S, Bhattacharya C (2009) Building relationships through corporate social responsibility. In: DJ MI, Park CW, Priester JR (eds) Handbook of brand relationships. M.E. Sharpe, New York

Smith M, Taffler R (1992) The chairman's statement and corporate financial performance. Account Finance 32:75–90. https://doi.org/10.1111/j.1467-629X.1992.tb00187.x

Smith M, Jamil A, Johari YC, Ahmad SA (2006) The chairman's statement in Malaysian companies – a test of the obfuscation hypothesis. Asian Rev Account 14:49–65. https://doi.org/10.1108/13217340610729464

Sosik JJ, Kahai SS, Piovoso MJ (2009) Silver bullet or voodoo statistics? A primer for using the partial least squares data analytic technique in group and organization research. Group Org Manag 34:5–36. https://doi.org/10.1177/1059601108329198

Subramanian R, Insley RG, Blackwell RD (1993) Performance and readability: a comparison of annual reports of profitable and unprofitable corporations. J Bus Commun 30:49–61. https://doi.org/10.1177/002194369303000103

Tschopp DJ (2005) Corporate social responsibility: a comparison between the United States and the European Union. Corp Soc Responsib Environ Manag 12:55–59. https://doi.org/10.1002/csr.69

van der Merwe AWAJ, Puth G (2014) Towards a conceptual model of the relationship between corporate trust and corporate reputation. Corp Reput Rev 17(2):138–156

Verboven H (2011) Communicating CSR and business identity in the chemical industry through mission slogans. Bus Commun Q 74:415–431. https://doi.org/10.1177/1080569911424485

Wanderley LSO, Lucian R, Farache F, de Sousa Filho JM (2008) CSR information disclosure on the web: a context-based approach analysing the influence of country of origin and industry sector. J Bus Ethics 82:369–378. https://doi.org/10.1007/s10551-008-9892-z

Ware BL, Linkugel WA (1973) They spoke in defence of themselves: on the generic criticism of apologia. Q J Speech 59:273–283

Weick K (1995) Sensemaking in organizations. Sage, Thousand Oaks

Wilson I (1975) What one company is doing about today's demands on business. In: Steiner G (ed) Changing business – society interrelationships. UCLA Graduate School of Management, Los Angeles, pp 121–140

Wong K (2013) Partial least squares structural equation modeling (PLS-SEM) techniques using SmartPLS. Marketing Bulletin 24: Technical Note 1

Wood DJ (2010) Measuring corporate social performance: a review. Int J Manag Rev 12:50–84. https://doi.org/10.1111/j.1468-2370.2009.00274.x

Ziek P (2009) Making sense of CSR communication. Corp Soc Responsib Environ Manag 16:137–145. https://doi.org/10.1002/csr.183

Part II
Environmental and Sustainability Performance Measurement and Management

Chapter 5
Managing Eco-efficiency Development for Sustainability: An Investigation of Top Carbon Polluters in Australia

Wei Qian, Amanpreet Kaur, and Stefan Schaltegger

Abstract Eco-efficiency as an important measure for integration of environmental and economic performance has been studied extensively in the past. However, previous studies are either conceptual or take a macro view of the empirical relationship between economic and environmental performance in an economy or industry. Little research has explored the actual integration in corporate practice. Using carbon emissions and their integration with corporate economic performance among Australian heavy polluters during 2009 and 2013, we analysed actual integration levels, improvements, patterns at the corporate level. Based on a typological classification of carbon efficiency developed in this study, we differentiate strong and weak eco-efficiency and identify the potential value drivers for the eco-efficiency results with regard to carbon emissions. The study finds that 54% of Australian top polluters have improved carbon efficiency since the implementation of Australian National Greenhouse and Energy Reporting (NGER) Act 2007. Among this, nearly 30% of companies achieve a strong carbon efficiency outcome. Economically strong carbon efficient firms (Golden Stars) are more common than environmentally strong carbon efficient firms (Green Stars). This pattern is consistent among weak carbon efficient and inefficient firms. Dirty Cash Cows whose focus is purely on economic growth while ignoring environmental images are a minority among the companies examined. For financially stressed companies, environmental engagement appears more likely to be a reaction to regulatory requirements. Consistently, the eco-efficiency improvement changes with the government carbon policy changes over the reporting periods, indicating an influence of regulatory pressures on corporate eco-efficiency.

W. Qian (✉) · A. Kaur
Centre for Sustainability Governance (CSG), School of Commerce,
University of South Australia Business School, Adelaide, SA, Australia
e-mail: wei.qian@unisa.edu.au

S. Schaltegger
Centre for Sustainability Management (CSM), Leuphana University Lüneburg,
Lüneburg, Germany

K.-H. Lee, S. Schaltegger (eds.), *Accounting for Sustainability: Asia Pacific Perspectives*, Eco-Efficiency in Industry and Science 33,
https://doi.org/10.1007/978-3-319-70899-7_5

Keywords Eco-efficiency · Carbon efficiency · Environmental performance

5.1 Introduction

Eco-efficiency has been proposed as one of the key sustainability performance indicators for over two decades. This indicator measures economic value added relative to environmental impacts generated. In a broader context, eco-efficiency calls for efficiency with which ecological resources are used to meet human needs. According to World Business Council for Sustainable Development's (WBCSD) definition, eco-efficiency is "achieved by the delivery of competitively-priced goods and services that satisfy human needs and bring quality of life, while progressively reducing ecological impacts and resource intensity to a level at least in line with the earth's estimated carrying capacity" (Schmidheiny and Stigson 2000, p. 4). Under this context, the significance of eco-efficient GDP (or green GDP) has been increasingly acknowledged (Korhonen and Seager 2008).

In the context of business corporations, Schaltegger and Burritt (2000, p. 358) define eco-efficiency as the "integration of economic information (the flow of financial funds such as income, expense, revenues and costs, which is linked to changes in stocks of funds [assets, liabilities and equities]) from conventional accounting with environmental information (environmental interventions such as emissions and resource use, which is linked with changes in eco-asset balances) derived from ecological accounting". Clearly, the essence of eco-efficient business is to integrate economic and environmental performance in core business strategies so as to achieve a "win-win" solution for sustainability. It is believed that business can do well by doing good or creating more value with less impact (e.g. Schaltegger 1997; Schaltegger and Müller 1998; Ehrenfeld 2005). The business case, i.e. win & win, is able to motivate a practical and incremental change for corporate sustainability (Schaltegger and Wagner 2006; Falck and Heblich 2007).

While today's business world has paid much more attention to environmental performance and impacts than the past, environmental and economic performances are still measured differently and managed separately. These two performances are often contained in different corporate reports with financials in annual reports and environmental issues in sustainability reports. Integration of the two in performance measurement is limited in early development of business reporting and management practice (de Villiers et al. 2014). In academic debate, eco-efficiency is more or less a conceptual term that has triggered many discussions in the past but few empirical investigations and evidences (Ehrenfeld 2005; Erkko et al. 2005; Ciroth 2009; Huppes 2009; Figge and Hahn 2013). Extant literature of social and environmental accounting is predominantly focused on corporate reporting, with little representation of environmental management accounting (EMA) or performance measurement research in mainstream accounting journals (see reviews in Parker 2005, 2011; Schaltegger et al. 2013). Empirical studies of corporate performance have made numerous attempts to justify the alignment of corporate economic value creation and environmental performance, and a positive or negative relationship between the two has been evidenced (see e.g., Konar and Cohen 2001; Derwall et al. 2005; Orsato 2006). However, an investigation into the actual integration, such as its levels, practices, improvements, differences and issues, is still uncharted water. An important question is unknown, that is, how companies are managing eco-efficiency, particularly the extent to which they are performing on a strong (i.e. increase both economic and environmental performances) or weak (i.e. increase either economic or environmental performance but the increase in one performance is larger than the decrease in the other) trajectory of eco-efficiency? Given that ever less businesses today can act with little regard or concern for their impacts on the environment and the demands for integration from not only internal business management but also external investors, lenders, suppliers and other stakeholders continue to increase, an investigation of corporate practice on eco-efficiency is clearly needed. Motivated by this research gap, we aim to examine the level and improvement of corporate carbon emissions and the integration of corporate carbon and financial performance among Australian heavy emitters.

With the international climate change agreements and the increased awareness and visibility of climate change and carbon pollution caused by industry development, the level of carbon emissions has become an important environmental indicator to business managers, government regulators as well as the community (Choi et al. 2013). Under Australian National Greenhouse and Energy Reporting Act 2007 (NGER 2007), top polluting companies have to disclose their annual carbon emissions and energy consumption to the public since 1 July 2008. The subsequent debates on Emission Trading Schemes (ETS) in 2009 and the enactment and then the repealing of Carbon Tax during 2012 and 2013 have provided Australian businesses enormous incentives as well as challenges and uncertainties to achieve eco-efficiency (in this case, carbon efficiency). Therefore, the central objective of this study is to develop a carbon efficiency typology and use this typological classification to reveal and understand how Australian top polluters manage carbon efficiency and to what extent they achieve a strong carbon efficiency outcome towards the ultimate goal of sustainability.

We collected Australian NGER emission data during 2009 and 2013 and integrated the 5-year emission data with financial data collected from the database Company 360 Select (financials). A systematic comparison and analysis were performed to understand carbon related eco-efficiency in corporate practice.

The chapter is organised as follows. Following the introduction and justification of this study, Sect. 5.2 reviews the concepts and debates of eco-efficiency and the empirical studies of corporate environmental and economic performances and their integration. In Sect. 5.3, we elaborate and develop a typological classification differentiating eco-efficiency levels and then link these with different corporate eco-efficiency profiles. Section 5.4 outlines the method used to collect and analyse data for this study. In Sect. 5.5, we critically evaluate and compare the eco-efficiency results across top polluting companies in Australia. The concluding remarks are provided in Sect. 5.6.

5.2 Literature Review

The notion of eco-efficiency has been defined and redefined by many previous studies and in many ways. In essence, it derives from the concept of efficiency which measures the relation between inputs and outputs. A service or activity is considered to be efficient if it provides higher levels of output for a given input or utilises lower levels of input for a given output (Schaltegger and Burritt 2000). When integrating economic and environmental performances into the input and output relationship, eco-efficiency focuses on creating more goods and services using fewer resources and/or generating less waste and pollution (Schaltegger and Sturm 1990). To a company, eco-efficiency measures its ability to generate more economic value with less environmental impacts, i.e. expressed as the ratio below (Schaltegger 1998; Schaltegger and Sturm 1990):

$$\text{Eco}-\text{efficiency} = \text{Economic value}\,\textit{added} \,/\, \text{Environmental impact}\,\textit{added}$$

In this definition economic value added represents financial performance of a company and – depending on the focus of analysis – can be expressed in both monetary terms (such as sales revenue and value added) and physical terms (units of production) (Schaltegger and Burritt 2000). Environmental impact added can be regarded as the sum of assessed environmental impacts generated by a company. Examples of eco-efficiency measures may include financial returns per tonne of CO_2 emissions and the contribution margin of a product relative to its greenhouse effect (CO_2 equivalents) (Schaltegger and Burritt 2006; Figge and Hahn 2013). The eco-efficiency of a company will increase when its environmental added value increases at a given level of environmental impacts and/or its environmental impact decreases at a given level of economic performance (Schaltegger 1998). The emphasis is on implementing environmental improvements and strategies that can yield parallel economic benefits. This concept urges business entities to seek innovation and opportunities which allow them to stay profitable while being environmentally responsible, thereby increasing their competitiveness for a longer term (Schmidheiny and Stigson 2000).The debate on the practicality of eco-efficiency and the alignment of environmental and economic performances has continued for two decades. Some prior studies repudiate the possibility of successful integration (i.e. being able to increase eco-efficiency) as they argue environmental management requires substantial corporate investments but financial returns on these investments are barely achieved (Walley and Whitehead 1994). In this strand of literature, initiatives to reduce environmental impacts are viewed as costly, risky and having a negative impact on economic value creation (Kiernan 2007; Aragon-Correa and Rubio-Lopez 2007). McDonough and Braungart (1998) even criticise eco-efficiency as an industrial buzz word as they consider the focus of eco-efficiency is still part of the industrial system that has caused environmental degradation. Hukkinen (2001) also questions the basic assumptions of eco-efficiency that an individual's concern for the environment can be decoupled from his or her material dependency on ecosystem services and eco-efficiency builds upon decoupling environmental governance from the local socio-economic and cultural context.

In contrast, the other stream of literature argues that environmental initiatives can bring a wide variety of benefits that outweigh their financial costs (Russo and Fouts 1997; Nakao et al. 2007; Sharfman and Fernando 2008; Molina-Azorín et al. 2009). For example, they may reduce regulatory compliance costs, increase image and reputation, and enhance consumer confidence, operating performance, shareholder value and stakeholder relationship (Derwall et al. 2005; Trudel and Cotte 2009; Figge 2005; Horváthová 2010; Guenster et al. 2011; Osazuwa and Che-Ahmad 2016; Al-Najjar and Anfimiadou 2012; Herold et al. 2016; Henri et al. 2016).

Empirical studies observing a positive relationship between economic and environmental performances have become more prevalent in literature (Klassen and McLaughlin 1996). Clarkson et al. (2011) find that pursing proactive environmental strategies leads to better financial performance among the most polluting industries. Karagozoglu and Lindell's (2000) study of environmental strategy and competitive advantage in high-tech and traditional manufacturing sectors also confirms that "win-win" outcomes do exist in different industries. Similar findings have been made by Porter and van der Linde (1995), Konar and Cohen (2001), Derwall et al. (2005), and Orsato (2006).

More recently, some studies have used larger samples or more robust evidence such as longitudinal data examinning the relationship between finanical and environmental performance. For example, Al-Najjar and Anfimiadou (2012) investigated 201 firms in the UK for a 10 year time period from 1999 to 2008 to reveal the positive association between eco-efficiency, environmental policy and firm value. Albertini (2013) conducted a meta-analysis of 52 studies over a 35-year period and the result also supports the positive relationship between financial and environmental performance. Osazuwa and Che-Ahmad (2016) analysed the content of annual reports by 667 Malaysian firms and in addition to confirm the association between financial and environmental performance, they also recognise the importance of stakeholder relationship in strengthening such association. In line with these empirical studies, Henri et al. (2016) examined the relationship between the management of environmental costs and financial performance. Their survey of 319 Canadian manufacturing firms reveals a positive and significant association between the tracking of environmental costs, the implementation of environmental initiatives and financial performance. They highlight that structural cost management can "align a firm's resources and associated cost structure with long term strategy" through the re-designing of the value chain and cost structure (pp. 277–278). Focusing specifically on carbon emissions, Busch and Hoffman (2011) find a positive relationship between carbon emission reduction and financial performance in their investigation of 2500 largest companies according to the Dow Jones Global Index. A series of King and Lenox's (2001, 2002) studies evidence that companies achieving lower emissions in their relevant industries are likely to experience higher market performance. Apart from large companies, Qian and Xing (2016) also confirm such positive relationship in private and smaller firms. However, most researchers supporting the rationale of eco-efficiency strategies believe that a business case for eco-efficiency is achievable but the change for the whole industry and the ecosystem will be incremental rather than overnight (Schaltegger and Wagner 2006; Falck and Heblich 2007; Wahba 2008).

While most empirics provide a strong support for eco-efficiency improvement in business practice, the focus of prior studies has largely been on testing the relationship between economic and environmental performances. As such, the two performances are treated and assessed separately. Limited studies have been undertaken to understand the actual integration, integration levels, changes and the way it is performed and achieved in individual firms. From the perspective of individual companies, practicing and reporting eco-efficiency still present a challenge. Erkko et al. (2005) find that despite discussing eco-efficiency as a broad concept, few Finnish companies actually quantify and operationalise the eco-efficiency concept, or report eco-efficiency indicators. Virtanen et al.'s (2013) study of an energy-intensive industry reveals many underdeveloped performance indicators in practice such as energy efficiency in production units or efficiency on a "product family" basis. Given the complexities involved in performance measurement, they highlight the need of further examination of eco-efficiency development. More recently, Passetti and Tenucci (2016) report a poor use of eco-efficiency measures in a study of 65 Italian companies. The study highlights that most companies possess only moderate understanding of eco-efficiency measurements. Therefore, the authors encourage companies to develop and use more articulated measurement and evaluation tools to analyse eco-efficiency performance. This echoes Burritt and Saka's (2006) case study of Japanese businesses which reveals that eco-efficiency measurements are still underutilised and there is a lack of a generally accepted format to facilitate eco-efficiency analyses and comparisons between companies.

5.3 Development of a Typological Classification of Eco-efficiency

To analyse and compare eco-efficiency performance, it is necessary to explore different levels of eco-efficiency development rather than simply looking at the relationship between economic and environmental performances. Several studies detailing the theory, concept and measurement of eco-efficiency, for example, Schaltegger (1998), Schaltegger and Burritt (2000), and Figge and Hahn (2013), provide valuable insights for this investigation. Ideally, eco-efficient companies are able to improve both economic and environmental performances, i.e. as suggested by previous empirical studies, to follow a positive linear relationship between the two performances. Schaltegger and Sturm (1998; see also Schaltegger and Burritt 2000) define this movement as *strong* eco-efficiency development, as illustrated in the upper right area (dark grey) in Fig. 5.1. Companies within this area are viewed as *green stars* (Schaltegger and Sturm 1998; Schaltegger 1998). They are able to use lean technology and management processes to achieve low environmental impact

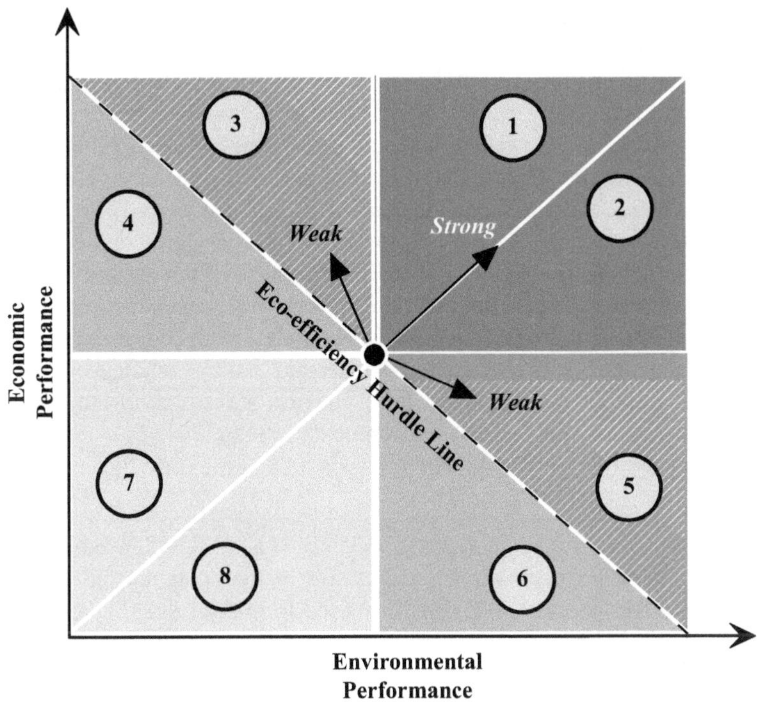

Fig. 5.1 Matrix of eco-efficiency development (Source: adapted from Schaltegger and Burritt 2000)

and cost, and consumers are willing to pay a price premium for their environmental achievements which lead to better economic performance (Schaltegger 1998).

However, value drivers for eco-efficiency may vary, which could lead to inconsistent development of efficiency in the use of economic and environmental resources (Figge and Hahn 2013). In this regard, companies may follow *weak* eco-efficiency development (striped areas) or fall into the inefficiency areas (areas to the left below the eco-efficiency hurdle line) as shown in Fig. 5.1. *Weak* eco-efficiency demonstrates one dimensional improvement, either economic or environmental, with the other dimension decreasing. If the value increase in one dimension is greater than the decrease in the other dimension, the eco-efficiency outcome may still be achieved, but this exhibits a weak sustainable improvement of eco-efficiency (Schaltegger and Burritt 2000). If the value increase in one dimension is lower than the decrease in the other, companies are clearly below the eco-efficiency line (the dashed line that separates the green and grey areas in Fig. 5.1). Broadly, Ilinitch and Schaltegger (1995) categorise companies with sound economic growth strategy and high profitability but high environmental impacts as *dirty cash cows* and the inverse as *green question marks*. Green question marks are environmentally friendly companies but they have relatively low economic performance which may raise questions on their long-term survival, in particular those falling below the eco-efficiency line. Companies that are not only economically uninteresting but also cause massive environmental damage are destructive. These "*dirty dogs*" struggle both financially and environmentally and are likely to be eliminated soon (Schaltegger 1998).

As the value drivers for eco-efficiency are not always congruent (Figge and Hahn 2013), economic efficiency may be significantly higher or lower relative to environmental performance in the same or different movement directions. This reflects the different focuses and strategies companies use to improve their eco-efficiency. For example, if the increase in economic performance is higher than the increase in environmental performance such improvement is considered an *economically strong* eco-efficiency improvement. If the increase in environmental performance is higher than the decrease in economic performance then such improvement is considered an *environmentally favourable* weak eco-efficiency improvement. As such, adapted and extended from the categorisation suggested by Schaltegger (1998), we develop eight areas of eco-efficiency improvements (or destructions) to reflect a full picture of corporate eco-efficiency developments in Table 5.1.

The explanation of the classification in each area of the eco-efficiency matrix is as follows:

1. *Golden stars*: This area includes companies that have achieved strong eco-efficiency improvements while the increase in the economic performance is higher than the increase in environmental performance. Such increase demonstrates an economically strong eco-efficiency improvement. Companies in this area are considered golden stars as their current development is characterized by a relatively stronger capital efficiency increase than the environmental improvement. They may have economic potential to contribute further towards environ-

Table 5.1 Typological classification of corporate eco-efficiency development

<table>
<tr><th>Performance</th><th>Classification</th><th>Eco-efficiency indicators</th><th>Area in eco-efficiency matrix</th><th>Direction and strength of change</th><th>Description</th></tr>
<tr><td rowspan="2">EconPerf ↑
EnvirPerf ↑</td><td>Golden stars</td><td>Econ↑ > Envir↑</td><td>1</td><td>++</td><td>Economically strong EE improvement</td></tr>
<tr><td>Green stars</td><td>Envir↑ > Econ ↑</td><td>2</td><td>++</td><td>Environmentally strong EE improvement</td></tr>
<tr><td rowspan="2">EconPerf ↑
EnvirPerf ↓</td><td>Greedy cash cows</td><td>|Econ↑| > |Envir↓|</td><td>3</td><td>+</td><td>Economically favourable weak EE improvement</td></tr>
<tr><td>Dirty cash cows</td><td>|Econ↑| < |Envir↓|</td><td>4</td><td>–</td><td>Economically favourable EE decrease</td></tr>
<tr><td rowspan="2">EconPerf ↓
EnvirPerf ↑</td><td>Green question marks</td><td>|Econ↓| < |Envir↑|</td><td>5</td><td>+</td><td>Environmentally favourable weak EE improvement</td></tr>
<tr><td>Red question marks</td><td>|Econ↓| > |Envir↑|</td><td>6</td><td>–</td><td>Environmentally favourable EE decrease</td></tr>
<tr><td rowspan="2">EconPerf ↓
EnvirPerf ↓</td><td>Dirty dogs</td><td>|Econ↓| < |Envir↓|</td><td>7</td><td>–</td><td>Destructive EE improvement</td></tr>
<tr><td>Stressed dogs</td><td>|Econ↓| > |Envir↓|</td><td>8</td><td>–</td><td>Destructive EE decrease</td></tr>
</table>

mental sustainability in the future as more capital resources may be available for future environmental performance improvements.

2. *Green stars*: This area includes companies that have shown strong eco-efficiency improvements while the increase in environmental performance exceeds their economic performance. These companies show high commitment to environmental sustainability and lead the industry for their environmental excellence. They are labelled as green star performers as environmental sustainability has been improved relatively more than the economic improvement as part of the eco-efficiency increase.
3. *Greedy cash cows*: This area comprises companies with improved economic performance but more environmental impact added. Greedy cash cows exist when the increase in economic performance is higher than the decrease in environmental performance. These companies have accepted a somewhat limited trade-off between economic improvement and environmental decrease. They are economically favourable weak eco-efficient performers. Their focus has been placed on increasing profitability but at the same time trying to limit their negative environmental impacts generated.
4. *Dirty cash cows*: Companies fall within this category if their damage to the environment outweighs the economic value created. Companies have clearly emphasised on economic value growth and are able to achieve favourable economic outcomes. However, their operations and management are based on strong trade-offs accepting large environmental impacts. Dirty cash cows are unsustainable and with the internalization of their environmental impacts may also prove to be economically inefficient in the long term.
5. *Green question marks*: This area includes companies with low economic performance but high environmental performance. Green questions marks are environmentally favourable weak eco-efficient performers, thus accepting a trade-off between environmental improvement and economic decrease. Their eco-efficiency improvement stems from the environmental dimension, but this has not triggered a more efficient use of financial resources and creation of adequate economic benefits. Strengthening economic performance presents a challenge but also an opportunity for companies to turn "weak" into "strong" sustainable performers.
6. *Red question marks*: This area exists when the increase in environmental performance is lower than the decrease in economic performance, thus resulting in an overall eco-efficiency decrease. This group includes companies that face financial difficulties but still make some marginal environmental improvements. Companies that are reactive to regulatory pressures to make necessary investments in green technologies may fall into this type of eco-efficiency development. However, these companies are under the radar (and the eco-efficiency hurdle) and may face high risk of shifting to destructive eco-efficiency zones in the future if the financial development persists.
7. *Dirty dogs*: This area comprises companies with destructive, negative eco-efficiency change. Such type of eco-efficiency development exists when the decrease in environmental performance is more than the decrease in economic

performance. Companies in this area may have chosen to reduce investments in environmentally friendly products in order to control the decrease in profitability.

8. *Stressed dogs*: This area includes companies with low economic performance and high environmental impacts. This means the companies have entered a destructive eco-efficiency decrease zone. The ongoing stress under both financial and environmental pressures may result in an eventual withdrawal of the companies from the market.

5.4 Research Method

Based on the review of the concept and measurement of eco-efficiency and the analysis and exploration of corporate eco-efficiency developments, we designed our research investigation as follows. The empirical data in this study were collected in Australia. Although eco-efficiency measurement and accounting practice and research have developed rapidly and extensively in various countries, Australia is still lagging behind (Zhou et al. 2016). Given that Australia has one of the highest per capita coal consumption in the world (Perry et al. 2015), it becomes critical to investigate eco-efficiency performance of Australian top polluters.

To apply the proposed eco-efficiency typology in the context of carbon emission management, we develop the following table defining the typological classification of carbon efficiency. As part of environmental performance, carbon performance specifically focuses on the reduction of carbon emissions. Therefore, carbon efficiency reflects the increase of economic performance relative to the reduction of carbon emissions (Table 5.2).

5.4.1 Sample

In Australia, business entities that exceed the specified thresholds[1] of greenhouse gas emissions are required to report emission and energy consumption information under the Australian National Greenhouse and Energy Reporting (ANGER) Act 2007 Act 2007. Our data coverage spanned 5 years between 2009 and 2013.[2] In 2009, when ANGER published its first carbon emission data, only 235 top polluters

---

[1] In 2009, entities that had total greenhouse gas emissions (CO2 equivalent or CO2-e) above 125 kilotonnes (KT) or total amount of energy produced or consumed above 500 terajoules (TJ) were required to report. The thresholds change to 87.5 KT and 350 TJ for 2010 and 50 KT and 200 TJ for later years.

[2] Under the NGER Act 2007 (Section 23), registered controlling corporations are obliged to report information on greenhouse gas emissions and energy consumption to the Greenhouse and Energy Data Officer (GEDO). The GEDO has published an extract of the information reported since 2009.

Table 5.2 Typological classification of corporate carbon efficiency

Classification	Definition	Description
Golden stars	Economically strong carbon efficiency improvement	Both economic and carbon performances increase, but the increase rate of economic performance is greater than that of carbon performance
Green stars	Environmentally strong carbon efficiency improvement	Both economic and carbon performances increase, but the increase rate of carbon performance is greater than that of economic performance
Greedy cash cows	Economically favourable weak carbon efficiency improvement	Economic performance increases while carbon performance decreases. The increase rate of economic performance is greater than the decrease rate of carbon performance
Dirty cash cows	Economically favourable carbon efficiency decrease	Economic performance increases while carbon performance decreases. The decrease rate of carbon performance is greater than the increase rate of economic performance
Green question marks	Environmentally favourable weak carbon efficiency improvement	Economic performance decreases while carbon performance improves. The improvement rate of carbon performance is greater than the decrease rate of economic performance
Red question marks	Environmentally favourable carbon efficiency decrease	Economic performance decreases while carbon performance improves. The decrease rate of economic performance is greater than the improvement rate of carbon performance
Dirty dogs	Destructive carbon efficiency improvement	Both economic and carbon performances decrease, and the decrease rate of economic performance is less than that of carbon performance
Stressed dogs	Destructive carbon efficiency decrease	Both economic and carbon performances decrease, and the decrease rate of economic performance is greater than that of carbon performance

were included. This number increased to 450 in 2013. Except for a small number of non-corporate entities such as local councils and universities, the majority of reporting entities are business corporations. As the focus of this study is on corporate carbon emissions and performance, we excluded all not-for-profit organisations such as local councils and universities. Companies that were involved with merge and acquisition or delisted during the study periods were also excluded. To capture the change of environmental performance, we included companies that contain at least three consecutive years of environmental and financial data. After sorting out the dataset, our final sample included 236 top polluting companies, within which 82 were public companies and 154 were private companies. Public companies were listed and traded at the Australian Stock Exchange (ASX) and private companies were non-listed companies involving private equity, state owned and foreign controlled companies. The companies selected covered ten major industry sectors, of

Table 5.3 Industry profile of sample companies

Industry	Total no.	No. of public companies	No. of private companies
Materials	68	28	40
Industrials	45	12	33
Consumer staples	28	8	20
Utilities	27	4	23
Consumer discretionary	21	9	12
Energy	19	5	14
Financials	19	11	8
Health care	6	4	2
Telecommunication services	2	1	1
Information technology	1	0	1
Total	236	82	154

which nearly one third of the companies came from the Materials sector. Table 5.3 shows the industry profile of ANGER companies selected.

Based on our sample data, around half of the top polluting companies were within the Materials and the Industrials sectors. Other high environmentally sensitive industries such as Utilities and Energy have relatively similar numbers of companies to some low sensitive industries such as Consumer Discretionary and Financials. Health Care, Telecommunication Services and Information Technology sectors have only a few reporting companies. Majority of the industry sectors have more private than public companies while this is reversed in Financials and Health Care.

5.4.2 *Measurements*

ANGER classifies carbon emissions into Scope 1 and Scope 2 emissions. Scope 1 emissions are greenhouse gases released to the atmosphere as a direct result of an activity or series of activities that constitute the facility, while Scope 2 emissions are greenhouse gases emitted at a second facility because of the electricity, heating, cooling or steam that is consumed at the facility (Australian Government 2007). In this study, we used *total emissions*, i.e. the aggregate of Scope 1 and Scope 2 emissions, to measure corporate environmental performance. High energy intensive entities such as utility firms may generate more Scope 1 (direct) emissions while low intensive firms such as banks may involve more Scope 2 (indirect) emissions. An environmentally responsible firm should take an overall responsibility to reduce both direct and indirect emissions. Therefore, we considered total emissions a better measure of environmental performance than single scope of emissions. This is consistent with the measurement of environmental performance used in previous studies such as King and Lenox (2002) and Busch and Hoffmann (2011).

As carbon emissions were size sensitive, i.e. the bigger firms tend to generate higher emissions than smaller firms, we scaled total emissions by total assets for each company. This changed carbon emissions to carbon emission intensity. However, to consider company size carbon emissions or emission intensities reflect corporate carbon pollution levels. Corporate carbon performance should be read as a reduction of their emission or intensity levels, i.e. negative change of emissions and intensities.

Economic data in this study were collected from company profile reports and statements contained in the database *Company 360° Select*. We used financial return on assets (ROA), i.e. earnings before interest and tax (EBIT) over total assets, to measure economic performance. This is consistent with prior studies (e.g. King and Lenox 2001; Clarkson et al. 2011; Qian and Xing 2016) which consider that the ROA measure reflects a firm's ability to use its assets to generate profit and revenue regardless of how assets are financed (interest bearing) or taxed. We calculated the changes of emission intensity and ROA for each company and compared the directions and absolute values of these changes. Both emission intensity and ROA were normalised by total assets. In actual calculations, we eliminated total assets in both performance measurements. In this regard, the change of economic performance was measured as the change of EBIT and the change of environmental performance was measured as the change of total emissions (the results were reversed as the reduction of emissions indicated an improvement of performance). Each company was then coded from "1" – Golden Stars, to "8" – Stressed Dogs, based on the typological classification defined in Table 5.2.

5.5 Result Analysis

We first analyse the proportion of companies falling within each carbon efficiency development over a 5 year reporting period. Figure 5.2 visualises this distribution.

For the time period from 2009 to 2013, we find about a quarter of NGER companies were Golden Stars, i.e. achieved overall economically strong carbon efficiency improvements. Only a small number of companies qualify as Green Stars (3%). However, altogether nearly *30%* of high emitters have made a "win-win" case for sustainability. The substantially larger number of Golden Stars than Green Stars shows that economic performance has improved relatively more among strong carbon efficient performers. This may reinforce the necessity and practicability of making a business case for corporate sustainability (Salzmann et al. 2005; Schaltegger and Wagner 2006; Falck and Heblich 2007). Reflecting from Schaltegger and Burritt's recent (2015) differentiation of motivations for business cases, significantly more Golden Stars than Green Stars appear to exhibit "technocratically responsible" business cases for sustainability among Australian top polluters. While they are able to create win-win improvements both for the environment and economically, their efficiency improvement and benefits are larger than their environmental improvements. However, when interpreting this result it is important to

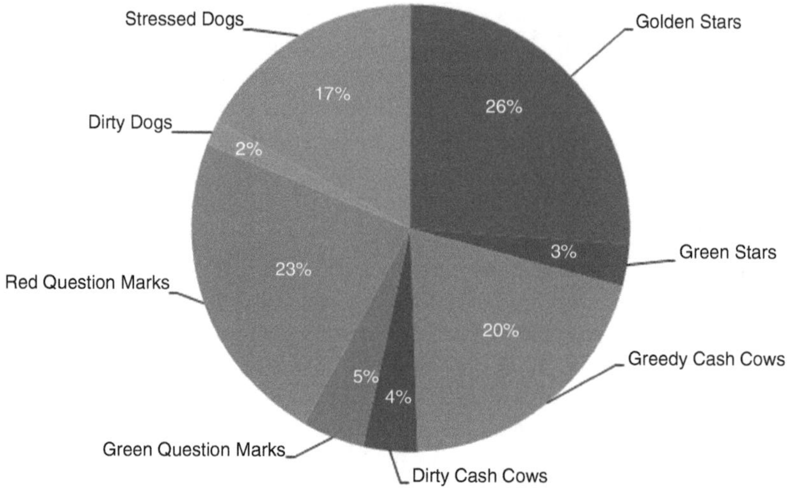

Fig. 5.2 Distribution of firms at different carbon efficiency levels

emphasize that for the natural environment it does not matter whether economic improvements which go along with the environmental improvement are larger or smaller in percentage. Of importance is that environmental improvements are created. Whether the economic improvements are larger in percentage is not relevant for the environment.

A similar pattern can be observed for companies that have achieved weak carbon efficiency developments. Twenty percent of the weakly carbon efficient firms are Greedy Cash Cows compared to 5% Green Question Marks. It appears that if companies are not able to overcome trade-offs and thus have to (or decide to) improve one dimension of efficiency at the cost of the other, they are more likely to improve economic benefits than environmental performance. This reflects conventional trade-off thinking in management decisions. Still, these companies seem to be able to limit the trade-off costs in a way that the overall carbon efficiency still improves, although weakly. When contrasting the 20% Greedy Cash Cows with the 4% Dirty Cash Cows, it seems that companies have moved away from being labelled as dirty and inefficient polluters with high energy use but low economic growth. For financially profitable companies, sacrificing environmental performance (with potentially related higher reputation risks) is relatively unpopular.

For financially challenged companies, the story is the other way around. The small number of Green Question Marks (5%) compared with nearly a quarter Red Question Marks (23%) indicate that few companies with weak carbon efficiency improvements are able to stay in business which favour environmental performance substantially over economic performance. Financially struggling firms are more likely to be reactive to environmental demands from regulatory authorities and other stakeholders. Their improvement of environmental performance or incurrence of environmental costs is likely to be used to protect business interests and maintain legitimacy and survival, and thus environmental management becomes costly and brings little or no economic benefits (Schaltegger and Burritt 2015). Most weak carbon efficiency improvements may also reflect a reactionary business case thinking where environmental improvements are only made at the last moment under pressure and thus result in costs which impact the conventional business case negatively. Taking *strong* and *weak* eco-efficient performers together, our data shows that 54% of Australian top polluters have managed their business eco-efficiently since the NGER Act 2007.

In carbon inefficient areas, companies are clearly struggling more with financial stress than environmental pressures. The data furthermore shows 17% Stressed Dogs and only 2% Dirty Dogs. This suggests that inefficient use of financial resources is a good indicator for failing to improve carbon efficiency. In a next analytical step we compare carbon efficiency development between reporting years (Table 5.4).

The comparison of annual carbon efficiency developments presents some interesting results. As a positive response to NGER Act 2007, the national carbon reporting requirement, nearly 40% of top polluters have managed to achieve strong carbon efficiency improvements (33% Golden Stars and 6% Green Stars) in their first movement during 2009 and 2010. The effect decreases in the following years, probably due to the three times rejection of the Emissions Trading Scheme (ETS) and the subsequent uncertainties in government climate change policy during 2010 and 2012. As a result, the strong carbon efficiency performers dropped to 26% in 2010–2011 and 24% in 2011–2012. In particular, Green Stars kept falling from 3% to 1%. However, for 2012–2013 the passage of Carbon Tax Bill in late 2011 and the implementation of carbon tax in 2012 seem to provide Australian companies another incentive to improve eco-efficiency. During 2012 and 2013, strong eco-efficiency performers have risen back to 32% and 5%, respectively, for Green Stars. With the repeal of the Carbon Tax in 2014, the uncertainty of carbon policy returns and this may lead to another change of corporate carbon efficiency developments.

While many carbon efficiency developments continue for the analysed reporting years, Table 5.4 also exhibits changes, particularly an increasing group of Red Question Marks. At one stage, Red Question Marks more than doubled (15% in 2009–2010 and 33% in 2011–2012). This may reflect the tightening of regulatory

Table 5.4 Annual eco-efficiency development

Area	Carbon efficiency levels	2009–2010 (%)	2010–2011 (%)	2011–2012 (%)	2012–2013 (%)
1	Golden stars	33	23	23	27
2	Green stars	6	3	1	5
3	Greedy cash cows	23	22	14	24
4	Dirty cash cows	5	6	3	4
5	Green question marks	5	5	6	3
6	Red question marks	15	19	33	23
7	Dirty dogs	0	1	4	1
8	Stressed dogs	15	21	17	15

pressures over years whereas financially stressed firms had to increasingly respond to their environmental challenges and demonstrate compliance and improvement. It may also reflect the management belief that trade-offs between economic and environmental performance are inevitable under the given regulatory conditions. This would explain carbon management activities which are in line with a reactionary business case thinking. As companies following a reactionary or reputational business case for sustainability will not go beyond compliance or pursue a forward thinking to integrate environmental consideration in business strategies, environmental activities are merely cost drivers rather than profit generators (Schaltegger and Burritt 2015).

As public firms only represent one third of the top polluters and two thirds of the sample are private firms which are significantly smaller and subject to much less public scrutiny for their environmental performance, we further investigate the difference of eco-efficiency developments between these two groups of companies.

As shown in Table 5.5, despite a few variations of carbon efficiency developments between public and private firms, the general of carbon efficiency development pattern is similar in each category. Both groups achieve around 30% strong carbon efficiency performers. However, public firms have a higher percentage of weak carbon efficiency improvement. While 30% of public firms have achieved weak carbon efficiency improvement, only 20% of private firms show the same development. This is mainly attributed to a much higher percentage of Greedy Cash Cows (27%) among pubic firms than private firms (15%), perhaps due to the greater ability of public firms to access economic resources through both internal and external fund providers. Nevertheless, high profitability of public firms is still built upon an increase rather than reduction of carbon emissions.

Table 5.6 compares the eco-efficiency development in different industries.

The results present some diversity of carbon efficiency development between industries. *Financials* clearly stands out as the best performer. Sixty eight percent of *Financials* have achieved eco-efficiency improvements, of which, 43% have achieved strong carbon efficiency and 25% weak eco-efficiency improvements.

Table 5.5 Carbon efficiency development of public and private firms

Area	Carbon efficiency levels	Public (N = 82) (%)	Private (N = 154) (%)
1	Golden stars	24	27
2	Green stars	4	3
3	Greedy cash cows	27	15
4	Dirty cash cows	3	4
5	Green question marks	3	5
6	Red question marks	20	25
7	Dirty dogs	1	2
8	Stressed dogs	16	18
Strong EE improvement		*28*	*30*
Weak EE improvement		*30*	*20*
Total eco-efficient firms		*58*	*50*

Table 5.6 Carbon efficiency development of different industries

Area	Carbon efficiency levels	Materials (%)	Utilities (%)	Energy (%)	Industrials (%)	Financials (%)	Consumer staples (%)	Consumer discretionary (%)
1	Golden stars	25	24	27	23	36	25	25
2	Green stars	3	4	7	4	7	1	0
3	Greedy cash cows	17	24	14	24	20	22	23
4	Dirty cash cows	4	5	7	5	5	0	4
5	Green question marks	4	7	3	6	5	5	0
6	Red question marks	26	16	17	20	21	26	37
7	Dirty dogs	1	2	2	3	0	3	4
8	Stressed dogs	20	18	24	16	5	18	9
Strong EE improvement		*28*	*28*	*34*	*27*	*43*	*26*	*25*
Weak EE improvement		*21*	*31*	*17*	*30*	*25*	*27*	*23*
Total eco-efficient firms		*49*	*59*	*51*	*57*	*68*	*53*	*48*

Being a strong economic dominator (most NGER reporting financial firms in Australia are publicly traded), the *Financials* sector maintains its ability to generate relatively high profit and growth with 36% Golden Stars and 7% Green Stars. The *Energy sector* comes second (34%) in achieving strong eco-efficiency results. It has less Golden Stars (27%) in comparison to the *Financials* sector, but the same percentage of Green Stars (7%). The weak eco-efficiency performers in the *Energy* industry, however, are the lowest (17%). *Utilities* and *Industrials* have slightly fewer strong carbon efficiency improving firms, but more weak carbon efficiently developing firms (both over 30%), which lead to totals of 59% and 57% carbon efficiency improving firms respectively in these two sectors. As current legislations in Australia only focus on direct emissions which are more likely generated by energy intensive industries such as *Energy* and *Utilities*, their above-average performance may reflect their responses to regulatory as well as social expectations. To illustrate, we map some examples of best performers (i.e. Leading Stars), continuously improving performers (i.e. Rising Stars) and continuously deteriorating performers (i.e. Falling Stars) over the 5-year reporting periods in Fig. 5.3.

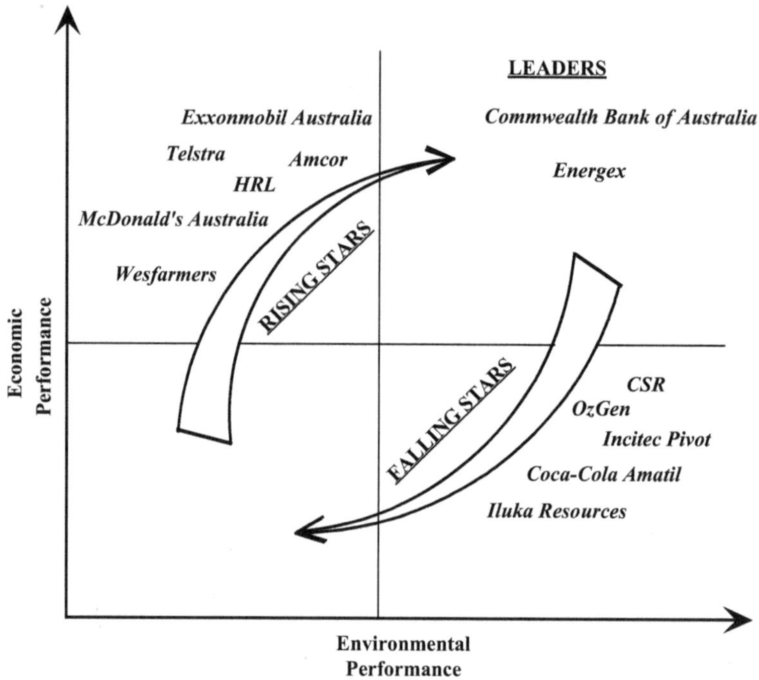

Fig. 5.3 Leading stars and rising/falling stars

Several companies are clearly leaders in managing eco-efficiency improvements. *Commonwealth Bank of Australia* (Financials) and *Energex Ltd.* (Utilities) have been noticeable for their strong eco-efficiency performance for every single year in the sample. Many large firms such as *Exxonmobil Australia* (Energy), *Wesfarmers* (Consumer Staples), *McDonald's Australia* (Consumer Discretionary), *Amcor* (Materials), *Telstra* (Telecommunication) and *HRL* (Industries) have started with a poor eco-efficiency performance, but became strong performers in later years. In contrast to these Rising Stars that are improving substantially, companies such as *OzGen Holdings Australia* (Utilities), *Coca-Cola Amatil* (Consumer Staples), *CSR Ltd.* (Industrials), *Iluka Resources* (Materials) and *Incitec Pivot* (Materials) have moved away from a win-win outcome. *Coca-Cola Amatil* as a food and beverage industry giant has fallen to a carbon efficiency destroyer (Stressed Dogs) in recent years, a warning signal for its business and environmental sustainability in both short and long terms.

5.6 Conclusions

This chapter is motivated by the recent debate and development of integration of environmental and economic performance and the discussion about business cases for sustainability. Eco-efficiency as an essential measure for integration has been studied extensively in the past, but mainly conceptually or in single case studies. Empirical examinations focus largely on the relationship between economic and environmental performances rather than the integration of the two to achieve "win-win" solutions. Although a positive relationship is increasingly reported as the result of large scale cross-sectional statistics, the actual business practice on integration is underexplored. Businesses may have paid much attention to environmental issues, especially environmental compliance costs. Yet, previous literature finds that managing eco-efficiency presents a different challenge (Burritt and Saka 2006; Erkko et al. 2005).

Extended from Schaltegger (1998), Schaltegger and Sturm (1998), and Schaltegger and Burritt (2000), we take corporate eco-efficiency development to the forefront of empirical investigation and propose a new typological classification for carbon efficiency development. Using carbon emissions and their integration with corporate economic performance among Australian heavy polluters during 2009 and 2013, we examine the actual integration levels, improvements, patterns, and more importantly, differentiate strong and weak carbon efficiency developments.

The study reveals that 54% of Australian top polluters have increased their eco-efficiency since the NGER Act 2007. Among this, nearly 30% of the companies have achieved a strong carbon efficiency improvement. Among the companies which have been able to create strong carbon efficiency improvements, more firms have increased their economic performance more strongly than their carbon performance (i.e. more *Golden Stars* than *Green Stars*). This pattern is consistent for firms which have improved their carbon efficiency weakly or which have become more inefficient. *Dirty Cash Cows* whose focus is purely on economic growth while ignoring environmental images are a minority among the companies examined. For financially stressed companies, environmental engagement appears more likely to be a reaction to regulatory requirements. Their reactive environmental/carbon compliance is not able to create profit or save costs, and thus potentially results in weaker economic performance.

Changes in carbon efficiency development seem to match against the government policy changes over the 5-year reporting periods. Almost 40% of companies achieved a strong carbon efficiency improvement subsequent to the reporting requirement under NGER Act 2007. This positive result was partially reduced in the following years. The visible decline of strong carbon efficiency performers during 2010 and 2012 may be attributed to the absence of clear climate change policies and the dismissal of ETS. Improvements were regained in 2012 under the new carbon tax motions. However, the repeal of carbon tax in 2014 may again cast some doubt on further corporate carbon efficiency improvements.

The comparison between public and private polluters does not indicate significant differences between these two groups, especially for strong carbon efficiency developments. The carbon efficiency development among industries clearly varies with *Financials* outperforming all other industries. Nearly 70% of the firms in the financial industry have improved their carbon efficiency during the reporting years, 43% of which have achieved strong carbon efficiency improvements. The *Financials* sector is followed by several high direct emission generators, such as *Energy* and *Utilities*. This may be due to their high environmental sensitivity and direct reporting and tax pressures on these direct emitters.

Taking the findings together, it seems that carbon regulations are likely to be an essential driver for corporate eco-efficiency development. As such, Australian top polluters have mainly reacted on regulations while a large group has been able to create technocratically optimized business cases. This highlights that companies are rather legitimacy oriented in their sustainability management and that profit-orientation is clearly not guiding the sustainability activities. These implications complement the recent findings by Schaltegger and Hörisch (2015) which reveal that the rationale of seeking legitimacy dominates corporate sustainability management practices. Companies predominantly react on societal pressure dealing with sustainability to secure legitimacy rather than to pursue economic success. Many companies do not seem to be able or willing to overcome trade-offs and are not integrating environmental and economic issues. This is particularly interesting because Australia has experienced most carbon regulatory changes and turmoils over the recent years. Future studies may extend the investigation of eco-efficiency developments after the abolishing of Carbon Tax in this country and the possible reintroduction of ETS under the new government.

References

Albertini E (2013) Does environmental management improve financial performance? A meta-analytical review. Organ Environ 26(4):431–457

Al-Najjar B, Anfimiadou A (2012) Environmental policies and firm value. Bus Strateg Environ 21(1):49–59

Aragon-Correa JA, Rubio-Lopez EA (2007) Proactive corporate environmental strategies: myths and misunderstandings. Long Range Plan 40(3):357–381

Australian Government (2007) National Greenhouse and Energy Reporting Act 2007. Canberra

Burritt RL, Saka C (2006) Environmental management accounting applications and eco-efficiency: case studies from Japan. J Clean Prod 14(14):1262–1275

Busch T, Hoffmann VH (2011) How hot is your bottom line? Linking carbon and financial performance. Bus Soc 50(2):233–265

Choi BB, Lee D, Psaros J (2013) An analysis of Australian company carbon emission disclosures. Pac Account Rev 25(1):58–79

Ciroth A (2009) Cost data quality considerations for eco-efficiency measures. Ecol Econ 68(6):1583–1590

Clarkson PM, Li Y, Richardson GD, Vasvari FP (2011) Does it really pay to be green? Determinants and consequences of proactive environmental strategies. J Account Public Policy 30(2):122–144

de Villiers C, Rinaldi L, Unerman J (2014) Integrated reporting: insights, gaps and an agenda for future research. Account Audit Account J 27(7):1042–1067

Derwall J, Guenster N, Bauer R, Koedijk K (2005) The eco-efficiency premium puzzle. Financ Anal J 61(2):51–63

Ehrenfeld JR (2005) Eco-efficiency. J Ind Ecol 9(4):6–8

Erkko S, Melanen M, Mickwitz P (2005) Eco-efficiency in the Finnish EMAS reports—a buzz word? J Clean Prod 13(8):799–813

Falck O, Heblich S (2007) Corporate social responsibility: doing well by doing good. Bus Horiz 50(3):247–254

Figge F (2005) Value-based environmental management. From environmental shareholder value to environmental option value. Corp Soc Responsib Environ Manag 12(1):19–30

Figge F, Hahn T (2013) Value drivers of corporate eco-efficiency: management accounting information for the efficient use of environmental resources. Manag Account Res 24(4):387–400

Guenster N, Bauer R, Derwall J, Koedijk K (2011) The economic value of corporate eco-efficiency. Eur Financ Manag 17(4):679–704

Henri J-F, Boiral O, Roy M-J (2016) Strategic cost management and performance: the case of environmental costs. Br Account Rev 48(2):269–282

Herold DM, Manwa F, Sen S, Wilde S (2016) It's the yeast we can do: untapping sustainability trends in Australian Craft Breweries. J Asia Entrep Sustain 12(2):82

Horváthová E (2010) Does environmental performance affect financial performance? A meta-analysis. Ecol Econ 70(1):52–59

Hukkinen J (2001) Eco-efficiency as abandonment of nature. Ecol Econ 38(3):311–315

Huppes G (2009) Eco-efficiency: from focused technical tools to reflective sustainability analysis. Ecol Econ 68(6):1572–1574

Ilinitch AY, Schaltegger SC (1995) Developing a green business portfolio. Long Range Plann 28(2):29–38

Karagozoglu N, Lindell M (2000) Environmental management: testing the win-win model. J Environ Plan Manag 43(6):817–829

Kiernan MJ (2007) Universal owners and ESG: leaving money on the table? Corp Gov 15(3):478–485

King AA, Lenox MJ (2001) Does it really pay to be green? An empirical study of firm environmental and financial performance: an empirical study of firm environmental and financial performance. J Ind Ecol 5(1):105–116

King A, Lenox M (2002) Exploring the locus of profitable pollution reduction. Manag Sci 48(2):289–299

Klassen RD, McLaughlin CP (1996) The impact of environmental management on firm performance. Manag Sci 42(8):1199–1214

Konar S, Cohen MA (2001) Does the market value environmental performance? Rev Econ Stat 83(2):281–289

Korhonen J, Seager TP (2008) Beyond eco-efficiency: a resilience perspective. Bus Strateg Environ 17(7):411–419

McDonough W, Braungart M (1998) The next industrial revolution. Atl Mon 282(4):82–92

Molina-Azorín JF, Claver-Cortés E, López-Gamero MD, Tarí JJ (2009) Green management and financial performance: a literature review. Manag Decis 47(7):1080–1100. https://doi.org/10.1108/00251740910978313

Nakao Y, Amano A, Matsumura K, Genba K, Nakano M (2007) Relationship between environmental performance and financial performance: an empirical analysis of Japanese corporations. Bus Strateg Environ 16(2):106–118

Orsato RJ (2006) Competitive environmental strategies: when does it pay to be green? Calif Manag Rev 48:127–143

Osazuwa NP, Che-Ahmad A (2016) The moderating effect of profitability and leverage on the relationship between eco-efficiency and firm value in publicly traded Malaysian firms. Soc Responsib J 12(2):295–306

Parker LD (2005) Social and environmental accountability research: a view from the commentary box. Account Audit Account J 18(6):842–860

Parker LD (2011) Twenty-one years of social and environmental accountability research: a coming of age. Account Forum 35(1):1–10

Passetti E, Tenucci A (2016) Eco-efficiency measurement and the influence of organisational factors: evidence from large Italian companies. J Clean Prod 122:228–239

Perry FN, Henry S, Perry ME, MacArthur L (2015) California green innovation index: international edition. Next 10 and Collaborative Economics, San Francisco

Porter ME, Van der Linde C (1995) Green and competitive: ending the stalemate. Harv Bus Rev 73(5):120–134

Qian W, Xing K (2016) Linking environmental and financial performance for privately owned firms: some evidence from Australia. J Small Bus Manag. https://doi.org/10.1111/jsbm.12261
Russo MV, Fouts PA (1997) A resource-based perspective on corporate environmental performance and profitability. Acad Manag J 40(3):534–559
Salzmann O, Ionescu-Somers A, Steger U (2005) The business case for corporate sustainability: literature review and research options. Eur Manag Rev 23(1):27–36
Schaltegger S (1997) Economics of life cycle assessment: inefficiency of the present approach. Bus Strateg Environ 6(1):1–8
Schaltegger S (1998) Accounting for eco-efficiency. In: Nath B, Hens L, Compton P, Devuyst D (eds) Environmental management in practice. Routledge, London, pp 272–287
Schaltegger S, Burritt R (2000) Contemporary environmental accounting: issues, concepts and practice. Greenleaf Publishing, Sheffield
Schaltegger S, Burritt R (2006) Corporate sustainability accounting: a catchphrase for compliant corporations or a business decision support for sustainability leaders? In: Schaltegger S, Bennett M, Burritt R (eds) Sustainability accounting and reporting. Springer, Dordrecht, pp 37–59
Schaltegger S, Burritt R (2015) Business cases and corporate engagement with sustainability: differentiating ethical motivations. J Bus Ethics. https://doi.org/10.1007/s10551-015-2938-0
Schaltegger S, Hörisch J (2015) In search of the dominant rationale in sustainability management: legitimacy or profit-Seeking? J Bus Ethics. https://doi.org/10.1007/s10551-015-2854-3
Schaltegger S, Müller K (1998) Calculating the true profitability of pollution prevention. In: Bennett M, James P (eds) The green bottom line: Environmental accounting for management: current practice and future trends. Greenleaf Publishing, Sheffield, pp 86–99
Schaltegger S, Sturm A (1990) Ökologische Rationalität: Ansatzpunkte zur Ausgestaltung von ökologieorientierten Managementinstrumenten. Die Unternehmung 4:273–290
Schaltegger S, Sturm A (1998) Eco-efficiency by eco-controlling. Vdf, Zurich
Schaltegger S, Wagner M (2006) Managing the business case for sustainability: the integration of social, environmental and economic performance. Greenleaf Publishing, Sheffield
Schaltegger S, Gibassier D, Zvezdov D (2013) Is environmental management accounting a discipline? A bibliometric literature review. Meditari Account Res 21(1):4–31
Schmidheiny S, Stigson B (2000) Eco-efficiency: creating more value with less impact. World Business Council for Sustainable Development, Switzerland
Sharfman M, Fernando CS (2008) Environmental risk management and the cost of capital. Strateg Manag J 29:569–592
Trudel R, Cotte J (2009) Does it pay to be good. MIT Sloan Manag Rev 50(2):61–68
Virtanen T, Tuomaala M, Pentti E (2013) Energy efficiency complexities: a technical and managerial investigation. Manag Account Res 24(4):401–416
Wahba H (2008) Does the market value corporate environmental responsibility? An empirical examination. Corp Soc Responsib Environ Manag 15(2):89–99
Walley N, Whitehead B (1994) It's not easy being green. Harvard Bus Rev 72:46–52
Zhou Z, Ou J, Li S (2016) Ecological accounting: a research review and conceptual framework. J Environ Prot 7(5):643–655

Chapter 6
The Role of Business Collaboration on Sustainable Performance: Evidence from Indonesia

Riana Sitawati and Lanita Winata

Abstract Competition in the hotel industry is very intense. To survive in this highly competitive market, hotels must sustain their better than average performance over time—so called 'sustainable performance'. To achieve and maintain such performance, hotels need to measure (monitor) their financial and non-financial performance. This paper argues that one way for hotels to achieve such performance is by collaborating with other organisations. Hence, the objective of the study was to examine the relationship between business collaboration and sustainable performance following the sustainability balanced scorecard concept, which includes financial, customer, internal business process, learning and growth, and social and environment perspectives. An online survey involving 85 hotel general managers was conducted to collect data from four- and five-star hotels located in Indonesia. Data analysis was performed using partial least squares. The results revealed that the relationship between hotel engagement in business collaboration and hotel sustainable performance in terms of internal business process, learning and growth, and social and environment perspectives was found to be positive and significant. Therefore, it can be concluded that business collaboration may assist hotels to improve their internal business processes, learning and growth, and social and environmentally related performances.

Keywords Business collaboration · Sustainable performance · Hotel industry · Sustainability balanced scorecard

---

R. Sitawati
Dharmaputra Economics Institute, Semarang, Indonesia

L. Winata (✉)
Griffith Business School, Griffith University, Gold Coast, Australia
e-mail: l.winata@griffith.edu.au

K.-H. Lee, S. Schaltegger (eds.), *Accounting for Sustainability: Asia Pacific Perspectives*, Eco-Efficiency in Industry and Science 33,
https://doi.org/10.1007/978-3-319-70899-7_6

6.1 Introduction

In the hotel industry, managers place more emphasis on financial indicators when evaluating performance (Chung and Parker 2008). The empirical evidence provided by research in chain-based European hotels (Harris and Mongiello 2001), British hotels (Atkinson and Brander 2000; Atkinson and Brown 2001) and Northern Cypriot hotels (Haktanir and Harris 2005) reveals that general managers (GMs) are more likely to use finance-related indicators when making their decisions. Similar results were reported in Australia, where GMs focus more on the financial dimension in evaluating subordinates' performance (Mia and Patiar 2001) or departments' performance (Patiar and Mia 2009). This empirical evidence raises concerns that hotels should also adopt non-financial indicators to avoid misleading decision-making by managers (Brown and McDonnell 1995; Geller 1985; Haktanir and Harris 2005; Harris and Mongiello 2001; Mia and Patiar 2001; Patiar and Mia 2009). The financial performance takes a narrow perspective on actual company activities (Gray and Bebbington 2000) and focuses only on the short term (Hayes and Abernathy 1980). Thus, focusing only on financial performance is less helpful to managers for recognising other significant non-financial elements such as market share, customer satisfaction, efficiency and productivity, product quality and employee satisfaction (Hoque 2004). By incorporating these non-financial aspects into the performance management, managers can 'recognize changes in the business environment, determine and assess progress towards business objectives, and affirm achievement of performance goals' (Hoque 2004, p. 486). This means that hotels will have a better chance to become sustainable. Corporate sustainability has been defined as the capacity of a firm to continue operating over a long period, depending on the sustainability of its stakeholder relationships (Perrini and Tencati 2006). By following this definition, the present study conceptualises hotel sustainable performance as 'a hotel's capacity to continue operating over a long period'.

Previous studies have recognised the importance of corporate sustainability relative to performance. Epstein (2008) summarised four main factors to explain why corporate sustainability is important: (1) regulations, when non-compliance with government regulations and industry codes requires companies to pay costs such as penalties, legal costs, lost productivity, potential closure of operations and the related effects on corporate reputation; (2) community relations, when the general public and activist non-government organisations become increasingly aware of sustainability and its impact on society and the environment; (3) cost and revenue imperatives, when sustainability practices create financial value for companies through enhanced revenues (increased sales resulting from improved company reputation) and lower costs (resulting from process improvements or decrease in regulatory fines); and (4) societal and moral obligations, when company activities affect the environment and society, which leads some executives and corporations to include sustainability in their company strategies.

To help companies maintain their performance, previous studies have suggested that sustainable performance should be measured based on the triple bottom line, which comprises economic, social and environmental aspects (Elkington 1998; Epstein and Wisner 2001; Figge et al. 2002; Perrini and Tencati 2006; Lee and Herold 2016). Perrini and Tencati (2006) explained that social performance describes the value added by all activities related to different stakeholder groups such as employees, financial partners, state and local authorities, the community and shareholders. An example of social performance information is the internal costs and benefits related to occupational health and safety management (Perrini and Tencati 2006). Environmental performance describes company activities related to environmental issues; for example, cost–benefit in relation to environmental management of a process or environmental management of the products (Perrini and Tencati 2006). Therefore, measuring performance by incorporating social and environmental indicators will give better support for a company to maintain its business operations in the long term (Epstein and Roy 2003; Schaltegger and Wagner 2006; Herold et al. 2016).

The above observations motivated this study, which was designed to investigate issues related to sustainable performance in the hotel industry. There is a need for such research into the hotel industry, as previous studies focused mostly on heavy industries such as mining, manufacturing and chemical industries (Chung and Parker 2008). This is because the hotel industry has the greatest potential for environmental destruction after the manufacturing industry, caused by its large resource consumption, mainly of energy and water (Bohdanowicz and Martinac 2007; Gil et al. 2001). Despite the hotel industry's impact on the environment, research related to hotel sustainability performance attracts less attention (Bader 2005; Chung and Parker 2008). It has been argued that the manufacturing industries have characteristics different from those of the hotel industry. These differences have been described by Winata and Mia (2005), Harris and Brown (1998), and Mia and Patiar (2001). Hence, studies related to sustainable performance in manufacturing industries might not generalise to the hotel industry.

In relation to the above discussion, it is argued here that there is a lack of research into company sustainable performance, particularly in the hotel industry. In examining the hotel industry in Indonesia, the present investigation uses the sustainability balanced scorecard (SBSC) approach to study sustainable performance, as this approach helps managers to identify the sustainable key performance factors and compare these factors to the company's strategic objectives (Epstein and Wisner 2001; Figge et al. 2002). The SBSC comprises five perspectives: financial, customer, internal business process, learning and growth, and social and environmental (Epstein and Wisner 2001; Figge et al. 2002); that is, it adds *social and environmental* into the original balanced scorecard's four perspectives. The results of this study will provide information to help Indonesian hotel managers better maintain their hotel's performance and improve sustainability.

The Indonesian government has a programme for improving the manufacturing industry's environmental performance, which has become a role model in the Southeast Asia region (Afsah et al. 1996, 2000; World Bank 2006; Tietenberg and Wheeler 1998). However, there is a lack of research related to corporate sustainability in the Indonesian business environment, particularly in the hotel industry, even though the tourism industry (including hotels) contributed to 4.23% of the national gross domestic product and created new jobs for around 12 million people in 2015 (Ministry of Tourism 2015). In 2015, tourism growth in Indonesia was above the world average (10.63%) which caused the country's tourism industry competitiveness position to move from rank 70 to rank 50 compared with the previous year, as acknowledged by the World Economic Forum (Ministry of Tourism 2015). Previous studies in the hotel industry were conducted in developed countries such as Europe, the United States and Australia. To the author's knowledge, no research has been done related into this area in Indonesia. Therefore, the present study emphasises the sustainable performance of hotels in Indonesia.

The increased demand for hotel services comes from both domestic and foreign customers. Data from the Ministry of Tourism (2015), for instance, showed that the number of domestic tourists in 2015 was 7,903,498, an increase of 1.57% from 2014. Additionally, the number of foreign tourists in 2015 was 10,406,759, an increase of 10.29% from 2014. This growing number of tourists affects higher competition in the hotel industry. In response, hotel managers need highly skilled employees to provide international standard customer service. Hotel managers also need to use other resources, such as technology that allows a flexible reservation procedure for their customers. However, sometimes a hotel cannot keep up with market demand if it does not have enough resources. This motivates hotel managers to engage in business collaboration, which results in a cooperative and mutual agreement between two (or more) parties for the purpose of securing a competitive advantage and long-term profitable value for all the cooperating parties (Hubbard et al. 2008; Winata 2005). Engagement in business collaboration enables companies to integrate their resources and gain greater value from the integration (Das and Teng 2000). By engaging in business collaboration, for instance, hotels may gain knowledge from their international partners and learn from their experience to employ international standard customer service and sophisticated reservation systems. Therefore, business collaboration is useful to support sustainable performance of hotels within the industry.

To summarise, a hotel needs to place considerable importance on building up collaborations with other organisations (e.g., other hotels, travel agents, and suppliers of inputs and services) to improve and maintain performance. However, the empirical research on the ways and means of improving hotel sustainable performance, specifically in developing countries like Indonesia, is scant. Consequently, hotel managers in countries like Indonesia may have limited knowledge of how they can help their hotel achieve sustainable performance. This study aims to help fill the knowledge gap of Indonesian hotel managers by providing empirical evidence on how business collaborations could play a role in improving sustainable performance. The SBSC approach was used to measure sustainable performance based on financial, customer, internal business process, learning and growth, and social and environmental perspectives.

6.2 Theoretical Framework and Hypothesis Development

6.2.1 Business Collaboration and Hotel Financial-Related Performance

Winata (2005) revealed that there was no positive relationship between the extent of a manufacturing firm's engagement in business collaboration and its financial performance in Indonesia. She argued that this situation may be caused by the Indonesian cultural characteristic of collectivism where people are more likely to work in a group than individually (Hofstede 1980). In a collectivist society, business collaboration itself may not be a competitive advantage that improves financial performance. It may happen because its competitors also engage in business collaboration along their supply chain (i.e., suppliers and customers). Thus, (1) a company may not obtain a cheaper price for its raw materials, and (2) a company may not obtain a good selling price for its product. As this study was conducted in the Indonesian manufacturing industry, caution is required when generalising because the manufacturing industry has different characteristics to the hotel industry.

Regarding the hotel industry, Boo and Mattila (2002) suggested that brand collaboration in the hotel restaurant context may have an impact on both partners in relation to their financial, managerial, and marketing performance. Another study by Chathoth and Olsen (2003) proposed that the use of technology will help the development of a strategic competitor collaboration, which in turn will improve the productivity and profitability (financial performance) of the allied companies. However, this proposition needs to be statistically tested. In a study about the Israeli hospitality industry, Preble et al. (2000) described an Israeli partner benefiting from the famous brand of its international partner. The famous brand may attract more customers, which in turn enhances company profit. This study also needs to be empirically tested to obtain a more reliable and valid result. Moreover, the Indonesian hotel industry may have different characteristics due to its different cultural and business environment, since it is a new emerging market compared to the markets of Israel. For example, Indonesia has a unique culture resulting from hundreds of local ethnic groups; these provide the country with enormous diversity that is manifested in the hundreds of local dialects and local cultures (reflected, for example, in dance, food, musical instruments and handicrafts; Picard 1997). Hotels in Indonesia may apply elements of this cultural diversity to add competitive value and so attract tourists. However, tourists in Israel may have religious motivations as the country has some important religious sites for Jews, Christians and Muslims (Preble et al. 2000). Therefore, the results of Preble et al.'s (2000) study must be treated with caution when being generalised to the Indonesian hotel industry.

Ozturen and Sevil (2009) conducted a study in Northern Cyprus to examine the effect of hotel collaboration with suppliers and customers on hotel performance. The authors revealed that a high level of collaboration with customers tends to improve hotels' net profits. Moreover, they suggested that hotel managers considered their suppliers as a source of profit increase through decreasing costs and improving input quality. However, they only used a single indicator (net profit) to measure financial performance. Applying more indicators to measure the impact of business collaboration would lead to a more accurate measure of a hotel's financial performance.

Concluding the discussion above, business collaboration is a key factor for the Indonesian hotel industry to compete in a highly competitive market. By collaborating, international partners may derive benefits from sharing knowledge and resources with their Indonesian partners (i.e., relating to natural and human resources, Indonesian culture and the local market), and overcome local regulation barriers (Sitawati 2004). Similarly, their Indonesian partners may benefit from association with an international brand and its advanced technology, such as its reservation system. As a result, the famous brand name and comprehensive reservation system may attract more customers, leading to a higher occupancy rate, thus improving profits. This is because business collaboration delivers a competitive advantage to its alliance members so they may obtain advantages from each other and decrease the competition among themselves (Winata 2005), leading to higher market shares (Sarkar et al. 2001) and increased profits (Contractor and Lorange 2002). Business collaboration also allows hotels to provide more services, such as in-house shops, restaurants, travel agents, beauty salons and medical centres, which increase the hotels' income. Therefore, it is arguable that hotels' engagement in business collaboration leads to a better financial performance. Based on the discussion above, Hypothesis 1_a is formulated:

Hypothesis 1_a There is a positive relationship between a hotel's engagement in business collaboration and its financial performance.

6.2.2 Business Collaboration and Hotel Customer-Related Performance

The empirical study conducted by Ozturen and Sevil (2009) to analyse the relationship between hotel collaboration and hotel performance found that collaborating with customers and travel intermediaries may have a positive impact on customer satisfaction. By having a close relationship with travel intermediaries or the customer, hotels may have better knowledge about customer expectations. Therefore, business collaboration may improve customer satisfaction, leading to customer loyalty and customer retention. Moreover, the authors found that collaborating with the customer is the most important step towards increasing the quality of hotel products such as customer service. Regarding hotel engagement with suppliers, Ozturen and Sevil (2009) revealed that collaborating with suppliers is imperative to improve the quality of hotel products. They stated that good input from hotel suppliers such as tour operators is crucial for providing good service to satisfy customers. By having a closer relationship with its suppliers, a hotel may improve its service quality. For example, hotels may cooperate with a tour operator (the hotel supplier) to include the hotel's name in a holiday package. Thus, customers need go to one place only (the tour operator) to arrange their holiday, including their accommodation. However, it should be noted that customer expectations might vary between countries. Therefore, the results need further consideration before being extended to hotels in other countries such as Indonesia.

A study of the Indonesian hotel industry (budget, standard and premium hotels) revealed that 'managers tend to over-estimate the customer value they deliver while customers under-estimate the customer value they experience' (Nasution and Mavondo 2008, p. 211). A gap was revealed between customer expectations and the hotel's actual performance (Nasution and Mavondo 2008). The service delivered by Indonesian hotels was considered below customers' expectations. These results suggest that hotels with a higher classification (i.e., standard and premium hotels) provide a higher level of customer satisfaction with respect to better service quality. Therefore, a good strategy is for local hotels to improve their quality by collaborating with international hotels that usually have a good brand image, superior managerial expertise and better customer service (Dev et al. 2007). Therefore, the present study's results may extend the Nasution and Mavondo (2008) study by extending the knowledge about the role of collaboration in improving customer satisfaction.

The study by Winata (2005) into the Indonesian manufacturing industry, mentioned previously, reported no relationship between engagement in business collaboration and a company's customer performance. The author suggested that this may be due to the geographical factor, in that Indonesia is divided into thousands of islands, which may cause communication difficulties between alliance partners. Another possible cause is that the Indonesian culture of collectivism means that engagement in business collaboration may not provide a competitive advantage anymore. However, Winata's findings should not be generalised to the Indonesian hotel industry, as this industry needs to cooperate with other parties to meet sophisticated customer demands. Unlike manufacturing companies, hotels deal directly with customers, who have different requirements and preferences (Winata and Mia 2005). To give faster and broader services, hotels need to be more involved with different types of service companies. Hotels may engage in business collaboration with travel agents and tour operators to speed up the customer reservation system. This results in customer satisfaction because of the time and cost saved when reserving a hotel room. Moreover, satisfied customers may result in customer loyalty because they are more likely to return to the same hotels in the future (customer retention). Thus, the presence of more customers leads to a higher market share. Hypothesis 1_b is formulated based on these discussions:

Hypothesis 1_b There is a positive relationship between a hotel's engagement in business collaboration and its customer-related performance.

6.2.3 Business Collaboration and Hotel Internal Business Process–Related Performance

Previous studies into the manufacturing industry pointed out the effect of business collaboration on the internal business process. A study by Monczka et al. (1998) revealed that manufacturing companies are likely to conduct collaboration for reasons such as improving the quality of the material purchased, gaining better access to new process technology, reducing time to market and reducing order cycle time. Lawson et al. (2009) found that sharing knowledge with suppliers may lead to improved product development outcomes. Moreover, Winata (2005) found that engagement in collaboration has a positive and significant association with internal business process performance in the Indonesian manufacturing industry. All these studies were conducted in the manufacturing industry, with a primary focus on production process efficiency. The results cannot be generalised to the hotel industry, which focuses mainly on people.

The hotel business must provide fast service directly to the customer, which leads to a better internal business process performance. One of the effective indicators for measuring internal business process performance in the hotel industry is the time required to complete key processes and tasks such as bookings and the check-in system (Denton and White 2000). To decrease the length of time required for a customer to place a booking, a hotel may engage in business collaboration in its marketing area. For example, a marketing alliance exists between seven large hotel brands: Dusit Hotels and Resorts; Kempinski Hotels; Landis Hotels and Resorts; Marco Polo Hotels; Omni Hotels; Pan Pacific Hotels and Resorts; and The Leela Palaces and Resorts (Chathoth 2008). This collaboration uses innovative technology to create synergy between these hotels so they gain better global access to the markets. At the same time, they run a one-stop Internet website that provides information such as the prices and products of all member hotels. Some member hotels also recognise other members' guest recognition programmes. Customers may then use their accumulative points at these hotels. Consequently, customers can make flexible and faster bookings by using this system. Overall, this innovation has improved the internal business process of the member hotels.

A study by Espino-Rodriguez and Padron-Robaina (2004) into the Canary Islands' hotel industry found that an outsourcing may improve services so that they are better, faster and more efficient. Outsourcing in the hotel industry could be for complementary services, such as health and sporting facilities, or a laundry service. By conducting outsourcing, a hotel can reduce the life cycle of services and add other functions to its basic service. When a hotel outsources its laundry activity, for instance, this gives the manager more time to focus on improving customer service activities, such as providing a faster response to customer complaints. Further, these complementary services can be perceived as a value added to the end service by customers. However, the Espino-Rodriguez and Padron-Robaina (2004) study focuses only on outsourcing. The current investigation extends their study by examining the influence of all types of collaboration on internal business process–related performance.

The hotel industry in Indonesia is intensely competitive. One reason for this is increasing customer demand. Consequently, hotel managers need to have a competitive advantage to meet customer expectations, thereby leading to enhanced customer satisfaction and attracting more customers. However, because of the lack of resources or knowledge, local hotels may engage in business collaboration to learn the required technology or skill from their partners, such as a sophisticated reservation system or customer database. Thus, Indonesian hotels may reduce the operation cycle time. It can be argued that after engagement in business collaboration, hotels may improve their operational efficiency, which leads to better internal business process performance. Hence, Hypothesis 1_c is formulated:

Hypothesis 1_c There is a positive relationship between a hotel's engagement in business collaboration and its internal business process–related performance.

6.2.4 Business Collaboration and Hotel Learning and Growth-Related Performance

Winata's (2005) study into the Indonesian manufacturing industry reported no relationship between engagement in business collaboration, a company's learning and innovation performance (i.e., number of new products, number of new patents, and time to market new products). Winata (2005) suggested that this may be because of the lack of trust and communication between alliance partners in the Indonesian manufacturing industry. Another reason she suggested was the Indonesian collectivist culture—that is, engagement in business collaboration is already commonplace in the Indonesian business environment. Therefore, engagement in business collaboration in Indonesia may no longer be used by companies as a competitive advantage.

Generalisation of this result to the hotel industry needs caution. For example, business collaboration in the manufacturing industry may focus on improving the production process, while the hotel industry is likely to emphasise the development of skills in human resources. Moreover, hotels need to cooperate with other parties within the tourism industry to provide a quality service to their customers (Pansiri 2009). For example, hotels may engage in business collaboration with their suppliers, such as tour operators, travel agents, airline companies or even other hotels to employ a sophisticated reservation system where customers can make reservations at these alliance partners when planning a holiday. Therefore, it is likely that engagement in business collaboration becomes a competitive advantage for hotels to survive in the highly competitive market.

Hotels may conduct business collaboration to learn from their partners. For example, Preble et al. (2000) proposed that local hotels in Israel might benefit from improved staff knowledge resulting from training provided by their foreign partner. Another benefit is that local hotels may learn about the comprehensive reservation system owned by their international partner. By being allied, the local hotel gains the benefit of learning this knowledge and technology, which may be difficult to obtain without business collaboration.

Because customer satisfaction with hotel services in Indonesia is lower than managers' perceptions of it (Nasution and Mavondo 2008), it is necessary to improve hotel service quality relating to customer expectations and needs. Skillful employees are needed to achieve this goal. In response, managers should focus on appointing staff who have a customer-oriented attitude and who understand the importance of service quality (Sparks and Weber 2008). This skill may be obtained from induction or training programmes emphasising customer service and service quality. In this case, managers may need external partners such as hotel consultants or they may need to form networks with foreign partners who can provide such staff training. By using another party's expertise, managers benefit by gaining better skilled employees. Ultimately, these more highly skilled employees can provide better customer service through their improved job performance, which in turn leads to lower employee turnover. It can be argued that business collaboration has a positive influence on company learning and growth performance. Hypothesis 1_d is formulated based on this argument:

Hypothesis 1_d There is a positive relationship between a hotel's engagement in business collaboration and its learning and growth-related performance.

6.2.5 Business Collaboration and Hotel Social and Environmentally-Related Performance

The hotel industry does not produce pollution like the manufacturing industry does. However, hotels affect their environment by consuming large amounts of energy such as electricity and water, resulting in high energy and water consumption costs. In response, some international hotels have learned to decrease their environmental costs by installing solar power panels, fitting energy-efficient light bulbs with motion detectors, or by recycling grey water for gardening, washing floors and flushing toilets, for instance (Molina-Azorin et al. 2009). Hotels may also outsource their laundry to their alliance partners and keep the hotels' environment green and clean. However, because of a lack of knowledge and skill or lack of professional advice, not all hotels have applied environmentally-related strategies (Chan 2008).

In Indonesia, the Ministry of Tourism provides a Green Hotel Award to four- and five-star hotels that apply environmental and sustainable development activities at their hotels. Therefore, hotels may need to learn from their competitors or partners how to be 'green'. Hotels will improve not only their environmental performance but also their social image by being green. For instance, hotels may learn from their alliance partners' experience about applying environmentally-related strategies relating to certain regulations, resulting in certification such as the 'eco-labels', which may attract environmentally sensitive tourists (Molina-Azorin et al. 2009). Hotels may also learn from their more experienced partners about how to quantify environmental savings and costs in their budget, and apply energy and water saving practices (i.e., how to make energy and conserve water). By practising these environmental management matters, hotels may achieve a safe, clean and healthy environment (Mensah 2006), which leads to higher appreciation from their employees and customers, and improved social and environmental performance. Hence, it is arguable that engagement in business collaboration has an impact on social and environmental performances. Hypothesis 1_e is formulated based on this discussion:

Hypothesis 1_e There is a positive relationship between a hotel's engagement in business collaboration and its social and environmentally-related performance.

Figure 6.1 below shows the model tested in this study (Table 6.1).

Fig. 6.1 Research model

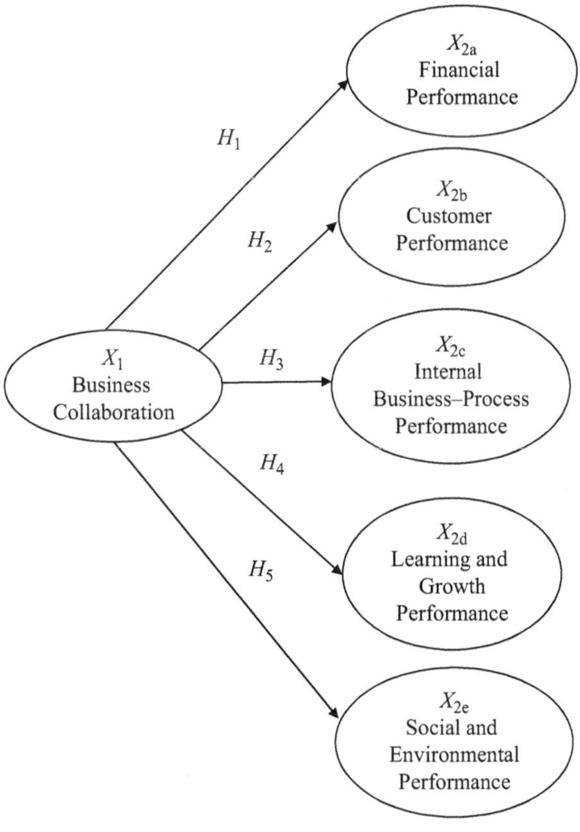

Table 6.1 Factor loadings from final partial least squares measurement model

	X_1	X_{2a}	X_{2b}	X_{2c}	X_{2d}	X_{2e}
X_1—Offer new or attractive hotel services/package	**0.580**	0.065	0.163	0.113	0.205	0.233
X_1—Market the services or hotel package	**0.890**	0.227	0.297	0.529	0.386	0.383
X_1—Improve hotel business process and human resources management	**0.752**	0.009	0.049	0.271	0.189	0.206
X_1—Conduct social and environmental management practice	**0.832**	0.164	0.220	0.388	0.389	0.298
X_{2a}—Occupancy rate	0.228	**0.828**	0.549	0.304	0.314	0.304
X_{2a}—Net profit ratio	0.176	**0.888**	0.568	0.384	0.384	0.402
X_{2a}—Revenue growth	0.111	**0.809**	0.555	0.308	0.366	0.358
X_{2a}—Return on assets	0.122	**0.859**	0.582	0.389	0.364	0.412
X_{2b}—Customer loyalty	0.172	0.526	**0.706**	0.387	0.425	0.501
X_{2b}—Customer satisfaction	0.131	0.550	**0.809**	0.465	0.467	0.554
X_{2b}—New customer acquisition	0.161	0.495	**0.872**	0.544	0.538	0.534
X_{2b}—Market share	0.227	0.573	**0.666**	0.345	0.305	0.364
X_{2b}—Service quality	0.352	0.503	**0.804**	0.515	0.562	0.517
X_{2c}—Customer background information compilation	0.327	0.278	0.425	**0.774**	0.331	0.388
X_{2c}—Management efficiency enhancement	0.189	0.281	0.340	**0.730**	0.307	0.404
X_{2c}—Time reduction of operation cycle	0.221	0.416	0.548	**0.642**	0.479	0.532
X_{2c}—Time reduction for handling customer complaints	0.528	0.274	0.388	**0.805**	0.491	0.500
X_{2d}—Employee ability to manage emergencies	0.203	0.221	0.376	0.326	**0.753**	0.521
X_{2d}—Employee satisfaction	0.305	0.379	0.513	0.483	**0.740**	0.552
X_{2d}—Employee ability to use IT products	0.251	0.461	0.557	0.421	**0.703**	0.503
X_{2d}—Knowledge and resource sharing among employees	0.245	0.168	0.349	0.350	**0.715**	0.482
X_{2d}—Employee productivity	0.353	0.240	0.387	0.363	**0.778**	0.490
X_{2d}—Employee professional ability	0.409	0.320	0.456	0.430	**0.744**	0.510
X_{2e}—Quantification of environmental savings and costs in hotel budget	0.265	0.340	0.507	0.470	0.534	**0.736**
X_{2e}—Ecological arguments for marketing campaigns	0.211	0.280	0.460	0.511	0.477	**0.745**
X_{2e}—Support for local community	0.194	0.272	0.392	0.452	0.435	**0.659**
X_{2e}—Diversity and equality	0.296	0.383	0.555	0.420	0.423	**0.650**
X_{2e}—Use of environmentally friendly materials	0.339	0.260	0.441	0.383	0.416	**0.743**
X_{2e}—Health and safety for workers	0.275	0.394	0.603	0.482	0.631	**0.845**
X_{2e}—Local recruitment priority for workers	0.202	0.233	0.410	0.413	0.467	**0.695**
X_{2e}—Applies energy and water saving practices	0.305	0.466	0.538	0.581	0.498	**0.772**
X_{2e}—Compliance with social/environmental regulation	0.310	0.291	0.499	0.462	0.511	**0.837**
X_{2e}—Employees training on social/environmental issues	0.401	0.325	0.477	0.407	0.538	**0.718**

X_1 = business collaboration; X_{2a} = financial performance; X_{2b} = customer-related performance; X_{2c} = internal business process–related performance; X_{2d} = learning and growth-related performance; X_{2e} = social and environmentally-related performance

6.3 Research Method

6.3.1 Sample

As previously mentioned, a programme called the 'Green Hotel Award' was launched by the Ministry of Tourism and Creative Economy in 2011 (Pembaruan 2011). Targeting four- and five-star hotels, this award has been given to hotels that practise environmental and sustainable development. Therefore, hotels of this category were selected as samples for this study since they are more likely to strive for an image as a green hotel (social-related performance) and achieve a better environmentally related performance.

An online survey was developed and subsequently distributed to four- and five-star hotel GMs in Indonesia. The survey was pilot tested: a sample was selected from the Indonesian Hotel and Restaurant Association (IHRA) using the systematic random sampling method, and responses were tested for validity. Eighty-five usable responses out of 350 delivered questionnaires (the final response rate was approximately 24%) were received. Results from the ANOVA test and the *t*-test indicate a non-response bias for the sample of the current study.

6.3.2 Measurement of Variables

6.3.2.1 Business Collaboration

The present study adopted the instrument from the study by Bucklin and Sengupta (1993), which was also used by Li and Atuahene-Gima (2001) and Winata (2005) to measure a company's engagement in business collaboration. It used a Likert-type scale, where 1 represented *strongly disagree* and 5 represented *strongly agree* (Bucklin and Sengupta 1993; Li and Atuahene-Gima 2001). The purpose of using a summated, multi-item scale such as a Likert-type scale is to improve the reliability of a construct for measuring self-efficacy (Maurer and Pierce 1998). Each respondent was asked to indicate the extent to which their company used business collaboration relative to their competitors over the last 3 years based on the following four items:

1. Entered into cooperative agreements with other firms to offer new or attractive hotel services/package
2. Collaborated with other firms to market the services or hotel package
3. Joined with other firms to improve hotel business process and human resources management
4. Collaborated with other firms to conduct social and environmental management practice.

Two items from the original Bucklin and Sengupta (1993) study were excluded because they focused on new product lines and research and development (which are not the main activities in the hotel industry).

6.3.2.2 Hotel Sustainable Performance

Hotel sustainable performance (HSP) in the present study was measured using an SBSC approach with five indicators (financial, customer, internal business, learning and growth, social and environmental). The HSP instruments were adapted from several relevant studies because of the lack of a common standard for measuring HSP in the hotel industry (Bohdanowicz and Martinac 2007; Clarke and Chen 2007; Evans 2005; Font 2002; Holcomb et al. 2007). The first four items of the SBSC (financial, customer, internal business process, and learning and growth performance) were adapted from items developed by Chen et al. (2011) based on Kaplan and Norton's balanced scorecard approach (Kaplan and Norton 1992, 1996, 2001). The fifth item, social and environmental performance, was adapted from items developed by Holcomb et al. (2007) and Gil et al. (2001), supported by in-depth interviews and a pilot study.

A lack of data on hotel social and environmentally-related performance may exist in the developing countries caused by relatively weak institutions, standards and appeal systems (Kemp 2001). To avoid this problem, in-depth interviews with open-ended questions were conducted asking five GMs about the social and environmental practices that they have applied in their hotels. Combining a survey with interviews 'enables the researcher to simultaneously answer confirmatory and exploratory questions, and therefore verify and generate theory in the same study' (Teddlie and Tashakkori 2003, p. 15).The selection of these GMs was based on their position as either the leader or representative of the IHRA in five provinces that were also in the top tourist destinations in Indonesia (namely, Yogyakarta, Bali, Central Java, West Java and East Java).For social-related performance items, answers from GMs were in line with Holcomb et al.'s (2007) suggestion that in terms of social practice, the community and the workforce were likely to be the major concerns emphasised by management. Therefore, four social-related performance items were developed for this study based on the interview results. These items were:

1. Diversity and equality in the workplace
2. Support for local community
3. Health and safety of workers
4. Priority to hire local staff.

For environmentally related performance items, this study used the environmental management instrument developed by Gil et al. (2001), which has also been adopted in other studies (Claver-Cortes et al. 2007; Molina-Azorin et al. 2009).

Gil's instrument of environmental management originally had seven items: (1) quantification of environmental savings and costs in hotel budgets; (2) employees' training on environmental issues; (3) priority to purchase ecological products; (4) using ecological arguments in hotel marketing campaigns; (5) facilitating customer collaboration in environmental protection; (6) energy and water saving practices; and (7) selective collection of waste items such as paper, oil, glass. Based on the pilot study results with the five Indonesian hotel GMs, the present study used six items. These were:

1. Use of environmentally friendly materials
2. Use of ecological arguments in marketing campaigns
3. Quantification of environmental savings and costs in hotel budgets
4. Employee training on social and environmental issues
5. Energy and water saving practices
6. Compliance with social and environmental regulations.

One item was modified (employee training on environmental issues) by including the social aspect; hence, the item became 'employee training on social and environmental issues'. One item was added based on the interview results: 'compliance with social and environmental regulations'. The modification and the addition were due to Indonesian government regulations. Hotels operating in Indonesia are required to follow certain environmental procedures—such as following the AMDAL (Analisis Mengenai Dampak Lingkungan/Analysis of Environmental Impact) and IPAL (Instalasi Pembuangan Air Limbah/Waste Water Disposal Installation)—before they can start business. After establishing their business, hotels need to report their environmentally related performance to the government. Hotels must also register their employees with the Labor Social Security Programme (Jamsostek) to secure their employees' rights to security, safety and welfare (Halim 2010). Moreover, hotels are required to provide an occupational health and safety management system to guarantee a safe working environment for their employees. Hence, adding one item to measure hotels' social and environmental performance based on their compliance with the government regulations is relevant in the Indonesian business environment.

The present study used subjective measures by asking the respondents to indicate their hotel's performance compared with that of their competitors. A Likert-type scale was used where 1 indicated *well below average* and 5 indicated *well above average*. Although some scholars criticise this self-insight approach, this method has been used in previous studies to measure organisational performance (Abernethy and Lilis 1995; Avci et al. 2011; Chen et al. 2011; Dess and Robinson 1984; Garrigos-Simon and Marques 2005; Hoque and James 2000; Jennings et al. 2003; Patiar and Mia 2008; Winata 2005). This method uses decision-makers such as top managers as respondents to improve the quality of managerial self-insight (Chenhall and Morris 1986; Larcker 1981; Wright 1977).

6.4 Statistical Tests and Results

The partial least squares (PLS) technique was used to test five hypotheses developed in this study (Chin 1998; World 1982). An evaluation of the PLS model was conducted following the procedure advised by Hulland (1999). At first, the PLS measurement model was analysed. Next, a hypotheses test was performed to evaluate the PLS structural model.

Table 6.2 describes the final factor loadings from the PLS measurement model. Table 6.2 provides a summary of the results for confirmatory factor analysis and discriminant validity analysis. Table 6.3 shows that the average variance extracted (AVE) for each variable was 0.50 and above and therefore demonstrated adequate convergent validity (Chin 1998; Hair et al. 2010, 2011). The composite reliability shown in Table 6.3 is above 0.70, which Hair et al. (2011) suggest supports good reliability of the constructs. Discriminant validity of the constructs was completed using a variance extraction test. In conclusion, the results from the PLS measurement model demonstrate that each construct in the current study exhibited satisfactory reliability and validity.

The structural model of PLS was used to test the hypotheses. Table 6.4 presents the path coefficients and the significance of the standardised β resulting from the analyses.

The results for Hypothesis H_{1a} indicate that business collaboration was not significantly associated with hotel financial performance. Thus, Hypothesis H_{1a} was not supported. A possible explanation for the lack of significant results is that Indonesia has a collectivist culture where people tend to work in a team. A previous scholar has suggested that a firm's engagement in business collaboration in a collectivist society such as Indonesia's is a common business trait (Winata 2005). Accordingly, the collaboration itself may not give a competitive advantage to the hotel and thus has no influence on financial performance. Hotels in Indonesia become members of the IHRA, which helps them to conduct business networking, especially with hotel competitors. Joining this association as a form of developing business collaborations does not represent a competitive advantage since every hotel should become a member to gain knowledge and expertise from the association's other members. A hotel may not sell its products or services at a better price than that of its competitors because the competitors might engage in similar collaboration with suppliers and customers. Moreover, in a collectivist country like Indonesia, managers are likely to put less focus on cost–benefit calculations when engaging in collaboration (Triandis 1995).

The results presented in Table 6.4 reveal that business collaboration did not have a significant influence on hotel customer performance. Therefore, Hypothesis H_{1b} was not supported. The reason for non-significant relationships between business collaboration and customer-related performance may relate to the Indonesian society's character of collectivism. In this type of society, engagement in business collaboration is a common business activity (Winata 2005). Therefore, being a member of a business collaboration in such a society may not enhance a hotel's customer-related performance straightaway.

Table 6.2 Factor loadings from final partial least squares measurement model

	X_1	X_{2a}	X_{2b}	X_{2c}	X_{2d}	X_{2e}
X_1—Offer new or attractive hotel services/package	**0.580**	0.065	0.163	0.113	0.205	0.233
X_1—Market the services or hotel package	**0.890**	0.227	0.297	0.529	0.386	0.383
X_1—Improve hotel business process and human resources management	**0.752**	0.009	0.049	0.271	0.189	0.206
X_1—Conduct social and environmental management practice	**0.832**	0.164	0.220	0.388	0.389	0.298
X_{2a}—Occupancy rate	0.228	**0.828**	0.549	0.304	0.314	0.304
X_{2a}—Net profit ratio	0.176	**0.888**	0.568	0.384	0.384	0.402
X_{2a}—Revenue growth	0.111	**0.809**	0.555	0.308	0.366	0.358
X_{2a}—Return on assets	0.122	**0.859**	0.582	0.389	0.364	0.412
X_{2b}—Customer loyalty	0.172	0.526	**0.706**	0.387	0.425	0.501
X_{2b}—Customer satisfaction	0.131	0.550	**0.809**	0.465	0.467	0.554
X_{2b}—New customer acquisition	0.161	0.495	**0.872**	0.544	0.538	0.534
X_{2b}—Market share	0.227	0.573	**0.666**	0.345	0.305	0.364
X_{2b}—Service quality	0.352	0.503	**0.804**	0.515	0.562	0.517
X_{2c}—Customer background information compilation	0.327	0.278	0.425	**0.774**	0.331	0.388
X_{2c}—Management efficiency enhancement	0.189	0.281	0.340	**0.730**	0.307	0.404
X_{2c}—Time reduction of operation cycle	0.221	0.416	0.548	**0.642**	0.479	0.532
X_{2c}—Time reduction for handling customer complaints	0.528	0.274	0.388	**0.805**	0.491	0.500
X_{2d}—Employee ability to manage emergencies	0.203	0.221	0.376	0.326	**0.753**	0.521
X_{2d}—Employee satisfaction	0.305	0.379	0.513	0.483	**0.740**	0.552
X_{2d}—Employee ability to use IT products	0.251	0.461	0.557	0.421	**0.703**	0.503
X_{2d}—Knowledge and resource sharing among employees	0.245	0.168	0.349	0.350	**0.715**	0.482
X_{2d}—Employee productivity	0.353	0.240	0.387	0.363	**0.778**	0.490
X_{2d}—Employee professional ability	0.409	0.320	0.456	0.430	**0.744**	0.510
X_{2e}—Quantification of environmental savings and costs in hotel budget	0.265	0.340	0.507	0.470	0.534	**0.736**
X_{2e}—Ecological arguments for marketing campaigns	0.211	0.280	0.460	0.511	0.477	**0.745**
X_{2e}—Support for local community	0.194	0.272	0.392	0.452	0.435	**0.659**
X_{2e}—Diversity and equality	0.296	0.383	0.555	0.420	0.423	**0.650**
X_{2e}—Use of environmentally friendly materials	0.339	0.260	0.441	0.383	0.416	**0.743**
X_{2e}—Health and safety for workers	0.275	0.394	0.603	0.482	0.631	**0.845**
X_{2e}—Local recruitment priority for workers	0.202	0.233	0.410	0.413	0.467	**0.695**
X_{2e}—Applies energy and water saving practices	0.305	0.466	0.538	0.581	0.498	**0.772**
X_{2e}—Compliance with social/environmental regulation	0.310	0.291	0.499	0.462	0.511	**0.837**
X_{2e}—Employees training on social/environmental issues	0.401	0.325	0.477	0.407	0.538	**0.718**

X_1 = business collaboration; X_{2a} = financial performance; X_{2b} = customer-related performance; X_{2c} = internal business process–related performance; X_{2d} = learning and growth-related performance; X_{2e} = social and environmentally-related performance

Table 6.3 Reliability and average variance extracted statistics, and correlations

Variable	Cronbach's alpha	Composite reliability	AVE	Correlations X_1	X_{2a}	X_{2b}	X_{2c}	X_{2d}	X_{2e}
X_1	0.764	0.846	0.585	*0.765*					
X_{2a}	0.870	0.910	0.717	0.184	*0.847*				
X_{2b}	0.836	0.882	0.601	0.264	0.634	*0.775*			
X_{2c}	0.724	0.828	0.549	0.477	0.415	0.595	*0.741*		
X_{2d}	0.834	0.879	0.548	0.410	0.422	0.609	0.546	*0.740*	
X_{2e}	0.909	0.925	0.554	0.382	0.441	0.576	0.616	0.516	*0.745*

From partial least squares model
X_1 = business collaboration; X_{2a} = financial performance; X_{2b} = customer-related performance; X_{2c} = internal business process–related performance; X_{2d} = learning and growth-related performance; X_{2e} = social and environmentally-related performance

Table 6.4 Results from partial least squares analysis (path coefficients, N = 85)

From	To	Path coefficient	*t* value	*p* value	Conclusion
X_1	X_{2a}	0.038	0.575	0.283	Not significant
X_1	X_{2b}	0.059	0.928	0.178	Not significant
X_1	X_{2c}	0.305*	3.812	0.000	Significant
X_1	X_{2d}	0.261*	2.909	0.002	Significant
X_1	X_{2e}	0.204*	1.971	0.026	Significant

X_1 = business collaboration; X_{2a} = financial performance; X_{2b} = customer-related performance; X_{2c} = internal business process–related performance; X_{2d} = learning and growth-related performance; X_{2e} = social and environmentally-related performance
*Significant at 0.05 level (one-tailed)

The results for Hypothesis H_{1c} indicate that a hotel's engagement in business collaboration was positively and significantly associated with its internal business process–related performance. An interpretation of the results is that a hotel's engagement in business collaboration enhances its internal business process–related performance. For example, a hotel engages in business collaboration with a tour operator and an airline company to create a particular holiday package to a specific tourist destination. Customers need go to only one place (e.g., the tour operator) to plan their holidays, including flight and accommodation. In this case, the hotel gives a faster reservation service to the customer. By gaining faster reservations through the booking system, the whole operation cycle becomes faster. Customers save more in costs and time, leading to a better hotel internal business process.

The results presented in Table 6.4 support Hypothesis H_{1d} that hotel engagement in business collaboration is positively and significantly associated with hotel learning and growth-related performance. Competitive advantage in business collaboration is achieved when the alliance partners obtain benefits from a synergy that they could not obtain when they perform individually (Teece 1992). This synergy is obtained when alliance partners exchange knowledge, skills or expertise that consequently improves their competitive advantage (Parkhe 1991). In the hotel industry, for example, a hotel may engage in business collaboration to gain access to a new market and to minimise the risks of entering another country (Chathoth and Olsen

2003; Preble et al. 2000). The local hotel may assist its partner by providing knowledge about a new market environment, local culture and government regulations. On the other hand, the local hotel may benefit from its partner's expertise in hotel management and technology (Preble et al. 2000). By achieving this mutual benefit after being engaged in business collaboration, the local hotel and its partner may enhance their learning and growth-related performance.

The results presented in Table 6.4 reveal that hotel engagement in business collaboration was positively and significantly associated with hotel social and environmentally-related performance. Therefore, Hypothesis H_{1e} was supported. Although hotels do not produce chemical waste the way that manufacturers do, hotels still need to manage their energy and water consumption (Molina-Azorin et al. 2009). This can be done by installing green energy equipment such as solar power panels or a recycling water system. Unfortunately, many hotels have not applied this environmentally friendly strategy because of a lack of knowledge and skills, or because of a lack of professional advice (Chan 2008). However, a hotel may acquire environmental knowledge, such as how to save energy and water consumption in daily operations, from its partner. Similarly, a hotel may also learn how to keep a safe environment—such as how to avoid accidents (e.g., caused by slipping on a wet floor) in the kitchen and restaurant. By applying an environmental strategy, a hotel may gain greater approval from its employees and customers resulting from its clean, safe and healthy environment. These actions lead to a hotel's higher social and environmentally-related performance.

6.5 Conclusion, Implications and Limitations

The present study aimed to reveal the relationship between business collaboration and HSP incorporating five perspectives of the SBSC. The results provide empirical evidence that business collaboration has a direct and significant relationship with some hotel performances: namely, internal business process, learning and growth, and social and environmentally-related performances. However, no relationship with financial and customer-related performances was found. Hence, hotel managers should not expect to increase their financial and customer-related performance straightaway after engaging in business collaboration.

The lack of significant results between business collaboration and financial performance indicates that a hotel's engagement in business collaboration is unlikely to influence its financial performance directly. All hotels engage in business collaboration to satisfy the growing sophistication and demands of their customers (Pansiri 2009). The results of the present study provide empirical evidence to support previous studies that have argued that there is no direct effect between engagement in business collaboration and financial performance (Anand and Khanna 2000; Bucklin and Sengupta 1993; Draulans et al. 2003; Lambe et al. 2002; Luo et al. 2007; Winata 2005). Thus, a mediating variable to support the impact of business collaboration on financial performance is needed.

In the case of the Indonesian hotel industry, membership of the IHRA may enhance opportunities for hotels to engage in business collaboration, especially with other hotels (competitors). However, mere engagement in business collaboration does not give the capability to attract customers, because all hotels do the same. A hotel manager needs to conduct further action after his or her engagement in business collaboration to draw this to the customers' attention. The current study provides empirical evidence to support Rindfleisch and Moorman's (2003) argument that business collaboration (particularly among competitors) may not have a positive effect on a company's customer orientation. This is caused by highly intensive collaboration, in which companies put more emphasis on how to do better than their partner–competitor instead of focusing on their customers (Gatignon and Deshpande 1994; Luo et al. 2007; Moorman 1995; Rindfleisch and Moorman 2003). The results of the current study extend the previous study in the Indonesian manufacturing industry by Winata (2005), who found no direct relationship between engagement in business collaboration and a company's customer performance. This current study also extends the work of Shrader (2001) who found no significant relationship between a company's engagement in business collaboration and its performance (sales growth, market share, R&D intensity and advertising intensity). Both studies argued that there are other factors that can moderate this relationship.

The positive and significant relationship found between business collaboration and a hotel's internal business process–related performance is in line with other studies, such as those of Lo and Yeung (2004), Lawson et al. (2009), and Winata (2005), who found that business collaboration has a positive and significant association with internal business process–related performance in the manufacturing industry. In the hotel industry, the results of the current study provide empirical evidence supporting Chathoth's (2008) study, which indicated that conducting business collaboration in the marketing area may result in better access to markets. Chathoth gave the example of a marketing alliance between several large hotels that run a one-stop Internet website. This website enables customer to check information and book services from any of the participating hotels, thus improving the hotels' internal business process. The current study also supports the study by Espino-Rodriguez and Padron-Robaina (2004), who suggested that outsourcing may have an impact by providing a better, faster and more efficient hotel service. The current study extends their study by adding six more items to measure hotel internal business process: customer background information compilation, hotel management efficiency enhancement, hotel product innovation and uniqueness, time reduction of the operation cycle, time reduction for handling customer complaints and an effective problem-solving percentage.

The current study provides results that are different from those obtained by Winata (2005) who reported no relationship between engagement in business collaboration and learning and innovation performance in the Indonesian manufacturing industry. This may be because the hotel industry has a different focus—such as a greater emphasis on the development of skills in its human resources—from that of the manufacturing industry, whose focus is more on improving the production process. Furthermore, the tourism industry (including hotels) is a highly integrated industry where there are almost no boundaries between the major players (hotels, airlines, travel agents, tour operators; Go and Appelman 2001; Poon 1993). Consequently, hotels need to engage in business collaboration with other players to survive in the global market. The results of the current study also offer empirical evidence to support Cheng et al.'s (2004) study, which proposed a model to explain the relationship between business collaboration employee satisfaction and commitment. It also supports Pansiri's (2009) statement that hotels need to engage in business collaboration with their suppliers, customers or competitors to survive in the highly competitive market.

The results of the current study support Espino-Rodriguez and Padron-Robaina's (2004) study, which revealed a positive relationship between outsourcing and hotel non-financial performance (measured by the hotel activity index). The current study also supports Ozturen and Sevil's (2009) study, which found a significant and positive relationship between supply chain practices (hotel relations with its partners, such as suppliers, travel intermediaries and customers) and hotel performance (market share, average annual sales growth, customer satisfaction, customer loyalty and quality of hotels' products). However, none of those studies measured the relationship between business collaboration and social–environmental performance. The current study did. The results also confirmed a previous study by Gil et al. (2001) who found that the application of environmental management techniques is more likely to be associated with high ranking (four- and five-star) hotels. By engaging in business collaboration, hotels may learn from their alliance partners' experience about how to improve their performance, based on social and environmental perspectives, to sustain their existence in Indonesia's highly competitive market.

There were three limitations in this study. The first limitation was that the sample size was relatively small (85 respondents). Future research should extend the population as well as the sample size to improve the generalisability of the results. Second, the current study focused on four- and five-star hotels. Data collected from lower hotel categories would expand understanding of the topic. Further, application of the theoretical model proposed by the current study to other service industries such as banking or the health industry would enrich the current literature related to corporate sustainability in this field. Finally, the hotel industry in the developing country of Indonesia was selected as the object of the current study. Replicating it for similar studies in other countries would be beneficial to test its applicability and make any necessary modifications.

References

Abernethy MA, Lilis AM (1995) The impact of manufacturing flexibility on management control system design. Acc Organ Soc 20(4):241–258

Afsah S, Laplante B, Makarim N (1996) Program-based pollution control management: the Indonesian PROKASIH program. Asian J Environ Manag 4(2):75–93

Afsah S, Blackman A, Ratunanda D (2000) How do public disclosure pollution control programs work? Evidence from Indonesia. Resource for the future discussion paper, 44

Anand BN, Khanna T (2000) Do firms learn to create value? The case of alliances. Strateg Manag J 21(3):295–315
Atkinson H, Brander BJ (2000) Performance measurement systems in the UK hotel industry: rethinking the folly of measuring the wrong things? In: Proceedings of the ninth annual CHME hospitality research conference, University of Huddersfield
Atkinson H, Brown J (2001) Rethinking performance measures: assessing progress in UK hotels. Int J Contemp Hosp Manag 13(3):128–135
Avci U, Madanoglu M, Okumus F (2011) Strategic orientation and performance of tourism firms: evidence from a developing country. Tour Manag 32(1):147–157
Bader EE (2005) Sustainable hotel business practices. J Retail Leis Prop 5(1):70–77
Bohdanowicz P, Martinac I (2007) Determinants and benchmarking of resource consumption in hotels—case study of Hilton International and Scandic in Europe. Energ Buildings 39(1):82–95
Boo HC, Mattila AS (2002) A hotel restaurant brand alliance model: antecedents and consequences. J Food Serv Bus Res 5(2):5–23
Brown JB, McDonnell B (1995) The balanced scorecard: short-term guest or long-term resident? Int J Contemp Hosp Manag 7(2/3):7–11
Bucklin LP, Sengupta S (1993) Organizing successful co-marketing alliances. J Mark 57(2):32–46
Chan ESW (2008) Barriers to EMS in the hotel industry. Int J Hosp Manag 27(2):187–196
Chathoth PK (2008) Strategic alliances in the hospitality industry. In: Olsen M, Zhao J (eds) Handbook of hospitality strategic management. Routledge, New York, pp 215–231
Chathoth PK, Olsen MD (2003) Strategic alliances: a hospitality industry perspective. Hosp Manag 22(4):419–434
Chen F-H, Hsu T-S, Tzeng G-H (2011) A balanced scorecard approach to establish a performance evaluation and relationship model for hot spring hotels based on a hybrid MCDM model combining DEMATEL and ANP. Int J Hosp Manag 30(4):908–932
Cheng EWL, Li H, Love PED, Irani Z (2004) Strategic alliances: a model for establishing long-term commitment to inter-organizational relations in construction. Build Environ 39(4):459–468
Chenhall RH, Morris D (1986) The impact of structure, environment, and interdependence on the perceived usefulness of management accounting systems. Account Rev 61(1):16–35
Chin WW (1998) The partial least square approach for structural equation modelling. In: Marcoulides GA (ed) Modern methods for business research. Lawrence Erlbaum Associates, Mahwah, pp 295–336
Chung LH, Parker LD (2008) Integrating hotel environmental srategies with management control: a structuration approach. Bus Strateg Environ 17(4):272–286
Clarke A, Chen W (2007) International hospitality management: concepts and cases. Elsevier, Oxford
Claver-Cortes E, Molina-Azorin JF, Pereira-Moliner J, Lopez-Gamero MD (2007) Environmental strategies and their impact on hotel performance. J Sustain Tour 15(6):663–679
Contractor FJ, Lorange P (2002) The growth of alliances in the knowledge-based economy. Int Bus Rev 11(4):485–502
Das TK, Teng B (2000) A resource-based theory of strategic alliances. J Manag 26(1):31–61
Denton GA, White B (2000) Implementing a balanced-scorecard approach to managing hotel operations. Cornell Hotel Restaur Admin Q 41(1):94–107
Dess GG, Robinson RB (1984) Measuring organizational performance in the absence of objective measures: the case of the privately-held firm and conglomerate business unit. Strateg Manag J 5(3):265–273
Dev CS, Brown JR, Zhou KZ (2007) Global brand expansion: how to select a market entry strategy. Cornell Univ 48(1):13–27
Draulans J, deMan A, Volberda HW (2003) Building alliance capability: management techniques for superior alliance performance. Long Range Plan 36(2):151–166
Elkington J (1998) Partnerships from cannibals with forks: the triple bottom line of 21st- century business. Environ Qual Manag 8(1):37–52

Epstein MJ (2008) Making sustanability work: best practices in managing and measuring corporate social, environmental and economic impacts. Greenleaf Publishing Ltd, Sheffield
Epstein MJ, Roy M (2003) Linking social and environmental actions to financial performance. J Corp Citizensh 9(1):79–96
Epstein MJ, Wisner PS (2001) Using a balanced scorecard to implement sustainability. Environ Qual Manag 11(2):1–10
Espino-Rodriguez TF, Padron-Robaina V (2004) Outsourcing and its impact on operational objectives and performance: a study of hotels in the Canary Islands. Int J Hosp Manag 23(3):287–306
Evans N (2005) Assessing the balanced scorecard as a management tool for hotels. Int J Contemp Hosp Manag 17(5):376–390
Figge F, Hahn T, Schaltegger S, Wagner M (2002) The sustainability balanced scorecard—linking sustainability management to business strategy. Bus Strateg Environ 11(5):269–284
Font X (2002) Environmental certification in tourism and hospitality: progress, process and prospects. Tour Manag 23(3):197–205
Garrigos-Simon FJ, Marques DP (2005) Competitive strategies and performance in Spanish hospitality firms. Int J Contemp Hosp Manag 17(1):22–38
Gatignon H, Deshpande R (1994) Competitive analysis. Mark Lett 5(3):271–287
Geller AN (1985) Tracking the critical success factors for hotel companies. Cornell HRA Q 25(4):76–81
Gil MJA, Jimenez JB, Lorente JJC (2001) An analysis of environmental management, organizational context and performance of Spanish hotels. Int J Manag Sci 29(6):457–471
Go FM, Appelman J (2001) Achieving global competitiveness in SMEs by building trust in interfirm alliances. In: Wahab S, Cooper C (eds) Tourism in the age of globalisation. Routledge, London, pp 183–197
Gray R, Bebbington J (2000) Environmental accounting, managerialism and sustainability: is the planet safe in the hands of business and accounting? Adv Environ Acc Manag 1(1):1–44
Hair JF, Black WC, Babin BJ, Anderson RE, Tatham RL (2010) Multivariate data analysis, 7th edn. Pearson Education, Upper Saddle River
Hair JF, Ringle CM, Sarstedt M (2011) PLS-SEM: indeed a silver bullet. J Mark Theory Pract 19(2):139–151
Haktanir M, Harris P (2005) Performance measurement practice in an independent hotel context: a case study approach. Int J Contemp Hosp Manag 17(1):39–50
Halim (2010) Jamsostek has yet to run optimally. Available from http://www.beritajakarta.com/english/NewsView.asp?ID=17607. Accessed 3 May 2016
Harris PJ, Brown JB (1998) Research and development in hospitality accounting and financial management. Int J Hosp Manag 17(2):161–181
Harris PJ, Mongiello M (2001) Key performance indicators in European hotel properties: general managers' choices and company profiles. Int J Contemp Hosp Manag 13(3):120–127
Hayes RH, Abernathy WJ (1980) Managing our way to economic decline. Harv Bus Rev 58(4):67–77
Herold DM, Manwa F, Sen S, Wilde S (2016) It's the yeast we can do: untapping sustainability trends in Australian craft breweries. J Asia Entrep Sustain 12(2):82
Hofstede G (1980) Culture's consequences: international differences in work-related values. Sage, Beverly Hills
Holcomb JL, Upchurch RS, Okumus F (2007) Corporate social responsibility: what are top hotel companies reporting? Int J Contemp Hosp Manag 19(6):461–475
Hoque Z (2004) A contingency model of the association between strategy, environmental uncertainty and performance measurement: impact on organizational performance. Int Bus Rev 13(4):485–502
Hoque Z, James W (2000) Linking balanced scorecard measures to size and market factors: Impact on organizational performance. J Manag Account Res 12(1):1–17
Hubbard G, Rice J, Beamish P (2008) Strategic management: thinking, analysis, action, 3rd edn. Pearson Education, Sydney

Hulland J (1999) Use of partial least squares (PLS) in strategic management research: a review of four recent studies. Strateg Manag J 20(2):195–204
Jennings DF, Rajaratnam D, Lawrence FB (2003) Strategy-performance relationships in service firms: a test for equifinality. J Manag Issues 15(2):208–220
Kaplan RS, Norton DP (1992) The balanced scorecard-measures that drive performance. Harv Bus Rev 70(1):71–79
Kaplan RS, Norton DP (1996) The balanced scorecard: translating strategy into action. Harvard Business School Press, Boston
Kaplan RS, Norton DP (2001) The strategy-focused organization. Harvard Business School Press, Boston
Kemp M (2001) Corporate social responsibility in Indonesia: quixotic dream or confident expectation? United Nations Research Institute for Social Development, Geneva
Lambe CJ, Spekman RE, Hunt SD (2002) Alliance competence, resources, and alliance success: conceptualization, measurement, and initial test. J Acad Mark Sci 30(2):141–158
Larcker DF (1981) The perceived importance of selected information characteristics for strategic capital budgeting. Account Rev 56(3):519–528
Lawson B, Petersen KJ, Cousins PD, Handfield RB (2009) Knowledge sharing in interorganizational product development teams: the effect of formal and informal socialization mechanisms. J Prod Innov Manag 26(2):156–172
Lee K-H, Herold DM (2016) Small and medium enterprises and corporate social responsibility practice: a Swedish perspective. Corp Soc Responsib Environ Manag 23(2):88–99
Li H, Atuahene-Gima K (2001) Product innovation strategy and the performance of new technology ventures in China. Acad Manag J 44(6):1123–1134
Lo VHY, Yeung AHW (2004) Practical framework for strategic alliance in Pearl River Delta manufacturing supply chain: a total quality approach. Int J Prod Econ 87(3):231–240
Luo X, Rindfleisch A, Tse DK (2007) Working with rivals: the impact of competitor alliances on financial performance. J Mark Res 44(1):73–83
Maurer TJ, Pierce HR (1998) A comparison of Likert scale and traditional measures of self efficacy. J Appl Psychol 83(2):324–329
Mensah I (2006) Environmental management practices among hotels in the greater Accra region. Int J Hosp Manag 25(3):414–431
Mia L, Patiar A (2001) The use of management accounting systems in hotels: an exploratory study. Hosp Manag 20(2):111–128
Ministry of Tourism (2015) Laporan akuntabilitas kinerja kementerian pariwisata tahun 2015. Available from http://www.kemenpar.go.id/userfiles/file/test/LAKIP-KEMENPAR%202015.pdf. Accessed 2 Nov 2016
Molina-Azorin JF, Claver-Cortes E, Pereira-Moliner J, Tari JJ (2009) Environmental practices and firm performance: an empirical analysis in the Spanish hotel industry. J Clean Prod 17(5):516–524
Monczka RM, Petersen KJ, Handfield RB, Ragatz GL (1998) Success factors in strategic supplier alliances: the buying company perspective. Decis Sci 29(3):553–577
Moorman C (1995) Organizational market information processes: cultural antecedents and new product outcomes. J Mark Res 32(3):318–335
Nasution HN, Mavondo FT (2008) Customer value in the hotel industry: what managers believe they deliver and what customer experience. Int J Hosp Manag 27(2):204–213
Ozturen A, Sevil G (2009) Supply chain management as a sustainable performance booster for the accommodation enterprises: evidence from North Cyprus tourism sector. Int J Bus Manag 4(2):97–111
Pansiri J (2009) Strategic motives for alliance formation in the travel sector of tourism. Int J Hosp Tour Adm 10(2):143–173
Parkhe A (1991) Interfirm diversity, organizational learning, and longevity in global strategic alliances. J Int Bus Stud 22(4):579–601

Patiar A, Mia L (2008) The interactive effect of market competition and use of MAS information on performance: evidence from the upscale hotels. J Hosp Tour Res 32(2):209–234
Patiar A, Mia L (2009) Transformational leadership style, market competitions and departmental performance: evidence from luxury hotels in Australia. Int J Hosp Manag 28(2):254–262
Pembaruan S (2011) Green hotel award menjadi nilai tambah standar pelayanan hotel. Available from http://www.suarapembaruan.com/home/green-hotel-award-jadi-nilai-tambah-standar-pelayanan-hotel/15036. Accessed 5 May 2016
Perrini F, Tencati A (2006) Sustainability and stakeholder management: the need for new corporate performance evaluation and reporting systems. Bus Strateg Environ 15(5):296–308
Picard M (1997) Cultural tourism, nation-building, and regional culture: the making of a Balinese identity. In: Picard M, Wood RE (eds) Tourism, ethnicity, and the state in Asian and Pacific societies. University of Hawaii Press, Honolulu, pp 181–214
Poon A (1993) Tourism, technology, and competitive strategies. CAB International, Wallingford
Preble JF, Reichel A, Hoffman RC (2000) Strategic alliances for competitive advantage: evidence from Israel's hospitality and tourism industry. Int J Hosp Manag 19(3):327–341
Rindfleisch A, Moorman C (2003) Interfirm cooperation and customer orientation. J Mark Res 40(4):421–436
Sarkar MB, Echambadi RAJ, Harrison JS (2001) Alliance entrepreneurship and firm market performance. Strateg Manag J 22(6–7):701–711
Schaltegger S, Wagner M (2006) Integrative management of sustainability performance, measurement, and reporting. Int J Account Audit Perform Eval 3(1):1–19
Shrader RC (2001) Collaboration and performance in foreign markets: the case of young high-technology manufacturing firms. Acad Manag J 44(1):45–60
Sitawati R (2004) Strategic motive and partner selection criteria in international joint ventures from Dutch and Indonesian perspectives. Hanzehogeschool and Anglia Ruskin University
Sparks B, Weber K (2008) The service encounter. In: Jones P (ed) Handbook of hospitality operations and IT. Elsevier, Oxford, pp 109–138
Teddlie C, Tashakkori A (2003) Major issues and controversies in the use of mixed methods in the social and behavioral sciences. In: Tashakkori A, Teddlie C (eds) Handbook of mixed methods in social & bchavioral research. Sage, Thousand Oaks, pp 3–50
Teece DJ (1992) Competition, cooperation, and innovation: organizational arrangements for regimes of rapid technological progress. J Econ Behav Organ 18(1):1–25
Tietenberg T, Wheeler D (1998) Empowering the community: information strategies for pollution control. World Bank Group, Washington, DC. Available from http://documents.worldbank.org/curated/en/431471468147870698/Empowering-the-community-information-strategies-for-pollution-control. Accessed 5 Apr 2015
Triandis HC (1995) Individualism and collectivism. Westview Press, Colorado
Winata LR (2005) Manufacturing automation, strategic alliance, information technology and organisational performance: evidence from Indonesia. Griffith University
Winata L, Mia L (2005) Information technology and the performance effect of managers' participation in budgeting: evidence from the hotel industry. Int J Hosp Manag 24(1):21–29
World H (1982) Systems under indirect observation using PLS. In: Fornell C (ed) A second generation of multivariate analysis, vol 1. Praeger, New York, pp 325–347
World Bank (2006) Environment matters: East Asia and Pacific region. Available from http://siteresources.worldbank.org/inteapregtopenvironment/resources/envmattersEAP06.pdf. Accessed 25 July 2015
Wright WF (1977) Self insight into the cognitive processing of financial information. Acc Organ Soc 2(4):323–331

Chapter 7
Final Ecosystem Services for Corporate Metrics and Performance

Charles Rhodes, John Finisdore, Anthony Dvarskas, Joël Houdet, Joel Corona, and Simone Maynard

Abstract Ecosystem services approaches are material to business performance. However, the lack of sufficiently detailed and commonly used ecosystem services classification systems prevents companies from benefitting fully from them. The *final ecosystem services perspective*, embodied by the Final Ecosystem Goods and Services Classification System (FEGS-CS) and the National Ecosystem Services Classification System (NESCS), offers a way through key bottlenecks to mainstreaming ecosystem services in corporate decision-making and accounting. Compared to other systems, these are easier to use, improve materiality analysis, and aid stakeholder engagement. In addition, their potential to improve the accuracy of valuation makes them preferable for natural capital accounting. Companies that adopt this final ecosystem services (FES) perspective are likely to gain these

C. Rhodes (✉)
U.S. EPA Office of Water, Washington, DC, USA
e-mail: charlesrrhodes@gmail.com

J. Finisdore
African Centre for Technology Studies (ACTS), Albert Luthuli Centre for Responsible Leadership – University of Pretoria (ALCRL – UP) and Synegriz, Johannesburg, South Africa
e-mail: John@SustainableFlows.com

A. Dvarskas
Stony Brook University, Stony Brook, NY, USA
e-mail: Anthony@SustainableFlows.com

J. Houdet
African Centre for Technology Studies (ACTS), Albert Luthuli Centre for Responsible Leadership – University of Pretoria (ALCRL – UP) and Synegriz, Johannesburg, South Africa
e-mail: j.houdet@iss-za.com

J. Corona
ORISE post-doctoral research fellow, participating at U.S. EPA Office of Water, Washington, DC, USA
e-mail: Corona.Joel@epa.gov

S. Maynard
Simone Maynard Consulting, Brisbane, QLD, Australia
e-mail: maynardsimone@gmail.com

K.-H. Lee, S. Schaltegger (eds.), *Accounting for Sustainability: Asia Pacific Perspectives*, Eco-Efficiency in Industry and Science 33,
https://doi.org/10.1007/978-3-319-70899-7_7

immediate benefits and first-mover advantage, as this FES perspective is poised to become standard practice.

Keywords Corporate performance · Ecosystem services · Final ecosystem services · Natural capital accounting · Business applications · Corporate sustainability · CSR · Environment · Natural resources · Sustainable accounting · Environmental risk

7.1 Ecosystem Services and Corporate Performance

An emerging consensus in sustainability accounting involves the terms *natural capital* and *ecosystem services*.[1] A basic understanding is that natural capital comprises stocks of natural assets, from which flows of ecosystem services contribute to benefits to people (See Fig. 7.1). For example, a forest is a subset of natural capital that provides timber for industry, while also purifying water for drinking, and offering a place for recreation.

Whether securing inputs of raw materials, managing soil for agriculture, or utilizing wetlands to mitigate the impacts from storms, companies depend on natural capital and the ecosystem services that flow from them. Changes in natural capital therefore impact business performance (see Table 7.1 for types of risks and opportunities). Some of the impacts are direct (such as changes in inputs to production) while others are more indirect (such as consumer preference shifts toward sustainable products, or the environmental effects on a surrounding community from site management). Reports[2] and case examples demonstrate their materiality (see Box 7.1).

Going a step further, the recently launched Science Based Targets initiative (SBTi 2017) demonstrates that corporate interest extends past near-term financial impacts. SBTi sets corporate targets within planetary boundaries. Carbon emissions are the present focus of SBTi, but their work is expanding into ecosystem services (Putt del Pino et al. 2016).

Firms select collect and report measurements relevant to decision-making. The ecosystem services paradigm intends to reveal and document human dependence on nature more discretely than past approaches. The paradigm is used for ecosystem services mapping, assessment, policy analysis, and accounting/recording. Achieving these paradigm objectives requires a process of identifying variables to include, selecting what to measure, and determining the best methodology for collecting measurements. Generally this process includes an attempt to estimate values for some of the ecosystem services. As the field matures, formalization and a thoughtful approach to each of the critical steps – identification, quantification, and valuation – will begin to pay off in larger ways.

[1] The views expressed in this chapter are those of the authors and do not necessarily represent the views or policies of the U.S. Environmental Protection Agency. The author team thanks Dr. Dixon Landers, Michael Trombley, anonymous chapter reviewers, and Dr. Ki-Hoon Lee for helpful comments.

[2] Porter and van der Linde (1996), Porter and Kramer (2011), Eccles et al. (2014), CDSB (2015) and Natural Capital Protocol (2016).

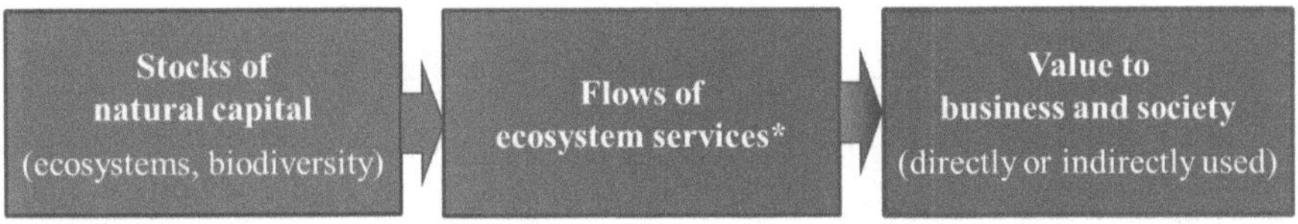

Fig. 7.1 Natural capital stock, flows, and value (Adapted from the Natural Capital Coalition's *Natural Capital Protocol* 2016)
*In the Natural Capital Protocol, "abiotic services" are flows from fundamental geological processes, including mineral ores, and these abiotic services are included alongside ecosystem service flows. The term is used differently by other references in this chapter

Table 7.1 Ecosystem-services-based opportunities and risks

Type	Opportunity	Risk
Operational	Increased efficiency and savings	Increase in scarcity and cost of inputs
		Disruption to operations
Regulatory and legal	Improved licensing processes	Extraction restrictions
	Services and products that meet new regulations	Fines, fees, and lawsuits
	Opportunities to influence public policies	Permitting and quota challenges
Reputational	Brand differentiation	Harm to brand or image
		Difficulty with "license to operate"
Market and product	Product and service innovations	Changes in customer preferences
	Market opportunities from certification	
	Markets for ecosystem services	
Financing	Investment from progressive leaders and socially responsible funds	Steeper lending requirements and capital costs

Adapted from Hanson et al. (2008)

The final ecosystem services (FES) perspective intends to narrow attention to goods and services from nature that directly affect people. The FES perspective can inform enable or focus a number of the steps needed for a sustainable approach to business.

Access to and/or use of these ecosystem services can be paid for by companies, received free of charge, or received at a steep discount, depending on the policy and legal environment. For example, water is often priced well below its true value. The heretofore unaccounted values that natural capital provides do impact the financial performance of business by creating both risks and opportunities (see Table 7.1). Impairment or destruction of natural capital, especially when it imposes spillover effects, can impose large (even if currently hidden) costs on an economy. TruCost PLC estimates that with a 2010 total of $3.7 trillion, 50% of unpaid natural capital costs globally may be attributed in Asia, and notes that allowing these unpaid costs to continue creates "perverse market incentives for unsustainable business" (TruCost PLC 2013).

Box 7.1: Case Examples of Natural Capital and Business Performance (WEF and PwC 2010)
General

- Water scarcity and biodiversity loss ranked as top risks by chief executive officers in 2010.
- Twenty seven percent of chief executive officers surveyed were extremely or somewhat concerned about biodiversity loss in 2010.
- Russia's Transneft pipeline project incurred delays and US$1 billion in additional costs due to the proximity of the pipeline to habitat of the endangered Amur Leopard.
- The gradual proliferation of ecologically certified materials by organisations such as the Marine Stewardship Council (MSC), Forest Stewardship Council, and Rainforest Alliance are indicative of the changing consumer demand for 'biodiversity-friendly' products. Consumer sales of these certified products are growing rapidly; sales of MSC-labelled products worldwide grew by 67% from April 2008 to March 2009.

Asia Pacific Region and Beyond

- In 2008, the Norwegian Pension Fund withdrew its £500 million stake in the mining giant Rio Tinto and excluded the company from its funds. The decision to withdraw was based on the activities of Rio Tinto's mining operations in Indonesia.
- Deforestation in the Agno River basin in the Philippines caused siltation, forcing the Binga hydroelectric facility to operate intermittently.
- Measures to control deforestation and conversion of forest to soy and palm oil production may significantly increase the prices of commodity soybeans and palm oil.
- The world's largest retailer, Walmart, will now only purchase farmed shrimp certified to Global Aquaculture Alliance standards, and has recently pledged to source only wild-caught fresh and frozen fish for North American stores from fisheries certified by the Marine Stewardship Council.

To address the different risks and opportunities in Table 7.1, companies have integrated natural capital accounting into a variety of business applications. Business applications generally represent these risks using a suite of indicators. The indicators can be qualitative or quantitative depending on the method used, needs of decision-makers, and data available. For example, the Lean Six Sigma method incorporates efficiency into the process of reducing production errors (McCarty et al. 2011), so could yield cost comparisons of different water-filtering technologies (e.g., deionizer, reverse osmosis, membrane filtration, wetland) or of a combination of these technologies (e.g., membrane filtration with a wetland for tertiary treatment). Alternatively, a more qualitative megatrends analysis may reveal long-term water shortages regionally, indicating that a company explore this trend in more depth. Regardless of the degree of quantification, using the right terms and classification of natural capital and ecosystem services matters.

7.1.1 Natural Capital and Ecosystem Services: Terms with Unrealized Potential to Highlight Business Risks and Opportunities

The terms natural capital and ecosystem services (ES) were proposed to bridge understanding between ecologists and social scientists, and to offer a framework for characterizing stocks and flows associated with human impacts and dependencies on the processes and provisions of nature. The terms were not generally known in corporate sustainability circles before *Nature's Services – Societal Dependence on Natural Ecosystems* (Daily 1997). That same year, the first attempt to value a critical set of the world's ES (Constanza et al. 1997) estimated global ecosystem services at US$16–54 trillion (averaged to US$33 trillion per year), when the global GNP was estimated at US$18 trillion annually.

These two efforts helped spur the Millennium Ecosystem Assessment (MA; MA 2005a; summary for business and industry: MA 2005b 2). The MA was a US$24 million effort involving 1300 experts and producing thousands of published pages that document the impact of human activities on natural systems globally. The MA effort projected how negative impacts could constrain human development, and added a new dimension to the corporate lexicon. Ecosystem services were soon promoted as a means to more fully integrate the risks and opportunities posed by ecosystem change into business applications. Moving beyond vague references to ecological functions, explicitly delineating ecosystem services offers a means of tracking business risks and opportunities to and from the natural environment (Bishop et al. 2012).

Despite an understanding of how ES perspectives can improve corporate performance, the ES paradigm has not been widely adopted in business applications. Reasons include:

- *Competing agendas and limited capacity*—Managers struggle to meet various environmental requirements with limited budgets and staff. International agreements and resource shortages take precedence over building new metrics and valuation systems.
- *Legal and regulatory uncertainty*—Ecosystem services is now a term in state, national, and internal deliberations, but few rules have been codified. This creates uncertainty and fear – misplaced or not – about how ES will be interpreted legally. The U.S. experience with Natural Resource Damage Assessments, the Deepwater Horizon oil spill being one example, paints a costly picture of what ES can mean to corporate bottom lines (Houdet and Germaneau 2011).

- *Unclear definitions of related environmental aspects*—Biodiversity, ecosystems, ecosystem services, and natural capital are often used interchangeably, and therefore imprecisely. This confusion may create the expectation that any effort to distinguish these terms has little utility.
- *Metrics, biophysical modeling, and valuation techniques can be difficulty to apply and are not applied uniformly*—Cross-disciplinary challenges associated with identifying, selecting, and measuring ecosystem services include complex ecological modeling of how ecosystems produce services, determining uses and users of the services, selecting appropriate metrics, and finally determining a value for these services to the users. Charting a reproducible course through these four components is a data-dependent, time-consuming process. Budgets and deadlines drive estimations and the choice of methods that meet decision-making needs, but do not drive the science forward.
- *Data shortages*—Accurate ecological production functions that describe how natural capital provides goods and services that people use (e.g., how wetlands and oyster beds reduce subsidence) require a great deal of ecological and economic data. Because most data for building the ecological component of production functions is collected on the ground rather than from remote observational data, it tends to be in short supply.

These shortcomings call for new accounting techniques to address them. A simplified example of such a technique would assume large errors in biophysical modeling and apply greater financial sensitivity analysis to decisions. Until more data and widely accepted principles are available, applying heuristics (learning or problem solving using a practical and sufficient short-cut) can help. Simply requiring a higher internal price (shadow price) for water or carbon in capital investment ledgers reduces the risk of underestimation in biophysical modeling (Topping et al. 2015). Similarly, multi-criteria stakeholder analysis can help balance the inaccuracy of measurement by including opinions from experts and stakeholders. When analyzing agricultural systems, land rental rates have been used to estimate the value of ecosystem services supporting crop growth (GTAP 6 data base 2006).

Some of these measurement and reporting challenges may best be addressed by improving how ecosystem services are defined. Definitions that distinguish between the existence of natural capital, the flows of services, and their value (as in Fig. 7.1), provide clearer boundaries for measuring ES and their impact on corporate performance.

7.2 Evolving from Grouping of Ecosystem Services to an Effective Identification Strategy

With the global promotion of ecosystem services spurred by the MA, four general types of ecosystem services began to be widely used:

- *Supporting services*—the natural processes that underlie and maintain other ecosystem services (e.g., nutrient cycling, primary production);
- *Provisioning services*—the goods or products from ecosystems used by people (e.g., water, timber, food);
- *Regulating services*—the benefits people receive from an ecosystem functioning to regulate natural processes (e.g., erosion control, temperance of flooding);
- *Cultural services*—the nonmaterial human benefits from ecosystems (e.g., recreation, inspiration) (MA 2005).

Within the MA four types, the "Supporting services" are deeper-cycling background processes in the environment that are set in the typology at a separate precursory level. They precede in function and enable the existence of Provisioning, Regulating, and Cultural services that link through various paths directly to "determinants and constituents of (human) well-being". The MA four types represented useful progress over a simple listing of ES, but the MA itself cautioned against considering the 1-and-3 grouping to be a classification or an exhaustive list of ES (Reid et al. 2003).

Embracing the progress and needing a way to qualify and define ES, public sector applications and corporate guidance documents referred to or used the MA-based four types as a classification system in publications.[3] The UN Environment Programme's The Economics of Ecosystems and Biodiversity (TEEB) used the MA types but cautioned that ecosystem services should not be equated with "benefits", because benefits to humans routinely involve combining ecosystem services with economically produced inputs (Bishop et al. 2012). TEEB then split out a 22-ecosystem-service "typology" (Bishop et al. 2012) within its direct assimilation of the four types. A few years later, the Common International Classification of Ecosystem Services (CICES, Haines-Young and Potschin 2013) doubled the number of services in the TEEB, but referred to the MA as a "typology" and not as a classification, noting that CICES offers a developed hierarchical structure for classifying ES.

The MA four types, while popular as a top-level sorting mechanism, did not offer definitions meeting certain economic and accounting needs. Accountants must consider that MA-based classification systems (TEEB and CICES) treat multiple points along a continuum of ecological production to be separate ecosystem services. This can invite cloudy classification boundaries and double-counting problems.

Other efforts were underway to further differentiate the broad notion of *ecosystem services* into (a) intra- and inter-ecosystem processes and functions (sometimes referred to as *intermediate ecosystem services*), and (b) *final ecosystem services* that directly enter the realm of human well-being (Boyd and Banzhaf 2007). Boyd and Banzhaf sought when defining ES to separate intermediate processes of an ecological system from elements that contribute to economic benefits, precisely to avoid the risk of double-counting benefits in economic accounting.

[3] The Corporate Ecosystem Services Review, Hanson et al. (2008); The Guide to Corporate Ecosystem Valuation, WBCSD 2010; the IFC Performance Standards, IFC 2012; IPIECA's Ecosystem Services Guidance: Biodiversity and Ecosystem Services Guide, IPIECA 2011; and the IUCN French Committee's Corporate Biodiversity Reporting and Indicators, IUCN French Committee 2014.

FES are defined at the point where the ecological product transitions from being predominately ecological to being an input that will often be mixed with man-made capital to produce an economic benefit. For example, if a fish hatches lives and dies in a remote lake or ocean trench, there is no direct human use or *service* to be had. There are billions of ecological relationships among phytoplankton, fungi, flora, fauna, and ecological features like biodiversity, water availability, and available carbon. Accounting for all interactions is unlikely to aid decision-making. A few ES generally weigh heavier on outcomes.

The FES perspective is practically implemented by focusing on the exact point where *ecological endpoints* are assigned an identity unique from the cycles and surroundings that made them. It is through human use or appreciation that an ecological element becomes an *endpoint* from the ecological point of view, because it enters the realm of human value. This is not then an intrinsic value, but what humans name because we use or appreciate it. The ecosystem service is then not just anything in nature, but is the transactional relationship between a human and an ecological endpoint (as a restaurant server's transactional relationship with a customer is a "food service"). This transaction yields *(ecosystem service) benefits*, which are the values for ecosystem services that pass directly to someone appreciating an ecological endpoint, or that pass into a product that also includes human-produced elements.

Consider that for a ready wild stock of ocean fish to make it to market, a boat, fishing supplies, fuel, and labor are needed. Only with the fisher's produced inputs and labor can the fish yield an ecosystem services benefit to the fisher or an *economic benefit* to a final consumer. In this example, the transition point occurs when the fish is *catchable* by the fisher. The transition point – from the ecological perspective to the economy, which is the transaction point from the economic perspective – is also determined by who is using the ecosystem service. To the fisher, the smaller creatures that his target fish eats are intermediate ecosystem services, but to a different fisher who harvests the smaller ones for bait, the ready catchability of these wild smaller fish are a final ecosystem service.

These same wild ocean fish depend on numerous environmental structures processes and functions, from habitat quality to nutrient cycling. Understanding these *ecological production functions* for this fish (/ecological endpoint), helps analysts gather appropriate data to predict dynamics in the fish population size, distribution, and individual quality. A focus on FES never ignores deeper ecological production processes nor the web of ecological relationships, it simply defines the endpoints.

Wild flowers are the product of an ecological production function, part of which was eons in the making, and part of which is weeks in the making. A person may find cut box and sell these wildflowers, but of course pays no money to "Nature" for the FES benefits the *picker* derives. The buyer of the boxed flowers receives no FES, because the FES has already been counted into the economy through the flower collector.

As defined here, FES are not marketed. Transaction quantities and values for FES tend to be unknown, as do common contextual elements of value such as those that impact the "value" for an economic good or service (e.g., individual and socially influenced preferences, scarcity, substitutability by other inputs, and access to use). Estimating quantities and values for flows of particular FES may well involve assumptions or modeling more complex and with more uncertainty than calculating estimating or modeling prices and quantities for economic transactions. Precisely defining the characteristics of a final ES can separate elements relevant to the estimation of value. Taking the extra step to characterize a flow of FES by the use and user of the ecological endpoint offers precision in the identification of flows that helps in the selection of more precise metrics – leaving less room for misspecification in sustainability accounting.

Understanding who uses or appreciates FES and how they are using an ecological endpoint, i.e., the "supply" and "demand" context, largely defines the FES perspective, providing an important distinction between ES classifications (Landers et al. 2016). The MA, TEEB, and CICES approaches do not internally include classifications of beneficiaries, or expressly match to them. Generating rigorous precise and reproducible results within the ecosystem services paradigm suggests use of a formal FES classification system, so it is worth considering which criteria qualify the most effective systems (see Box 7.2).

Box 7.2: What Makes for an Effective ES Classification System?

A classification is a system and process for grouping things according to shared properties, qualities, or characteristics. Ranking classified elements within a hierarchy is a powerful and common method for organizing categories. Commonly known hierarchical classifications include the taxonomic ranking system for species (Kingdom, Phylum, Class, Order…) and the International Standard Industrial Classification System (sector, subsector…).

Applying principles of classification and known and consistent rules can make an ES classification appealing for accounting – results are as clear and reproducible as possible.*

Essential elements of an ES classification useful for sustainable accounting:

- *Exhaustive and Mutually Exclusive*—can uniquely classify all types of ecological endpoints (products or inputs from nature, not humans) that humans use or appreciate, allowing that judgment of business impact is a secondary process;
- *Non-Duplicative*—focuses attention and measurement on final ecosystem services (versus ecological structures processes and functions), to avoid double-counting.

Appealing elements of an ES classification useful for sustainable accounting:

- *Practical for Users*—separates and groups candidate elements using clear definitions and hierarchies that allow for breaking out or aggregation, offering easy-to-track and reproducible results, without fuzzy classification boundaries, or unnecessary complexity;

(continued)

Box 7.2 (continued)

- *Helpful for Selecting Appropriate Metrics*—identifies key value-relevant elements for precise flows of FES, including beneficiaries, and how they use the ecological endpoints;
- *Appropriate to be a Standard*—is stable, its rules for use well-explained, and it is practical enough to serve as the standard for many types of applications;
- *Modular*—interfaces with other standard classification systems or ecosystem service tools without extensive exceptions and patching.

* The UN SEEA Central Framework (2012) lays out criteria using most of these concepts in its praise of the UN Food and Agriculture Organization's Land Cover Classification System (page 177 of 347).

7.2.1 FES Classification Systems with Beneficiaries/Users

Following the FES perspective, researchers at the US Environmental Protection Agency developed two classification systems: the Final Ecosystem Services Classification System (FEGS-CS), and the National Ecosystem Services Classification System (NESCS[4]). Both systems include beneficiaries, supporting improved measurement of ecosystem services as they enter the economy, and both allow every FES they identify to be assigned a numeric code linking to aggregable categories in nested hierarchies.[5]

FEGS-CS sub-divides a hierarchy of Environments of the earth, where each type is a complex reservoir of natural capital from which final ecosystem services may be derived (Landers and Nahlik 2013). A two-digit code for characterizing the *Environment* to the sub-class level combines with a four-digit code for characterizing types of *Beneficiaries*, so each set of very similar Final Ecosystem Goods and Services (*FEGS*) carries its own unique six-digit code (see Fig. 7.2). Compared to the MA, TEEB, CICES, or ad-hoc naming of ES, the FEGS-CS methodology tightens the definition of what is counted as a final ES, offering a mechanism for standardization. FEGS-CS identifies 338 relevant types of FEGS (the shorthand "FEGS" is used for the ecological endpoints that link an Environment with a Beneficiary, and separately for the six-digit codes). This goes some way in helping people define useful metrics.

[4]"NESCS" is often vocalized as "nexus" for ease of pronunciation, and to emphasize the tool's intended function of linking ecologic and economic systems.

[5]Practitioners have experimented with creating numeric codes for CICES rows, again to date without a user/beneficiary component. CICES, FEGS-CS, and NESCS all claim to incorporate the essential elements from Box 7.2, and all of the appealing elements (although there is debate among ES classification developers about whether competing systems hold this or that property). It is worth noting that these are the only "formal" (F)ES classifications the authors have discovered, in the sense that other commonly used ES typologies (MA and TEEB) do not claim to incorporate the elements of formal classification listed in Box 7.2, and lack developed (nested) hierarchies that are characteristic of formal classifications. Ad hoc typing of a few ES is a common practice in academic work, but does not attempt to rise to formal classification.

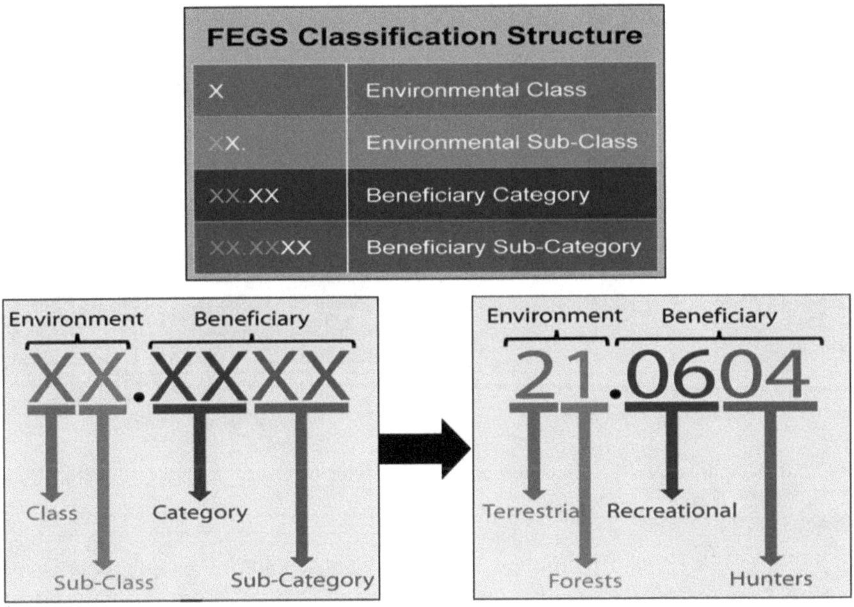

Fig. 7.2 FEGS-CS classification structure with coding example (Landers and Nahlik 2013)

NESCS (USEPA 2015) has a core structure of four classification groups: Environment, Ecological End-Products, Uses, and Users (see Fig. 7.3).[6] NESCS is flexible in identifying potential *Flows of Final Ecosystem Services* (*FFES*), as each of the four groups is a nested hierarchy capable of broad categorization or of further nesting. For a *potential* FFES to be identified using NESCS (only measurement can confirm if there is an *actual* supply from the environment and flow to the economy), there must be a selection from each of the four groups in its structure. This at first appears complex, but this complexity dissolves to a highly useful template for identifying context characteristics relevant to biophysical and valuation measurements. Where, What, Why, and Who are answered by identifying an element from Environment, Ecological End-Products, Uses, and Users in the NESCS structure.

The *Environment* group within NESCS uses the same Environment Classes and Sub-Classes as FEGS-CS. The second group, *Ecological End-Products*, comprises nine ecological endpoint sub-categories, such that every FES will fit in one of these categories.[7] The NESCS third group is *Uses* (of the Ecological End-Products), and the fourth group is the Users. *Users* are Industries, Households, or Government. Because Uses and Users are separate (unlike the coupling of the two in "Beneficiaries"

[6] In this chapter, *ecological endpoints* substitutes for Ecological End-Products as named in the NESCS report, because accountants understand something more specific by "end-*product*" than do ecologists and some economists.

[7] It is not as clear that the MA and TEEB typologies share the properties of exhaustiveness or uniqueness in an adequately rigorous sense within the FES perspective.

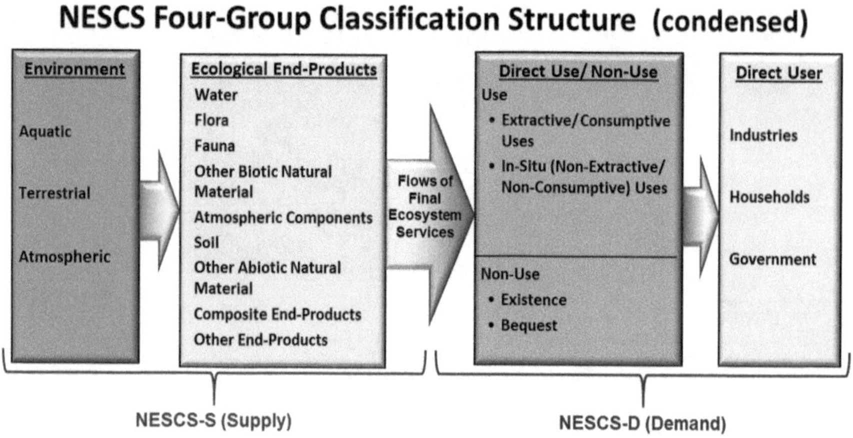

Fig. 7.3 Simplified NESCS classification structure without coding example (Adapted from USEPA 2015, cover)

in FEGS-CS), a User with different Uses of the same ecological endpoint may have multiple unique potential FFES identified, which also holds for different Users having the same Use.

A corporation or government agency using NESCS may find it very useful to add their own nesting level, sub-dividing within classification categories, for different Uses within different operations under the same management (same User at higher levels of sub-class). For U.S. applications, Industries are defined by the North American Industry Classification System (NAICS). NESCS is intentionally modular, in that the Environment classification could be traded out for another classification or typology of environments (land covers, land uses) that produce endpoints that people use or value. Similarly, the NAICS classification could be substituted out for the International Standard Industrial Classification (ISIC) or another industrial classification, plus as in the core structure, the User categories Household and Government. This modularity eases the integration of FES into existing analytic methods.

NESCS was designed to trace how flows of FES would be affected under different policy, environmental, or temporal scenarios, so that (US federal) policy makers could make informed decisions. Not all FES available in NESCS will be appropriate for all applications – national accountants, for example, have expressed little desire to include FES that cannot have exchange values (e.g., *existence values* for penguins in a place few people go) – but NESCS presents a four-group template through which *any* FES may be identified, encouraging analysts to identify any and all FES that could be affected by an action before they consider limitations constraining the measurement and valuation steps of analysis. A common core objective of the ES and sustainability paradigms is to introduce more elements that impact sustainability into formal decision-making over time, so NESCS's exhaustive identification strategy should assist in facing this challenge.

Coding for FFES can be as coarse as 4 digits, or if expanded through subcategories (NAICS codes are up to 6 digits), can be up to 15 digits. As with FEGS-CS, numeric coding intends to engage consistency and reproducibility in defining and accounting for FES.[8] The Restricted Case Application to Indonesian Palm Oil Production (below) may help clear any confusion, and demonstrate how NESCS flexibly accommodates user needs.

From the FES perspective, FEGS-CS and NESCS thoroughly separate components of natural capital from ecosystem services. By requiring their users to focus on the ES transaction point, ecological endpoint, and beneficiary, strong FES classifications help to:

1. *Reduce double counting*—Following an MA-based classification system for an agriculture setting, one may identify ecosystem services including insect pollination, soil carbon, and the crop itself. Two types of problem may arise. First, the two regulating ecosystem services (pollination and the existence of soil carbon) are subcomponents of the primary ecosystem service in these typologies, the crop. This may not be an issue when doing biophysical measurements of the agriculture systems for crop management purposes, but if one moves to valuation and natural capital accounting, the value of the crop already contains regulating services and the regulating services may be double counted. Second, an FES classification system would focus on, as one example, valuing how soil nutrients contribute to crop production, separate from and without classifying as ES flows or the value from them, the purchased inputs and labor that humans add to cultivation. The distinction avoids any double counting associated with calling a cultivated crop an *ecosystem* service, when the crop is obviously a benefit owing to contributions from the ecological and the economic spheres.
2. *Speed the identification of analytical techniques because beneficiaries are identified early in the process*—Clearly stating the beneficiary, for example between "water for a farmer" verses "water for manufacturing", allows practitioners to immediately consider the most appropriate ecological modeling and valuation techniques. This should better orient budgeting and planning of the analysis, and draw attention to human well-being throughout the study.
3. *Improve stakeholder engagement*—Limiting technical jargon will allow companies to more clearly discuss common ecological endpoints such as water, soil quality, and recreational opportunities with regulators, communities, or other direct users of effected final ecosystem services.
4. *Integrate ecological information into work with sociologists, health professionals, finance teams, and strategy experts*—By beginning with environmental aspects that readily connect to human use, teams working on business applica-

[8] Developers of both FEGS-CS and NESCS note for those cleaving to the MA four types of ES, that post-classification assignment of one of the four types to any of the objects defined as FES is simply done. Anyone wishing to call a 11.0103 (water from a river to feed grazing livestock) from FEGS-CS, or a 11.12.1105.1112 (water from a river to animal cultivation by an animal production subsector) from NESCS, a "provisioning service", can easily do so without violating any of the organizing principles of either system.

tions such as environmental impact assessments or strategic planning analysis should find it easier to use FES as a common language.

These four improvements should offer managers a more effective framework for integrating natural capital and ecosystem services into corporate decision-making.

7.3 Applying Principles to Business Applications

7.3.1 A Way to Think of Natural Capital Stocks and Flows: The New and Not-So-New

A first building block of accounting is estimating asset values. How one estimates the net present value (NPV) of natural capital will be influenced by how one defines the flows from that capital, which we here call final ecosystem services – where a longer list of flows probably implies a higher NPV.[9] Figure 7.4 presents a schematic that adds natural capital and economically relevant flows from it to the produced, financial, human, and social capitals with which companies operate.

In Fig. 7.4, the upper-right box indicates the traditional place in standard national and business accounting that economic inputs and products derived from natural materials have been found. Sustainability accounting ("ecosystem accounting"/"natural capital accounting" in national accounting circles) suggests advantage in re-naming some of these elements in order to separate dependencies on natural stocks and processes from dependencies on human-produced and -cultured inputs. Sustainability accounting looks for accounting flows from natural, regenerative, and biological processes. The bottom row in Fig. 7.4 suggests the identification of flows that will have

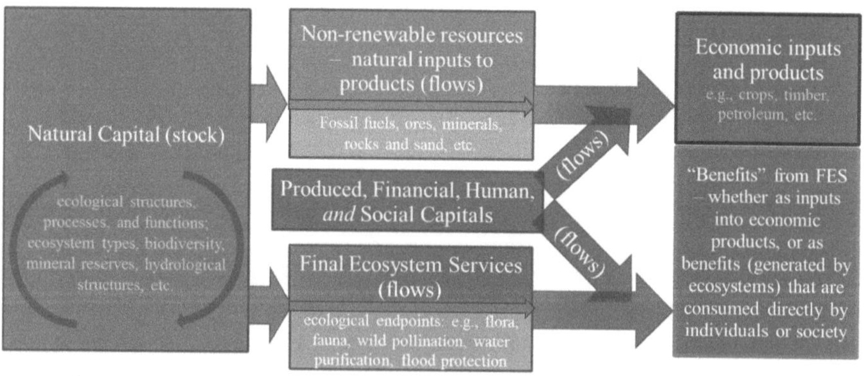

Fig. 7.4 Getting from natural capital to inputs, products, and "Benefits"

[9]The Natural Capital Protocol lists "abiotic services" including mineral ores and fossil fuels as "ES", whereas the CICES, FEGS-CS, and NESCS do not, because these are not renewable by an ecosystem roughly within a human lifetime.

to be measured and recorded, and for identified "benefits" in the bottom right box, recording will necessitate both flows not previously in business accounts, and the separation of elements of natural productivity that in previous accounts had been bundled in with man-made productivity. The FES perspective is suited to assist in this process.

Further, the orientation of elements in Fig. 7.4 provokes the questions "What part of our input and product streams do we owe to nature?", and for ecosystem services particularly, "What part of our input and product streams do we owe to the renewable elements of nature?" It is in more carefully assessing what nature provides us, that we may, while using these resources, seek to understand the production dynamics of nature, and begin to understand how to maintain sustainable flows of natural inputs into economic processes.

This is not an entirely new perspective, but to apply this perspective at a new scale scope and level of integration with standard accounts does pose some significant accounting challenges. At the level of national accounts, the United National Statistics Division has worked with others for years to carefully define ways to extend the Standard National Accounts to include a System of Environmental-Economic Accounting (SEEA). The SEEA Central Framework was published in 2012 (United Nations 2012), and the SEEA Experimental Ecosystem Accounting (SEEA-EEA) framework, meant to acknowledge flows that result from the complexity of ecosystems (this would exclude non-renewable resources), remains at a promising but adolescent stage of development (United Nations 2013, as a White-Cover Publication, subject to official editing). The ability of corporate sustainability accounts (naturally much narrower in many dimensions than national accounting requires) to easily match or merge with the form of international-standard national accounts may prove a useful feature before long.

The national accounting and corporate sustainability accounting challenges are similar in that a new perspective demands upgraded management and reporting processes, new accounting structures, and new data and analytical approaches. Accordingly, both share a common drive to better assess and manage scarce resources and the continued productive capacity of natural capital. The perspectives diverge in that national accounting will be recording very broad states conditions and flows, while companies must strategically manage resource dependencies and navigate complex legal and political environments to stay competitive in global markets.

7.3.2 Moving from Theory to Practice

A theoretical application of FES highlights the advantages and challenges of mainstreaming the FES into corporate decision making. The most effective way to do this is by integrating FES perspectives into existing business applications. These can be very diverse, from trends analysis, to compliance risk assessment, to Lean Six Sigma analysis. These applications seek to synthesize and analyze relevant information to aid in decision-making. For example, environmental management systems (e.g., ISO 14000, EU Eco-Audit and Management Scheme) have continuous improvement systems that drive companies to consider improvements on a regular basis, regardless of performance.

7.3.2.1 Megatrend Analysis

Corporations facing complex decision-making environments are analyzing expected social, market, and political developments (Mittelstaedt et al. 2014). Applications such as the Megatrend Analysis and Portfolio Strategy (MAPS) embody this work, as do publications by the World Economic Forum (WEF 2016), Institute for Future Insights, and the consultancy McKinsey. This research names urbanization, the smart connected world, rising economic power, and the "sustainability imperative" as key forces that will impact business performance.

The WEF, for example, effectively lumps the loss of biodiversity, ecosystems, and the services they provide into a single category that can create business risks and opportunities. In a risk survey ranking high threats over the coming decade, "biodiversity loss and ecosystem collapse" is noted along with water crises and failure of climate-change mitigation and adaptation (see Fig. 7.5). The report notes the overlap among these risks and discusses them interchangeably.

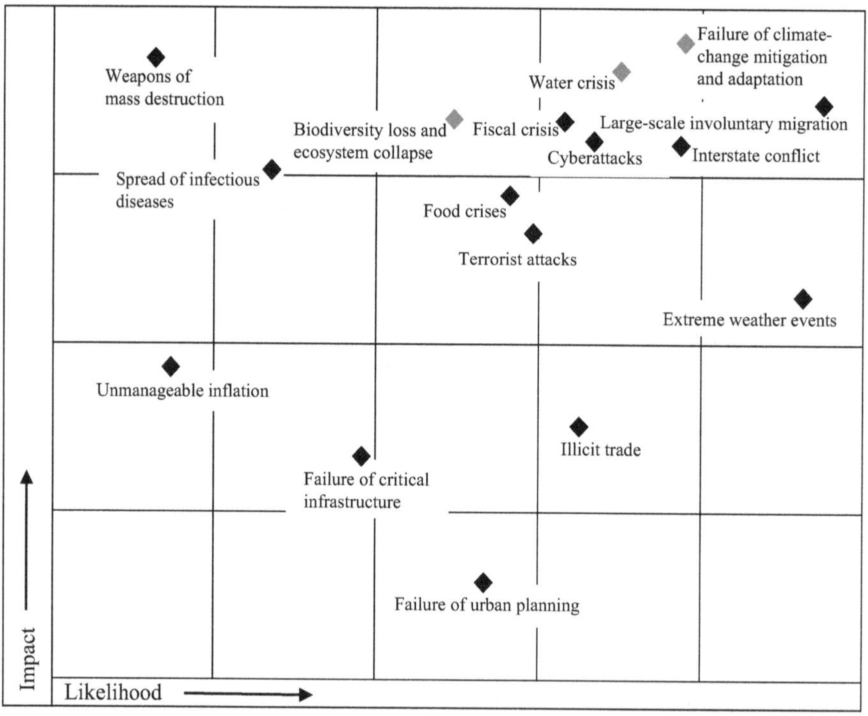

Fig. 7.5 Biodiversity in the global risk landscape (Adapted from World Economic Forum 2016)

A shrimp-farming example demonstrates the importance of considering such forces. Commercial clearing of mangroves for shrimp farming in Southeast Asia reduced both biodiversity and coastal storm protection these ecosystems provide (Lewis et al. 2003). A 2004 Tsunami caused more damage to areas that experienced this loss (Dahdouh-Guebas et al. 2005). The 2004 damage and similar coastal damage across Southeast Asia spurred governments to increase regulation, consumers to change buying habits, and other market changes that negatively impacted the shrimp industry. This example begs that other industries consider similar long-term trends from the commercial transformation of natural environments and the loss of biodiversity.

This research shows that at a conceptual level the FES perspective can add value to business strategy. By separating biodiversity, or the existence of species and ecosystems, from the services that ecosystems and their characteristic biodiversity can provide – coastal protection in this case – a more accurate risk analysis can be conducted. The risks associated with the loss of biodiversity to the shrimp industry are largely regulatory, and confined to local permitting. The risk associated with the loss of coastal protection, however, is larger, impacting a wider set of markets. Without this clear demarcation, managers are left with a murkier view of the risk landscape.

7.3.2.2 Natural Capital Accounting

Working papers on natural capital accounting recommend developing accounts for the condition of natural capital stocks, for their flows of services, and for the value of these flows to the company and stakeholders. Some mention *final* ecosystem services and note the advantages of avoiding double counting and understanding how value is derived from the use of ecosystem services (eftec 2015; Houdet et al. 2012). FES would help that process by clearly defining beneficiaries and avoiding double-counting with associated economic transactions (e.g., labor). Research on accounting for wildlife in conservation and ecotourism organizations has been published with similar thematic intent (Burritt and Cummings 2002; Wentzel et al. 2009).

To remove the capital and labor associated with crops and livestock in food production, simply subtracting the value of labor and capital inputs could provide a reasonable first estimate of value for the related bundle of FES. Developing biological measures for specific FES could be considered a second step. These measures are needed for management of a field, and for comparison of revenue from alternative uses of land. A theoretical demonstration of results from an MA- and an FES-based classification system when valuating an agriculture system may clarify the risk of double counting (see Fig. 7.6).

The MA-based system yields \$155 of double-counted ecosystem services, including crops, pumped groundwater, and hired pollinators.

MA-based classification system

Land for crops	
Crops	$120
Pollination	$20
Soil	$30
Rainwater	$15
Pumped groundwater	$20
Presence of farm for views by residents	$50
Total	**$ 255**

FES-based classification system

Land for crops	
-	-
Non hired pollination	$5
Soil for farming	$30
Rainwater for farming	$15
-	-
Presence of farm for views by residents	$50
Total	**$100**

Fig. 7.6 Constructed comparison of classifying as ecosystem services elements with and without substantial direct human inputs

7.3.2.3 Reporting

Communicating a firm's environmental risks and strategic responses is a key function of sustainability professionals. Required disclosures (e.g., SEC 10K requirements, King III Report on Corporate Governance), voluntary reporting guidelines (e.g., GRI, IIRC, SASB), and awards and rankings (e.g., CERES-ACCA Reporting Awards, Dow Jones Sustainability Index) all influence what environmental aspects firms track and publicly share. These standards mention ecosystem services, mostly associated with water. Efforts are underway to expand this set (Houdet et al. 2016; MacNair et al. 2014) including considering FES, and how they relate to biodiversity and drivers of ecosystem change (IUCN French Committee 2014).

7.3.2.4 Product Certification

Most product certification systems measure both intermediate and final ecosystem services without distinction (Milder et al. 2015; CDSB 2015). Generally, they refer to ecosystem services that are used by communities. However, FEGS-CS and NESCS would not classify many of these as "final". Making the FES approach standard could sharpen definitions within certification systems, providing clearer guidelines to farmers, for example, on what they need to do on their farms to increase community benefits. For example, the ecosystem services of non-timber forest products (NTFPs), water, soil carbon, and recreational values would be simplified into the FES of NTFPs, water purification, and recreational values. Soil carbon would be classified as an ecosystem function related to soil management.

7.3.2.5 Impact Assessments and Offsets

Best practices in impact assessments call for the mitigation hierarchy when considering impacts on biodiversity and ecosystem services, which are often defined using the MA groups (International Finance Corporation 2012). Using the FES perspective would provide greater distinction between the threatened and endangered species, ecosystems, and the services they provide. This could simplify the current process by:

- Largely eliminating the supporting and many regulating ecosystem services from the International Finance Corporation (IFC) lists.
- Focusing analysis on the ecological production functions of the priority ecosystem services. This process could simplify data collection, as field sampling could be focused on the producers and traits that drive priority ecosystem services (Andrew 2015). Further, as the IFC Performance Standards are one of the few codified standards relating to ecosystem services, and they generally require field sampling, it is an ideal place to advance modeling and mapping.
- Making beneficiaries a larger part of the ES assessment process by coupling them with definitions of environmental attributes from the outset.

A few examples demonstrate recent applications of this perspective. Grupo Argos used FEGS-CS to help organize a site's existing biological research, allowing it to recognize clear compelling risks to the firm. The consultancy ERM developed an ecosystem services decision tool in Maine, finding helpful the FEGS-CS call for a focus on beneficiaries (MacNair et al. 2014).

7.3.3 Restricted Case Application to Indonesian Palm Oil Production

The Indonesian palm oil industry presents challenges opportunities and risks, including for corporate sustainability accounting. A short background and highlight of challenges will be accompanied by a brief illustrative comparison of some of the differences between attempting to identify final ES using an MA-based approach versus an explicitly FES classification.

7.3.3.1 Case Context

As an oilseed, oil palm is ten times more commercially productive per hectare than soybeans (which are second), making oil palm cultivation "one of the most lucrative land-uses in the tropics" (Morel et al. 2016, along with facts in related paragraphs, unless otherwise noted; quote p. 12). Oil palm prospers in humid tropical lowland soils, thriving in soils more acidic than most other crops can tolerate. A tree's economic production cycle lasts about 25 years (from approximately 4 to 30 years after seedlings establish). On-site or localized oil extraction is very water- and labor-intensive, and routinely fueled by burning oil palm biomass. For export, extracted oil is trucked to domestic refineries or directly to ports for refinement by importers.

Southeast Asia dominates world palm oil production, with Indonesia leading in crude and refined export volume, and Indonesia and Malaysia together accounting for 84% of world supply. Indonesia's palm oil production expanded nine fold between 1980 and 2010, and Indonesia passed India in 2013 as the world's largest consumer. The Indonesian government has in recent years incentivized investment in domestic refinement. Due in part to explicit government effort, growers are a mix of smallholders, "plasma farmers", and plantations, with the nine largest companies holding 20% of oil palm area, and producing 35% of Indonesia's crude palm oil.

The lucrative nature of the industry has drawn significant land conversion from peatland forests – co-opted peatland acreage increased 20-fold from 1967 to 1997, with a 110k ha/year growth in oil palm plantation area between 2005 and 2010 (Morel et al.). A strict financial calculation shows low return for peatland forest but high return for oil palm, corn, or rubber. However, an economic return that considers option values, indirect benefits, ecosystem services, and non-use uses (e.g., existence values, bequest values, etc.) can not only demonstrate a high return for peatland forest, but due to the loss of carbon sequestration and critical habitat when converting the lowland peat forest to farms, can demonstrate a negative total economic return to oil palm, corn, or rubber farming (Narayan et al. (Abt Associates, Inc.) 2014).

The loss of ecosystem services runs deeper. Lowland peat forest not only stores very large amounts of carbon and organic matter, but does so generally underwater. Draining peatland exposes the organic matter to oxygen, accelerating decomposition and emitting greenhouse gases carbon dioxide and methane (Morel et al.). But there is a further cascade beyond this when the land is farmed. The drainage and conversion of peatland affects the hydrology, suppressing the peatland's ability to mitigate drought when rains fail, and to absorb vast amounts of water and prevent flooding when rains are heavy. In dry conditions, the high-organic-matter dry material burns easily and long, with significant smoke. El Niño years (1982, 1997, 2006, 2009) tend to bring drought conditions, along with fires, and haze (Morel et al.). Fires in 1997 burned 2–3% of the entire land area of Indonesia, causing at least $9 billion in damage and affecting commercial timber, farmland, plantations, tourism, commerce, and health care costs (Narayan et al.) – with more than ten percent of the 450 million people in Southeast Asia exposed to unsafe levels of particulates in their air. More than 100,000 deaths per year are attributed to particulate air pollution from forest and peat fires in Southeast Asia (Morel et al.).

With peatland gone, farms and surrounding homes and businesses are susceptible to flooding, and ironically also to drought and fire. The ecosystem's mitigating power to suppress these extreme events (a set of FES) has been removed by conversion and cultivation. Conversion can affect Indonesia's rich biodiversity and high number of endemic species. The loss of habitat native to the (charismatic megafauna) orangutans has been used to incite end-customer action, impacting oil palm plantation operations. A 2010 campaign by Greenpeace targeted palm oil products from Sinar Mas, one of the largest conglomerates in Indonesia, for association with habitat destruction, focusing particularly on a Nestlé candy bar. Nestlé stopped purchasing palm oil from Sinar Mas, and committed to purchasing 100% certified sustainable palm oil by 2015 (Morel et al.).

7.3.3.2 Restricted ES Identification Comparison

This case can demonstrate a few aspects of the FES perspective. One can immediately see the danger with orthodox accounting, where measurement may stop at the company's fence, or at the fences of its suppliers or immediate clients. Sustainability accounting demands some consideration of the scope of the FES *beneficiary-scape* as perhaps *much* larger than a company's commercial property boundary. Consider a plantation sitting on converted peatland and proposing expansion. There is among the elements that may be included in a sustainability account the plantations' own land; the neighboring land being assessed for conversion; the local population (which according to Narayan et al. may find 70% of its employment in the oil palm fields and local mills); other local farms and businesses that may be deprived of water and burned, or flooded, or both in turn; the entire region that may suffer from inhalation of air particulates from fires associated with peatland drainage; the regional scale and volume of carbon dioxide and methane; and the long-term global impact from increased greenhouse gas emissions. Other FES may include species being displaced or left without adequate habitat. Note also that following conversion of the peatland, some effects involve a reduction in what had been FES, but only in later accounting years. Properly applying the FES perspective involves multiple dimensions, including the scale of place-based effects (e.g., how wide will flooding effects be?), the time scale, and the chosen scope of the FES "beneficiary-scape".

A rough comparison of taking an MA-based approach, the FEGS-CS approach, or the NESCS approach to defining FES associated with this case affords insights into the FES perspective. A European Union commitment to map and assess ecosystem services EU-wide developed the Mapping and Assessment of Ecosystems and their Services (MAES) program. MAES has released a series of useful tools and publications, all of which to date follow the MA typology, including a comparison of ecosystem service categories across three MA-based typologies (see Table 7.2). As the 2013 Guidance Manual for TEEB Country Studies, version 1.0 (Wittmer et al. 2013) recommends CICES v.4.3, we will focus on that, and at the Class Type level, using Table 7.2 as a general comparative guide.[10] We will refer also for comparison to a subset of the FEGS-CS Matrices (see Table 7.3),[11] and to the NESCS Four-Group Structure (see Fig. 7.7).

[10] Wittmer et al. note that "stakeholders often identify a much more differentiated set of services than any of the classifications listed above" (p. 52). This may indicate some appeal to practitioners in the quest for a standard from the more articulated FEGS-CS and NESCS systems, which were not published at that time (the *exhaustive* element from Box 7.2).

[11] The full spread of 6-digit FEGS combinations appear in a 50-page set of matrices, accessible online with the FEGS-CS report.

Table 7.2 MA-based ecosystem-services types and categories

MA categories	TEEB categories	CICES v4.3 Group
Food (fodder)	Food	Biomass [Nutrition]
		Biomass (Materials from plants, algae and animals for agricultural use)
Fresh water	Water	Water (for drinking purposes) [Nutrition]
		Water (for non-drinking purposes) [Materials]
Fibre, timber	**Raw materials**	**Biomass (fibres and other materials from plants, algae and animals for direct use and processing)**
Genetic resources	Genetic resources	Biomass (genetic materials from all biota)
Biochemicals	Medicinal resources	Biomass (fibres and other materials from plants, algae and animals for direct use and processing)
Ornamental resources	Ornamental resources	Biomass (fibres and other materials from plants, algae and animals for direct use and processing)
		Biomass based energy sources
		Mechanical energy (animal based)
Air quality regulation	Air quality regulation	[Mediation of] gaseous/air flows
Water purification and water treatment	Waste treatment (water purification)	Mediation [of waste, toxics and other nuisances] by biota
		Mediation [of waste, toxics and other nuisances] by ecosystems
Water regulation	**Regulation of water flows**	**[Mediation of] liquid flows**
	Moderation of extreme events	
Erosion regulation	Erosion prevention	[Mediation of] mass flows
Climate regulation	Climate regulation	Atmospheric composition and climate regulation
Soil formation (supporting service)	Maintenance of soil fertility	Soil formation and composition
Pollination	Pollination	Lifecycle maintenance, habitat and gene pool protection
Pest regulation	Biological control	Pest and disease control
Disease regulation		

(continued)

Table 7.2 (continued)

MA categories	TEEB categories	CICES v4.3 Group
Primary production, nutrient cycling (supporting services)	Maintenance of life cycles of migratory species (incl. nursery service)	Lifecycle maintenance, habitat and gene pool protection
		Soil formation and composition
		[Maintenance of] water conditions
	Maintenance of genetic diversity (especially in gene pool protection)	Lifecycle maintenance, habitat and gene pool protection
Spiritual and religious values	Spiritual experience	Spiritual and/or emblematic
Aesthetic values	Aesthetic information	Intellectual and representational interactions
Cultural diversity	Inspiration for culture, art and design	Intellectual and representational interactions
		Spiritual and/or emblematic
Recreation and ecotourism	**Recreation and tourism**	**Physical and experiential interactions**
Knowledge systems and educational values	**Information for cognitive development**	**Intellectual and representational interactions**
		Other cultural outputs (existence, bequest)
MA provides a classification that is globally recognised and used in sub global assessments	TEEB provides an updated classification, based on the MA, which is used in on-going national TEEB studies across Europe	CICES provides a hierarchical system, building on the MA and TEEB classifications but tailored to accounting

Adapted from Biodiversity Information System for Europe, MAES

For a large firm considering how conversion of new large tracts of peatland forest may affect flows of ecosystem services, let's restrict focus to just a few of these, including those associated with the oil palm crop itself, reduced regulation of drought and flood, and threat to orangutans. From the FES perspective, there may be many dozens of other sets of potential FES to consider, so the following is illustrative, not exhaustive or with complete attempts to exactly match the product of one typology or classification to the others. Our physical natural capital account will cover the land and the ecology on the land that either remains peatland or is converted to oil palm farming. These land units may in their different states be assessed an ecological condition in a linked account, indicating their productive capacity to generate FES flows.

For this restricted set, in the MA, TEEB, and CICES, we will begin through the third row in Table 7.2 Fibre–Raw Materials–Biomass. For CICES, while there is reference in other rows to cultivated crops and cultivated livestock for nutrition, we must go through Provisioning–Energy– ([Class]"Biomass based energy sources"–[Class Type]"Plant based sources"). The regulation of drought represents a path taken through the ninth row, as again does the same path for reduced flood risk,

Table 7.3 Extracted case rows from FEGS-CS matrices, for Indonesian oil palm example

Beneficiary categories and sub-categories	General beneficiary description	FEGS	Importance of FEGS to the beneficiary
21.02 Terrestrial—forests—commercial/industrial			
21.0206 Resource-dependent businesses	Without the environment, this beneficiary would not have the opportunity for businesses, including marinas, stables, and ecotourism (e.g., rafting companies, hot air balloon companies, beach resorts, hot springs, ice hotels) – but not farm or forest land	Presence of the environment	Opportunity for placement of infrastructure and reduced/increased risk of erosion, fire, and pest infestation on the property
21.06 Terrestrial—forests—recreational			
21.0601 Experiencers and viewers	This beneficiary views and experiences the environment via an activity such as scenery gazing, hiking, bird watching, botanizing, ice skating, rock climbing, flying kites, etc. This beneficiary does not have physical contact with water	Presence of the environment	Opportunity to view the environment and organisms within it
		Viewscapes	Landscape that provides a sensory experience
		Flora, fauna, fungi	Organisms (i.e., flowers, plants, etc.) that can be viewed (flora, fauna, fungi)
		Sounds and scents	Sounds and scents that provide a sensory experience
21.08 Terrestrial—forests—learning			
21.0802 Researchers	Researchers are interested in the environment for academic and applied purposes and as a group do not discriminate over which parts of the environment are of interest	Presence of the environment	Research opportunities
21.09 Terrestrial—forests—non-use			
21.0902 People who care (Option/bequest)	Option/bequest non-use beneficiaries consider that they or future generations may visit or rely on the environment. This includes beneficiaries that value the traditional aspects or features of an activity or FEGS	Presence of the environment	Knowing that the environment exists

(continued)

Table 7.3 (continued)

Beneficiary categories and sub-categories	General beneficiary description	FEGS	Importance of FEGS to the beneficiary
22.01 Terrestrial—agroecosystems—agricultural			
22.0106 Farmers	Farmers may plant annual crops (e.g., corn, soybeans, rice) or introduce cultivars that produce perennial long-term crops (e.g., hay, grapes, cranberries, watercress, Christmas trees). Note that Farmers and Irrigators are different beneficiaries	Soil	Suitable soil in which annual or perennial crops (NOT crops themselves) can be grown
		Open space	Suitable conditions (i.e., land) in which to grow annual or perennial crops (NOT crops themselves)
		Pollinators	Wild pollinators and depredators that provide opportunity to grow annual or perennial crops
		Depredators and (pest) predators	
22.02 Terrestrial—agroecosystems—commercial/industrial			
22.0206 Resource-dependent businesses	Without the environment, this beneficiary would not have the opportunity for businesses including marinas, stables, and ecotourism (e.g., rafting companies, hot air balloon companies, beach resorts, hot springs, ice hotels) – but not farm or forest land	Presence of the environment	Opportunity for placement of infrastructure and reduced/increased risk of erosion, fire, and pest infestation on the property

Adapted from Landers and Nahlik (2013)

“Water Regulation–Regulation of Water Flows *and* Moderation of Extreme Events (2) –Mediation of liquid flows”. While the match is far less clear for the orangutans, the last two rows, one for visiting them wild or in parks Recreation and ecotourism–Recreation and tourism–physical and experiential interactions (CICES [Class]“non-consumptive experiential uses” –[Class Type]“…of…animals…or locations”), and one for appreciating that the orangutan are there (without visiting Indonesia) Knowledge systems and educational values–Information for cognitive development–Intellectual and representational interactions (CICES [Class]“other cultural outputs”–[Class Type]“Existence”).

The FEGS-CS and NESCS “rows” from their respective systems will be asking where exactly the FES transaction takes place (or for nonuse-type uses, such as existence, will be asking where the FES exists), and who uses the FES and how, as this is expected to affect the choice of valuation, and probably also biophysical, metrics. The required focus separates natural productivity from human-produced productivity (through purchased inputs, active management, etc.), and identifies some number more candidate FES for each ecological endpoint considered (that each would generally still fall within the broader types that TEEB or CICES describe without naming beneficiaries).

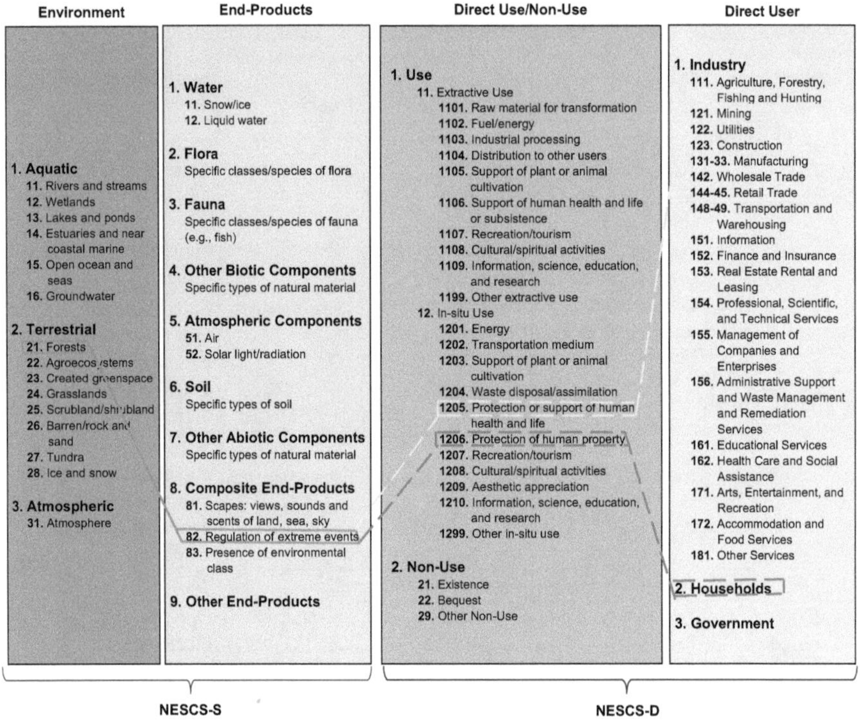

Fig. 7.7 NESCS four-group structure illustrating NESCS coding system with two representative "Traces" (Adapted from USEPA 2015)
Note: the last two digits for Industry (in the Direct User Column in this diagram) represent 2-digit North American Industrial Classification System (NAICS) sectors. We omit NAICS 814 (Private Households) and NAICS 92 (Public Administration). See https://www.census.gov/cgi-bin/sssd/naics/naicsrch?chart=2012 for definitions. We include separate categories for Households and Government to ensure we capture a broader range of uses than that implied by the NAICS definition. The representative traces are: 21.82.1205.111, and 21.82.1206.201

This matters. While the MA and TEEB seem extremely broad in treating all fibrous raw materials as ecosystem services, the CICES allows greater specificity, restricting to plant-based-biomass-energy as a provisioning service. But they all include the *cultivated* crop as an ecosystem service, when farmed oil palm fruit is undoubtedly the product of natural and human inputs. Counting all of the value of a cultivar or livestock as an ecosystem service when doing an ES assessment sets up a lopsided and *false trade-off* between the commercial value of the extractable oil and the value of the peatland that was displaced for the farm. There is proposed movement in the current revision process for CICES (version 5.0) to correct this double- or cross-counting issue provoked by a lax definition.

FEGS-CS paths for natural productivity associated with oil palm production will include at a minimum sets of FEGS from Agroecosystems with (commercial, not subsistence) Farmers as beneficiaries – not of the crops themselves (crops being a joint product of humanity and nature), but of suitable soil, suitable conditions, wild pollinators, and wild depredators, where these examples are within the set: 22.0106.

NESCS will have at a minimum sets beginning from Agroecosystems, across a range of endpoints, including (non-irrigation) water, soil, and possibly atmospheric components (natural sunlight that could be blocked by man-induced fires) and combined end-products (other suitable conditions, as a set). Most of these endpoints will be used in-situ (as opposed to "extractive use") to support plant cultivation, by the commercial farmer (agricultural industry). In appropriate combinations, 22.12.1105.111, 22.6.1203.111, 22.52.1203.111, and 22.83.1203.111 would be part of this set of candidate flows of FES. Note that including the class of endpoint in the identification provides flexibility for specific identification within the same Environment, by the same User subclass, suggesting biophysical metrics in some cases that may vary by Use-User combination.

For the regulating service of suppression of drought or flood (which was variants of two paths through the same row in CICES), FEGS-CS and NESCS require a designation for the exact transaction, to determine whether the service is intermediate or final, and a designation of the exact beneficiary type. There is some question whether FEGS-CS offers a different possible solution than 22.0106 above. A Resource-Dependent Business enjoys a reduced risk of (harm to/) destruction of that business from fire, pest infestation, or the like, as 22.0206, where the descriptive detail in Table 7.3 explains that. Usually in FEGS-CS the same firm or person can have multiple beneficiary types, just as someone can be a hunter and a painter of landscapes in the same forest. But in the case of 22.0206, farms and forests have been excluded, to discourage double counting. This may require a revision of that description, but 22.0206 definitely still applies to *other* businesses in the area that could suffer from drought or flood – which depending on the legal and political environment, the oil palm plantation holder may wish to consider.

For both the FEGS-CS and NESCS candidate flows, the peatland regulating service is more likely to be "intermediate", and a part of the ecological production function that includes favorable (or unfavorable) growing conditions to the oil palm farmer, than an actual final service. But if the absence of a peatland regulating service requires an economic investment to offset (including local engineering to replicate the function, or new purchase of insurance against property damage), then this regulating function is an FES.

NESCS will assign the palm oil farmer 22.82.1203.111 (Agroecosystems—Combined End-Product Regulation of extreme events—Supports plant cultivation—Commercial Agriculture), but can also have many other combinations of Uses or Users in the area who benefit from mitigation of drought or flood to protect life (Use 1205) or property (Use 1206), or for tourism (Use 1207) etc. Some of the Users could be businesses (111) or Households (201). So of the many possible latter combinations of Uses and Users of these "water mitigating" FES, there would be Users of co-located or immediately adjacent peat forest regulation of water flows, such as 21.82.1205.111, 21.82.1206.201, etc. *Traces* of these particular two 11-digit-level potential FFES through the four groups, are represented on the NESCS structure in Fig. 7.2.

Properly using FEGS-CS or NESCS provokes the question whether local people care about the orangutans or not (when they need jobs in the oil palm fields). This is a scoping and measurement question for the managers and analysts applying such a tool. Does your beneficiary-scape include only local residents, citizens of the nation, or people who might travel to Indonesia as eco-tourists? FEGS-CS allows for different beneficiaries to appreciate fauna in a (peatland forest): 21.0206 (local tour guides), 21.0601 (recreational viewers), 21.0802 (researchers), and 21.0902 (people who care, and [psychologically] hold an Option value for future visit). NESCS again allows many possible combinations, among those just tied to the orangutans or other species in the native peatland forest: 21.3.1207.201 (recreation by tourists); 21.3.1207.301 (state or national park revenues); 21.3.1210.161 (domestic or foreign university research of orangutans, traveling to native habitat); 21.3.1207.171 (tour services), etc.

7.3.3.3 Closing Notes Relevant to Restricted Comparison Within the Case Context

- This was by design a restrictive exercise – the "lines" of ES identified here are not comprehensive to the case for any of the typologies or classifications, and final ES in one system may be named that may or may not have equivalents in the others. The focus was on a few points of contrast, not every such point. None of the systems focus on *habitat* (part of an ecological production function), but rather on the actual species, so in a sense there may be no avoiding some degree of buy-in to the FES perspective.
- The "groundwater" effects from peatland drainage are complicated. Groundwater is usually an element of the ecological production function rather than an FES under the FEGS-CS and NESCS approaches. However, corporate use of a shadow price for groundwater in planning (Trucost 2016) is not discouraged by the FES perspective. Groundwater is a key element affecting the dynamics of many FES in oil palm growing areas. In fact, appreciation of the different ES flows, each tied to the full spectrum of beneficiaries drawing flows of FES that are affected by groundwater, is likely to make (localized) shadow pricing more accurate.
- Framing accounting measurement questions with an eye to stakeholders and specific beneficiary types early on may have significant ramifications. Speaking specifically to an Indonesian palm oil case, Narayan et al. (2014) note that benefits from reducing greenhouse gas emissions and forest conservation accrue at a much larger institutional scale (internationally) than do the financial returns from using land at a community scale (corporate or small business). Rectifying these interests when the institutional decision-making does not occur at the same level creates a particular challenge to achieving full social benefits. Tying ecosystem services flows under different scenarios to stakeholders whose incentives and returns accrue at different scales, and who may not communicate effectively, has the capacity to allow managers to consider a wider constellation of factors when planning corporate strategy.

- The policy environment in Indonesia is complex and dynamic (Morel et al. 2016), so understanding the FES beneficiary-scape is one way to anticipate where alliances or resistance may arise. Institutional complexities affected by FES flows may not be appreciated if scoping is too narrow. As the Greenpeace-Nestlé-Sinar Mas case shows, hedging reputational risk required the appreciation of economic end-consumers of products made with FES flows that were captured (or disrupted) by Sinar Mas, or the small farmers it sourced from (often the FES beneficiaries). Pressure from OECD economic beneficiaries of Southeast Asian products generated with FES inputs has contributed to zero-deforestation commitments by 96% of the palm oil trade (by volume). However, enforcing commitments is not trivial, as many small growing enterprises and subsidiaries sell to large traders, and groups and agencies scoring oil palm companies for ecological-friendliness or "sustainability" certification have not awarded many good or high scores (Morel et al. 2016). As end-consumers in industrialized nations increasingly demand environmental and sustainably-raised certifications on products as minimum standards, there will be greater reward to standardization of corporate sustainability accounting practices, and eventually less chance for older exploit-nature-for-commodity-volume producers to price punish firms that maintain sustainability commitments.
- Even working through these few rows reveals that using an FES classification suggests consideration of relevant stakeholders and value-context elements that an MA-based typology does not in the first order identify. Frequency of modest drought or flooding may negatively affect some beneficiaries worst, while any high single flood may devastate a different beneficiary. The choice of how to measure drought or flood risk on the biophysical side may be affected by who the FES User is, and the specifics of the Use.
- The FEGS-CS and the NESCS approaches to identification of FES get accountants, managers, and executives) to think more specifically, and perhaps thereby to consult natural and social scientists and stakeholders earlier in the scoping phase, than MA-based ES identification, by its constructs, suggests. In this manner, formal and detailed classification templates for FES may engender improved scoping measurement and reporting processes and structures.

7.4 Discussion

FES-based classifications, such as FEGS-CS and NESCS, can be less confusing than the alternatives, and may prove easier to integrate into existing business applications (MacNair et al. 2014). For example:

- Regulatory compliance processes typically measure pollution (e.g., nitrogen, copper). The FES perspective focuses on how these pollutants affect the environment in ways people care about.

- FES are more similar to environmental aspects or metrics used in strategic planning and corporate sustainability goals (e.g., characteristics of water flow important to the company, or community access to non-timber forest products).
- Reporting processes, such as those advocated by the Global Reporting Initiative, utilize metrics found in both regulatory and strategic business applications, and MA-based classification systems straddle these groups. The FES perspective offers an opportunity for sustainability reports to more clearly show how sustainability programs are reducing risks and improving human well-being.
- People with expertise outside the environmental arena will find the FES easier to understand as it focuses on aspects directly used by industry, governments, and communities, such as water, coastal protection, and soil quality, by linking FES to beneficiaries/users. Specialists from different disciplines will be able to more directly link the natural environment to a business application's or a community's needs.

Rigorous and useful FES identification may make the choice of metrics clearer, squarely preparing tool users to identify data needs. While FES identification may help to more efficiently recognize precise data gaps, it will not fill them. Data gathering is a step each team must take.

The cost of transitioning practitioners from an MA-based perspective to an FES perspective need not be high, and will be more than offset by methodological efficiencies the FES approach offers. As noted above, anyone wanting to label FEGS from FEGS-CS or FFES from NESCS by one of the MA four types, post-classification, should find this an easy task.

The emphasis on beneficiaries/users in the FES perspective allows the "definition" phase of process scoping to merge with a stakeholder-driven process. Stakeholder-driven systems:

- Can better identify or confirm links between FES and beneficiaries;
- Can resolve problems such as the overlap between the aesthetic FES, and the existence value of endangered species or ecosystems;
- Can create ownership/empowerment/social-learning among individuals and across stakeholder groups;
- Can create better understanding of other people's values among stakeholders and more quickly identify topics for negotiation and compromise;
- Can create better understanding of the decision-making processes, reducing risk of conflicts; and
- Can identify and address data and information gaps through qualitative inputs.

As with all progress-oriented endeavors, the perfect should not be the enemy of the good.

In 2015, Economics for the Environment Consultancy Ltd. (eftec) prepared with PricewaterhouseCoopers LLP (UK) "Developing Corporate Natural Capital Accounts – Guidelines For the Natural Capital Committee" (eftec 2015). They lay out three main practical steps to prepare corporate natural capital accounting: Planning, Development, and Review. The FES perspective treats natural capital as a stock that yields flows of final ecosystem services, and requires identifying beneficiaries for each specific FES flow, in a way that affects scoping, boundary, timescale, and data measurement and valuation choices, all listed by eftec as important scoping questions at the planning stage of building a corporate natural capital account. By design, FES classifications provide guidance for executing the beginning of eftec's Development step: "identify assets and their services". This suggests a useful pragmatism endemic to having the FES perspective built into definitions and classification.

7.5 Current Status

Ultimately, the adoption of the FES perspective will come through voluntary private use and government action. These examples demonstrate some efforts to date.

7.5.1 DOW, TNC, and the ESII Tool

The Nature Conservancy (TNC) and The Dow Chemical Company (Dow) recently collaborated to demonstrate how integrating the value of nature's benefits into decision-making could improve business decisions and outcomes. At the forefront of this new shift in corporate strategy, this effort shows that nature can benefit the bottom line of businesses:

> Dow has established a new framework to identify, implement, and value projects that are good for both nature and Dow. In April [2015], Dow released its new set of 2025 Sustainability Goals, including a goal to Value Nature, which aims to begin delivering systematic and widespread investments in nature across the company. This transformative approach at Dow requires not only changes to the business environment and culture, but also the knowledge base and tools to assess the value of nature that the work of the Collaboration has helped to develop (TNC & Dow, p. 3).

With the input of TNC, Dow commissioned what became the Ecosystem Services Identification and Inventory (ESII) tool – designed to help companies across the world quantify ecosystem services.[12] The Dow Collaboration team:

> is deploying the ESII tool at sites around the globe to both quantify the benefits from and impacts on nature and improve projects by enhancing ecosystem services and reducing impacts on the environment….[and Dow hopes] that the momentum from our work is sufficient to show the importance of valuing nature so that it becomes mainstream for companies, governments and non-governmental organizations (p. 3).

As part of a Global Resilience Partnership project, the ESII Tool is being used to help assess community flood risk reduction and mitigation strategies on the Indonesian island of Java. The tool will help local communities understand the

[12] The tool launched at the GreenBiz conference in February 2016, and is now available for download by companies and individuals in the Apple App Store.

impact of various upstream land management scenarios on downstream flood risk. ESII Tool outputs will be used to inform cost-benefit analyses regarding various flood prevention opportunities.

Upon being exposed to the NESCS tool, ESII tool developers immediately appreciated the utility of the structure for a field-ready ES assessment tool, and are considering absorbing the NESCS into the identification portion of the ESII tool.

7.5.2 *Grupo Argos*

The Colombian conglomerate, Grupo Argos used the FEGS-CS in the environmental baseline assessment of its property on Barú Island near Cartagena. The assessment used FEGS with the Corporate Ecosystem Services Review method. It provided a basis for organizing all of the research, and yielded clear, compelling risks to Argos' development plans. The assessment lead, Ecoral S.A.S., found the method more effective than the MA-based alternatives.

7.5.3 *Peru's Natural Capital Accounting*

Conservation International has worked with Peru's Ministry of Environment to develop natural capital accounts for San Martin Peru, using FEGS-CS to identify the FES to be valued over time. In addition they are linking these FES to the International Standard Industrial Classification System so that the values can be directly incorporated into national accounts. This should allow Peru to understand how ecological changes to the San Martin area will impact the broader economy.

7.6 Recommendations for Practitioners

7.6.1 *Short-Term Tactics*

The difficulties of creating a global standard, combined with the advantages of experimentation and the organic development of standards, means that a unified standard ecosystem services classification may not emerge soon. Therefore, managers should be aware of the different classification systems and their advantages. It is recommended that in their ecosystem services assessments, practitioners:

1. Define (unique) ecological endpoints as tightly as may be appropriate.
2. Note the difference between ecosystem processes and economic production inputs in any ecosystem services assessment. For example, when valuing an agroecosystem, note the economic functions of machinery, technology, and labor

that are components of crop value. In addition much crop value is driven by the actual ecosystem services of wild pollination, soil quality and naturally-sourced water inputs, etc. Humans may create a space where ecological processes may flourish, but ecological endpoints are what nature creates without a constant human touch on that space. Human inputs are never ES.

3. Note, and if possible in some detail, who the beneficiaries of FES are. In the case of wild pollination it is the farmer. This will help integrate respective stakeholders with their own value contexts into studies, earlier in the process.

7.7 Conclusions

Economic growth is more stable and sustainable when there are diverse sectors contributing, and not just natural-resource-intensive sectors. This is a problem common enough to have its own idiom: the natural resource curse. Without clear accounting of how sectors, industries, and operations are contributing *on net* to economies (including among all factors, value added minus FES, and subtracting degradation of renewable resources) neither corporations, governments, nor international agencies are likely to have sufficiently accurate facts from which to move development from theory to praxis. Planning for the future – a modus operandi of well-functioning corporations and nations – is simply less possible without accurate accounting and reporting systems, and sustainability accounting will become part of these systems. This suggests that one ask: Who will lead, and how? Will followers be presented with new systems and standards that lead them to wish they had done more to shape them?

FES-based classification systems will likely prove easier to integrate into existing business applications than the alternatives. The FES perspective:

- *Fits better into business processes*—regulatory compliance processes typically measure pollutants, while the FES perspective focuses on how pollutants affect well-being;
- *Is similar to aspects used in strategic planning and reporting*—e.g., water used by the company, easing integration of environmental data into planning and communication;
- *Is easier to understand*—than MA-based systems; and
- *Focuses valuation efforts*—reducing uncertainty and creating greater consistency between corporate and public ecosystem services accounting.

There are challenges associated with adopting the FES perspective. Any system must prove relevant to managers, and a flexible approach is encouraged. This will allow learning to occur over time (Maynard et al. 2015). Like other ES assessment tools and approaches, the FES perspective requires large quantities of high-quality data and complex ecological modeling that are as yet in short supply. Some stakeholders (e.g., small-scale farmers) may not have access to the data or resources (e.g., expertise, finances) needed to apply complex ecological modeling.

The FES perspective embodied in FEGS-CS and NESCS likely provides corporate managers an improved system for understanding, quantifying, and responding to risks related to ecosystem services. The FES perspective helps reduce overlap of ecological and economic production functions in analysis, and identifies beneficiaries early in analysis, emphasizing the value to humans of benefits from the environment.

References

Biodiversity Information System for Europe: ecosystem service categories. (A project of the European Union's MAES). Available online at: http://biodiversity.europa.eu/maes/ecosystem-services-categories-in-millennium-ecosystem-assessment-ma-the-economics-of-ecosystem-and-biodiversity-teeb-and-common-international-classification-of-ecosystem-services-cices. Accessed 13 Apr 2017

Bishop J, Evison W, White O (2012) The economics of ecosystems and biodiversity in business and enterprise. Available at: http://www.teebweb.org/media/2012/01/TEEB-For-Business.pdf. Accessed 15 Oct 2016

Boyd J, Banzhaf S (2007) What are ecosystem services? The need for standardized environmental accounting units. Ecol Econ 63:616–626

Burritt R, Cummings L (2002) Accounting for biological assets—the experience of an Australian conservation company. Asian Rev Account 10(2):17–42

Climate Disclosure Standards Board (CDSB) (2015) CDSB framework for reporting environmental information & natural capital. Available at: http://www.cdsb.net/sites/cdsbnet/files/cdsb_framework_for_reporting_environmental_information_natural_capital.pdf. Accessed: 15 Sept 2016

Costanza R, D'Arge R, De Groot R, Farber S, Grasso M, Hannon B, Naeem S, Limburg K, Paruelo J, O'Neill R, Raskin R, Sutton P, van den Belt M (1997) The value of the world's ecosystem services and natural capital. Nature 387:253–260

Dahdouh-Guebas F, Jayatissa L, Di Nitto D, Bosire J, Lo Seen D, Koedam N (2005) How effective were mangroves as a defence against the recent tsunami? Curr Biol 15(14):1337–1338

Daily G (ed) (1997) Nature's services: societal dependence on natural ecosystems. Island Press, Washington, DC

Eccles R, Ioannou I, Serafeim G (2014) The impact of corporate sustainability on organizational processes and performance. Manag Sci 60(11):2835–2857

eftec (2015) Developing corporate natural capital accounts—final report for the natural capital committee. Natural Capital Committee, London. Available at: http://nebula.wsimg.com/fded24fcf05ff18ecaf8ddafc776532f?AccessKeyId=68F83A8E994328D64D3D&disposition=0&alloworigin=1. Accessed 7 Jan 2017

G4 Sustainability Reporting Guidelines. Available online at: https://www.globalreporting.org/information/g4/Pages/default.aspx. Accessed Apr 2017

GTAP 6 data base (2006) Center for global trade analysis. Department of Agricultural Economics, Purdue University. Available at: https://www.gtap.agecon.purdue.edu/databases/v6/v6_doco.asp. Accessed 21 Sept 2016

Haines-Young R, Potschin M (2013) Consultation on CICES 4, 2012, 34. Available online at: https://unstats.un.org/unsd/envaccounting/seearev/GCComments/CICES_Report.pdf. Accessed 18 Aug 2016

Hanson C, Ranganathan J, Iceland C, Finisdore J (2008) The corporate ecosystem services review: guidelines for identifying business risks and opportunities arising from ecosystem change.

World Resources Institute, Washington, DC. (2012), Version 2.0 (of same authors and report name from 2008). Available at: www.wri.org/ecosystems/esr. Accessed 10 July 2016

Houdet J, Germaneau C (2011) The financial implications of BP's response to the deepwater horizon oil spill. Comparing damage valuation approaches & highlighting the need for more reliable environmental accounting and reporting. Case study 2011-01, Synergiz—A@L Integrated Sustainability Services. Available at: http://www.synergiz.fr/wp-content/uploads/2011/04/Case-study-BP-gulf-oil.pdf. Accessed 19 Oct 2016

Houdet J, Trommetter M, Weber J (2012) Understanding changes in business strategies regarding biodiversity and ecosystem services. Ecol Econ 73:37–46

Houdet J, Quétierb F, Ding H (2016) Net impact accounting for renewable natural capital—pathways for corporate level disclosure. Working Paper 2016-01. Synergiz, African Centre for Technology Studies, University of Pretoria, Albert Luthuli Centre for Responsible Leadership, & Integrated Sustainability Services. Available at: http://naturalcapitalcoalition.org/wp-content/uploads/2016/07/Synergiz_Net-impact-accounting.pdf. Accessed 18 Oct 2016

International Finance Corporation (2012) Environmental and social performance standards and guidance notes. IFC, Washington, DC. Available at: http://www.ifc.org/wps/wcm/connect/topics_ext_content/ifc_external_corporate_site/ifc+sustainability/our+approach/risk+management/performance+standards/environmental+and+social+performance+standards+and+guidance+notes. Accessed 19 Oct 2016

IUCN French Committee (2014) Corporate biodiversity reporting and indicators. Situation analysis and recommendations. Paris, France. Available online at: http://www.uicn.fr/IMG/pdf/IUCN_ReportingBiodiversity_en.pdf. Accessed 22 Oct 2016

Landers D, Nahlik A (2013) Final ecosystem goods and services classification system (FEGS-CS). U.S. Environmental Protection Agency, Washington, DC. Available online at: https://www.epa.gov/eco-research/final-ecosystem-goods-and-services-classification-system. Accessed 25 Oct 2016

Landers D, Nahlik A, Rhodes C (2016) The beneficiary perspective—benefits and beyond. In: Potschin M, Haines-Young R, Fish R, Turner RK (eds) Routledge handbook of ecosystem services. Routledge, London

Lewis R, Phillips M, Clough B, Macintosh D (2003) Thematic review on coastal wetland habitats and shrimp aquaculture. World Bank, NACA, WWF and FAO Consortium Program on Shrimp Farming and the Environment. Available at: http://library.enaca.org/Shrimp/Case/Thematic/FinalMangrove.pdf. Accessed 27 Nov 2016

MacNair D, Tomasi T, Freeman M (2014) US EPA classification system for final ecosystem goods and services. Presentation, prepared for a community on ecosystem services annual conference, Washington, DC, 2014. Available at: http://www.erm.com/globalassets/documents/publications/2015/erm-ecosystem-valuation-white-paper.pdf. Accessed 21 Oct 2016

Maynard S, James D, Davidson A (2015) Determining the value of multiple ecosystem services in terms of community wellbeing: who should be the valuing agent? Ecol Econ 115:22–28

McCarty T, Jordan M, Probst D (2011) Six sigma and sustainability—how organizations design and deploy winning environmental programs. McGraw-Hill, New York

Milder J, Arbuthnot M, Blackman A, Brooks SE, Giovannucci D, Gross L, Kennedy ET, Komives K, Lambin EF, Lee A, Meyer D, Newton P, Phalan B, Schroth G, Semroc B, Rikxoort HV, Zrust M (2015) An agenda for assessing and improving conservation impacts of sustainability standards in tropical agriculture. Conserv Biol 29:309–320

Millennium Ecosystem Assessment (2005a) Ecosystems and human well-being: synthesis. Island Press, Washington, DC. Available at: http://www.millenniumassessment.org/documents/document.356.aspx.pdf. Accessed 25 Oct 2016

Millennium Ecosystem Assessment (2005b) Ecosystems and human well-being: opportunities and challenges for business and industry. World Resources Institute, Washington, DC. Available at: http://www.millenniumassessment.org/documents/document.353.aspx.pdf. Accessed 25 Oct 2016

Mittelstaedt JD, Shultz CJ, Kilbourne WE, Peterson M (2014) Sustainability as megatrend: two schools of macromarketing thought. J Macromarketing 34(3):253–264

Morel A, Friedman R, Tulloch D, Caldecott B (2016) Stranded assets in palm oil production: a case study of Indonesia. Working paper, Sustainable Finance Programme at the University of Oxford's Smith School of Enterprise and the Environment, Oxford, UK. Available online at: http://www.smithschool.ox.ac.uk/research-programmes/stranded-assets/Stranded_Assets_in_Palm_Oil_Production.pdf. Accessed 10 Mar 2017

Narayan T, Besedin E, Hyson M, Haskell J, Peak K, Wicaksono A, Bahtiar R (2014) Ecosystem valuation based strategic environmental assessment: Muaro Jambi Case Study, 16. Available online at: http://abtassociates.com/AbtAssociates/files/83/83fdcb11-dece-4cc2-973a-76bde787c455.pdf. Accessed 10 Mar 2017

Natural Capital Coalition (2014) Valuing natural capital in business. Taking stock: existing initiatives and applications. Available online at: http://www.naturalcapitalcoalition.org/js/plugins/filemanager/files/Valuing_Nature_in_Business_Part_2_Taking_Stock_WEB.pdf. Accessed 27 Dec 2015

Natural Capital Coalition (2016) Natural capital protocol. Available online at: www.naturalcapitalcoalition.org/protocol. Accessed 27 Dec 2017

Natural Capital Declaration (2015) Towards including natural resource risks in cost of capital, state of play and the way forward, natural capital declaration. Available online at: http://www.unepfi.org/fileadmin/documents/NCD-NaturalResourceRisksScopingStudy.pdf. Accessed 28 Dec 2015

Natural Capital Hub (2015) Available online at: http://www.naturalcapitalhub.org/web/natural-capital-business-hub/make-the-case. Accessed 28 Dec 2015

Porter M, Kramer M (2011) Creating shared value. Harvard Business Review. 89, 1–2 (January–February 2011). Available online at: https://hbr.org/product/creating-shared-value-hbr-best-seller/R1101C-PDF-ENG?cm_sp=Article-_-Links-_-Buy%20PDF. Accessed: 28 Dec 2015

Porter M, van der Linde C (1996) Green and competitive: ending the stalemate. In: Welford R, Starkey R (eds) The earthscan reader in business and the environment. Earthscan Publications Ltd, London

Putt del Pino S, Cummis C, Lake S, Rabinovitch K, Reig P (2016) From doing better to doing enough: anchoring corporate sustainability targets in science. Working Paper. Washington, DC: World Resources Institute and Mars Incorporated. Available online at: http://www.wri.org/publications/doing-enough-corporate-targets. Accessed 26 Mar 2017

Reid W et al (2003) Millennium ecosystem assessment: ecosystems and human well-being. Island Press: Washington, DC. Available at: http://pdf.wri.org/ecosystems_human_wellbeing.pdf. Accessed 28 Dec 2017

SBTi (2017) SBTi call to action guidelines. 14 Mar 2017. Available at: http://sciencebasedtargets.org/wp-content/uploads/2017/03/SBTi-C2A-Guidelines-March-15-2017.pdf. Accessed 7 Apr 2017

TEEB – The Economics of Ecosystems and Biodiversity (2013) Guidance manual for TEEB country studies. Version 1.0. Job Number: DTI/1662/GE. Available at: http://www.teebweb.org/media/2013/10/TEEB_GuidanceManual_2013_1.0.pdf. Accessed 8 Apr 2016

The Nature Conservancy and The Dow Chemical Company (2015) 2015: year in review, working together to value nature—a collaboration of the nature conservancy & the dow chemical company. Available online at: https://www.nature.org/about-us/working-with-companies/companies-we-work-with/dow/2015-year-in-review.pdf. Accessed 27 Apr 2017

Topping N, Cushing H, Law S, Pierce L (2015) Carbon pricing pathways toolkit: navigating the path to 2°°C. CDP and the we mean business coalition. Available at: https://www.wemeanbusinesscoalition.org/sites/default/files/CPP%20Executive%20Summary.pdf. Accessed 12 Nov 2017

TruCost PLC (2013) Accounting for Asia's natural capital—driving the transition to a resource-efficient green economy. Available online at: https://www.trucost.com/publication/accounting-asias-natural-capital/. Accessed 12 Nov 2016

TruCost PLC (2016) Growing business value in an environmentally challenged economy—natural capital data informs business questions along the value chain. Available online at: https://www.trucost.com/publication/growing-business-value-environmentally-challenged-economy/. Accessed 2 Feb 2017
United Nations (2012) System of environmental-economic accounting 2012—central framework. United Nations, United Nations. Available online at: https://unstats.un.org/unsd/envaccounting/seearev/seea_cf_final_en.pdf. Accessed 28 Oct 2016
United Nations (2013) System of environmental-economic accounting 2012—experimental ecosystem accounting. United Nations, United Nations. Available online at: https://unstats.un.org/unsd/envaccounting/eea_white_cover.pdf. Accessed 28 Oct 2016
United States Environmental Protection Agency (USEPA) (2015) National ecosystem services classification system (NESCS): framework design and policy application. EPA-800-R-15-002. United States Environmental Protection Agency, Washington, DC. Available online at: https://www.epa.gov/eco-research/national-ecosystem-services-classification-system-framework-design-and-policy. Accessed 28 Oct 2016
Wentzel WJ, Reilly BK, Reilly Y (2009) Measurement and recognition of wildlife in the financial statements of public sector entities: a South African perspective. Eco-efficiency Ind Sci 24(IV):283–300
World Business Council for Sustainable Development (WBCSD) (2011) Guide to corporate ecosystem valuation. World business council for sustainable development, International union for the conservation of nature, ERM and PwC. Available online at: http://www.wbcsd.org/pages/edocument/edocumentdetails.aspx?id=104&nosearchcontextkey=true. Accessed 28 Dec 2015
World Economic Forum (2016) The global risks report 2016. Switzerland. Available online at: http://www3.weforum.org/docs/Media/TheGlobalRisksReport2016.pdf. Accessed 30 Apr 2017
World Economic Forum and PricewaterhouseCoopers (PwC) (W. Evison and C. Knight, coordinating authors, 2010). Biodiversity and business risk—a global risks network briefing. Available online at: http://www.pwc.co.uk/assets/pdf/wef-biodiversity-and-business-risk.pdf. Accessed Dec 2015

Part III
Environmental Management Accounting: Material Flows, Cost Accounting, and Business Cases

Chapter 8
Cost Behavior of Environmental Protection and Social Contribution Activities: Korean Evidence

Keun-Hyo Yook and Il-Woon Kim

Abstract In this study, we focus on the corporate social responsibility (CSR) management of Korean firms and examine whether their CSR costs (particularly environmental protection and social contribution costs) are properly and effectively managed. Results of the study suggest that the disclosure of environmental capital and social contribution spending does not appear to be a function of quantitative materiality, on average and across time. It is also shown that environmental conservation costs (ECC) and social contribution costs (SCC) demonstrate symmetric behavior while R&D costs show asymmetric behavior, which implies that when sales are decreasing, ECC and SCC decrease proportionately but R&D costs decrease less than the percentage of sales decrease. SCC is stickier for firms that have a share of foreign investment, which implies that foreign investors require management to increase or maintain SCC. CSR activities measured with ECC, SCC, and R&D costs do not change as the ownership of major shareholders changes. Finally, no difference has been found between environmentally sensitive industries and non-sensitive industries in terms of the cost behavior of environmental conservation and social contribution activities.

Keywords Corporate social responsibility · Environmental conservation costs · Social contribution costs · R&D costs

K.-H. Yook
Busan University of Foreign Studies, Busan, South Korea
e-mail: yook@bufs.ac.kr

I.-W. Kim (✉)
The University of Akron, Akron, OH, USA
e-mail: ikim@uakron.edu

K.-H. Lee, S. Schaltegger (eds.), *Accounting for Sustainability: Asia Pacific Perspectives*, Eco-Efficiency in Industry and Science 33,
https://doi.org/10.1007/978-3-319-70899-7_8

8.1 Introduction

Corporate social responsibility (CSR), once a fad of corporate public relations, has recently become an important part of the global business strategy of large firms. International organizations, such as the United Nations and OECD, and many economic institutions around the world have been emphasizing the importance of CSR and have published numerous CSR policies and/or guidelines. According to *The 2016 CSR Trend in Korea* published by the BISD (Business Institute of Sustainability Development),[1] primary issues facing CSR managers and experts in Korea in 2016 are environmental and climate changes (24.4%) and contribution to local communities (10.7%), followed by fair trade with customers and corporate supply chain partnerships. While following these issues, the BISD's report made two suggestions related to the role of corporations in CSR. First, corporations are expected to go beyond simple participation in environmental and social programs, eventually becoming providers of solutions to the problems. Second, they should also consider adopting an SOI (Sustainability-Oriented Innovation) strategic approach where CSR is part of a sustainable corporate culture and naturally incorporated into product innovation.

Apparently, as corporate social responsibility is becoming increasingly important, investment in environmental protection and social contribution has become a major strategic decision, with firms feeling pressure from investors, consumers, and various other interest groups to increase the level of investment. Traditionally, however, business leaders around the world believe that the additional financial burden and added costs for firms serve as constraints in regard to improving their CSR performance, and this perception seems to be dominant in many business sectors (Pinkse and Kolk 2010; Weinhofer and Hoffmann 2010; Lee et al. 2015). This was especially true for Korea's manufacturing industry until 2003 because Korean firms, following the government's policy of high economic growth, focused on investment in physical facilities and accordingly delayed environmental and social investment (Min 2011). Beginning in 2003, the level of investment in Korea has been increasing gradually, and recent statistics show that many firms tend to maintain or increase CSR budget and activities. Specifically, 31.1% of the surveyed firms are maintaining roughly the same level of CSR budget and activities and 55.6% have increased the level, with 4.4% having a significant increase of more than 20% (*The 2016 CSR Trend in Korea*). Although it is expected that Korean firms will continue to increase the amount of their CSR budgets and activities, they are still short of firms in OECD countries.

Prior research on environmental protection and social contributions focused on two broad areas. The first area addressed a governmental policy inducing firms to voluntarily make environmental and social investments. The second area concerned investment performance with respect to environmental performance (e.g., reduction of environmental waste, energy efficiency, etc.), economic benefits (e.g., cost reduction

[1] This report was published in 2016 based on a survey of 100 corporate managers and 50 experts in charge of CSR, which was conducted by BISD (Business Institute of Sustainability Development) in Korea.

and long-term profitability) and intangible benefits such as improving the corporate image (Orlitzky et al. 2003; Wu 2006). Numerous research papers have been published in these two areas, but no empirical evidence has been documented about the efficacy of environmental protection and social contribution costs.

For business, cost management is important because the cost is a key element in improving a firm's competitive position and therefore should always be considered in the strategic decision-making process (Kaplan and Cooper 1998). It can even be argued that the value of a firm is created through effective cost management which will lead to a firm's success. Hence, understanding the behavior of a firm's CSR costs can have significant implications on the nature and characteristics of its management decision-making. Additionally, international organizations, such as the UNFCCC (United Nations Framework Convention on Climate Change) and NGOs, and many economics institutions around the world have been recently stressing the importance of CSR or sustainability. Under this environment, it is important to study the economic feasibility decision on investment management and cost management because investment and cost are direct measure of the level of CSR activities of each firm.

In this study, we plan to focus on CSR management of Korean firms and examine whether their CSR costs (particularly environmental protection and social contribution costs) are properly and effectively managed. The behavior of environmental protection and social contributions costs will be empirically analyzed with regard to asymmetric cost behavior or cost stickiness which is very common in business. More specifically, the objectives of the study are three fold. First, we classify the sample firms into two groups based on the change in sales (i.e., increase or decrease) and, through regression analyses explaining the rate of change in cost based on the rate of change in sales, examine the efficiency of cost management of each group, including the issue of cost stickiness of environmental and social contribution costs. Second, we examine how internal factors, such as corporate governance structure and industry characteristics (e.g., pollution industry) affect the behavior of CSR costs. Third, because each cost item contains different information, we undertake a comparative analysis of each cost item not only with ECC (environmental conservation costs) and SCC (social contribution costs) but also with R&D (research and development) costs.

Results of the study suggest that the disclosure of environmental capital and social contribution spending does not appear to be a function of quantitative materiality, on average and across time. It is also shown that both ECC and SCC demonstrate cost symmetric behavior while R&D costs show asymmetric behavior, which implies that when sales are decreasing, ECC and SCC decrease proportionately but R&D costs decrease less than the percentage of sales decrease. SCC is stickier for firms that have a share of foreign investment, which implies that foreign investors require management to increase or maintain SCC. Furthermore, R&D costs are stickier for firms that have higher foreign investors' ownership. CSR activities (ECC, SCC, R&D costs) do not change as the ownership of major shareholders changes. Finally, no difference has been found between environmentally sensitive industries and non-sensitive industries in terms of the cost behavior of environmental conservation and social contribution activities.

It is expected that the results of this study will demonstrate the impact of these costs on the sample firms' environmental and financial performance. More importantly, the results will provide empirical evidence on the appropriate level of cost management efficiently and some insight into the justification and sustainability of CSR programs. Also, we can now better understand how the quality of corporate governance can determine the degree of cost stickiness. Specific contributions are to provide (1) useful information to managers for decision making in CSR investment as the market environment changes, (2) reference data to the government in setting environmental policies and regulations, and (3) opportunities for further academic research approaching environmental issues from the accounting perspective.

8.2 Literature Overview and Hypotheses

8.2.1 Prior Research Related to Cost Behavior

Traditionally, researchers made a simple assumption on the firm's symmetric cost behavior in which costs move up and down symmetrically in response to the changes in the level of activities (Banker and Johnston 1993; Noreen and Soderstrom 1997). The results of past studies were divided, showing either stickiness or anti-stickiness.[2] Cost stickiness occurs when certain costs increase more when the activity level rises than they decrease when the activity level falls by an equivalent amount. An implication of these results is that the change in costs is not proportional to the change in activity. The first study focusing on cost stickiness was conducted by Anderson et al. (2003), who found that selling, general, and administrative (SG&A) costs increase more as sales activity increases than they decrease as sales activity decreases of corresponding magnitude (Anderson et al. 2003). Anderson et al. attribute such findings to managers deliberately adjusting their firm's resources in different circumstances. Banker et al. (2014) add more evidence to support deliberate managerial decisions and cost behavior. They show that cost stickiness is conditional on a prior sales increase and cost anti-stickiness is conditional upon a prior sales decrease (Fig. 8.1).

Based on the results of previous studies, cost stickiness can be explained from three different perspectives. The first is the accounting perspective in which, for the firms with many fixed costs, the percentage of cost decrease with a sales decrease will be less than the percentage of costs increase with a sales increase of the same magnitude. Anderson et al. (2007) show that the stickiness of SG&A costs is more prevalent in those firms with high fixed costs than those with low fixed costs. The second is the economic perspective, which states that cost stickiness can occur when costs do not decrease immediately because of managers' belief that a sales decrease is temporary and the future outlook is positive and when costs do not decrease

[2] Costs are termed anti-sticky if they increase less when activity rises than they decrease when activity falls by an equivalent amount (Weiss 2010).

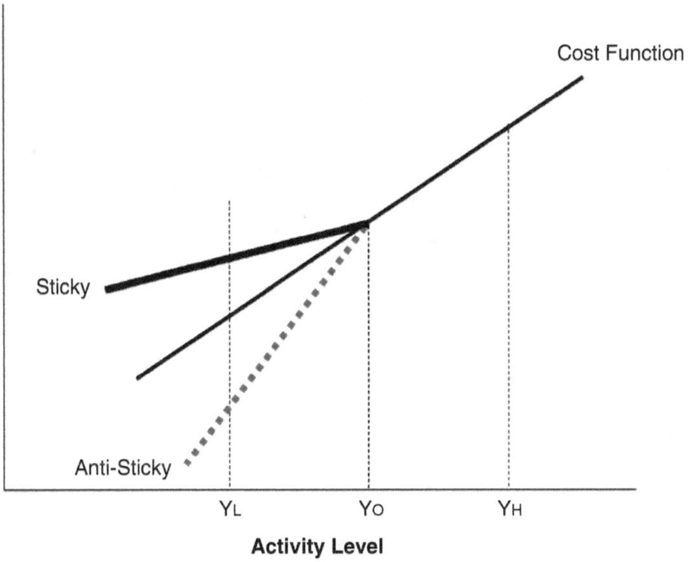

Fig. 8.1 Sticky and anti-sticky cost functions
Note: The figure depicts sticky and anti-sticky cost functions based on an example by Balakrishnan et al. (2004). The bold cost function illustrates sticky costs assuming that activity level Y_0 is high-capacity utilization. The dashed cost function illustrates anti-sticky costs assuming excess capacity for activity level Y_0 (Weiss 2010)

immediately due to a large amount of adjustment costs[3] (Anderson et al. 2003). Finally, according to the behavioral perspective, cost stickiness occurs because corporate managers as agents place their own priorities over those of the stockholders as owners (Balakrishnan et al. 2004; Chen et al. 2012).

Prior studies can be classified into three categories based on their topical issues addressed. In the first group, the existence of asymmetric cost behavior was investigated, and it was confirmed that cost stickiness existed not only in the manufacturing industry but also in the retail, banking and service industries (Subramaniam and Weidenmier 2003); the operational costs of medical institutions were also empirically shown to demonstrate cost stickiness (Balakrishnan and Gruca 2008). Basically, the same result was obtained based on the analysis of data from different countries (Calleja et al. 2006; Banker et al. 2014). The second group of studies focused on the determining factors of cost stickiness. The factors identified were facility utilization rate, managers' forecast of future sales, EPL (employment protection legislation strictness), and corporate governance structure (Balakrishnan et al. 2004; Banker et al. 2013; Chen et al. 2012). The third group of studies examined the impact of

[3] Adjustment costs refer to the costs of altering the level of output or the costs associated with making any changes within a firm. Examples are costs for hiring a new employee and costs of lost production in the event of layoffs. All firms have some types of adjustment costs, especially when they seek to increase efficiency.

cost stickiness in business. Banker and Chen (2006) showed that the accuracy of the profitability forecast model was improved once cost stickiness was incorporated into the model, Anderson et al. (2007) analyzed the market response to the change in cost behavior, and Kim and Prather-Kinsey (2010) and Weiss (2010) tested the influence of cost behavior on the profit forecast of analysts.

Most of these studies used selling, general and administrative costs, operating expenses, and/or labor costs to analyze the cost behavior of the sample firms. Our study, however, will include comparative cost behavior analyses of each cost item in ECC and SCC which will provide different information to different CSR interest groups and will also extend the scope of the research to include R&D costs.

8.2.2 Prior Research Related to ECC and SCC

Among the costs associated with CSR, we use ECC and SCC in this study because both have been most controversial in CSR accounting research and practice, and have therefore been used as research topics in many studies. ECC is important in environmental accounting research because ECC was used as a proxy in some studies to measure the degree of the firm's voluntary environmental protection efforts or indicate government environmental regulation (Sueyosh and Goto 2009). In fact, voluntary capital expenditures in ECC, have been positively valued in the stock market (Clarkson et al. 2004; Johnston 2005). Another reason for the importance of ECC is that managing ECC effectively is critical for firms producing eco-friendly products in terms of product pricing competitiveness and market share expansion. As top managers recognize the importance of strategy on sustainability, it is shown that the magnitude of firms' CSR expenditure has been increasing (Christmann 2000; Chan-Fishel 2002). Unlike ECC, the concept of SCC is not well defined. According to the OECD Library, social contributions are actual or imputed payments to social insurance schemes to make provision for social insurance benefits. Hence, social contributions can include social security contributions by employees, employers, and self-employed individuals, as well as other contributions whose source cannot be determined. SCC also includes actual or imputed contributions to social insurance schemes operated by governments. SCC (including donations) is unique in that it is part of operating expenses[4] for external matters and has nothing to do directly with a firm's financial performance. SCC also has dual faces in that it will increase the firm value if it can enhance its public image as an intangible benefit for profit maximization and decrease the value if it is used simply to improve the personal utility of top managers. Except during the financial crisis period of 2007–2008, the magnitude of ECC and SCC has been continuously increasing in Korea (Ministry of Environment of Korea 2015). It would be interesting to see how ECC and SCC behave in Korean firms under such a business environment.

[4] In contrast, ECC has the characteristics of both capital expenditure and operational expenses.

Prior research on ECC can be divided into two groups: studies on the drivers of environmental protection activities and studies on the impact of these activities in business. In the first group, the drivers are not determined consistently to all firms but rather contingent upon various internal and external factors concerning the environmental management. In the second group of studies, two issues have been examined: financial impact and environmental impact. Increasing operations and maintenance expenditures and conducting environmental assessments of capital projects can benefit the environment, thereby moving the overall economy toward sustainable development (Gupta et al. 1995). It can also be argued that firms with environmental expenditures have better efficiency and productivity, which may help them improve their performance (Wang et al. 2014). However, it has been shown that financial impact is negative in the short term and becomes positive in the long term (Hassel et al. 2005; Sueyosh and Goto 2009). Most studies on SCC have focused on the drivers of SCC, their determinants, and the level of SCC. Recent studies on SCC used the agency theory approach (Barnea and Rubin 2006; Brown et al. 2006) or signaling theory approach (Fisman et al. 2006; Goyal 2006). Barnea and Rubin (2006) reported a conflict between top managers and stockholders in that managers invest in CSR activities to enhance their personal reputation as good citizens. Other studies show that CSR could be used as a signal of vertical differentiation (Fisman et al. 2006) or as simply a positive signal of firms that have direct investment in other countries (Goyal 2006).

Most prior research on CSR has analyzed the drivers and determinants of CSR activities or costs and the impact of the costs of CSR activities on firms' financial performance. In this study, we will examine the cost structure and behavior of ECC and SCC (and R&D costs) of Korean firms. Specifically, we plan to provide empirical evidence on the effectiveness of cost management for environmental protection and social contribution activities in response to the changes in the business environment.

8.2.3 Development of Hypotheses

When managers do not properly control the amount of inputs for manufacturing based on the change in production needs, production (and sales) can decrease without a corresponding decrease in costs; consequently, cost stickiness will occur. In Korea, managers generally view the costs of CSR activities as an additional burden, rather than a long-term investment for sustainability, which does not have a positive impact on financial performance. Historically, they have focused on investment in physical facilities directly related to production, with much less emphasis on investment in CSR activities. Hence, it can be conjectured that Korean managers will actively cut the costs of CSR activities to be flexible when sales decrease, which will show cost stickiness for these costs.

Hypothesis 1 The costs of CSR activities will demonstrate cost stickiness in their behavior.

One of the main characteristics for Korean firms' corporate governance is the control of the founder and/or the founder's immediate family members as major shareholders, through their participation in management directly or indirectly as top managers. This control issue is not unique only to Korean firms, but rather common in many Asian countries. As Claessens et al. (2000) stated, there are serious agency problems in East Asian firms between major shareholders as owner-managers and minority shareholders. Hence, it can be forecasted that, as the ownership percentage of managers becomes higher, their opportunistic behavior for personal spending will decrease and cost stickiness will naturally decrease. In addition, a high presence of foreign ownership is viewed as a positive signal in corporate governance because they are expected to participate in management with a long-term perspective and exercise their power to monitor managers' opportunistic behavior or moral hazard so that shareholders' wealth can be maximized (Aggarwal et al. 2005; Leuz et al. 2003; Lee and Herold 2016). It can be concluded that cost stickiness caused by managers' opportunistic behavior will decrease as the ownership percentage of foreign investors and major shareholders is increasing. In addition, investment on CSR in Korean firms is still not viewed as an improvement on sustainability but as an additional expense that does not lead to improved financial performance. There is also a study showing that major shareholders tend to try to decrease CSR activities when sales decrease. It would be necessary to test Korean firms how CSR activities change as the ownership of major shareholders and foreign investors changes.

Hypothesis 2 Cost behavior depends on the percentage of foreign ownership and major shareholders.

Depending on the industry, the costs related to CSR activities can be regarded as a discretionary decision item by managers or as a required input for business. For example, the firms in an environmentally sensitive industry[5] are more likely to view the costs as a required input than firms in a non-sensitive industry (Wood and Loss 2006); therefore, they have a higher probability of demonstrating cost stickiness. Hence, the following hypothesis is developed:

Hypothesis 3 Cost stickiness of CSR-related costs is more significant with the firms in an environmentally sensitive industry.

8.3 Research Design

8.3.1 Research Model and Definition of Variables

The main objective of this study is to investigate the change in cost management practice based on the change in demand. Change in demand is measured by the change in sales, and the change in cost management practice can be measured by the

---

[5]Environmental sensitive industries include food, textile, paper, plastics and rubber, chemical, mining, petroleum, energy, primary metal, utilities, and resource (Davidsdottir and Fisher 2011).

change in cost behavior. In testing CSR-related cost asymmetry, we use the models similar to those used by Anderson et al. (2003). Equation 8.1 is the basic model to be used, which is an empirical model that can measure the COST (i.e., ECC, SCC, and R&D) in response to contemporaneous changes in sales revenue and discriminates the periods of increase in sales and decrease in sales.

$$\Delta \mathbf{\mathit{lnCOST}}_{i,t} = \beta_0 + \beta_1 \Delta \mathbf{\mathit{lnSALES}}_{i,t} + \beta_2 \mathbf{\mathit{DecDummy}}_{i,t} \Delta \mathbf{\mathit{lnSALES}}_{i,t} \quad (8.1)$$

Equation 8.2 will be used to test the hypothesis stating that the corporate governance structure can mitigate the cost stickiness caused by managers' opportunistic decision making. The basic assumption behind this equation is that, if a firm has effective control and monitoring systems, the agency costs will be reduced and manager's opportunistic incentives will be restrained due to tight governance systems. It can be expected that strong corporate governance is effective to mitigate the degree of cost stickiness.

$$\begin{aligned} \Delta \mathbf{\mathit{lnCOST}}_{i,t} = {} & \beta_0 + \beta_1 \Delta \mathbf{\mathit{lnSALES}}_{i,t} + \beta_2 \mathbf{\mathit{DecDummy}}_{i,t} \Delta \mathbf{\mathit{lnSALES}}_{i,t} \\ & + \beta_3 \mathbf{\mathit{DecDummy}}_{i,t} \Delta \mathbf{\mathit{lnSALES}}_{i,t}{}^* \mathbf{\mathit{FORE}} \\ & + \beta_4 \mathbf{\mathit{DecDummy}}_{i,t} \Delta \mathbf{\mathit{lnSALES}}_{i,t}{}^* \mathbf{\mathit{OWE}} \\ & + \mathbf{\mathit{Year\ Dummy}} + \mathbf{\mathit{Industry\ Dummy}}_t + \varepsilon \end{aligned} \quad (8.2)$$

where $\Delta \mathbf{\mathit{lnCOST}}_{i,t} = \Delta \mathbf{\mathit{lnCOST}}_{i,t} - \Delta \mathbf{\mathit{lnCOST}}_{i,t-1}$ is the log-change in costs of firm i in year t; $\Delta \mathbf{\mathit{lnSALES}}_{i,t} = \Delta \mathbf{\mathit{lnSALES}}_{i,t} - \Delta \mathbf{\mathit{lnSALES}}_{i,t-1}$ is the log-change in sales revenue; the interaction variable, $DecDummy_{i,t}$ takes the value of 1 when sales revenue decreases between periods t-1 and t, and 0 otherwise; and $\boldsymbol{\varepsilon}$ is an error term. Coefficient β_1 indicates the percentage increase in costs (ECC, SCC, and R&D) for a 1% increase in sales revenue; the sum of coefficients β_1 and β_2 indicates the percentage decrease in costs for a 1% decrease in sales revenue. FORE (foreign ownership) is the percentage of shares held by foreign investors out of total outstanding shares of a firm. OWE (major shareholders) is the percentage of shares held by major shareholders out of total outstanding shares. The three-way interaction term β_3 represents the percentage decrease in costs, following 1% decrease in sales with the increase of foreign ownership, and the interaction term β_4 represents the percentage decrease in costs, following a 1% decrease in sales with the increase of major shareholders.

8.3.2 Sample Firms and Data Collection

Sample firms were initially selected from the Korean Stock Exchange based on the availability of CSR-related costs and other data required for this study's statistical analyses from 2009, when reports on environment and sustainability were first officially published by the Korean government until 2014. Firms that were merged and acquired or converted into holding companies were excluded after these events during the testing period. Two commercial banks and three non-profit institutions were dropped because of the unique nature of their business and different accounting standards. Firms that did not have the data continuously for at least 4 years were excluded. In total, 62 firms were initially selected, but the final sample size was 37 firms with 297 accounting periods (or firm-year observations). Due to the small sample size, all of the original data were used except for very limited outliers (top and bottom 0.5%). Financial data of the sample firms were obtained from KIS-Value,[6] information on ECC and SCC from each firm's environmental sustainability report, and all other data for empirical testing from FN-Guide.[7]

8.4 Empirical Findings

8.4.1 Descriptive Statistics

In examining the behavior of ECC and SCC, time-series analysis would be appropriate considering the unique nature of each firm's environment and business practices. In Korea, however, long-term data are not readily available even though reports on CSR or sustainability have been published for more than 10 years. We use combined data of time-series and cross-sectional analyses.

Table 8.1 presents the descriptive statistics of our sample firms, including the distribution of sales revenue, CSR costs, and corporate governance. For the entire 297 firm-year observations, the average of total sales is $14,562 million, and the averages of ECC and SCC are $187 million and $28 million, respectively. The percentage of ECC to sales is 0.9% on average, and the median is 0.26%. The percentages of SCC and R&D to sales are 0.23% and 3.5%, respectively, and their medians are 0.1% and 1.6% each. The average percentage of major shareholders is 39.6% and that of foreign investors' ownership is 26.5%.

Correlations between the variables used in this study are shown in Table 8.2. There is a positive correlation between the change in sales (V1) and three variables: change in ECC (V2), change in SCC (V3) and change in R&D (V4). The change in sales also has a positive correlation with the major shareholders variable (V6) which has a significant positive correlation with change in ECC (V2). The major shareholder variable (V6) has a positive correlation with all cost variables but significantly correlated only with the change in ECC (V2). Foreign investor's ownership (V5) has a negative correlation with all cost variables, but without significance.

Table 8.3 presents the percentage changes of ECC, SCC, and R&D costs with two groups of the firms: increasing sales and decreasing sales from the previous year. It is interesting to note that the average change of all three cost variables is

[6] This is the credit and financial information service database by NICE group in Korea.

[7] This is the cyber financial data library operated by FnGuide company.

Table 8.1 Descriptive statistics of the sample firms (thousand dollars)

	Mean	Standard deviation	Median	Minimum	Maximum
Sales	14,562,666	21,936,347	6,000,780	508,600	158,372,000
ECC	186,514	625,150	190,230	167	4,737,800
SCC	27,669	55,254	9515	80	349,000
R&D	529,290	1,804,446	73,265	3784	13,755,900
ECC/S	.0090	.01839	.00263	.00002	.1096
SCC/S	.00229	.00402	.00101	.00001	.0304
R&D/S	.03529	.147129616	.01646	.00028	2.0729
FORE	.2649	.18039	.2357	.0000	.7000
OWN	.3964	.2101	.3512	.0533	1.0000

Note: ECC, SCC and R&D are total environmental conservation costs and social contribution costs, research and development costs. FORE is foreign investor's ownership and OWE is major shareholders, and both are measured by the number of shares held by foreign investors and major shareholders divided by the total shares outstanding at the end of the fiscal year

Table 8.2 Pearson's correlation analysis of key variables

	V1	V2	V3	V4	V5	V6	V7
V1	1						
V2	0.116***	1					
V3	0.206***	0.231***	1				
V4	0.269***	0.120*	0.370***	1			
V5	−0.083*	−0.041	−0.028	−0.076	1		
V6	0.254**	0.130*	0.057	0.157	−0.332*	1	
V7	0.059	0.055	−0.011	0.118*	−0.053	−0.020	1

Note:
V1: change in sales between year t and year t−1;
V2: change in environmental conservation costs between year t and year t−1;
V3: change in social contribution costs between year t and year t−1;
V4: change in research and development costs between year t and year t−1;
V5: ratio of foreign ownership divided by the total shares;
V6: ratio of major shareholders divided by the total shares;
V7: 1 when the firms belong to environmental intensive industry and 0 otherwise;
***, **, and * indicate the significance at the 1%, 5%, and 10% levels, respectively (two-tailed)

Table 8.3 Comparative statistics of sales increase group and sales decrease group

	Sales increase group			Sales decrease group		
	Mean	Minimum	Maximum	Mean	Minimum	Maximum
ECC_t/ECC_{t-1}	1.053	0.231	1.992	0.957	0.140	1.665
SCC_t/SCC_{t-1}	1.087	0.311	1.982	0.958	0.305	1.523
$R\&D_t/R\&D_{t-1}$	1.171	0.592	2.360	1.097	0.626	1.796

greater than 1 for the sales increase group: 1.053 for ECC, 1.087 for SCC, and 1.171 for R&D costs. Apparently, both ECC and SCC are increasing when sales increase. When sales are decreasing, both decrease with an average of less than 1: 0.957 for ECC and 0.958 for SCC. R&D costs, however, do not decrease proportionately as sales decrease, which demonstrates cost stickiness.

8.4.2 Results of Empirical Tests

Materiality is a "cornerstone" concept in financial reporting (Lee 1984) that determines the importance of an item for information users (FASB 1975). The SEC's Accounting Series Release No. 41 identifies the materiality guideline for separate disclosure of balance sheet items as "10 percent or more of their immediate category or more than 5 percent of total assets" (FASB 1980, p. 70). We examine the extent to which disclosure of environmental capital and social contribution spending may be driven by materiality. Table 8.4 shows a summary of percentage of CSR expenditures in relation to total assets and total capital expenditures separately. This table is intended to verify the importance of capital spending for environmental conservation and social contribution relative to R&D costs and total capital expenditure (e.g., equipment investment). As noted in Table 8.4, annual environmental capital spending ranges from a low of 0.01% to a high of 5.56% of total assets. The average across all firm-year observations is 0.57%. Based on total capital expenditures, the firm-year environmental capital spending ranges from a low of 0.08% to a high of 64.95%. The average across all firm-year observations is 7.28% of total capital expenditures. Furthermore, only 3 of the 37 companies making a disclosure of an environmental capital and social contribution expenditure amount at least for one year have spending averages of more than 1% of total assets. According to SEC (Securities & Exchange Commission) guidelines, these low percentages do not appear to make a very strong case that CSR spending would be considered material relative to firms' total assets or capital expenditures (Cho et al. 2012). Accordingly, on average and across time, our results suggest that the disclosure of environmental capital and social contribution spending does not appear to be a function of

Table 8.4 CSR expenditures in relation to total assets and total capital expenditures

	Percentage of total assets			Percentage of total capital expenditure		
Cost category	Mean (%)	Minimum (%)	Maximum (%)	Mean (%)	Minimum (%)	Maximum (%)
ECC	0.57	0.01	5.56	7.28	0.08	64.95
SCC	0.15	0.01	1.21	2.40	0.03	32.45
R&D	2.12	0.04	8.79	9.49	0.22	66.05

Notes: n = 37 firms with 292 firm-year observations for total assets and with 290 firm-year observations for total capital expenditures

Table 8.5 Results of regressing cost growth rate on sales growth rate

Variable	Expected sign	Dependent variable: cost log change		
		ECC	SCC	R&D costs
		Coefficient (t-statistic)	Coefficient (t-statistic)	Coefficient (t-statistic)
Intercept (β_0)	?	1.172	1.115	0.117
		(−1.69)*	(−2.29)**	(−0.23)
Sales log change (β_1)	+	0.164	0.277	0.307
		(2.99)***	(3.33)***	(1.77)*
Decrease dummy* Sales log change (β_2)	+, −	−0.021	−0.034	−0.251
		(−1.31)	(−1.63)	(−2.14)**
Industry dummies	Included			
Year dummies	Included			
Adjusted R^2		0.08	0.09	0.13
N		242	253	294

Note:
***, **, and * indicate the significant at the 1%, 5%, and 10% levels, respectively (two-tailed)
Cost log change = log change in ECC, SCC, and R&D cost (thousand dollar)
Sales log change = log change in sales (thousand dollar)
Decrease dummy = 1 if sales is year t are less than sales in year t−1, and 0 otherwise

quantitative materiality. Hence, it can be argued that the choice to disclose CSR expenditure amounts by Korean firms is not based on a quantitative materiality threshold.

We estimate the model described in Eq. 8.1 on a yearly basis and the results of estimating the basic ABJ regression model[8] on ECC, SCC, and R&D costs are presented in Table 8.5. Year dummy and industry dummy variables are included to control the industry-fixed effect and year-fixed effect. Estimated coefficients for ECC, SCC, and R&D costs exhibit a positive and significant β1 (0.164, 0.277, and 0.307, respectively) which is the change in ECC, SCC, and R&D costs following increased sales revenue. Our coefficient estimate for β2, which shows the estimated change in costs following a decline in sales revenue, is negative but not significant except for R&D costs. As shown in Table 8.5, apparently all CSR costs exhibit sticky cost behavior, although the degree of stickiness of ECC and SCC is much lower (−0.021 and −0.054 as the coefficient of β2, respectively) than that of R&D costs (with coefficient of −0.251). These estimated coefficients indicate that ECC and SCC increase on average 0.16% and 0.27%, respectively, per 1% increase in sales but ECC and SCC decrease 0.14% and 0.24%, respectively, per 1% decrease in sales. This means that ECC and SCC demonstrate cost symmetry while R&D costs show cost asymmetry, which implies that with the decrease in sales, ECC and SCC will decrease proportionately but decrease in R&D costs are less than the decrease in sales revenue. In the firms with sales decreasing, top managers probably

[8] The ABJ regression model was the model used by Anderson et al. (2003) in their first study of cost stickiness. Many follow-up studies used the same model.

Table 8.6 Results of regressing cost growth rate on sales growth rate with corporate governance

Variable	Expected sign	Dependent variable: cost log change		
		ECC	SCC	R&D costs
		Coefficient (t-statistic)	Coefficient (t-statistic)	Coefficient (t-statistic)
Intercept (β_0)	?	1.154	1.110	0.105
		(−1.69)*	(−2.37)**	(3.18)***
Sales log change (β_1)	+	0.151	0.247	0.274
		(2.22)**	(2.41)**	(3.25)***
Decrease dummy* Sales log change (β_2)	+, −	−0.014	−0.027	−0.182
		(−1.54)	(−1.75)*	(−1.85)*
Decrease dummy*Sales log change* Foreign Ownership (β_3)	+	−0.015	−0.077	−0.063
		(−0.31)	(−1.88)*	(−2.05)**
Decrease dummy*Sales log change*Major Shareholders (β_4)	+	0.058	0.083	0.088
		(1.19)	(1.47)	(1.13)
Industry dummies	Included			
Year dummies	Included			
Adjusted R^2		0.09	0.10	0.16
N		242	253	294

Note:
***, **, and * indicate significance at the 1%, 5%, and 10% levels, respectively (two-tailed)
Variable definitions:
Cost log change = log change in ECC, SCC, and R&D costs (thousand dollar)
Sales log change = log change in sales (thousand dollar)
Decrease dummy = 1 if sales in year t are less than sales in year t−1, and 0 otherwise

get involved in making a discretionary decision to cut ECC and SCC without considering current environmental and social activities. Managers most likely believe that ECC and SCC are not necessary inputs for business and investment in CSR activities is less important than production and selling and administrative costs.

Table 8.6 reports the impact of the corporate governance on the asymmetric cost behavior of the sample firms. First, the ECC regression coefficient of β2 is −0.014 without significance, which indicates that the change in ECC is affected by the corporate governance. Coefficients of β3 and β4 are −0.015 and 0.058, respectively, without significance. With respect to SCC, the coefficients of β2 and β3 are −0.027 and −0.077, respectively, and both are statistically significant. The result shows that SCC are stickier for firms that have higher foreign investors' ownership. It appears as though foreign investors require management to increase or maintain SCC. Finally, the coefficient β2 for R&D costs is −0.182 and statistically significant, indicating cost stickiness with a decrease in sales. The coefficient of β3 is −0.063 and significant which supports the argument of more cost asymmetric behavior with higher foreign investors' ownership. However, among the dependent variables of ECC, SCC, and R&D, the coefficient of β4 is not significant, which indicates that CSR activities do not change as the ownership of major shareholders changes. This result can be interpreted that managers continue to invest in R&D for future performance even when sales are decreasing. The results of this study provide clear empirical

Table 8.7 Cost stickiness of environmental sensitive industries versus non-sensitive industries

	Dependent variable: cost log change					
	Environmental sensitive industry			Environmental non-sensitive industry		
	ECC	SCC	R&D costs	ECC	SCC	R&D costs
Variable	Coefficient (t-statistic)	Coefficient (t-statistic)	Coefficient (t-statistic)	Coefficient (t-statistic)	Coefficient (t-statistic)	Coefficient (t-statistic)
β_0	0.228	0.607	0.841	−0.592	0.117	−0.059
	(1.99)*	(1.41)	(1.24)	(−2.29)**	(0.73)	(−1.23)
β_1	0.288	0.277	0.374	0.455	0.307	0.462
	(2.09)**	(3.73)***	(3.28)***	(3.33)***	(2.79)**	(3.81)***
β_2	−0.008	−0.044	−0.139	0.007	0.022	−0.110
	(0.78)	(1.74)*	(1.87)*	(0.97)	(1.53)	(−1.81)*
Adj- R^2	0.08	0.09	0.13	0.07	0.10	0.13
N	171	168	202	71	85	92

Note:

***, **, * indicate the significance at the 1%, 5%, and 10% levels, respectively (two-tailed)

Standard errors are clustered by the firm

Variable Definitions:

$\beta 1$ = Sales log change

$\beta 2$: Decrease dummy* Sales log change

evidence regarding how the quality of corporate governance can determine the degree of cost stickiness.

Table 8.7 shows the statistical results of the cost stickiness analysis of ECC and SCC for environmentally sensitive industries and non-sensitive industries. For both groups, the coefficient of $\beta 1$ is positive and statistically significant. Coefficients of $\beta 2$ for both ECC and SCC are negative for the environmentally sensitive group and positive for the non-sensitive group. However, the coefficients of $\beta 2$ are very small and statistically insignificant, and it appears that the behavior of cost stickiness does not differ between environmentally sensitive industries and non-sensitive industries.

8.5 Conclusion

The main purpose of this study was to present empirical evidence on the appropriateness and effectiveness of cost management regarding environmental protection and social contribution activities, thereby enhancing the value of CSR management and providing insight into the sustainability of CSR. We examined the existence of cost stickiness behavior in Korean firms with respect to environmental protection and social contribution costs and the determinants of such cost behavior.

Our results suggest that the disclosure of environmental capital and social contribution spending does not appear to be a function of quantitative materiality, on average and across time. We find that both ECC and SCC clearly demonstrate cost symmetric behavior while R&D costs show asymmetric behavior. This result implies that when sales are decreasing, ECC and SCC decrease proportionately but R&D costs decrease less than the percentage of sales decrease. The result of the impact analysis of corporate governance on cost behavior shows that SCC are stickier for firms that have a share of foreign investment, which implies that foreign investors require management to increase or maintain SCC. Furthermore, R&D costs are stickier for firms that have higher foreign investors' ownership. However, CSR activities measured with ECC, SCC, and R&D costs do not change as the ownership of major shareholders changes. The results of this study provide empirical evidence regarding how the quality of corporate governance can determine the degree of cost stickiness. Finally, no difference has been found between environmentally sensitive industries and non-sensitive industries in terms of the cost behavior of environmental conservation and social contribution activities.

In summary, it is less likely for managers to view ECC and SCC as necessary inputs for business, compared to R&D costs; they are more likely to regard investment in CSR activities to be less valuable than production costs and general and administrative costs.

The results of this study have made several contributions to the accounting literature related to environmental research. First, this was the first study linking CSR and sustainability management issues with management accounting; it provided insights for CSR management from an accounting perspective. Second, this study went beyond examining the structure CSR costs (i.e., ECC and SCC) and analyzed strategic control issues of managers concerning CSR costs. Third, the findings and methodology of this paper contributed to a better understanding of the studies on firms' asymmetric cost behavior and CSR cost management; they also provided a base for future research on CSR management from an accounting perspective.

Because asymmetric cost behavior can differ by period and industry, or due to the unique characteristics of individual firms, these factors should be taken into account in future studies. To better understand cost management practices in the real business world, it would also be interesting to study how cost behavior changes in response to changes in external factors, such as market demand and economic situations.

References

Aggarwal R, Klapper L, Wysocki PD (2005) Portfolio preferences of foreign institution investors. J Bank Financ 29(12):2919–2946

Anderson MC, Banker RD, Janakiraman SN (2003) Are selling, general, and administrative costs "sticky"? J Account Res 41(1):47–63

Anderson MC, Banker RD, Huang R, Janakiraman SN (2007) Cost behavior and fundamental analysis of SG&A costs. J Acc Audit Finan 22(1):1–28

Balakrishnan R, Gruca T (2008) Cost stickiness and core competency: a note. Contemp Account Res 25(4):993–1006

Balakrishnan R, Peterson M, Soderstrom N (2004) Does capacity utilization affect the "stickiness" of cost? J Acc Audit Finan 19(3):283–299

Banker RD, Chen L (2006) Predicting earnings using a model based on cost variability and cost stickiness. Account Rev 81:285–307

Banker RD, Johnston HH (1993) An empirical study of cost drivers in the U.S. airline industry. Account Rev 68(3):576–601

Banker RD, Byzalov D, Threinen L (2013) Determinants of international differences in asymmetric cost behavior. Working paper, Temple University

Banker RD, Byzalov D, Ciftci M, Mashruwala R (2014) The moderating effect of prior sales changes on asymmetric cost behavior. J Manag Account Res 26(2):43–79

Barnea A, Rubin A (2006) Corporate social responsibility as a conflict between share- holders, Working paper, University of Texas at Austin

BISD (2016) 2016 CSR Trend of Korea, Business Institute of Sustainability Development

Brown WO, Helland E, Smith JK (2006) Corporate philanthropic practices. J Corp Finan 12:855–877

Calleja K, Steliaros M, Thomas D (2006) A note on cost stickiness: some international comparisons. Manag Account Res 17:127–140

Chan-Fishel M (2002) Survey of climate change disclosure in SEC filings of automobile, insurance, oil and gas, petrochemical, and utilities companies. Friends of the Earth US, Washington, DC

Chen CX, Lu H, Sougiannis T (2012) The agency problem, corporate governance, and the asymmetrical behavior of selling, general, and administrative costs. Contemp Account Res 29(1):252–282

Cho CH, Freedman M, Patten DM (2012) Corporate disclosure of environmental capital expenditures. Account Audit Account J 25(3):486–507

Christmann P (2000) Effects of 'Best Practices' of environmental management on cost advantage: the role of complementary assets. Acad Manag J 43(4):663–680

Claessens S, Djankov S, Lang LHP (2000) The separation of ownership and control in East Asian corporations. J Financ Econ 58:81–312

Clarkson PM, Li Y, Richardson GD (2004) The market valuation of environmental capital expenditures by pulp and paper companies. Account Rev 79(2):329–353

Davidsdottir B, Fisher M (2011) The odd couple: the relationship between state economic performance and carbon emission economic intensity. Energy Policy 39(8):4551–4562

FASB (1975) Materiality: discussion memorandum. Stamford

FASB (1980) SFAC 2 concepts statement No. 2 qualitative characteristics of accounting information. Issue Date 5/1980

Fisman R, Heal G, Nair VB (2006) A model of corporate philanthropy, Working paper, University of Pennsylvania

Goyal A (2006) Corporate social responsibility as a signaling device for FDI. Int J Econ Bus 13:145–163

Gupta S, Miranda K, Parry I (1995) Public expenditure policy and the environment: a review and synthesis. World Dev 23(3):515–528

Hassel L, Nilsson H, Nyquist S (2005) The value relevance of environmental performance. Eur Account Rev 14:41–61

Johnston D (2005) An investigation of regulatory and voluntary environmental capital expenditures. J Account Public Policy 24(3):175–206

Kaplan RS, Cooper R (1998) Cost & effect: using integrated cost systems to drive profitability and performance. Harvard Business Press, Boston

Kim M, Prather-Kinsey JJ (2010) An additional source of financial analysts' earnings forecast errors: imperfect adjustments for cost behavior. J Acc Audit Finan 25(1):27–51

Lee T (1984) Materiality: a review and analysis of its reporting significance and auditing implications. Auditing Practices Committee of the CCAB, London

Lee KH, Herold DM (2016) Cultural relevance in corporate sustainability management: a comparison between Korea and Japan. Asian J Sustain Soc Responsib 1–21

Lee KH, Min B, Yook K (2015) The impacts of carbon (CO2) emissions and environmental research and development (R&D) investment on firm performance. Int J Prod Econ 167:1–11

Leuz C, Nanda D, Wysocki P (2003) Investor protection and earnings management. J Financ Econ 69:505–527

Min S (2011) An efficiency analysis of Korea's CGEI and IPEP in the manufacturing industries. J Environ Policy 20(2):61–93
Ministry of Environment (2015) ECOREA environmental review 2015. Korea
Noreen E, Soderstrom N (1997) The accuracy of proportional cost models: evidence from hospital service departments. Rev Acc Stud 2:89–114
Orlitzky M, Schmidt FL, Rynes SL (2003) Corporate social and financial performance: a meta-analysis. Organ Stud 24(3):403–441
Pinkse J, Kolk A (2010) Challenges and trade-offs in corporate innovation for climate change. Bus Strateg Environ 19:261–272
Subramaniam C, Weidenmier ML (2003) Additional evidence on the sticky behavior of costs. Working Paper
Sueyosh T, Goto M (2009) Can environmental investment and expenditure enhance financial performance of US electric utility firms under the clean air act amendment of 1990? Energy Policy 37:4819–4826
Wang W, Lu W, Wang S (2014) The impact of environmental expenditures on performance in the U.S. chemical industry. J Clean Prod 64:447–456
Weinhofer G, Hoffmann V (2010) Mitigating climate change – how do corporate strategies differ? Bus Strateg Environ 19:77–89
Weiss D (2010) Cost behavior and analysts' earnings forecasts. Account Rev 85(4):1441–1471
Wood D, Loss DG (2006) Environmental social controls and capital investments: Australian evidence. Account Financ 46(4):677–695
Wu ML (2006) Corporate social performance, corporate financial performance, and firm size: a meta-analysis. J Am Acad Bus 8(1):163–171

Chapter 9
Application of MFCA with LEAN to Improve Pajama Production Process: A Case Study of Confederate International Co., Ltd

Wichai Chattinnawat, Warangkana Suriya, and Parichat Jindapanpisan

Abstract This research aims to present an application describing how to integrate the widely accepted productivity improvement technique of LEAN with the environmental accounting management tool of Material Flow Cost Accounting (MFCA). This research followed the steps of LEAN thinking approach by identifying the hidden, non-value added activity and wastes throughout the manufacturing process. This research identified and eliminated the typical seven wastes, by examining the details of each process and operation for greater understanding of the current status of each process. This research used Value Stream Mapping and Material Flow Model to depict the efficiency and effectiveness of the current process stream. This research then converted both physical wastes and hidden system wastes into monetary units and applied the MFCA technique to identify and rank the sources of material, energy, and system inefficiency. Discrete system simulation was used to capture and simulate the uncertainty of the process in terms of varying processing time and random quality level of each manufacturing stage. The MFCA cost was then used to determine both negative and positive costs by accounting for the variances of the process and the quality. Next, the concept of system efficiency and continuous flow was used to improve and re-engineer the interrelationships between manufacturing processes. This resulted in waste minimization programs which can be considered as environmental improvement. Quality imperfection, defectives, and all material, energy, and wastes were analyzed and resolved with a sustainable improvement program. This waste minimization implementation approach helped the team to outline and select improvement alternatives consisting of process design, work design, product, process, quality improvement, etc. The waste minimization programs and the system optimization were justified with respect to the MFCA cost scenarios. The improvement solutions were implemented and evaluated with respect to the MFCA cost structure. The case study of the pajamas production process was

W. Chattinnawat (✉) · W. Suriya · P. Jindapanpisan
Department of Industrial Engineering, Chiang Mai University, Chiang Mai, Thailand
e-mail: chattinw@eng.cmu.ac.th

K.-H. Lee, S. Schaltegger (eds.), *Accounting for Sustainability: Asia Pacific Perspectives*, Eco-Efficiency in Industry and Science 33,
https://doi.org/10.1007/978-3-319-70899-7_9

used to illustrate the implementation of MFCA with LEAN application. This research study demonstrates how one can integrate MFCA with LEAN. Thus, this application leads to both productivity improvement and a sustainable production system.

Keywords LEAN · VSM · MFCA · Productivity improvement · Simulation

9.1 Introduction

9.1.1 Productivity Background and Its Movement in Asia

Productivity is a critical driver for many Asian countries in their attempt to meet the global increase in demand and consumption. The past 50 years have seen a shift towards productivity maximization, and related movements in the Asia-Pacific region. In Asia, productivity and its growth have been monitored by the Asian Productivity Organization (APO) since the late 1960s in its capacity as a regional intergovernmental organization. The APO works with member countries and has strong direction in promoting green manufacturing and technologies, and stimulating green consumption demand, green products, as well as green services. After World War II, there have been significant and impressive changes in the economic performances of Asian countries, in that they have been continually increasing in GDP and trade expansion. For instance, the Association of Southeast Asian Nations, or ASEAN, is ranked as "the second-fastest growing economy in Asia after China, expanding by 300% since 2001 and exceeding the global growth average in the past 10 years. Today, ASEAN has a combined GDP of $2.4 trillion and a consumer base of 626 million."[1] The major sources of this rapid economic growth in these newly industrialized Asian countries, are capital movement and capital accumulation from foreign countries into the region. Technical progress is considered another factor that drives the productivity expansion in Asia (Kim and Lau 1994; Zhang 2001). These two factors play key roles in supporting the total factor productivity growth and trade expansion for the Asia-Pacific region as well. The Organization for Economic Co-operation and Development (OECD) suggests that low productivity contributes to wealth and income disparities, and if compounded by a global financial crisis, will have a negative impact on the growth of productivity and the economies. Hence, there is a strong need to increase the productivity level of a country in order to harmonize its production with the growth in demand and consumption around the world.

In order to increase productivity, a country needs to consider several factors such as labor, resources, demographics, and technology. There are reports provided by the Asian Productivity Organization (APO) which point out that a country's produc-

[1] Source: https://www.usasean.org/why-asean/what-is-asean

tivity organizations have been one of the major factors that influences the changes in productivity and its movements (APO 2015). Government policies play a critical role that not only drives the productivity outcomes, but also shapes the direction of its dynamic. For example, a policy on increasing foreign direct investment has contributed to greater total factor productivity growth through technological catching-up and technological diffusion as well as innovations for the host. The innovative knowledge embedded in the technologically international transfer can directly promote productivity growth in the Asian economies through enhanced and skilled labor force (Chang and Luh 1999). However, different demographic and topological structures have lead Asian countries to direct their distinct industry development policies in varying manners which, in turn, has resulted in different economic growth patterns, as well as productivity changes among themselves. For example, because of the scarcity of its resources, the Singapore government has heavily encouraged and deployed an open foreign investment policy, in order for local entrepreneurs to absorb technology and add value to their products, whereas the Taiwan government has constantly gained improvement on the design, production, and manufacturing skills of their electronic products and computers (Hobday 1995). In the past, several productivity policies for newly industrialized Asian countries have been deployed without any concern regarding their impact on society and environment.

During the late nineteenth century, in the 1980s and the 1990s, many countries adopted strategies that focused on productivity and efficiency to cultivate economic growth in order to ensure successful industrialization and trade expansion. However, there are several reports that relate the progress of industrialization to global environmental digression. For instance, the rapid economic growth in China in the past two decades has been attributed to the positive total factor productivity growth of the world. However, this high economic performance has induced severe environmental pollution and related health damage. A recent OECD analysis claims that, without new sustainability policies and actions, the global greenhouse gas emissions are likely to increase by 70% by 2050. Therefore, one should not simply capitalize on the traditional total factor productivity index, as it tends to favor technological advancement while disregarding the various kinds of environmental pollution caused (Cao 2007).

Productivity is a key to maintaining competitiveness between countries, and is still considered the main driver of economic growth and well-being. However, rather than adopting the old notion of more input for more output, we must emphasize on a new paradigm of doing more with less, through investment in innovation and knowledge-based capital. However, incremental and traditional methods of productivity improvement may not always result in sustainable productivity, since social and environmental considerations may be omitted by the traditional concepts of productivity measure and improvement. Therefore, we must ensure that the notion of sustainable, socioeconomic and environmental development is embedded in every stage of production and hence constantly applied. There exist several ambitious and environmentally conscious measures such as the new Sustainable Development Goals (SDGs) derived by OECD that are "calling on all countries—be they upper, middle, or low income—to make tangible improvements to the lives of their citizens." The SDGs take into consideration the social, environmental, and economic aspects of development. Therefore, environmentally friendly production and management are incorporated into its efficient productivity paradigm (Rusinko 2007; United Nations 2015).

9.1.2 Productivity Background and Policy in Thailand

Thailand, ranked among the upper-middle-income countries in 2011, is positioned among the top 50 economies, as reported by the World Bank on October 28, 2015. Based on the "Thailand Industrialization and Economic Catch-up: Country Diagnostic Study" report by the Asian Development Bank (ADB) in 2015, "Thailand is now the second largest economy with the 4th highest income per capita in the Association of Southeast Asian Nations." The Economy of Thailand has shifted from agriculture to export-oriented manufacturing. The industry sectors account for 42% of the overall GDP, with the manufacturing subsectors accounting for about 75% of the industrial output. Similar to many developing countries in Asia, industries in Thailand are more capital intensive than agriculture intensive (Diao et al. 2005). Therefore, the manufacturing and industry sectors play a major role in driving productivity growth and, thereby, Thailand's economy. The major industries producing the most exported manufactured products are textiles and garments, agricultural processing, beverages, tobacco, cement, lightweight manufacturing such as jewelry and electric appliances, computers and parts, integrated circuits, furniture, plastics, automobiles, and automotive parts. Thailand has been considered a production-based country for automobiles, electronics, and garments. Based on the report published by the World Economic Forum, Thailand's current competitiveness index has a score of 4.64 points out of 7 on the 2015–2016 global competitiveness, which is an increase from the average of 4.60 points in 2007. However, Thailand, like other countries such as Vietnam, the Republic of China, Cambodia, and the Philippines, has been placing strong emphasis on both improving and enhancing productivity, in order to boost competitiveness in fulfilling the increasing consumer demand in regions such as Asia, North America, and Europe. In May 2003, Prof. Michael E. Porter visited Thailand and addressed significant points in scaling Thailand's competitiveness, by creating the foundation for higher productivity. In the viewpoint of Prof. Porter, "Competitiveness is determined by the productivity with which a nation uses its human, capital, and natural resources. Productivity sets a nation's or region's standard of living (wages, returns to capital, and returns to natural resource endowments). Productivity depends both on the value of products and services (e.g., uniqueness, quality) as well as the efficiency with which they are produced. It is not what industries a nation competes in that matter for prosperity, but how firms compete in those industries. Productivity in a nation is a reflection of what both domestic and foreign firms choose to do in that location. The location of ownership is secondary for national prosperity. The productivity of "local" industries is of fundamental importance to competitiveness, not just that of traded industries." This perspective of valuation has produced results as regards value creation and productivity improvement since 2003. Since then, productivity enhancement in the manufacturing and service industries has been a national target for every Thai government in the past decade, especially for local, and small and medium enterprise (SME) sectors. Since Thailand's competitiveness is strongly related to and has to be equated with national productivity or GDP growth, the increase of Thailand's productivity in all sectors is very important and has been one of the top national priorities.

In recent years, Thailand has been facing a challenge in competing with neighboring countries such as Vietnam and Laos who have an abundance of material and labor resources (ADB 2015). Based on interview data collected from top executives of manufacturing firms belonging to the Federation of Thai Industry (FTI), six criteria have been appointed as a measure of national competitiveness; quality, customer-focus, delivery, flexibility, know-how, and costs are recognized as important priorities that enhance the competitiveness of manufacturing firms and countries. Moreover, Thailand now has its emphasis on how to sustain improvement through innovation (Phusavat and Kanchana 2007, 2008). This study led Thai Governments to direct policies that emphasize enhancing productivity and efficiency, and sustaining the outcome for greater competitiveness. The enhancement of productivity across the nation is now driven by many major government agencies, especially the Thailand Productivity Institute (TPI). The TPI is also the national body member of the APO, operating under the supervision of the Ministry of Industry. It has primarily been entrusted with the following tasks: (i) measuring and conducting activities to improve productivity and competitiveness, (ii) promoting national productivity and executing the policies for productivity promotion set by the Royal Thai Government. The main function of the TPI is to help increase the competitiveness of the Thai industry and service sectors in the world marketplace. Nevertheless, having major campaigns for improving those competitive factors of quality, customer-focus, delivery, flexibility, know-how, and costs alone may not be sufficient drivers for Thailand. This is as sustainable development is now a defining component for the world economy, and thus directly affects Thailand's competitiveness on the global stage. The world market condition has shifted tremendously toward sustainability, where green and eco-friendly products have become crucial to the competition. This has resulted in shifting countries toward sustainable and high-value productivity growth, and thus, the notion of sustainable production has been continuously adopted by many industry sectors around the globe, including Thailand.

9.1.3 Sustainable Production Policy in Thailand

One commonly used definition of sustainable development is "the development that satisfies the needs of the present without compromising the ability of future generations to meet their own needs" (United Nations World Commission on Environment and Development [WCED] report, Our Common Future 1987). As environmental and ecological degradation became major factors that define the course of agricultural and industrial production, sustainability arose as an important criterion to be met. As Thailand considers the growth of productivity, the country must meet its society's economic, social, as well as environmental needs. Among the scores of existing environmental indexes, air pollution, the rise of CO_2 levels, and the greenhouse effect have been considered key indexes, as they are considered major causes of health concerns (Jacobson 2008). Among other environmental impacts, the rise of CO_2 emissions is 1 of the 12 major pillars or main drivers that determine the Global Competitiveness Index, an indicator developed by the World Economic Forum. "In particular, the way that the physical environment is managed can have a serious impact on future productivity. The extent to which it is well managed can be measured by factors such as the efficient use of resources and, more generally, by environmental quality. Countries that do not properly manage their environmental assets face direct risks to the productivity of their human resources base by damaging the health of the workforce" (World Economic Forum: The Global Competitiveness Report 2011–2012, page 59). The World Bank's report on the tendency of the rapid rise of greenhouse gas emissions in Thailand (Fig. 9.1) has suggested that Thailand needs to call for sustainable production and practice from all industries and service sectors. As a result, there have been pressing calls not only for Thailand but also for other countries around the world to practice sustainable production, as well as sustainability improvement in their production and manufacturing process.

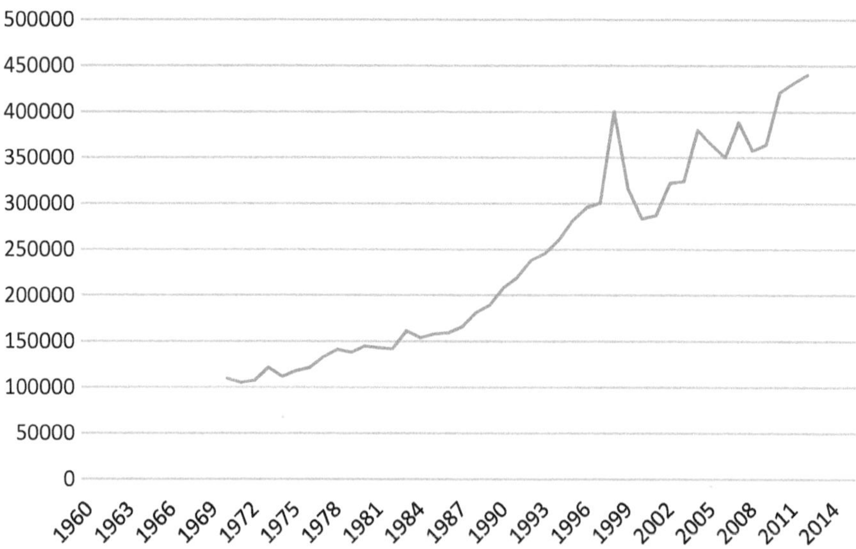

Fig. 9.1 The total green house gas emission (kton of Co_2 equivalent) in Thailand
Data Source: World Development Indicators, last updated date 7/22/2016 http://data.worldbank.org/country/thailand?view=chart

Sustainable production could be effectively and systematically achieved, if governments set clear policies toward greener economies, and provide mechanisms for industries to raise the efficiency of their resources and energy usage. Since Thailand is a leading global producer of products such as automobiles, hard disks, and garments, various sectors are being solicited for the implementation of the green productivity concept. This includes the garment industry, who is being called on to include environmental considerations as part of its productivity improvement analysis. For instance, in order to abide by sustainable development and stay competitive, the Thai government is directing its industrial development policy to promote a value-added green economy, in compliance with Industry 4.0's vision for a sustainable and value-based economy. This requires all manufacturing sectors and industries to deploy autonomous production, innovation, and Internet of Things into their processes, in order to maximize both efficiency and productivity, while reducing impact on the environment. This research aims to study how we can improve productivity while considering the environmental impact and its cost. This research adapted MFCA, an Environmental Management Accounting (EMA) tool supported by ISO14051 standard, which can systematically quantify the flow of all materials and wastes throughout the system. MFCA helps in providing information on material flow that can be used to identify opportunities to reduce the environmental impact. Moreover, MFCA can disclose how the environmental cost is associated with the current operation. The monetary information and its flow generated from MFCA can be used to justify and determine the most suitable improvement options. Therefore, this research, with a combined use of the LEAN and the MFCA tools, would provide an way forward to green productivity improvement, in which economic and environmental performance can be concurrently improved. The structure of this research is as follows: the concept of productivity improvement, especially via LEAN, is explained in the next section, while the methodology regarding how to apply MFCA with the LEAN concept is explained in Sect. 9.3. This research exemplifies this combined application using a pilot case study of pajamas production process at the Confederate International Co., Ltd. The conclusion is provided toward the end, which is followed by the discussion section.

9.2 Literature Review

9.2.1 Productivity Improvement at Corporate Level Through LEAN Concept

Japan has taken a leading role in applying productivity enhancement and improvement as the key success drivers of competitiveness at both organizational and country levels. These successful applications of productivity enhancement and improvement are partly based on integration of socioeconomic development with sustainability. From the economic production theory viewpoint, the productivity of a production process is defined in terms of how efficiently the process can transform inputs into outputs. Productivity indexes are, therefore, generally defined as "the ratios of an aggregate output index to an index of either single or total factor use" (APO 2015). However, over the past year, the concept of productivity and the notion of improvement have evolved from simply an efficiency ratio to cover broader issues of effectiveness in quality, cost, safety, social concerns, and social responsibility. Additionally, sustainability and productivity are strongly tied to business excellence, governance, corporate social responsibility, and environmental protection productivity (Tuttle and Heap 2008). The notion of productivity enhancement via sustainable production is sometimes referred to as green productivity, or GP, by the APO (Lee 2009; Hur et al. 2004). Today, productivity concepts also extend to include social, and productivity and knowledge concepts. There are different concepts and definitions of productivity enhancement and improvement (Muthiah and Huang 2006). The standard concept of productivity improvement promoted by APO emphasizes on increasing both effectiveness and efficiency. An efficient production process must produce a value-created product of high quality at the lowest possible cost. This suggests that productivity enhancement and improvement should maximize the goods and services, or the output, while minimizing the input (Huang et al. 2002). This concept of productivity improvement can definitely enhance corporate and organization competitiveness, but a proper set of tools and guidelines must be strategically and correctly applied, such as the Toyota production system and the LEAN production.

There have been various successful cases of LEAN production application in Asian countries. The LEAN production system has been defined as a philosophy or a strategy, using a set of practices to minimize waste in order to improve an enterprise's performance (Womack and Jones 1996, 2003; Bhasin and Burcher 2006; Manea 2013). The LEAN production principle helps corporations and enterprises to improve their entire production processes, and business operations to improve quality, reduce error and defects, shorten lead time and speed up delivery, reduce cost, increase customer satisfaction, and enhance business performance and competitiveness (Holweg 2007). The LEAN production system can be adopted at the enterprise level (Powell et al. 2013) as well as the factory level (Agus and Hajinoor 2012). The LEAN production system evolved from shop-floor improvement and innovation at the Toyota Motor Corporation (Shingo 1981; Ohno 1988). LEAN is sometimes referred to as the just-in-time (JIT) production system. The LEAN production system focuses on the concept of value creation, thus it starts with the identifying of non-value-added activities or processes, and the elimination of what is conventionally called the basic seven deadly wastes, or "mudas." These seven wastes consist of overproduction, inventory, motion, waiting, overprocessing, defects, and transportation, as shown in Fig. 9.2. By eliminating these mudas, the company can reduce unnecessary defects and reworks and, thus, reduce cost, delivery time, inventory, and rework (Melton 2005; Pettersen 2009; Manea 2013).

A LEAN system uses a variety of tools and techniques to eliminate those mudas in order to increase resource utilization, improve productivity and quality, reduce the delivery and manufacturing cycle time and hence lead time, reduce stock, improve inventory efficiency and management, and increase planning flexibility and

Fig. 9.2 The list of *mudas*, or conventional basic seven wastes

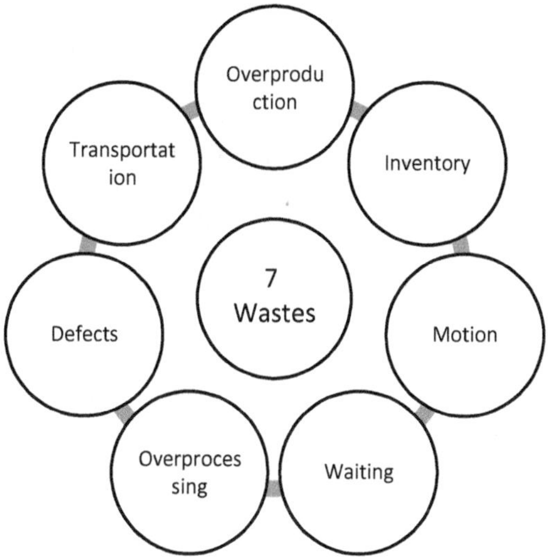

agility of process for greater delivery performance. The major tools and techniques used in the LEAN production system consist of Value Stream Mapping (VSM), 5S, small lot production, pull production system using Kanban, single unit piece flow, cellular manufacturing together with multi-skilled workforce, cycle time reduction, Total Productive Maintenance (TPM), quick setup or Single Minute Exchange of Die (SMED), Jidoka and process perfection, Total Quality Management (TQM), and defective elimination (Womack and Jones 1996; Shah and Ward 2003). These tools are applied in coherence with others under a continuous improvement or Kaizen program/event—a major total employee participation mechanism at all levels, to constantly identify the problems, solve the problems, and improve the system (Shah and Ward 2003, 2007). The results of the improvement are then considered standardized working instructions, which in many cases are combined with automated or mistake proofing called poka-yoke.

The fundamental principle of LEAN is to focus on value creation and waste reduction. Womack and Jones (1996, 2003) outlines the principal steps regarding how to implement the LEAN system. The authors clearly suggest that the VSM must first be carried out in order to identify the value-added and the non-value-added activities and processes. This will lead to initiatives on re-engineering the business and the processes, resulting in a shortened lead time or manufacturing cycle time, and reduced throughput time. The VSM is a major tool that can visualize not only the value-added/non-value-added activities but also the efficiency of the flow of process and the material. VSM acts as a visual representation for the managers to identify and analyze the value flow of the whole system, so that wastes can be identified and eliminated (Andrade et al. 2016). The VSM is used to analyze the current state of a production process, so that a more efficient production process with maximum flow can be proposed (Seth and Gupta 2005).

The next principle of LEAN is to maximize the continuous flow of a system. When the system or the process flow is hindered by bottle neck activities, wastes in the form of waiting and inventory are normally incurred. This leads to increased costs and environmental wastes, or, in other words, high degradation. In the LEAN production system, efficiency is typically measured based on the throughput rate, amount of output per unit time, as well as the time the product spends within the system. For example, the imbalance of the production line will limit the continuous flow and decrease the throughput of material in the system (Domingo et al. 2007). The manufacturing and operation lead time will then be unnecessarily increased, leading to higher costs of production due to induced waiting, a non-value-added activity. An imbalanced production system can also lead to high accumulation of inventory and work in process (WIP) within the system, inducing unnecessary management of inventory and costs. To maximize the flow, one needs to identify bottleneck processes and activities. Measures of improvement of the process such as cycle time reduction, and quality improvement, can then be adopted in order to reduce high production or cycle time.

9.2.2 Combining LEAN and MFCA

MFCA is an environmental accounting tool which has been increasingly adapted by industries (Nakajima 2011; ISO 14051: 2011; METI 2011; Wagner 2015; Christ and Burritt 2015; Schaltegger and Zvezdov 2015; Kokubu and Kitada 2015). By comparing the total amount of material outputs with the inputs at each stage of production, MFCA helps in identifying the losses throughout the process or system. The differences in the material inputs and outputs are considered as wastes which directly reveal the efficiency of the operation and the process (Jasch 2008; ISO 14051: 2011; Schmidt and Nakajima 2013). Wastes, in general, are part of a production process which consumes material and energy, including other direct and indirect resources; significant proportions of input costs are also incurred in those wastes. The greater the waste, the higher the wastage of the process investment costs. Hence, these wastes need to be further investigated, analyzed, and then minimized.

MFCA focuses on the flow of materials and costs associated within a system. The physical units of all material will be traced and quantified, and will be used for cost calculation in the later steps. The constructed costing structure provides businesses with opportunities to improve their operation and process to reduce adverse effects on the environment. MFCA helps the process engineer to reveal both the quantity and the location of the material and energy losses (Schmidt 2015). In order to effectively and systematically identify the source of the losses, MFCA should be applied throughout the manufacturing stream of the system, starting from the receiving of the material to the shipping of the final product. MFCA allows a company and its investigating team to disclose the inefficiency of material, energy, and other resources throughout the entire process and system (Schaltegger and Zvezdov

2015). These wastes are typically high, not only in material value (Jasch 2008; Kasemset et al. 2015) but also in system value (Chattinnawat et al. 2015). In many industries, the processing and system cost invested and accumulated in the product also forms a major proportion of the investment, especially with regard to labor-intensive industries such as the garment industry. Thus, identification and quantification of wastes is the first step toward green productivity improvement (Nakajima 2011; Chattinnawat 2013).

Even though MFCA originated in Germany as an environmental protection tool, its contents and procedures were further developed, standardized, and successfully practiced in Japan as an improved Kaizen tool to benefit both the environment and cost saving (METI 2011; Schmidt 2015). In Thailand, there have been several research studies that have applied MFCA to small and medium enterprises (Kasemset et al. 2015; Chompu-inwai et al. 2015). However, the application of MFCA under LEAN remains very limited (Chattinnawat et al. 2015). Recently, the concepts of sustainability, sustainable production, and GP have received active support from the current Thai government. GP has been defined as a strategy for enhancing productivity and environmental performance for sustainable, socioeconomic development; it consists of various applications of productivity tools, techniques, and technologies to reduce the environmental impact of an organization's activities, products, and services. MFCA can be considered as one of the green productivity improvement tools. It would be very advantageous for a company to integrate the LEAN concepts and green productivity improvement into its system. Integrating MFCA with LEAN could help organizations improve productivity, increase efficiency, and reduce cost while minimizing the environmental impact.

9.3 Methodology

The LEAN and the MFCA principles can be integrated to enhance productivity, and increase a business's competitiveness while cultivating sustainability. The integration of MFCA with productivity improvement techniques such as TPM (Nakajima 2008), quality inspection system design (Chattinnawat 2013), simulation (Takakuwa et al. 2014) have been presented in research literature. The application of MFCA in production has also been adopted by major companies such as Toyota, Nitto Denko, and Cannon Company. (Nakajima 2009). The implication of adopting MFCA with productivity improvement techniques is that it clearly leads to higher process efficiency. The fundamental strategy behind implementing MFCA with LEAN is the evaluation of the operations and the activities in terms of efficiency and environment concurrence.

This research argues arbitrarily that LEAN mechanism is the key driver for applying MFCA under the productivity improvement framework, owing to the well-defined, systematic and constructive structure of LEAN, with many explicitly proven tools for analyzing the system. This long-evolved, novel improvement strategy of LEAN has been proven effective by the success of many world class corporations. In contrast, the implementation of MFCA, according to ISO14051 (2011), is defined in general Plan-Do-Check-Act (P-D-C-A) stages. At the Plan (P) stage, management engagement is required to support the provision of resources for the project. Identification of the system boundary and the Quantity Center (QC) needs to be defined, so that the input and the output material analysis including its monetary flow can be quantified in the Do (D) stage. MFCA calculation report must be used to communicate and disclose the current performance of the system during the Check (C) stage. The ISO14051 (2011) simply defines the Act (A) stage as identification and assessment of improvement opportunities, without giving any explanation of the concept of improvement. This research thus employed the LEAN mechanics to gear both system and material efficiency.

This research implemented MFCA under the LEAN thinking by incorporating the MFCA tools during each step of implementation of LEAN. Based on the five major steps of conventional LEAN thinking (Bhasin and Burcher 2006), this research was carried out in three main steps, as shown in Fig. 9.3, starting from values and wastes. First, this research identified and eliminated non-value-added activities and the typical seven wastes by examining the details of each process and operation for greater understanding of the current status of each process. Next, this research used VSM together with the material flow model technique of MFCA to determine the efficiency and the environmental impacts of the current process stream. The difference between the inputs and the outputs for each processing step was quantified and depicted using the material flow model. This research then converted both material wastes and hidden system wastes into monetary units and applied the MFCA technique to report the current performance based on the MFCA cost matrix. This MFCA costing structure matrix can then be used to study how the system efficiency interacts with the EMA

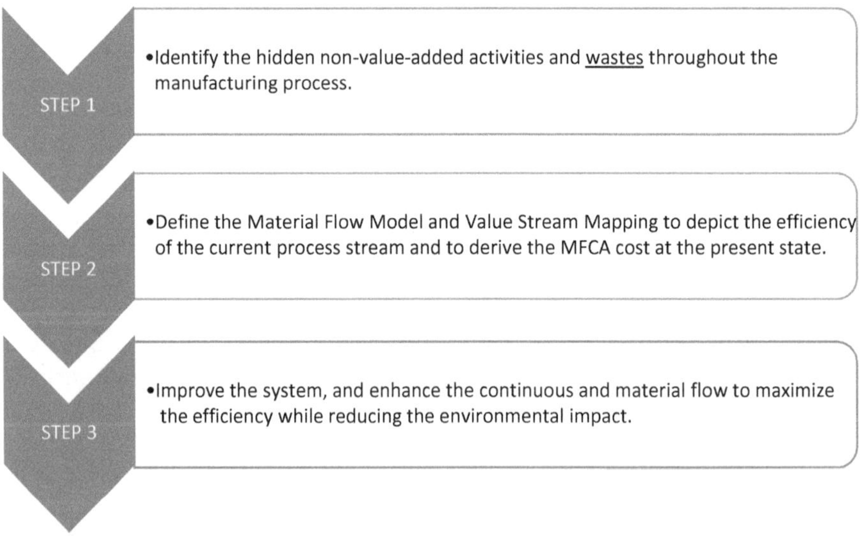

Fig. 9.3 The steps of application of MFCA with LEAN

cost. This was used to identify the cost drivers and rank the improvement programs. This MFCA cost information has great benefits in that it can be used to evaluate and justify improvement options developed according to the LEAN analysis.

The objective of applying MFCA with LEAN is to make the production system more efficient, which will result in a minimal lead time or maximum throughput, with reduced environmental impact and cost. The system and energy costs are directly related to the amount of time the product is processed through all the operations. If the operations and the processes are all efficient, then mudas resulting from inefficient system and process will be minimal, leading to shorter production lead time and lower system and energy costs. This directly results in a rapid responsive production system with low production cost, which, therefore, yields highly competitive products. Similarly, the material wastes generated from each production process indicates that the effectiveness of the operations needs to be increased. The higher the amount and the sources of waste, the less effective the current operation and process is. Thus, a waste minimization program must be initiated. This focus on system effectiveness and efficiency should be done simultaneously, in order for the two to self-supplement each other. The final step is to sustain and continuously improve the system with Kaizen programs. The identification of waste minimization programs and system optimization are justified with respect to the economic and environment perspective under different MFCA cost scenarios. The improvement solutions can then be implemented and evaluated with respect to the MFCA cost.

9.4 Results

9.4.1 Background of the Case Study: A Pajama Manufacturing Company

This research demonstrates the implementation of MFCA under LEAN steps by using the case study of a pajama manufacturing company located in northern Thailand. This company has approximately 150 employees working in different departments. All of their leading products are exported to the markets of North America and Europe.

Before applying MFCA tools and techniques, this research used the process flow chart technique to define the flow of activities, works, and materials across all operations. The process flow chart helps in revealing the connection between operations and their relationships. The process requirements and resources can be determined preliminarily using this technique. This process flow chart also provides insight into the flows of materials and is the basis for the material flow model of the process.

Next, comprehensive data collection was carried out by the researcher. The business process of this case study system starts with receiving orders from customers. Then samples and patterns are designed and sent to the customer for approval. If approved, raw materials are then acquired from suppliers and processed through the

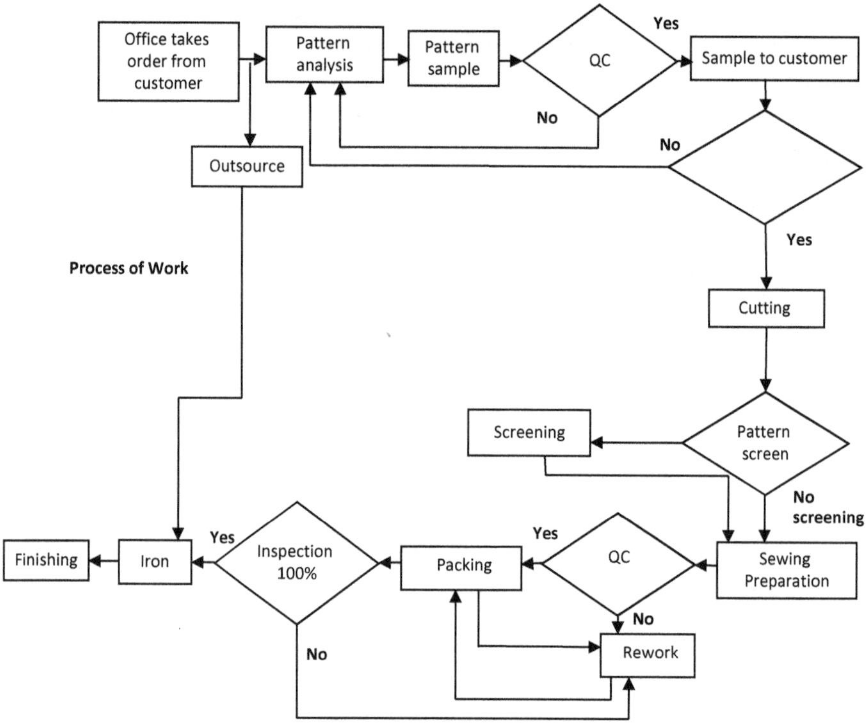

Fig. 9.4 The business flow chart of the case study

serial stages of cutting, screening, sewing, ironing, and packing, and, finally, finishing. The operation processes are depicted in Fig. 9.4. Fabric, the raw material, is cut according to the pattern generated. Some cut pieces are further processed with screening, while the assembled pieces need to be kept on hold for matching. Since the screening operation is outsourced, in this research, the lead time of the screening operation is fixed and, hence, excluded from the improvement analysis. Once the screened pieces arrive and the complete set is obtained, it is processed and sewn by the sewing department. Thus, any delays occurring at the screening or the sewing process will cause other operations, including delivery, to be delayed. All major operations, including patterning, cutting, and sewing are considered the critical path of the production process. These major operations also consume energy; hence, the system and the energy costs are incrementally absorbed along the production stages.

Based on the process flows constructed, the research study then analyzed how the product or service value was created along the business operation. Information on production and system efficiency was then disclosed. This case study company encountered typical productions problems of longer lead time, high inventory, and high Work In Process (WIP), excessive defects leading to high material wastes, and high production cost (Fig. 9.5). The company frequently missed delivery schedules and encountered higher production costs because of extreme overtime periods.

Fig. 9.5 The current status of the case study process

Along the production stage, there occurred several instances of waste, that is, at the cutting, the screening, and the sewing operations. These material wastes were collected and processed as negative products. This research identified the system's efficiency and used material waste as a measure for initiating LEAN MFCA to improve the production process efficiency, as well as using LEAN, MFCA and the discrete event system simulation techniques to reduce the production and environmental costs.

9.4.2 Implementing of MFCA Under LEAN

9.4.2.1 Step 1: Identifying Hidden Non-value-added Activities and Wastes Throughout Manufacturing Process

At this stage, the researcher adopted the value engineering principle to identify wastes and mudas at each operation. The Kaizen technique of elimination of the seven wastes, ECRS, time study, and visual control were applied. The wastes and mudas were sorted out and eliminated. For example, at the sewing stage, the output rate was inconsistent due to, for instance, inefficient material or "big lots part transportation" between workers. Communication between leaders and workers regarding the production sequence and the productivity status was not effective, leading to frequent idle time and waiting periods. Also, the fact that the workers had varying levels of competency, there were variations in the output rate. This research then adopted and used the multi-skilled worker technique, and regrouped the workers according to the sewing load and pattern. This helped in leveling the work and the output load significantly. The productivity was observed to improve, as did communication due to the use of visual control. The dedicated material transportation was with small lot sizes for each worker cell, whose output was constantly monitored using a visual control board (Fig. 9.6). The resulting output was found to increase at the sewing process, from an average of 625 units per day to 723 units per day (15% increase in the output), leading to a labor cost saving of 31.53%.

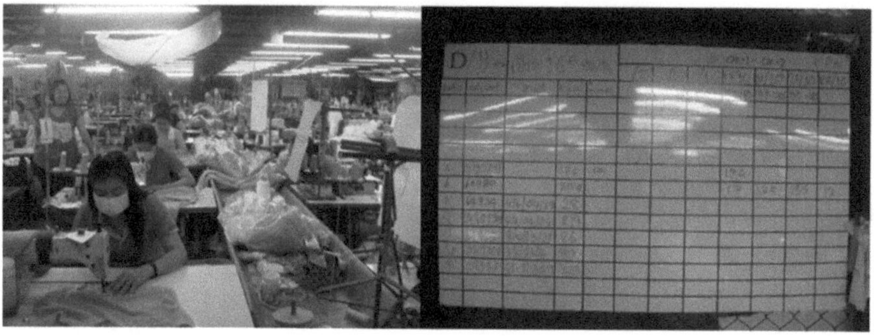

Fig. 9.6 Visual control and dedicated material transport for each worker cell

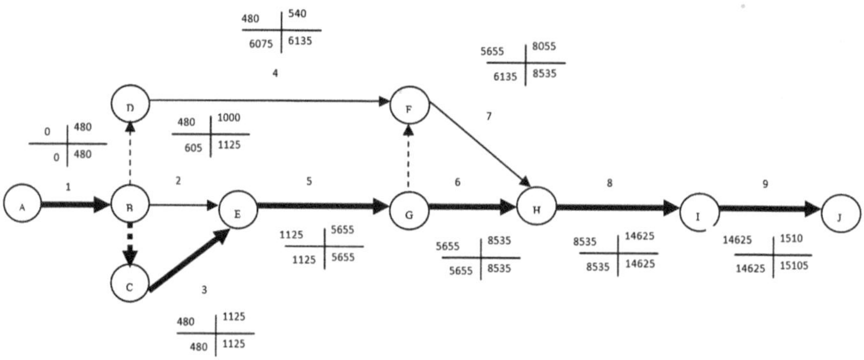

Fig. 9.7 Application of PERT to define critical path operations and improve the monitoring scheme

Moreover, to reduce the delay in delivery, this research applied the Project Evaluation and Review Technique (PERT) to identify the critical path, as shown in Fig. 9.7. This helped the researcher to set up a monitoring scheme for other orders. Consequently, the planning of internal operations could be monitored and improved. In summary, identification and reduction of system wastes and non-value-added activities in the very first step helped in increasing the throughput of the processes, thus minimizing the system cost per unit of product. However, the relationships between activities and operations along the business chain need to be further analyzed systematically. The following section explores the second step of the LEAN MFCA methodology.

9.4.2.2 Step 2: Defining Material Flow Model and Value Stream Mapping to Depict Efficiency of Current Process Stream

The next step is to identify the interconnectivity of the internal operations with manufacturing. This is best accomplished by using the Value Stream Mapping, or VSM, tool which has been vastly used by the LEAN school. VSM can help with

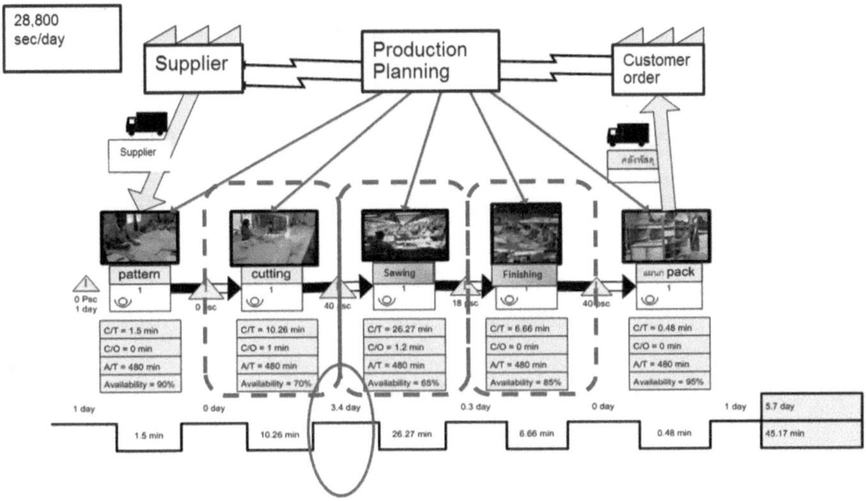

Fig. 9.8 The VSM of the business and the manufacturing operations of the case study

depicting and identifying the current material flow, information flow, inventory stored throughout the system, and the interaction between the demand and the production supply mechanism. The VSM of the business and the manufacturing operations of the case study, as shown in Fig. 9.8, revealed high level of inventory waiting for the sewing process. This was the main cause for delivery delays and was partly caused by inefficient capacity of the sewing department. Moreover, VSM also indicated that the largest proportion of system cost was at the sewing process which accounted for the highest processing time per lot. Hence, a detailed analysis of the sewing process, its cycle time at each sewing step, and the overall line balance needed to be investigated; this is explained in the next step.

In order to identify the sources of waste, this research study followed the MFCA procedure, by starting with identifying the material losses and wastes from the entire production process. The material flow model was drawn to identify the sources of the material inputs and outputs including the sources of wastes generated, as shown in Fig. 9.9. In this research, the process consisted of six QCs represented by each main process of cutting, screening, sewing, finishing, outsourcing, and packing.

Next, the material inputs and outputs were determined for each QC represented by each process. The difference between the inputs and the outputs for each processing step was quantified and reported. Based on the available material cost per unit, the material cost (MC) could then be determined for the total cost of material (per lot), cost of positive material (per lot), and cost of wasted material (per lot). For example, the material balance table of the cutting process, or QC1, was as shown in Table 9.1. The material cost calculation was done for all QCs.

The researcher then used the information obtained from the LEAN VSM analysis in terms of cycle time, to determine the System Cost (SC). The amount of energy consumed by each QC was also determined and calculated for Energy Cost (EC). For example, the MFCA cost allocation for MC, SC, and EC of QC1: cutting

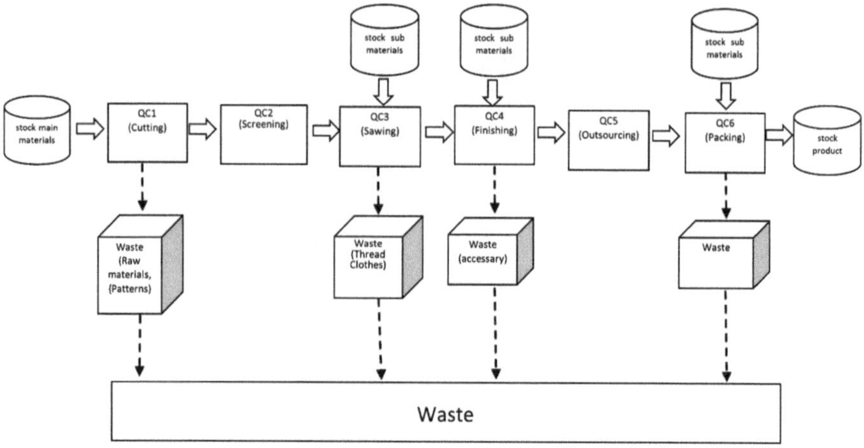

Fig. 9.9 The material flow model of the manufacturing operations of the case study

Table 9.1 Material balance table of QC1: cutting process

Material balance table (QC1: cutting process)					
Input: material used		**Output: waste**		**Output: company products**	
Major materials	Quantity	Waste (negative product)	Quantity	Company products	Quantity
CK-155	190 yd	CK-155	38 yd	CK-155	152 yd
UNI top	12 yd	UNI top	2.4 yd	UNI top	9.6 yd
UNI bottom	219 yd	UNI bottom	43.8 yd	UNI bottom	175.2 yd
Plastics	70 kg	Plastics	14 kg	Plastics	56 kg
Patterns	180 pieces	Patterns	36 pieces	Patterns	144 pieces
Quantity percentage	**100%**	**Quantity percentage**	**20%**	**Quantity percentage**	**80%**
Cost of input materials		Cost of wasted materials (negative product)		Cost of materials (positive product)	
Total	**25,468.9**	**Total**	**50,93.79**	**Total**	**20,375.1**

process is shown in Fig. 9.10. Since the physical units of the input materials are different, this research study allocated the MFCA cost based on the proportion of the material input values, rather than the proportion of the physical weight.

This MFCA cost allocation was done for all the six QCs, which gave rise to the MFCA cost matrix, as shown in Table 9.2 and graphed in Fig. 9.11. The MFCA cost structure revealed that the MC accounted for almost 70% of the total cost, whereas the SC accounted for almost 30%. This clearly suggested that the total cost depended not only on the material but also the processing time. Hence, it can be concluded that flow efficiency had a great impact on the MFCA cost structure. If the production

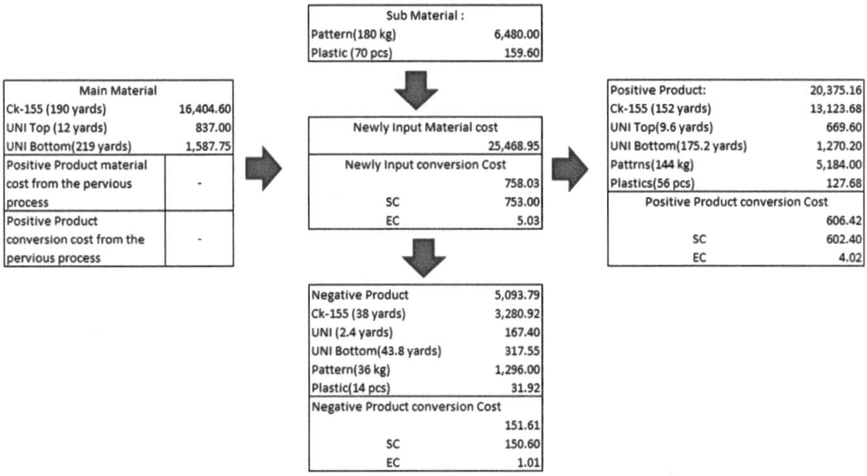

Fig. 9.10 The MFCA cost allocation for MC, SC, and EC of QC1: cutting process

Table 9.2 MFCA cost structure (per lot) of case study (before improvement)

MFCA cost matrix	MC (%)	SC (%)	EC (%)	WC (%)	Total (%)
Positive product	53.67	27.29	0.99	0.00	82
Negative product	15.41	1.72	0.06	0.87	18
Total	**69.08**	**29.01**	**1.04**	**0.87**	**100**

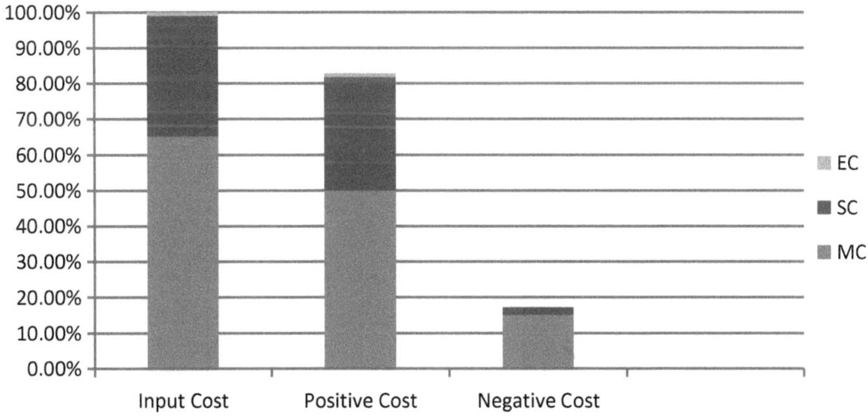

Fig. 9.11 The graphical representation of the MFCA cost (before improvement)

was improved according to the continuous flow concepts of LEAN, the total cost of production could be reduced.

Note that the information from LEAN in terms of VSM can be directly used for MFCA analysis to draw the material flow model. The processing time indicated in the VSM can be used to compute SC and EC, since the amount of energy consumed is directly proportional to the cycle time. Together with the information generated from MFCA, all MC, SC, EC, and WC can be determined for all QCs. Hence, LEAN helps in providing the principal structure for MFCA, whereas their combination generates a model that can be used to study the interaction between system efficiency and environmental impact. This engineering model can therefore be used to analyze how a system variable interacts with the MFCA cost structure. This research study shows that LEAN and MFCA support each other.

9.4.2.3 Step 3: Improving System, and Enhancing Continuous and Material Flow to Maximize Efficiency

The results of the analysis from VSM and material flow, as illustrated in Figs. 9.8 and 9.9, indicate that the sewing process was the bottleneck process which caused inventory to accumulate. The production lead time was necessarily increased from many hidden non-value-added activities, and inappropriate lot size movement causing large amounts of inventory and long waiting times among the sewing operators. This leds to high proportion of the system cost. The large amounts of inventory led to higher chances of error and defect since WIP was inspected only after production.

The sewing process was operated currently as the push system. Each pajama required several cut pieces of different parts of the product, such as neck, shoulder, front piece, and back piece. At the sewing process, there were nine sewing operations, each station employing one worker. The cycle time of each sewing station, as

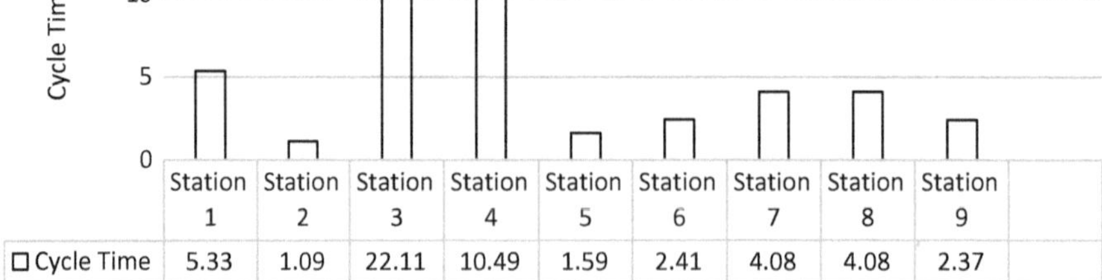

Fig. 9.12 The cycle time of each sewing station

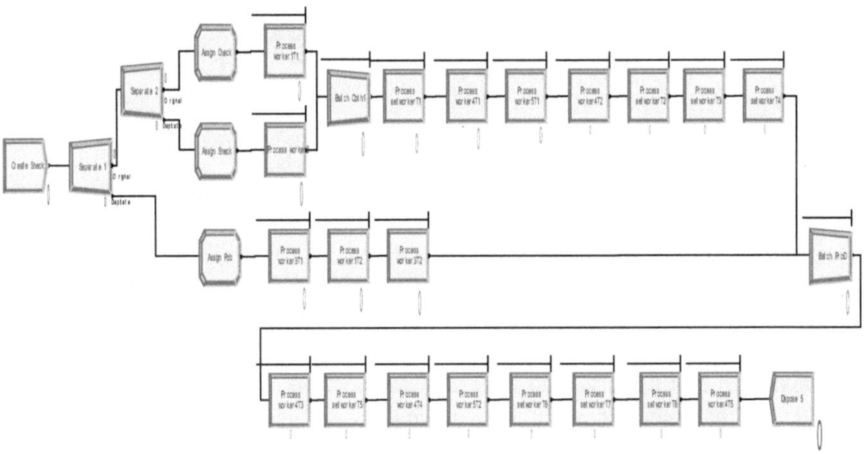

Fig. 9.13 The representation of the sewing processes using discrete event simulation

presented in Fig. 9.12, revealed that the line balance needed to be improved. Sewing station no. 9 had the longest cycle time which could lead to a long waiting time and WIP within the sewing department. The LEAN MFCA solution was to improve and rearrange the sequence of the sewing operations, in order to eliminate the bottleneck process which accounted for the long cycle time.

In order to account for the random fluctuations of the operation condition while improving the efficiency and the continuous flow, the analysis of the process flow chart and the cycle time of each sewing station was modeled using the discrete simulation technique with the Arena program. Discrete event simulation was used to represent the flow of the process, as shown in Fig. 9.13. This model was used to study the interaction between the cycle times and the outputs of the process. In our simulation verification, the model was run to determine the estimated production lead time at the sewing process for a single lot size of 200 pajamas. The simulation revealed that the amount of time spent on a single lot at the sewing department was an average of 33 h (4 days), and that it could be as high as as 66 h (8 days). The total number of WIPs was an average of 241 pajamas, and it could be as high as 721 pajamas. This corresponded with the VSM which showed a shorter cycle time for the previous station, screening. Hence, this would cause the inventory of WIP to be stacked up at the sewing process.

Thus, to improve the system efficiency and continuous flow, we needed to reduce the cycle time of the sewing system and apply the line balancing technique to eliminate the bottle neck situation. Upon rearranging the workloads between station 2 and station 3, the system cycle time was found to have reduced, but the line could not be perfectly balanced because of some sewing constraints. The simulation was run again to compare the results between before and after improvement. The improved line balance, as shown in Table 9.3, helped to reduce the production lead

Table 9.3 MFCA cost structure (per lot) of case study

	Before (h)	After (h)
Average total time	33	20.28
Maximum total time	66.6	42

time of a single lot from an average of 33 h (4 days) to an average of 20.28 h, and from what could be as high as 66 h (8 days) to a maximum total time of 42 h (5 days), which was equivalent to 38.55% reduction. With respect to the MFCA cost structure, this reduction in the sewing time corresponded to the reduction in the system cost. The MFCA cost structure was then improved with a smaller proportion of the negative system cost.

The improvement analysis also gave rise to waste minimization programs, which were considered as environmental improvement with regard to the whole operation. The current operations were analysed with reference to material losses and wastage. A typical problem found was quality imperfection; this and the occurrence of defects at the sewing process were the main sources of wastage and negative products. This wastage of material, energy, and system processing was resolved with a waste minimization program.

9.4.3 Initiating Waste Minimization Programs

The analysis of the wastes generated from the process indicated that the greatest source of material waste was the cutting process. The amount of waste was dependent on the pattern generated, and it could be improved if the pattern-generating software was modified and improved. At the time the research was carried out, the company was unable to modify its pattern-generating software. Thus, the team focused on the next two main sources of waste: the sewing and finishing processes.

Before the improvement, there was no quality control program dedicated to the sewing process. Because of that reason, the pajamas needed to be inspected at the finishing stage. This led to inefficient monitoring and communication regarding defects caused during the sewing process. Moreover, there were also defects that were inherent to the screened parts and the raw material fed into the sewing department. This research study designed a quality control program for the sewing department, by installing a technique for inspecting the incoming raw material, in order to avoid accepting defective input, and having an in-process inspection to closely monitor the defects and effectiveness of the sewing operations. These quality control programs have led to a reduction in waste and negative products. In addition, the case study company experimented by improving the competency and the skills of the sewing workers with training programs. This training also helped reduce the number of defective items, generated from incorrect sewing. Thus, it was evident that the two waste minimization programs at the sewing department helped reduce

Table 9.4 Comparison of MFCA cost structures (per lot) after improvement

MFCA cost matrix		MC	SC	EC	WC	Total
Positive product	After	54.70%	29.11%	0.90%	0%	85%
	Before	(53.67%)	(27.29%)	(0.99%)	(0.00%)	(82%)
Negative product	After	13.72%	0.98%	0.02%	0.57%	15%
	Before	(15.41%)	(1.72%)	(0.06%)	(0.87%)	(18%)
Total	**After**	**68.43%**	**30.08%**	**0.92%**	**0.57%**	**100%**
	Before	**(69.08%)**	**(29.01%)**	**(1.04%)**	**(0.87%)**	

waste at both the sewing process, from 5% to 2%, and the finishing process, from 2% to 1%. The improved operations have led to lower proportions of negative product cost. The proportion of positive products computed for a single lot was found to have increased from 82% to 85%. The proportions of material, system, and energy were also observed to have increased, and the proportions of the negative products were all found to have decreased, as shown in Table 9.4. The implementation of both LEAN and waste minimization led to an overall cost reduction of 3.6%, and a reduction of negative cost by 18%. The ratio of positive cost to negative cost was observed to have improved from 82%:18% to 85%:15%.

This waste minimization helped the team to outline and select improvement alternatives consisting of process design, work design, product, process and quality improvement. The identification of waste minimization programs and system optimization, was again justified with respect to the economic and environmental perspective under different MFCA cost scenarios. The company continued to launch programs to eliminate wastage and inefficiency within the process. Even though modification of the pattern-generating software was not possible, an arrangement of the cutting pattern to minimize waste was. The company also defined an improvement program of waste reduction at the cutting department which would be followed up in the next round of implementation. The possibility of generating defective items, which were discovered at the screening process, was also planned to be eliminated by applying quality control and improvement techniques, seven quality control tools, and design of experiment to identify the root causes of the problem. Implementation of the next LEAN MFCA cycle was also defined and planned.

The waste minimization programs led to a reduction of material losses, thus reducing the amount of chemicals and energy used at the cutting and the screening processes. Energy consumption per lot was observed to have reduced, as did environmental impacts caused by wasted material and the use of chemicals. The environmental management program and the treatment of waste could be improved, thanks to the reduction of material usage, which is the core concept of MFCA among the 3R concepts.

9.5 Discussion and Conclusion

This research study presented an application of LEAN MFCA in which MFCA was implemented under the LEAN methodology. This application demonstrated how to embed and integrate the widely accepted productivity improvement technique of LEAN with the sustainable production concept of MFCA. This research study applied the LEAN MFCA technique to a real case study: that of a pajama manufacturer located in northern Thailand. The implementation followed the LEAN thinking steps. The first step was identifying and eliminating the hidden non-value-added activities and typical wastes including material and energy wastes throughout the manufacturing process; this led the company to identify basic improvement methods of all processes and operations. However, the overall system and its interactions needed to be optimized, which was done by using the well-known LEAN and MFCA tools of VSM and the material flow model to depict the efficiency and effectiveness of its current state. This system analysis was also reported in an economic view through MFCA lens, which helped identify and rank the sources of inefficiency contributing to the greatest negative cost.

The solution to improve the overall system efficiency and continuous flow was provided jointly with the waste elimination programs. The typical problems of quality imperfection, defects, and all material, energy, and wastes were minimized. Identification of waste minimization programs and system optimization were justified with respect to MFCA cost scenarios. The solutions for improvement were experimented, implemented, and evaluated with respect to the MFCA cost. The waste minimization programs at the sewing department helped reduce waste at both the sewing process and the finishing process. The improved operations have led to a lower proportion of the negative product cost. The proportions of the material, system, and energy were also found to have increased, while the proportions of negative products were all observed to have decreased. The overall total cost of production and the total negative cost were all found to have reduced, while the ratio of the positive cost to the negative cost was observed to have increased. Such application of green and sustainable improvement could help the team to improve the system, the economy, and the environment simultaneously. The presented application has brought about an integrated LEAN and MFCA model, which concurrently takes into account efficacy and economizing. This research application has thus paved way for an improved productivity and a sustainability-oriented production system.

Note that the proposed methodology aligns the MFCA tools with the essence of the LEAN concept in differentiating between value-added and non-value-added activities, eliminating all wastage and mudas, and improving system efficiency with VSM and continuous flow for greatest efficiency. The MFCA measure in terms of MFCA costing was used mainly to tie the physical with the monetary efficiency of the current operation. In fact, several other environmental measures could also be applied, such as Ecovalue08, Eco indicator 99, and cumulative energy demand. These indicators can be applied to LEAN MFCA to gain wider a perspective on environmental impacts.

In addition to the core LEAN benefits, this proposed methodology focuses on and brings into consideration the physical, material, energy, and resource wastes. This is essential to the green productivity improvement concept; it also extends the meaning of waste beyond its traditional definition, and the system to the entire range of negative products generated. This integration helps businesses strategically manage operations, and look at the design of the product and the process. There are other considerations that can also be included. For example, the authors have evaluated that the new improved condition has been found to reduce carbon footprint, due to reduced material loss, use of chemicals, and consumption of energy.

The waste minimization program can lead to the redesigning of the products, processes, and raw materials used. This will help improve the planning of new products and the processes, as well as any planning programs used during the design phase. This research study employed industrial engineering tools such as PERT, discrete simulation, line balancing, lot sizing, visual control, quality control, to improve the process conditions. Other tools such as environmental and energy sciences can also be used. This research study evaluated and selected improvement methods based on the economic performance reported, and the structure according to the MFCA disclosure. Nevertheless, the social aspect could be included in the evaluation, which would help in expanding the LEAN MFCA toward sustainable improvement. This research finally demonstrates the application of combining the EMA tool with productivity improvement, which led to an increase in the material, system, and environmental efficiency. The findings of this research could be used as a basis for theoretical development of a new paradigm for improvement of sustainable productivity in the future.

Acknowledgment This research was supported by the Research Administration Center, Office of the President, Chiang Mai University, Thailand.

References

Agus A, Hajinoor MS (2012) LEAN production supply chain management as driver towards enhancing product quality and business performance: case study of manufacturing companies in Malaysia. Int J Qual Reliab Manag 29(1):92–121

Andrade PF, Pereira VG, Del Conte EG (2016) Value stream mapping and lean simulation: a case study in automotive company. Int J Adv Manuf Technol 85(1):547–555

Asian Development Bank (ADB) (2015) THAILAND industrialization and economic catch-up country diagnostic study report of Asian Develop Bank

Asian Productivity Organization (APO) (2015) Productivity in the Asia-Pacific past, present, and future

Bhasin S, Burcher P (2006) LEAN viewed as a philosophy. J Manuf Technol Manag 17(1):56–72

Cao J (2007) Measuring green productivity growth for China's manufacturing sectors. Asian Econ J 21(4):425–451

Chang CC, Luh YH (1999) Efficiency change and growth in productivity: the Asian growth experience. J Asian Econ 10(4):551–570

Chattinnawat W (2013) Identification of improvement for multistage serial processes with respect to material flow cost accounting via dynamic programming. In: Proceedings of the 2013 EMAN-EU conference on material flow cost accounting, Germany, pp 30–33
Chattinnawat W, Teeratanasombut M, Kammoon C (2015) Development of analysis method of material flow cost accounting using LEAN technique in food production: a case study of Universal Food Public (UFC) Co., Ltd. KKU Eng J 42(2):155–172
Chompu-inwai R, Jaimjit B, Premsuriyanunt P (2015) A combination of material flow cost accounting and design of experiments techniques in an SME: the case of a wood products manufacturing company in northern Thailand. J Clean Prod 108(Part B):1352–1364
Christ KL, Burritt RL (2015) Material flow cost accounting: a review and agenda for future research. J Clean Prod 108(Part B):1378–1389
Diao X, Rattsø J, Stokke HE (2005) International spillovers, productivity growth and openness in Thailand: an intertemporal general equilibrium analysis. J Dev Econ 76(2):429–450
Domingo R, Alvarez R, Peña MM, Calvo R (2007) Materials flow improvement in a lean assembly line: a case study. Assem Autom 27(2):141–147
Hobday M (1995) East Asian latecomer firms: learning the technology of electronics. World Dev 23(7):1171–1193
Holweg M (2007) The genealogy of LEAN production. J Oper Manag 25(2):420–437
Huang SH, Dismukes JP, Shi J, Su Q, Wang G, Razzak MA, Robinson DE (2002) Manufacturing system modeling for productivity improvement. J Manuf Syst 21(4):249–259
Hur T, Kima I, Yamamoto R (2004) Measurement of green productivity and its improvement. J Clean Prod 12(7):673–683
ISO 14051 (2011) Environmental management – material flow cost accounting – general framework. ISO, Geneva
Jacobson MZ (2008) On the causal link between carbon dioxide and air pollution mortality. Geophys Res Lett 35:L03809. Available at. https://doi.org/10.1029/2007GL031101
Jasch CM (2008) Environmental and material flow cost accounting: principles and procedures. Springer, Dordrecht
Kasemset C, Chernsupornchai J, Pala-ud W (2015) Application of MFCA in waste reduction: case study on a small textile factory in Thailand. J Clean Prod 108(Part B):1342–1351
Kim J, Lau LJ (1994) The source of growth of the East Asian newly industrialized economies. J Jpn Int Econ 8(3):235–271
Kokubu K, Kitada H (2015) Material flow cost accounting and existing management perspectives. J Clean Prod 108(Part B):1279–1288
Lee KH (2009) Why and how to adopt green management into business organizations? The case study of Korean SMEs in manufacturing industry. Manag Decis 47(7):1101–1121
Manea D (2013) LEAN production– concept and benefits. Rev Gen Manag 17(1):164–171
Melton T (2005) The benefits of LEAN manufacturing: what LEAN thinking has to offer the process industries. Chem Eng Res Des 83(A6):662–673
Ministry of Economy, Technology and Industry (METI) (2011) MFCA case examples 2011. Japanese Ministry of Economy, Trade and Industry, Tokyo. Available at: http://www.jmac.co.jp/mfca/thinking/data/MFCA_Case_example_e2011_new.pdf
Muthiah KMN, Huang SH (2006) A review of literature on manufacturing systems productivity measurement and improvement. Int J Ind Syst Eng 1(4):461–484
Nakajima M (2008) The new development of Material Flow Cost Accounting (MFCA): MFCA analysis in power company and comparison between MFCA and TPM (Total Productive Maintenance). Kansai Univ Rev Bus Commer 10:57–86
Nakajima M (2009) Evolution of Material Flow Cost Accounting (MFCA): characteristics on development of MFCA companies and significance of relevance of MFCA. Kansai Univ Rev Bus Commer 11:27–46
Nakajima M (2011) Environmental management accounting for cleaner production: systematization of material flow cost accounting (MCFA) into corporate management system. Kansai Univ Rev Bus Commer 13:17–39

Ohno T (1988) The Toyota production system: beyond large-scale production. Productivity Press, Portland

Pettersen J (2009) Defining LEAN production: some conceptual and practical issues. TQM J 21(2):127–142

Phusavat K, Kanchana R (2007) Competitive priorities of manufacturing firms in Thailand. Ind Manag Data Syst 107(7):979–996

Phusavat K, Kanchana R (2008) Competitive priorities for service providers: perspectives from Thailand. Ind Manag Data Syst 108(1):5–21

Powell D, Alfnes E, Strandhagen JO, Dreyer H (2013) The concurrent application of LEAN production and ERP: towards an ERP-based LEAN implementation process. Comput Ind 64(3):324–335

Rusinko C (2007) Green manufacturing: an evaluation of environmentally sustainable manufacturing practices and their impact on competitive outcomes. IEEE Trans Eng Manag 54(3):445–454

Schaltegger S, Zvezdov D (2015) Expanding material flow cost accounting. Framework, review and potentials. J Clean Prod 108(Part B):1333–1341

Schmidt M (2015) The interpretation and extension of Material Flow Cost Accounting (MFCA) in the context of environmental material flow analysis. J Clean Prod 108(Part B):1310–1319

Schmidt M, Nakajima M (2013) Material flow cost accounting as an approach to improve resource efficiency in manufacturing companies. Resources 2(3):358–369

Seth D, Gupta V (2005) Application of value stream mapping for LEAN operations and cycle time reduction: an Indian case study. Prod Plan Control 16(1):44–59

Shah R, Ward PT (2003) Lean manufacturing: context, practice bundles, and performance. J Oper Manag 21(2):129–149

Shah R, Ward PT (2007) Defining and developing measures of lean production. J Oper Manag 25(4):785–805

Shingo S (1981) Study of the Toyota production systems. Japan Management Association, Tokyo

Takakuwa S, Zhao R, Ichimura H (2014) Analysis of manufacturing systems using simulations in terms of material flow cost accounting. Int J Comput Intell Syst 7(2):44–51

Tuttle T, Heap J (2008) Green productivity: moving the agenda. Int J Product Perform Manag 57(1):93–106

United Nations (2015) Sustainable consumption and production: a handbook for policymakers, global edition, United Nations Environment Programme. Available at: https://sustainabledevelopment.un.org/content/documents/1951Sustainable%20Consumption.pdf

United Nations World Commission on Environment and Development (WCED) (1987) Our common future/Brundtland Report

Wagner B (2015) A report on the origins of Material Flow Cost Accounting (MFCA) research activities. J Clean Prod 108(Part B):1255–1261

Womack JP, Jones DT (1996) LEAN thinking: banish waste and create wealth in your corporation. Simon & Schuster, New York

Womack JP, Jones DT (2003) LEAN thinking: banish waste and create wealth in your corporation, 2nd edn. Simon & Schuster, London

Zhang KH (2001) Does foreign direct investment promote economic growth? Evidence from East Asia and Latin America. Contemp Econ Policy 19(2):175–185

Chapter 10
Is Japanese Material Flow Cost Accounting Useful To Vietnam? A Case Study of a Vietnamese Seafood Processing Company

Den Thi Thu Nguyen

Abstract Environmental Management Accounting (EMA) is a crucial method used in environmental management systems by many Japanese companies for targeting cleaner production and sustainable development. Among various EMA tools, Material Flow Cost Accounting (MFCA) is determined to be the most useful approach. Existing studies have shown numerous successful cases of MFCA applications in Japan; however, there are only a few reported cases about EMA applications in Vietnam. This paper aims to ascertain the viability of using MFCA as an EMA method for Japan in order to determine this tool's applicability to Vietnamese companies in their pursuit of sustainable development. Using the case study method, this paper discusses the usefulness and applicability of the Japanese MFCA approach in a Vietnamese context. In this work, a case study is used to answer the research question. The company under study is a small company from the seafood processing industry, which currently causes serious environmental problems in Vietnam. Using MFCA analysis, the results of the study show that the actual and hidden losses and waste in the production process of a company can be identified.

Keywords Applicability · Material flow cost accounting · Japan · Seafood processing industry · Vietnam

10.1 Introduction

Material Flow Cost Accounting (MFCA) is one of three elements of material flow accounting (UN 2001), which integrates physical and economic information for various dimensions of management. From an ecological economics perspective,

D.T.T. Nguyen (✉)
Graduate School of International Social Sciences, Yokohama National University, Yokohama, Japan
e-mail: nguyen-den-ym@ynu.jp

K.-H. Lee, S. Schaltegger (eds.), *Accounting for Sustainability: Asia Pacific Perspectives*, Eco-Efficiency in Industry and Science 33,
https://doi.org/10.1007/978-3-319-70899-7_10

MFCA is a tool of Environmental Management Accounting (EMA) to enhance material efficiency in quantity and value, and to bring economic and environmental benefits to enterprises (Schaltegger and Zvezdov 2015; Jasch 2009; Kokubu and Nakajima 2004; UN 2001), so this is an environmentally friendly approach of management.

MFCA was developed in the late 1990s by the Institut für Management und Umwelt (IMU) in Augsburg, Germany (Berger et al. 2003; Kokubu and Nakajima 2004) and has attracted the attention of the Japanese government and researchers since the year 2000 (Kokubu and Nakajima 2004; Nakajima 2010). This was in response to the promotion initiatives of the Japanese governmental agency to bridge the gap between environmental reporting (ER) and EMA applications in Japanese companies. Indeed, this is because the EA guidelines of Japanese government agencies had focused more on disclosing information and satisfying external stakeholders than internal decision making during the government's early years of promoting Environmental Accounting (EA) development in Japan. Thus, a project that promoted EMA was implemented in Japan in 2000 and MFCA was one of five tools used in this project. This approach was patterned after the practices in Europe and the United States in order to make it applicable to the environmental management practices of Japanese companies (Kokubu and Tachikawa 2013; Kokubu and Nakajima 2004). Aside from the encouragement of the government, MFCA has become an essential tool of EMA and has been widely and quickly adopted in Japan because of its own distinctive advantages, which are supportive of cleaner production and sustainable development. In 2011, the MFCA was included under the ISO (International Organization for Standardization). Since the ISO 14015 publication, MFCA has been recognized as the foremost tool of EMA and an assistance technique for individual organizations or the total supply chain (Christ and Burritt 2016; ISO 2011; METI 2011; Nakajima et al. 2015). Standardization of MFCA is essential for management because this tool reflects environmental impacts from business activities and helps to increase economic returns by means of decreasing production costs (Schaltegger and Zvezdov 2015; Rieckhof et al. 2014). Regarding the establishment of ISO 14051 in 2011, which is an advocated framework of MFCA implementation, Japan has made valuable contributions from practical experiences (Kokubu et al. 2009; METI 2011; Schmidt 2015).

MFCA is a technique that enables one to identify more losses than the conventional accounting method and offers a new definition of losses; not only losses because of spoiled products at the end of the production process, but other losses at each stage throughout the process as well (Jasch 2009). Consequently, MFCA enables higher material efficiency or resource efficiency, and better economic and environmental performance in sustainable development (Schaltegger and Zvezdov 2015). In the manufacturing industry, the material purchase value of non-product output comprises the largest proportion of environmental costs (Jasch 2009), so identifying the exact amount and value of material loss is, therefore, a critical responsibility for cleaner production and sustainable development (Jasch 2009; Nakajima 2011). It is a fact that the Vietnamese manufacturing and Malaysia, have shown the benefits of MFCA (Kasemset et al. 2015; Sulong et al. 2015). From the cleaner production point of view, MFCA appears to be the dominant approach because of its insight into the material inefficiencies throughout the production process (Schaltegger and Zvezdov 2015; Nakajima 2011; Schmidt et al. 2015). Furthermore, to deal with the scarcity of resources and pressures of environmental pollution, MFCA has also proven to be a viable tool because it detects avoidable losses and hidden wastes through the flows of production, as well as throughout the supply chain (Jasch 2009; Nakajima 2009; Schaltegger and Zvezdov 2015). Essentially, firms operating in developing countries like Vietnam are part of the supply chain, so it is possible to successfully introduce the MFCA concept to them.

Japanese firms have attained zero or nearly zero losses by institutionalizing MFCA (METI 2011). By contrast, Vietnamese companies are struggling from a variety of economic and environmental issues. For example, in the seafood processing industry, most firms have been operating unproductively with as much as 60% material losses, while disposing large amounts of waste and emissions to the environment. Needless to say, it is essential to seek a viable and sustainable solution for this situation in Vietnam. This paper, therefore, aims to examine whether Japan's MFCA approach may be useful and integrated into the Vietnamese setting, by introducing MFCA analysis in the production process of a Vietnamese seafood processing company and testing whether this tool can identify abnormal on-the-spot losses. The reason why Japan's experience in MFCA could be suitable for Vietnamese companies is that, although MFCA was developed in Germany, its breakthrough happened in Japan and has been recognized widely in the country (Schmidt et al. 2015; Guenther et al. 2015). Japanese companies succeeded in their first pilot projects of MFCA implementation (Schmidt et al. 2015; Nakajima 2009, 2010) in 2000 and the number of applications has exceeded 300 cases to date (Nakajima 2010). Furthermore, many companies have successfully integrated their own MFCA applications to existing information systems and programs, even in terms of MS Excel (Kokubu and Kitada 2010). Japan has also extended the use of MFCA to small- and medium-sized enterprises (SMEs) to achieve targets of reducing losses and increasing material productivity. As a matter of fact, according to a Japanese report from METI (2011) about EMA–MFCA applications, SMEs such as Nippon Film Company, Ltd. and IBEX Company, Ltd., in addition to large-sized companies such as Canon Corporation and Nitto Denko Corporation, have reduced their waste and losses, as well as improved their environmental performance, using MFCA applications (see METI 2011 for further information). Therefore, it could be said that the Japanese MFCA approach has characteristics that may be adaptable to companies in developing countries like Vietnam, regardless of size, capital, or current productivity levels.

By incorporating the feasible approach of Japanese companies that uses MFCA, it is anticipated that Vietnamese companies will be able to address their environmental and economic inefficiencies in their production processes. Additionally, this paper may complement APO project 14-IN-22-GE-WSP-B in order to expand

MFCA applications in developing countries in the Asia-Pacific region.[1] Moreover, this paper can possibly contribute to the body of empirical research on EMA applications, particularly in discerning the effectiveness of EMA tools in resolving the environmental and economic problems of companies from developing countries.

In order to reach its research targets, the paper is structured as follows. After the introduction, the research questions and methods are discussed in detail. The third section explains the development of MFCA as the primary EMA tool in Japan and explores the characteristics of the Japanese MFCA approach related to its applicability to Vietnamese companies. The fourth section recommends a trial application of MFCA analysis to a Vietnamese company; in particular, the case of a seafood processing business. Conclusions derived from the research and future research prospects about MFCA implementations in Vietnam are drawn and comprise the last section of this paper.

10.2 Research Design

There are very limited studies on EMA applications in Vietnam. One of the few notable studies is the work of Schaltegger et al. (2012) about the application of EMA on the Vietnamese beer brewing industry. In their study, they highlighted the inefficiency in the management of the production facility and the industry's energy consumption. In particular, they analyzed the physical accounting information of material and energy through a material and energy flow accounting (MEFA) system, which was patterned after the EMA framework of Burritt et al. (2002). In this paper, the emphasis will be on how the Japanese MFCA approach is valuable in analyzing a company in the Vietnamese seafood processing business.

The paper adopts an exploratory case study approach to identify the usefulness of Japanese MFCA in Vietnam. Information about the application of MFCA in Japanese companies is collected from previous research. Based on these sources, the author is able to identify the distinctive characteristics of the MFCA approach for Japan according to the IMU and determine the variable parameters that may be useful in Vietnam. By analyzing these characteristics and practical applications, the MFCA approach in Japan was discerned to be more preferable in constructing a trial model of MFCA analysis for a Vietnamese firm in the seafood processing industry. Through the case study method, this model was applied to a real life scenario in terms of the production process of a Vietnamese seafood company.

Data for the case study are from multiple sources (Yin 2013), so the required information was obtained from various documents in the accounting and production department of the company. In addition, clarifications about the data were verified through direct interviews with managers from the production, technology, and accounting department. Discrepancies of material flow information between the

[1] There was an agreement between 12 countries, including Vietnam and Japan, on developing and disseminating MFCA with the support of the National Productivity Organization, APO, and Japanese experts in 2015 in Indonesia.

accounting documents and actual production were also examined via these interviews. Furthermore, during the research period, the author visited the company many times to observe and understand the actual production process. In order to eliminate any randomness due to production fluctuations and worker behavior during different periods, monthly data was used in the analysis. The MFCA implementation steps are introduced into the practical production process of the case study. In order to simplify MFCA to suit the small Vietnamese company, this paper particularly focused on analyzing only one among three elements of MFCA—raw materials. Consequently, the actual and abnormal material losses and wastes of the process are indicated and presented by MFCA calculations and matrix flows. Later, based on MFCA analysis and the Plan-Do-Check-Act (PDCA) cycle, the solutions for improvement are proposed and implemented.

10.3 MFCA in Japan

To understand the specifics about the Japanese MFCA, the history of MFCA development in Japan, as well as the criticisms about the distinctive characteristics of Japan's MFCA approach compared to Germany's approach, are discussed hereunder.

10.3.1 History of MFCA Development in Japan

During the early years of EA development, Japanese companies focused on reporting environmental information to external stakeholders rather than using EA as a management tool (Kokubu and Nakajima 2004; Nakajima et al. 2003). The reason is that the EA guidelines of the Japanese Ministry of Environment (MOE) were more focused on external factors than internal ones (Kokubu et al. 2003; Kokubu and Nakajima 2004; METI 2002). To settle this situation for Japanese companies, the government; in particular, the Ministry of Economy, Technology, and Industry (METI) implemented projects to develop suitable EMA for Japanese companies by studying the EMA practices in North America and Europe that could also enhance the internal functions of EA and become a tool in which to improve the internal communication of environmental information for decision making (Kokubu and Nakajima 2004; Wagner 2015). MFCA was developed as a result of these projects and has been considered as a major tool of EMA for sustainable development (Nakajima et al. 2013). The METI project lasted from 1999 to 2002 and developed environmental management accounting tools that fit Japanese companies (Kokubu and Nakajima 2004). At first, MFCA was introduced into some Japanese companies (such as Nitto Denko, Canon, Tanabe, and Takiron) as case studies and, later on, was evaluated for its effectiveness in terms of the Japanese METI project in 2001 (Nakajima 2004). The results revealed that such companies gained positive results with lower losses and lower waste emissions. Japan determined that MFCA could be used as a tool of EMA–a kind of EA for internal management–in order to protect the environment and to enhance material productivity (Nakajima 2003; Kokubu and Nakajima 2004).

At present, MFCA is widely used in Japan. As a matter of fact, several Japanese companies such as Canon and Tanabe Seiyaku have become notable examples of companies that espouse MFCA. Definitely, Japan is the first country to achieve large-scale MFCA applications (Schmidt and Nakajima 2013). According to a report from the Asian Productivity Organization (APO 2014), more than 300 companies in Japan have adopted MFCA.

10.3.2 Japan's MFCA Approach

Although Japan's MFCA and Germany's MFCA originate from one source, Japan further revolutionized the concept so that it was more practically useful. Therefore, in terms of practical usage, there are some discrepancies between Japanese version and the original (Nakajima 2004).

Japan's MFCA, for example, has primarily been concerned with each product line or process (IFAC 2005). The German version, on the other hand, was more interested in constructing company-wide information systems such as the Enterprise Resource Planning (ERP) system (IFAC 2005). Therefore, MFCA in Japan is usually first applied to a single process as a trial run and then expanded to other processes until it pervades the entire system. This action enables further analysis of process improvements, investment, and innovation (IFAC 2005).

In Japan, most companies use Microsoft (MS) Excel for performing MFCA calculations (Kokubu and Kitada 2015). In their research on MFCA applications in Japanese companies, Kokubu and Tachikawa (2013) mentioned that, in Japanese companies, manual information preparation by paper or post-it-notes is as effective as computer programs (Christ and Burritt 2015). By contrast, Strobel and Redmann (2002) believed advanced information technology options and ERP systems are essential for MFCA applications in German companies. Germany's MFCA is combined with advanced information technology, even in the first project of expanding MFCA applications in Germany (Wagner 2015); meanwhile, Japan's MFCA may be useful in current information systems without the support of high-tech software. This makes Japanese MFCA user-friendly and adaptable to small- and medium-sized companies (Kokubu et al. 2009). This can also be explained by the most distinctive characteristic of management between Japanese and Western companies. While Western companies are more focused on breakthrough innovations, Japanese companies prefer continuous step-by-step improvements (Imai 1991).

In addition, MFCA applications in Germany seem to focus more on large-sized companies, while MFCA projects in Japan are introduced to companies of all sizes (Kokubu and Nakajima 2004; METI 2011). Indeed, among 32 companies in the METI (2011) report of MFCA case examples, 15 cases were SMEs.

Japanese companies combined MFCA analysis and the PDCA cycle. This combination was first established through practical applications to Japanese companies such as Canon and Nitto Denko (Kokubu and Kitada 2015; Higashida et al. 2013; Nakajima 2009; Schmidt and Nakajima 2013). This experience was a valuable contribution to the official publication of ISO 14051–Environmental management – MFCA standardization. According to APO (2014), MFCA may enhance the efficiency of the Environmental Management System (EMS) by using the PDCA cycle. PDCA is an endless process of improving environmental and economic performance based on continuous plans, activities, and inspection. "Plan" means setting environmental targets and policies; "Do" requires preparation of resources and actions for implementing the plan; "Check" aims to evaluate and justify actions, if necessary; and "Act" is the review for the next environmental plan. In the Japanese style, information from MFCA analysis is used for management based on the PDCA cycle. To date, the PDCA cycle is published in ISO 14051 as a guideline for implementing MFCA. Based on the information from MFCA analysis, Japanese companies employ continuous PDCA cycles to carry out countermeasures against material losses and environmental impacts. The combination between MFCA and PDCA cycles also includes the characteristics of Kaizen in MFCA. Indeed, Japanese companies recognized MFCA as the "Green Kaizen" (Nakajima et al. 2013; Schmidt and Nakajima 2013). Therefore, when using the Japanese MFCA approach, continous and incremental improvements are made in small steps.

Overall, Japanese practical applications indicate that MFCA can be applied without advanced information technology and in enterprises of all sizes, as well as in various industries (Kokubu et al. 2009; Kokubu and Nakajima 2004). Adding such abovementioned characteristics to the MFCA approach may lead to breakthroughs in MFCA applications in Japan and make such Japanese adaptions more amenable to SMEs in developing countries like Vietnam, where there are mainly small- and medium-sized companies with poorly equipped facilities and information systems.

10.4 MFCA Application for the Vietnamese Case

10.4.1 Environmental Issues Due to the Vietnamese Seafood Processing Industry

In Vietnam, environmental protection has not been addressed by many businesses. Many companies violated environmental regulations and dumped wastewater into rivers or creeks and the surrounding environment without subjecting them to any treatment. In particular, only approximately 70% of the seafood processing industry companies is equipped with wastewater treatment systems. The seafood processing industry is disposing a large amount of waste into the environment. According to the Vietnam Research Institute for Marine Fisheries, in order produce 1 ton of product, firms dispose 0.75 tons of waste for shrimp and 0.8 tons of waste for tra fillet (Tran

Nguyen 2014). These amounts do not include wastewater and emissions. Furthermore, the disposal from this industry is extremely toxic to the environment because of high organic impurities from fish intestines and shrimp cells; for example, in surimi production, the indices of Biochemical Oxygen Demand (BOD) and Chemical Oxygen Demand (COD) in wastewater were as high as 3120 mg/l and 4890 mg/l, respectively. In addition, according to information about problems in the seafood processing industry, the average wastewater disposal from only one seafood processing firm is around 50,000 m^3/day. With this trend, polluted water sources may cause serious impacts on human life and well-being in Vietnam in the near future.

It is clear that the seafood processing industry has caused substantial and severe environmental degradation in Vietnam. Hence, immediate actions to overcome these environmental impacts should be taken in Vietnam.

10.4.2 Challenges to the Seafood Processing Industry

Due to recent international protocols on sustainable development, the Vietnamese government has imposed decrees on natural resources management and environmental protection. Among them were decrees and decisions on maritime resource management and regulations for fishing, thus restructuring the production of seafood processing firms. Because of more stringent governmental laws relating to the fish catch, Vietnamese firms in the seafood processing industry have to deal with a dearth of materials and higher input prices. In addition, the shortage of materials in the seafood processing industry has been caused by salinity intrusions and drought into many aquaculture areas, so the yields of shrimp and tra fish have been decreasing in recent years. According to the Vietnam Steering Committee for Climate Change Mitigation and Adaption, in the first months of 2016 “shrimp die because of drought and saltwater intrusion, and the salinity is over 30%.”

Another challenge is that seafood processing consumes huge volumes of water; thus, seafood processing firms usually have high expenses for water consumption and wastewater treatment. For instance, in surimi production, a seafood processing company needs approximately 70 m^3 of water for producing 1 ton of product. However, according to the latest research on surimi production (Park 2013), a reasonable level is merely 20–25 m^3. This illustrates that the Vietnamese seafood industry is overusing water. Additionally, according to official reports from the Vietnamese Ministry of Finance (2016) and in compliance with new environmental laws, the fee rate for wastewater treatment in the seafood processing industry will be higher. This means that the seafood processing firms may have extremely higher expenses for wastewater disposal.

In a global competition perspective, the price of seafood products from Vietnam is relatively lower compared to countries such as Indonesia, India, and Thailand. The exporting turnover of Vietnam is also lower compared to these countries because of the unstable yields of aquaculture (VASEP 2016). Meanwhile, inferring from the strategy of *developing Vietnam seafood to 2020*, the returns of the seafood industry are expected to increase 8–10% per year and exports are planned to reach nine billion USD by 2020. This trend puts pressure on the seafood production industry in Vietnam. To achieve this target, Vietnam's seafood industry should attain higher competitive advantages in its exports, more efficient operations, and cleaner production.

These challenges indicate that the Vietnamese seafood businesses will have to gain higher productivity yields and cleaner production to relieve the pressures of material shortages, global competiveness, and higher environmental fees.

10.4.3 Case Study Design for Introducing MFCA to a Vietnamese Seafood Processing Company

10.4.3.1 Background of the Case Study

The small-sized company in this case study is located in an industrial zone in a large coastal city in the central area of Vietnam. Its main product is surimi, which is a kind of seafood that is produced from fish fillets. All products are exported. It employs 135 people, 120 of which are blue-collar workers and 15 are employed in the general management department.

Characteristics of Production

In this seafood process, fish represent the material and they have to remain in specific conditions–under low temperature to keep the material fresh and in good quality up to consumption. This costs the company a lot for energy and for water (ice making and storage). Furthermore, this process also generates a high volume of wastewater. Moreover, the proportion of material waste is very high because only fish fillets become the finished product, while the remaining fish parts are deemed as waste.

Manufacturing Process

The manufacturing process for surimi–the main product of the case study–includes five steps: namely, first washing and temporary storage; preliminary processing; refining and processing; blending and quality checks, shaping and PE packaging; and freezing and metal checking, box packaging, and frozen storage (Fig. 10.1). During this process, the sub-product is weighed after each phase. This action aims to control the desirable quantity for the machine and to balance the amount of water.

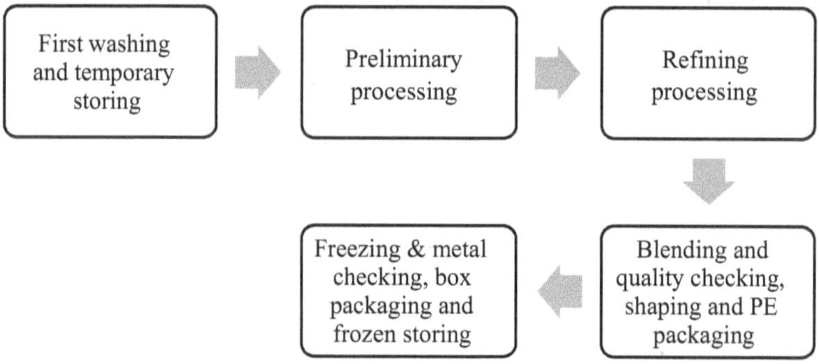

Fig. 10.1 Surimi production process

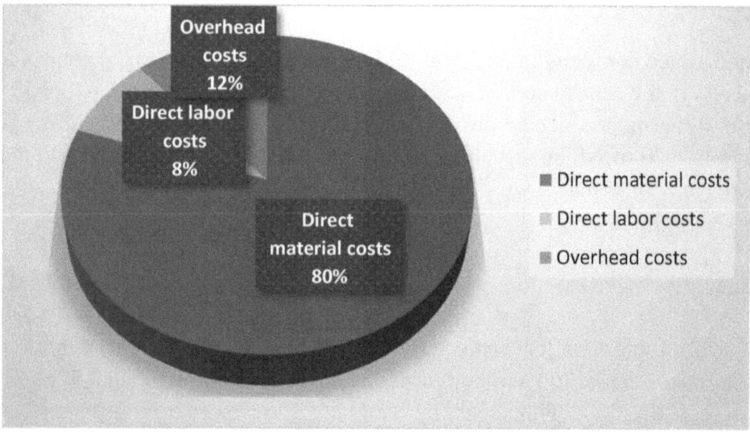

Fig. 10.2 Proportion of production costs in the case study

Proportion of Production Costs in the Case Study

According to information from the current accounting system, the production costs consist of up to 80% for the material costs, 12% for the overhead costs, and only 8% for the direct labor costs (Fig. 10.2). Moreover, the percentage of the finished product to the material inputs is very low at about 50%. This means that 1 ton of material produces a half ton of product. This actual characteristic poses a great challenge for this company in the cases of seafood price fluctuations and a lack of raw materials.

1. **First washing and temporary storage**

   This step includes two tasks. First, cold water is used to remove the possible impurities that cling or are attached to the fish skin. Then, the fish are stored in ice, while waiting for the next step of the production process.

2. **Preliminary processing (heading, gutting, boning, and washing).**
   Unlike the production of surimi from cold water fish, which is large enough to process mechanically, tropical fish, as in this case, are too small to cut mechanically. Therefore, the fish are beheaded and gutted manually. However, the beheaded and gutted fish are deboned by machine. In this step, the intermediate products are also washed to eliminate the undesirable fish parts, excluding the fish flesh.
3. **Refining and processing (mincing, washing, and dewatering).**
   Fillets are minced, washed, and then dewatered before proceeding to the next step.
4. **Blending, quality checking, shaping, and PE packing**
   The fillets are blended with some substances at a fixed rate, according to fish meat quantity. This step is done by machines and takes around 10 min for each turn. After blending, the sample of minced meat is taken to test for moisture. Later, the minced meat is extruded into PE bags with 10 kg per bag and shaped by a tray to become a block.
5. **Freezing and metal checking**
   Freezing is done to satisfy the required temperature for intermediate products and in preparation for checking whether the products have any metal traces after processing.
6. **Packaging and frozen storage**
   In this phase, two blocks of products are put into one carton box and stored under low temperatures. Storage requires the space between boxes to be high enough; that is, around 10–20 cm. The carton box is designed according to the particular customer's requirement and the box is subsequently ordered by the customer.

Specific Characteristics of Waste Disposal and Treatment of the Seafood Processing Company

The main material is raw fish. Only the fish fillets are used in production, while the other parts (including the heads, fins, entrails, and tails) are thrown away. Although the solid waste will be recycled as food for aquaculture, these kinds of waste (especially viscera) cause high rates of bacteria and organic materials, such as BOD and COD in the wastewater, and also create a large amount of sludge. Consequently, the seafood processing company has extremely high costs for wastewater treatment and disposal. In addition, the odor from processing is also unfavorable and may endanger the surrounding environment in the case of a low-quality deodorizing system.

Regarding wastewater treatment, all wastewater after first treatment inside the firm has to be piped into common treatment tanks for all seafood processing companies in the industrial zone. At present, the seafood processing company uses biotechnology for waste treatment, including treatments for odors, water, and sludge.

10.4.3.2 MFCA Analysis

From the current research perspective, MFCA is probably one of the major tools of EMA and may be applied to all sizes of company in various industries, regardless of the country where they operate. Therefore, it is presumed that an analysis of the Japanese MFCA approach could indicate abnormal losses in the production processes of Vietnamese companies. In this case analysis, to simplify the MFCA model for a SME, the focus will only be on the raw materials; i.e., fish. Other elements used in production, such as water, energy, and other system costs will not be analyzed. Introducing MFCA as a trial example in this case study will be implemented using the following steps.

Step 1

The boundary, time period, and quantity center are identified. In this case, the boundary of the material flow in the company is surimi processing. The study is conducted in 1 month. The quantity centers that are evaluated will consist of five phases of the production process: namely, first washing and temporary storage; preliminary processing; refining and processing; blending and quality checking, shaping and PE packaging; and freezing and metal checking, box packaging, and frozen storage.

Step 2

In this step, there are two main responsibilities. First, the inputs and outputs for each quantity center must be defined and calculated in physical units by the principle of material mass balance–"total material inputs should be equal to total material outputs." Second, these inputs and outputs are calculated in money terms using the formula "*Material costs = weight of material × unit price of material,*" in which the unit price is a constant value in the process.

Based on the information of this case study, this step can be displayed, as in Table 10.1. The unit price of 1 kg of fish is 14,000 Vietnam Dong (VND).

Step 3

In this step, the flow chart of MFCA (Fig. 10.3) is drawn, based on the production process and information of the inputs and outputs in step 2 (Table 10.1). This flow chart clearly indicates how much material is transferred to the next phase and lost after each phase throughout the process.

The information of inputs and outputs of the raw materials is also expressed in a type of cost matrix table (Table 10.2) that shows how raw materials are lost in each quantity center.

Step 4

From the information of the material flow matrix (Fig. 10.3) and material cost matrix (Table 10.2), the actual quantity of material losses and hidden losses in the existing accounting information system can be detected.

The MFCA flow cost matrix reveals some solid waste flowing into the effluent streams in the preliminary and the refining and processing steps.

Table 10.1 Input–output information of the raw materials in the MFCA case study

Quantity center	Input	Output
First washing and temporary storing	Raw fishes (2,285,628 kg; 31,998,792 thousand Vietnam Dong (VND)	Raw fishes (2,285,628 kg; 31,998,792 thousand VND)
	Cool water, ice (Liter)	Wastewater (Liter)
Preliminary processing	Raw fishes (2,285,628 kg; 31,998,792 thousand VND)	Fillets (1,028,875 kg; 14,404,250 thousand VND)
		Head, bone, intestine (recycled) (972,782 kg; 13,618,948 thousand VND)
		Solid waste (283,971 kg; 3,975,594 thousand VND)
	Cool water (Liter)	Wastewater (Liter)
Refining processing	Fillets (1,028,875 kg; 14,404,250 thousand VND)	Minced meat (817,627 kg, 11,446,778 thousand VND)
		Fish fat (recycled) (114,281 kg; 1,599,934 thousand VND)
		Solid waste (96,967 kg; 1,357,538 thousand VND)
	Cool water (Liter)	Wastewater (Liter)
Blending and quality checking, shaping and PE packaging	Minced meat (817,627 kg, 11,446,778 thousand VND), Substances (5,314 kg; 74,396 thousand VND)	Surimi (822,532.5 kg; 11,515,455 thousand VND)
	PE bag (bags)	Waste for quality checking (408.5 kg; 5719 thousand VND)
Freezing and metal checking, box packaging and frozen storing	Surimi (822,532.5 kg; 11,515,455 thousand VND)	Surimi (822,532.5 kg; 11,515,455 thousand VND)
	Carton box (boxes)	

Note: The paper focuses on identifying the loss in raw materials, so the information of inputs and outputs of energy and other systems costs are not presented in this table

10.4.3.3 Implementing Countermeasures Based on the PDCA Cycle Tool and MFCA Analysis

In this case study, MFCA analysis showed that a rather considerable amount of solid waste was ignored and it drained into the wastewater, which caused more wastewater pollution, higher costs for wastewater treatment, and lower returns from selling solid waste. From the MFCA data (Table 10.2), it is clearly seen that the solid waste drained into the wastewater during preliminary processing and during refining and processing. Analyzing the root of the problem, the company recognized that, in preliminary processing, the cause of losses is that workers drop fish heads, fins, and intestines onto the floor, and then the cleaning workers sweep them into the drain (see Fig. 10.4a, b). During refining processing, losses were caused by the net of the rackets used to dredge for fish fat (see Fig. 10.5a, b). The company plans to

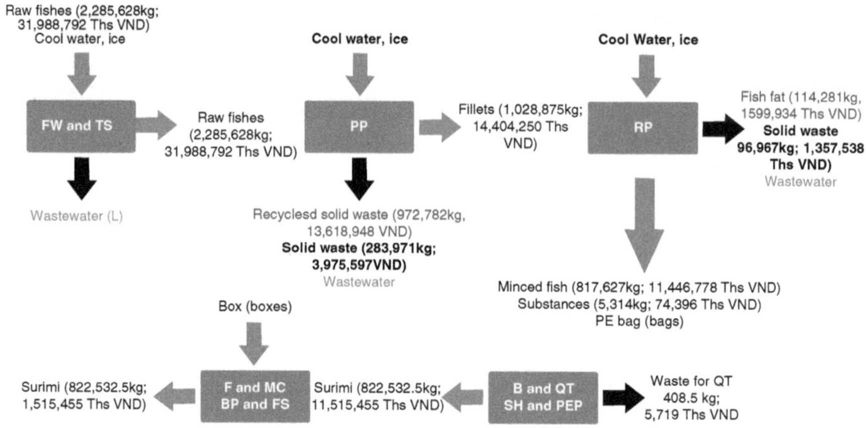

Fig. 10.3 Material flow cost accounting of the case study

Table 10.2 Material cost matrix

	Product		Non-product			
			Non-recycle		Recycle	
Quantity center	Quantity	Cost 1000 VND	Quantity	Cost 1000 VND	Quantity	Cost 1000 VND
FW and TS	Raw fishes		None		None	
	2,285,628	31,998,792				
PP	Fillets		***Solid waste***		Head, intestine, bone	
	1,028,875	14,404,250	*283,971*	*3,975,594*	972,782	13,618,948
RP	Minced fish		***Solid waste***		Fish fat	
	817,627	11,446,778	*96,967*	*1,357,538*	114,281	1,599,934
B and QC, SH and PEP	Surimi		Waste for quality checking		None	
	822,532.5	11,515,455	408.5	5,719		
F and MC, BP and FS	Surimi		None		None	
	822,532.5	11,515,455				

implement suitable solutions to reduce the losses of solid waste into the wastewater with its available human, facility, and financial resources in a step-by-step process. Thus, the company will try to adopt the PDCA cycle for its environmental management (Fig. 10.6). In the Plan step, the company wants to focus on collecting more solid waste in the preliminary processing phase and then, in a straightforward manner, the company will add requirements to the tasks of the cleaning workers in the preliminary Do step.

Instead of only keeping things clean during the preliminary step, the workers should filter the solid waste, while sweeping the floor. In order to check whether the solid waste has been collected, the quantity of solid waste will be weighed after each phrase of the production process and compared with the ratio of input materials and

a b

Fig. 10.4 Solid waste drained into wastewater in the preliminary processing step (**a**) Due to fish that are manually beheaded and gutted, (**b**) due to parts that are swept into a pipe

solid waste outputs from 1 month to the next. In the Act step, the company will continue to propose solutions to reduce losses in the preliminary phase and to improve the dredged fish fat using nets in order to reduce losses during the refining process. According to the company's management plan, the PDCA cycle will be reformulated continuously to reduce losses as much as possible. Regarding forthcoming actions of the continuous PDCA to achieve an environmental plan of reducing the solid waste that drains into wastewater, some action plans are being discussed, such as adding an edge for the working tables in the preliminary processing step (see Fig. 10.4a, where the table for heading and gutting fish is without an edge), using a thicker net, and changing the nets that collect the fish fat in the refining and processing step more frequently. The managers believe they can try these solutions because such approaches do not cost much; by contrast, they can earn greater returns by collecting more solid waste and reducing polluted wastewater disposal. Concurrently, they can protect the environment and join the green food supply chain.

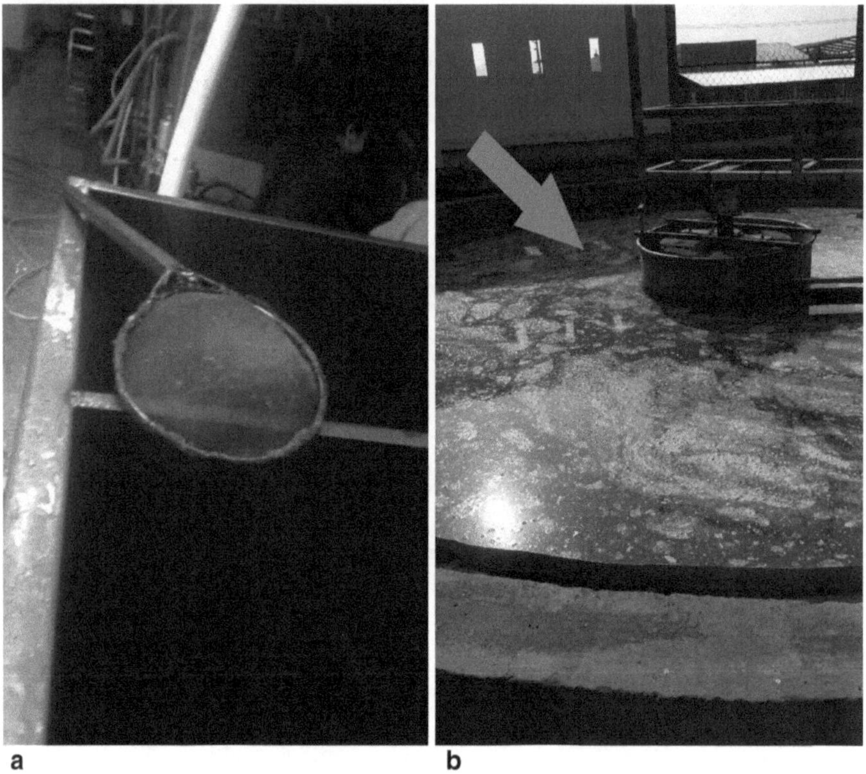

Fig. 10.5 (a) Racket used to filter fish fat during the refining and processing step, (b) solid waste drained into wastewater due to refining and processing

10.4.3.4 Results

In this case study, the data in the material flow matrix and material cost matrix tables show that some solid waste flowing into the effluent stream was not recorded, while the lost solid waste made the wastewater more polluted and reduced the returns from recycling this waste. Indeed, in the lens of the existing cost accounting system, the non-recycled solid waste is ignored; meanwhile, in the MFCA cost system, this can be observed and calculated. Based on MFCA data, the company can identify the hidden losses and waste in its production process and combine such data to find solutions to reducing the losses of solid waste using the continuous PDCA cycle (Fig. 10.6). In the first round of PDCA implementation, the company has achieved its plan to collect more solid waste in the preliminary process and reduce the amount of polluted wastewater without adding cost. Regarding the efficiency of this solution, the quantity of collected solid waste increased 3% and the cost of wastewater treatment decreased 5%. This result shows the efficiency of MFCA analysis and the adoption of PDCA in a company situation. By employing a continuous PDCA cycle,

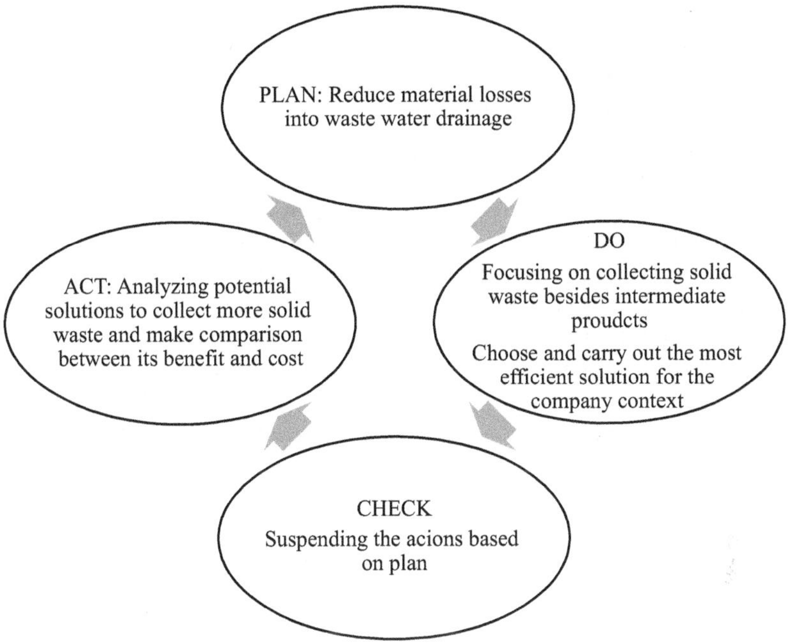

Fig. 10.6 PDCA cycle of the case study

plans and solutions to reduce solid waste losses will continue, so the Vietnamese company should continue to improve its production management system and increase its economic benefits, while protecting the environment in a better fashion.

10.5 Conclusions and Discussions

Empirical studies illustrate that MFCA can increase economic incomes by reducing material losses and waste costs (e.g., Kokubu and Kitada 2010). In this paper, the trial experiment also shows that more material losses have been recognized by MFCA than the existing cost accounting system of the company in the case study. Thanks to the lens of MFCA, the company can recognize large amounts of abnormal losses (the solid waste that drained into the wastewater stream), which had not been recorded by the existing accounting department. Based on data in the MFCA table or flow chart, this company can propose solutions to reduce the loss. As a result, the company can reduce the costs and gain higher returns. For example, the company could pay lower fees for wastewater treatment because of less-polluted wastewater caused by solid waste and earn more from selling its solid waste. Moreover, MFCA analysis does not require new information systems, as all data were collected via an existing accounting system and production department. Therefore, it could be said that MFCA analysis is useful and adaptable to Vietnamese companies. Consequently, it is expected that MFCA application could support Vietnamese companies to overcome hurdles to achieve higher productivity and better environmental performance. On the one hand, MFCA clearly shows material losses and waste. On the other hand, MFCA applications do not require further investment in information systems. Therefore, Vietnamese seafood processing companies or other Vietnamese companies could benefit from MFCA applications. However, it should be noted that MFCA is a tool in which to observe the data, not solve the problems by itself. The success of MFCA may depend on the cooperation of managers, accountants, and employees in the company.

The results of this application may contribute toward some positive impacts. Firstly, this company gained some valuable experience for itself. This made management reconsider its management views on economic performance and environmental protection. In addition, the practical application of this case study may be a useful example for other Vietnamese companies to follow. The paper clearly shows the implementation steps for MFCA applications and explains the principles by giving typical examples. This advancement may encourage firms from developing countries like Vietnam, where the majority of enterprises operate with underdeveloped information technology, because MFCA data can be calculated using an MS Excel program (Kokubu and Kitada 2015). Additionally, this study adds to the case studies of EMA applications for SMEs in developing countries, which is a research area that still lacks attention compared to large-sized companies in developed nations (Herzig et al. 2012; Lee 2009). This case from Vietnam may be a particularly interesting additional example of EMA applications in developing countries because measures for cleaner production in developing countries are currently attractive to researchers (Schaltegger et al. 2012). This research is also expected to inspire Vietnamese SMEs in future projects on MFCA applications in Vietnam within the APO. As mentioned above, the Vietnamese government has signed an agreement on MFCA promotion in Vietnamese SMEs with the aid of APO and the assistance of Japanese experts.

However, the paper is affected by limitations in terms of the number of case studies, the time period, and the MFCA approach. The study was carried out to discover the advantages and distinctive characteristics of Japanese companies, although no new cases of Japanese companies were shown. Nonetheless, the previous literature indicates that most characteristics of the Japanese MFCAs could be adaptable to the Vietnamese case, so there is sufficient evidence for using the Japanese MFCA approach. Another limitation is that the MFCA model was examined during a 1 month processing period. However, monthly data may be reasonable for our analysis because the input and output ratio of materials does not change dramatically from 1 month to the next. Therefore, data for 1 month could represent the pattern of practical production for any case study rather than using data for a random period. As expected, further research could be conducted with the promotion of the Vietnamese government and with nongovernment organizations like APO's project, as mentioned above. This paper is also limited by showing the flows for raw materials and overlooking other elements of MFCA, including water, energy, system costs, and disposal/delivery costs. Nevertheless, in this seafood case study, the cost of raw materials surpasses other cost elements, as mentioned above, so the model is acceptable and it is possible for small companies to simplify and adopt the MFCA model (Nakajima 2009). Moreover, gradually small improvements are better for Vietnamese companies who are not very willing to change and adopt new theories.

Regarding the implications of MFCA applications in the Vietnam context, there may be some advantages and disadvantages. On the one hand, by using this approach to obtain MFCA information, a Vietnamese company does not need to make any changes to its production processes and investments, while the approach may immediately show higher economic benefits and less environmental impacts. In addition, many samples of MFCA applications and guidelines for MFCA have been published by the Japanese government, as well as other organizations, such as ISO. Thus, by learning from these experiences, managerial solutions for MFCA implementation by Vietnamese companies may be more feasible and efficient. Furthermore, the Vietnamese government has signed an agreement to promote MFCA in Vietnamese SMEs, along with the support of APO and assistance of Japanese experts. By next year, this will open up opportunities for Vietnamese SMEs to access and employ MFCA as a management tool for reaching their economic and environmental goals. However, on the other hand, in order to foster MFCA expansion in Vietnam, there may be some challenges. First, the fine for breaking environmental laws is still lower than the cost of environmental investment. Therefore, this does not place pressure on business organizations to become cleaner manufacturers or become concerned about environmental impacts due to their activities. This means that managers may easily ignore the benefits of MFCA applications when the adoption of MFCA really needs the commitment of top managers. Second, cross-functions and communication between departments are very poor in Vietnamese companies. The employees mainly carry out their duties and solely report their results to top managers individually. Thus, a Vietnamese company may struggle and have more difficulties in combining MFCA information with existing management information. Finally, further development of MFCA needs a full understanding of MFCA by top managers (Nakajima 2011); however, to satisfying this condition takes a long time and requires official education and expert support. In sum, to promote the implementation of MFCA in Vietnam, one needs governmental factors such as environmental taxes, environmental management, and environmental management training for enterprises, in addition to major concerns about the cleaner production processes of Vietnamese enterprises.

Although MFCA implementation in this case study may only accomplish an on-the-spot achievement, the study is expected to promote the application of EMA tools in Vietnam. Thanks to the hard evidence from this case study, many more companies may become aware of the benefits of MFCA and be willing to try EMA tools in order to solve their problems regarding materials, energy costs, and waste disposal. Therefore, this response may also foster the spread of voluntary participation by Vietnamese companies in the application of MFCA or other EMA tools, and the gradual conventional cognizance of the trade-off between economic benefits and environmental protection in most Vietnamese companies may be replaced. From the perspective of theory, this paper presents the first evidence of the applicability of the

Japanese MFCA approach to SMEs in Vietnam and it supports the findings of earlier studies using the MFCA approach and EMA tools for developing countries (e.g., Chompu-inwai et al. 2015; Schaltegger et al. 2012; Sulong et al. 2015).

References

APO–Asian Productivity Organization (2014) Manual on environmental flow cost accounting: ISO 14051. Japan. http://www.apo-tokyo.org/publications/ebooks/manual-on-material-flow-cost-accounting-iso-14051/. Accessed 10 Dec 2015

Berger M, Enzler S, Kammerer-Kirch E, Luger M, Müller U, Redmann C, Strauß T, Strobel M, Wagner B (2003) Flow management for manufacturing companies sustainable re-organisation of material and information flows. Imu Augsburg GmbH & Co. KG und Zentrum für Weiterbildung und Wissenstransfer, Augsburg

Burritt RL, Hahn T, Schaltegger S (2002) Towards a comprehensive framework for environmental management accounting—Links between business actors and environmental management accounting tools. Aust Account Rev 12(27):39–50

Chompu-inwai R, Jaimjit B, Premsuriyanunt P (2015) A combination of material flow cost accounting and design of experiments techniques in an SME: the case of a wood products manufacturing company in northern Thailand. J Clean Prod 108:1352–1364

Christ KL, Burritt RL (2015) Material flow cost accounting: a review and agenda for future research. J Clean Prod 108:1378–1389

Christ KL, Burritt RL (2016) ISO 14051: a new era for MFCA implementation and research. Rev Contabilidad 19(1):1–9

Guenther E, Jasch C, Schmidt M, Wagner B, Ilg P (2015) Material flow cost accounting–looking back and ahead. J Clean Prod 108:1249–1254

Herzig C, Viere T, Schaltegger S, Burritt RL (2012) Environmental management accounting: case studies of South-East Asian companies. Routledge, London

Higashida A, Kokubu K, Shinohara A (2013). Introducing material flow cost accounting and creating visibility–analyzing MFCA in practice based on a longitudinal case study. In: Proceedings of the seventh Asia Pacific interdisciplinary research in accounting conference, pp 26–28

IFAC–International Federation of Accountants (2005) International guidance document: environmental management accounting. IFAC, New York

Imai M (1991) The key to Japan's competitive success, 2nd edn. McGraw-Hill/Irwin, New York

ISO International Standard Organization (ISO 14051: 2011). Environmental management–material flow cost accounting–general framework. BSI Standard Publication, Geneva

Jasch CM (2009) Environmental and material flow cost accounting: principles and procedures. Springer, Dordrecht

Kasemset C, Chernsupornchai J, Pala-ud W (2015) Application of MFCA in waste reduction: case study on a small textile factory in Thailand. J Clean Prod 108:1342–1351

Kokubu K, Kitada H (2010) Conflicts and solutions between material flow cost, accounting and conventional management thinking. In: 6th Asia-Pacific interdisciplinary perspectives on accounting research (APIRA) conference at University of Sydney on, pp 12–13

Kokubu K, Kitada H (2015) Material flow cost accounting and existing management perspectives. J Clean Prod 108:1279–1288

Kokubu K, Nakajima M (2004) Sustainable accounting initiatives in Japan: pilot projects of material flow cost accounting. In: Seiler-Hausmann JD, Liedtke C, von Weizsäcker EU (eds) Eco-efficiency & beyond: towards the sustainable enterprise. Greenleaf, Sheffield, pp 100–112

Kokubu K, Tachikawa H (2013) Material flow cost accounting: significance and practical approach. In: Kauffman J, Lee K-M (eds) Handbook of sustainable engineering. Springer, Dordrecht, pp 351–369

Kokubu K, Nashioka E, Saio K, Imai S (2003) Two governmental initiatives on environmental management accounting and corporate practices in Japan. In: Bennett MD, Rikhardsson PM, Schaltegger S (eds) Environmental management accounting—purpose and progress. Springer, Dordrecht, pp 89–113

Kokubu K, Campos MKS, Furukawa Y, Tachikawa H (2009) Material flow cost accounting with ISO 14051. ISO Manag Syst 9(1):15–18

Lee K-H (2009) Why and how to adopt green management into business organizations? Manag Decis 47(7):1101–1121

METI–Ministry of Economy, Technology and Industry (2002) Environmental Management Accounting (EMA) workbook. Tokyo, Japan

METI–Ministry of Economy, Technology and Industry (2011) MFCA case examples 2011 Japanese Ministry of Economy, Trade and Industry, Tokyo. http://www.jmac.co.jp/mfca/thinking/data/MFCA_Case_example_e2011_new.pdf. Accessed 10 Dec 2015

Nakajima M (2003) Introducing material flow cost accounting for environmental management accounting system. In: International symposium on environmental accounting. Japan

Nakajima M (2004) On the differences between material flow cost accounting and traditional cost accounting: in reply to the questions and misunderstandings on material flow cost accounting. Kansai Univ Rev Bus Commer 6:1–20

Nakajima M (2009) Evolution of material flow cost accounting (MFCA): characteristics on development of MFCA companies and significance of relevance of MFCA. Kansai Univ Rev Bus Commer 11(March 2009):27–46

Nakajima M (2010) Environmental management accounting for sustainable manufacturing: establishing management system of material flow cost accounting (MFCA). Kansai Univ Rev Bus Commer 12(March 2010):41–58

Nakajima M (2011) Environmental management accounting for cleaner production: systematization of material flow cost accounting (MCFA) into corporate management system. Kansai Univ Rev Bus Commer 13(March 2011):17–39

Nakajima M, Kokubu K, Okajima J, Nashioka E, Saio K (2003) Case study I: Nippon Paint Co., Ltd. In: International symposium on environmental accounting. Japan

Nakajima M, Kimura A, Oka S (2013) MFCA management as sustainable management. In: Proceedings of the 7th Asia Pacific interdisciplinary research in accounting conference, vol 276. Kobe University, Japan

Nakajima M, Kimura A, Wagner B (2015) Introduction of material flow cost accounting (MFCA) to the supply chain: a questionnaire study on the challenges of constructing a low-carbon supply chain to promote resource efficiency. J Clean Prod 108:1302–1309

Park JW (2013) Surimi and surimi seafood. CRC Press, Boca Raton

Rieckhof R, Bergmann A, Guenther E (2014) Interrelating material flow cost accounting with management control systems to introduce resource efficiency into strategy. J Clean Prod 108:1262–1278

Schaltegger S, Zvezdov D (2015) Expanding material flow cost accounting. Framework, review and potentials. J Clean Prod 108:1333–1341

Schaltegger S, Viere T, Zvezdov D (2012) Tapping environmental accounting potentials of beer brewing: information needs for successful cleaner production. J Clean Prod 29:1–10

Schmidt M (2015) The interpretation and extension of Material Flow Cost Accounting (MFCA) in the context of environmental material flow analysis. J Clean Prod 108:1310–1319

Schmidt M, Nakajima M (2013) Material flow cost accounting as an approach to improve resource efficiency in manufacturing companies. Resources 2(3):358–369

Schmidt A, Götze U, Sygulla R (2015) Extending the scope of material flow cost accounting–methodical refinements and use case. J Clean Prod 108:1320–1332

Strobel M, Redmann C (2002) Flow cost accounting, an accounting approach based on the actual flows of materials. In: Environmental management accounting: informational and institutional developments. Springer, Dordrecht, pp 67–82

Sulong F, Sulaiman M, Norhayati MA (2015) Material flow cost accounting (MFCA) enablers and barriers: the case of a Malaysian small and medium-sized enterprise (SME). J Clean Prod 108:1365–1374

Tran N (2014) Seafood processing: solving environmental pollution. http://www.thuysanvietnam.com.vn/che-bien-thuy-san-giai-quyet-van-nan-o-nhiem-moi-truong-article-9682.tsvn. Accessed 20 Dec 2015 (in Vietnamese)

UN–United Nation (2001) Environmental management accounting: procedures and principles. United Nations, New York

VASEP–Vietnam Association of Seafood Exporters and Producers (2016) Opportunities and challenges of seafood exporters in globalization. http://vasep.com.vn/Tin-Tuc/1217_43509/Co-hoi-va-thach-thuc-cua-thuy-san-Viet-Nam-khi-hoi-nhap.htm. Accessed 01 Apr 2016

Vietnamese Government (2013a) Decree No. 103/2013/ND-CP on Regulations on administrative sanctions in the fisheries activities. http://www.moj.gov.vn/vbpq/lists/vn%20bn%20php%20lut/view_detail.aspx?itemid=28645. Accessed 20 Dec 2015 (in Vietnamese)

Vietnamese Government (2013b) Decree No. 179/2013/ND-CP on Punishment on violence action on environmental protection. http://www.moj.gov.vn/vbpq/lists/vn%20bn%20php%20lut/view_detail.aspx?itemid=24938. Accessed 20 Dec 2015 (in Vietnamese)

Vietnamese Government (2015) Decree No. 38/2015/ND-CP on Waste and scrap management. http://www.moj.gov.vn/vbpq/lists/vn%20bn%20php%20lut/view_detail.aspx?itemid=30396. Accessed 20 Dec 2015 (in Vietnamese)

Vietnamese Ministry of Finance (2016) http://www.mof.gov.vn/webcenter/portal/btc/r/cd/dtvb/ctdtvb?centerWidth=0%25&id=11721&leftWidth=100%25&rightWidth=0%25&showFooter=false&showHeader=false&_adf.ctrl-state=1gdyu0nlc_4&_afrLoop=4825572454433572#!%40%40%3F_afrLoop%3D4825572454433572%26centerWidth%3D0%2525%26id%3D11721%26leftWidth%3D100%2525%26rightWidth%3D0%2525%26showFooter%3Dfalse%26showHeader%3Dfalse%26_adf.ctrl-state%3D9x1v465m5_4. Accessed 15 Apr 2016 (in Vietnamese)

Wagner B (2015) A report on the origins of Material Flow Cost Accounting (MFCA) research activities. J Clean Prod 108:1255–1261

Yin RK (2013) Case study research: design and methods. Sage, Beverly Hills

Part IV
Sustainability Reporting: Challenges and Approaches

Chapter 11
The Functional Differentiation Between the International Integrated Reporting Council (IIRC) and the Global Reporting Initiative (GRI) in the Sphere of Sustainability Reporting

Kensuke Ogata, Sadako Inoue, Atsuki Ueda, and Hiroyuki Yagi

Abstract The International Integrated Reporting Council (IIRC) and Global Reporting Initiative (GRI) have concurrently issued guidelines for an alternative to current corporate reporting. The former issued *International Integrated Reporting Framework*, while the latter *Sustainability Reporting Guidelines ver.4*. As some commentators pointed out, the IIRC shifted its emphasis from sustainability-related information, which it shared with GRI, to investor-oriented information. Did GRI and IIRC plan to bifurcate their roles? If so, how did they do that? This paper aims to answer these questions with a focus on organizational structures, based on the strategy-structure–performance paradigm of organizational theory. Thus, shedding light on the differences in organizational structure can reveal the direction in which an organization is headed, as well as the strategies they would implement. Based on the results of organizational structure analysis and network theory, while GRI formed a network open to various stakeholders for creating new sustainability reporting practices, IIRC built a network that was dominated by financial stakeholders to apply the GRI guideline to investor-oriented guideline, in accordance with IIRC's main purpose.

K. Ogata (✉)
Osaka City University, Osaka, Japan
e-mail: ogata@bus.osaka-cu.ac.jp

S. Inoue
University of Marketing and Distribution Sciences, Kobe, Japan
e-mail: Sadako_Inoue@red.umds.ac.jp

A. Ueda
Senshu University, Tokyo, Japan
e-mail: a-ueda@isc.senshu-u.ac.jp

H. Yagi
Yokohama National University, Yokohama, Japan
e-mail: baum8@ynu.ac.jp

K.-H. Lee, S. Schaltegger (eds.), *Accounting for Sustainability: Asia Pacific Perspectives*, Eco-Efficiency in Industry and Science 33,
https://doi.org/10.1007/978-3-319-70899-7_11

Keywords IIRC · GRI · IIRF · G4 · Strategy-structure–performance paradigm · Social network analysis

11.1 Introduction

The International Integrated Reporting Council (IIRC) has attached attention as a new global coalition for developing a novel form of corporate reporting since its foundation in October 2010. The two leading organizations in the field of sustainability accounting, Prince's Accounting for Sustainability Project (A4S) and the Global Reporting Initiative (GRI), have contributed significantly to the establishment of IIRC. A4S, which was founded in 2004, aims to link the finance and accounting communities from business, government, academia and the capital markets, in order to develop the institutions, systems, tools, and approaches needed to build a sustainable economy (A4S 2015). In addition, GRI was established in 1997 for providing "a trusted and credible framework for sustainability reporting that can be used by organizations of any size, sector, or location," with the symbolic phrase "triple bottom line" (GRI 2011: 3 and 8). Both the organizations share a common vision of contributing to sustainable social and economic development through the improvement of corporate reporting, which incorporates existing economic information into environmental, social, and governance (ESG) information. IIRC was founded to carry out this task. In the press release that A4S and GRI issued with regard to the creation of IIRC, its purpose was explained as follows (A4S and GRI 2010):

> The IIRC's remit is to create a globally accepted framework for accounting for sustainability. A framework which brings together financial, environmental, social and governance information in a clear, concise, consistent and comparable format – put briefly, in an "integrated" format. The intention is to help with the development of more comprehensive and comprehensible information about an organization's total performance, prospective as well as retrospective, to meet the needs of the emerging, more sustainable, global economic model.

After its creation, IIRC has viewed itself as "an international coalition of leaders from the corporate, investment, accounting, securities, regulatory, academic and standard-setting sectors as well as civil society" (IIRC and GRI 2013: 1), with the following three goals to achieve: (a) create a globally accepted Integrated Reporting framework that provides all material information about an organization's strategy, governance, impacts, performance and prospects, in a clear, concise and comparable format; (b) ensure the adoption of Integrated Reporting by report preparers; and (c) acquire the support of regulators and investors (IIRC 2012). To fulfill the most significant mission of developing a framework, IIRC issued a Discussion Paper in September 2011 (IIRC 2011), subsequently publishing a Consultation Draft in April 2013. IIRC deliberated on the comments received from various stakeholders, eventually promulgating the *International Integrated Reporting Framework* (IIRF) in December 2013 (IIRC 2013).

However, there was heavy criticism of IIRF for overemphasizing the viewpoint of investors, being overpowered by the accountancy professionals and multinational enterprises, thus abandoning the idea of sustainability reporting (Flower 2015). On the other hand, in May of the same year that IIRF was published, GRI also issued its own guideline, *Sustainability Reporting Guidelines ver.4* (G4), in order to help the reporters prepare sustainability reports that contain valuable information about the organization's most critical sustainability-related issues (GRI 2013). These two things—IIRC's apparent disconnect from its original policy and GRI's development of its own guideline—were probably the result of a potential division of their roles. In effect, IIRC and GRI issued a *Memorandum of Understanding* (*MoU*), clarifying the differences between integrated reporting and sustainability reporting (IIRC and GRI 2013).

Hence, it is evident that the framework for integrate reporting, initiated by IIRC, never pursues the new sustainability-related information content. However, it likely makes use of the sustainability reporting framework developed by GRI in shaping its framework. How did GRI and IIRC divide their roles? This paper aims to answer this question with evidence based on the organizational structure. According to the strategy-structure–performance (SSP) paradigm of traditional organizational theory, an organization is believed to reform its structure for achieving their purposes or aims. Based on this premise, studying the aspects of structural change can reveal the direction in which an organization is headed or the strategies they would implement. It has some implications that a particular type of regulator or rule maker might change in order to achieve its own goals, similar to for-profit companies. This indicates that we can enhance the predictability of the regulatory behaviors of regulators and standard setters.

In addition, IIRF and G4 brought forth important guidelines regarding sustainability reporting for companies in the Asia-Pacific region. To embed these guidelines into the disclosure system or to encourage various companies in different countries to adopt them, it is crucial to analyze the backgrounds of IIRC and GRI, with their governance structures, while clarifying the differences in their basic characteristics and stances. Understanding these things can help promote proper use of these guidelines. Thus, this paper contributes to the effective utilization of IIRF and G4.

11.2 Theoretical Basis

11.2.1 Background

11.2.1.1 Missions and Formal Organizations of IIRC

The main mission of IIRC is to develop a framework for the new disclosure medium—integrated report—and to promote it to the public. According to the IIRC, the integrated report could communicate "how an organization's strategy, governance, performance and prospects, in the context of its external environment, lead to the creation of value over the short, medium and long term" (IIRC 2013: par.1.1).

IIRC presumes that the development of the framework would obtain the approval of preparers, as well as support from regulators and investors (IIRC 2012: 3). To ensure this, IIRC has organized the following four internal bodies: Council, Working Group, Secretariat, and Board.

The first internal body, the Council, has three main responsibilities: to advise IIRC on its mission, role and governance practices; to provide thought leadership, intellectual contribution and strategic insights on IIRC's initiatives and activities; and to lend weight and credibility to IIRC's profile. The second, the Working Group, provides practical guidance in developing positions and for making recommendations as appropriate to the Board and Council, especially in relation to the development of the framework; the promotion of adopting integrated reporting by relevant government and regulatory bodies, preparers, and investors; and the determination of long-term institutional arrangements for IIRC. The third, the Secretariat, assumes the planning, coordination and execution of initiatives, activities and interactions. The fourth, the Board, directs IIRC's affairs, notably to oversee the coordination and interaction among the Council, the Working Group and the Secretariat, as well as with external stakeholders and other parties (IIRC 2013).

11.2.1.2 Missions and Formal Organizations of GRI

On the other hand, with growing social concerns about global issues such as climate change and human rights, GRI, which was created in 1997 with the efforts of the Coalition of Environmentally Responsible Economies and the United Nations Environment Program, is an international network-based NPO, involved with thousands of professionals and organizations from many sectors, constituencies and regions (GRI 2013). The mission is to provide a trusted and credible framework for sustainability reporting that could improve the existing disclosure system that attaches too much significance to economic performance. Therefore, GRI places more importance on social and environmental viewpoints, required to "create innovative approaches to address global issues, such as climate change and human rights" (GRI 2014b: 4).

GRI comprised of the following four internal groups until 2014: Board of Directors, Stakeholder Council, Technical Advisory Committee, and Secretariat. The Board of Directors has the final decision-making authority on GRI's organizational strategy and framework development; with its members representing a range of regions and constituencies. The Stakeholder Council is a formal stakeholder policy forum of GRI, representing a wide range of regions and constituencies to offer strategic recommendations on future policy and business planning of GRI. The Technical Advisory Committee is made up of international experts in the fields of environment, human rights, labor, economics and finance, reporting and accountancy, to oversee the content of the framework. The Secretariat fulfills the work plan set out by the Board. The GRI emphasizes "multi-stakeholder approach," as evident from the membership of GRI's internal groups (GRI 2013, 46). In January 2015, GRI changed the governance and management structure to strengthen the independence and management of the standards, while meeting the requirements of a public standard setter, as follows: Board of

Directors, Global Sustainability Standards Board (structural change from Technical Advisory Committee), Independent Appointments Committee (newly-created), Due Process Oversight Committee (newly-created), Stakeholder Council, Governmental Advisory Group (newly-created) and Secretariat (GRI 2014a).

11.2.1.3 Functional Differentiation Between the IIRC and the GRI

In accordance with the remit of IIRC that A4S and GRI described during the foundation of IIRC, as mentioned previously, IIRC would be requested to adopt a new reporting style called integrated reporting, which should include not only the financial information of organizations, but also the environmental, social and governance information. This might have caused an overlap with the sustainability reporting initiated by GRI, disrupting corporate reporting practices. Recognizing this concern, IIRC and GRI issued an *MoU* to clarify the differences between integrated reporting and sustainability reporting in February 2013, immediately before the issuance of G4 and IIRF (IIRC and GRI 2013). In the *MoU*, the following three points, with regard to the relationship between the two types of reporting, have been mentioned. Firstly, sustainability reporting delivers components that are integral to integrated reporting, as a key pillar on which integrated reporting is based. Secondly, the development and implementation of integrated reporting is materially relevant to the ongoing enhancement of sustainability reporting practices. Thirdly, the active involvement and support of organizations that promote sustainability reporting are relevant to the development and implementation of integrated reporting (IIRC and GRI 2013: 2–3).

Taking into account the relationship between both the corporate reporting styles, GRI has developed guideline on ESG information, to provide for a wide range of stakeholders surrounding the organizations, while IIRC is involved in transforming the sustainability reporting guideline developed by GRI into other uses, like reporting for providers of financial capital. Thus, GRI can be called the "developer" of sustainability reporting guideline, while the IIRC is an "applied ruler."

11.2.2 Previous Studies

There are fewer academic studies on integrated reporting because this type of reporting is an emerging phenomenon (Stubbs and Higgins 2014). Instead, accountants and consultants have normatively referred to the benefits and practical problems expected from the promotion of integrated reports (cf. Cheng et al. 2014; IMA and ACCA 2016; Fried et al. 2014; Krzus 2011; Smith 2014a, b; Soyka 2013). Apart from these, there were case studies focusing on simulated adoption and early adoption of integrated reporting, which included case studies of Australian listing companies (ACCA and Net Balance Foundation 2011), South African companies that have been mandated by the listing rules of the Johannesburg Stock Exchange to prepare integrated reporting (Setia et al. 2015; van Zyl 2013).

With regard to Asia-Pacific region, Jonathan Labrey, IIRC's Chief Strategy Officer and Head of Asia Pacific, said that Asian countries, except for Japan, where over 200 companies have produced integrated reports, have had a low participation. Among these countries, the prime minister and regulators in Malaysia are attempting to embed integrated reports within their capital market, having stipulated companies to adopt such reports. In India, the Securities and Exchange Board of India called on the business associations to develop a program for adopting integrated reports (Labrey 2016). Specifically, in the case of Malaysia, a research report of the Malaysian Institute of Accountants (MIA) and the Association of Chartered Certified Accountants (ACCA) indicated that the number of companies which are considering the adoption of integrated reports has increased, while users also expect to improve information on a company's value and value generation potential through the adoption of such reports (MIA and ACCA 2016). With regard to Singapore, according to a survey of Chiat et al. (2013), since Singapore government and Singapore Exchange have encouraged listed companies to produce sustainability reports since around 2010, most companies have published these reports in conformity with GRI's guideline. This trend has not changed, with a low number of companies producing integrated reports (Labrey 2016).

Labrey mentioned that Japan has "the biggest IR success story in the world outside South Africa" (Labrey 2016), based on over 200 companies producing integrated reports. However, our preliminary inquiry into the integrated reporting practices of major Japanese companies that produced integrated reports on their own indicated that many companies' reports simply combined their annual reports and sustainability reports, resulted in insufficient information on the companies' values and value generation processes.

As mentioned above, although its popularity is increasing all over the world, the availability of IIRF has shown little progress in the Asia-Pacific region. In embedding the IIRF or GRI's guideline into the disclosure system or encouraging companies to adopt either guideline, presenting the difference in the basic characteristics and stances of both, IIRF and G4, along with the governance structures of both IIRC and GRI, can contribute to the effective utilization of IIRF and G4.

Not everyone supported the recent activities of IIRC. Several commentators directed their criticism at IIRC for shifting its focus from sustainability reporting to business and investors (Dumay et al. 2016). Milne and Gray (2013) suggested that IIRF does not include sustainability issues. Flower (2015) mentioned that, although the original IIRC represented high stakes in the disclosure regarding organizations' ESG perspective, such an approach gradually reduced. In addition, he pointed out that IIRC membership did not adequately represent stakeholders focusing on ESG issues. Instead, accountants dominated the central positions in IIRC. The dominance of accountants within IIRC was also noted by Fried et al. (2014). Adams (2015) and Thomson (2015) countered Flower's critique on the grounds that his opinion was not based on adequate evidence.

Recent studies focusing on the IIRF-making process have been carried out. Reuter and Messner (2015) suggested the active involvement of large multinational companies, preparers and accounting professional bodies in the process through content analysis in comment letters toward IIRC's Discussion Paper (IIRC 2011). In addition, Humphrey et al. (2017) examined the various mechanisms and strategies through which IIRC has encompassed a broad range of stakeholder groups to support the fundamental concept of integrated reporting, based on Suddaby and Viale's theorization of how professionals reconfigure organizational fields.

Our paper is one of the studies focusing on the institutionalization of IIRC, with an interest in its organizational structure, including governance organizations, which previous studies have not addressed. This is because, as pointed out by traditional theorists like Rumelt (1974) and Miles and Snow (1978), organizations have a high probability of changing their structure in order to execute specific strategies, consequently changing their performance. This is called Strategy-Structure-Performance paradigm (SSP paradigm). According to Defee and Stank (2005), recent studies based on the SSP paradigm stress that external and internal contingency factors should be considered when developing updated strategies. In other words, it can be said that the organizational structure is a crucial first step in implementing its strategy. There were some studies based on the importance focusing on the strategic behavior of accounting standard setters, such as the Financial Accounting Standards Board and International Accounting Standards Board. These studies indicated that these setters have modified the composition of the board members or have selected members from specific stakeholders in order to resolve the problems that they faced (cf. Mattli and Büthe 2005; Perry and Nöelke 2005; Zeff 2005).

11.2.3 Theoretical Foundation

To understand the features of organizational structure, many studies have used social network analysis, which focuses on relationships among social entities, including individuals and organizations, and on the patterns and implications of these relationships, from a quantitative perspective and in a graphical presentation (Wasserman and Faust 1994). According to a review paper on social network analysis until the early 2000s, summarized by Borgatti and Foster (2003), the analysis was applied across a wide range of categories, like social capital, embeddedness, network organizations, and board interlocks. The scope of this analysis covers a wide range from studies on individuals to studies on issues at a global-scale. Social network analysis emphasizes that structure matters. For example, at an individual level, outcomes of a node, which means an individual actor or an organization, can depend in part on its position in the network structure; or the outcomes can be explained on the basis of an individual's social environment through influential or leveraging processes (Borgatti et al. 2009).

One of the most well-known concepts employed in social network analysis is "structural hole." It means the absence of a tie between a pair of nodes in the network. The network in which many structural holes are present suggests that the relationships among nodes are not closely connected. This is called an *open* network. In contrast, the network which contains a few structural holes suggests that the relationships are closely connected, which is called a *closed* network (Borgatti et al. 2009; Perry-Smith 2006).

Perry-Smith (2006) argues about the two network types as follows. It can be commonly seen that innovations are accomplished by collaborating with other people having diverse values and ideas. To promote innovations, some organizations form a network comprised of heterogeneous people with different backgrounds and visions. It is intended to improve access for actors in the network to a wide range of perspectives and diversified information. Therefore, these organizations shape the network through people with heterogeneous backgrounds and visions, constructing an *open network*, which shares a weak relationship among members. On the other hand, in some cases, organizations need to share a similar vision, to deepen the knowledge and information among members. In doing so, the organizations require close communication and seamless coordination among its members with homogeneous backgrounds and visions. Thus, the organizations would create a *closed network*, in which the actors' contacts are bound together.

11.2.4 Hypotheses Formation

Based on the above arguments, with a higher stake from a financial perspective, IIRF might not express an interest in ESG issues. In contrast, G4 highlights ESG issues. It means that the arguments were in line with the role sharing between integrated reporting and sustainability reporting suggested in the *MoU*, with GRI being the "developer" of sustainability reporting guideline with regard to ESG issues, while IIRC functions as the "applied ruler" that uses the sustainability reporting guideline developed by GRI. Thus, both organizations might attempt to fulfill the assigned roles in authentic way.

According to the argument of Perry-Smith (2006), appropriate organizational structure can vary depending on situation. This means, an organization requiring innovation calls for obtaining access to a diversified range of values and ideas. To do so, it develops a network comprised of people with heterogeneous backgrounds and visions, constructing an *open network*, which has weak relationships among its members. In contrast, for an organization that is required to share visions and information among members, to deepen knowledge, close communication and cooperation are crucial. Therefore, it attempts to create a *closed network*, in which the relationship among members is strong. Being required to transform ESG-related information to information for investors, IIRC had to establish a strong working relationship between the stakeholders interested in ESG issues and the securities markets representatives. On the other hand, in the case of GRI, which attempts to develop innovative ESG-related information, it seems that GRI needed to involve people with diverse values. Thus, the following two hypotheses could be derived.

(H1) IIRC formed a closed network in order to apply the sustainability reporting guideline developed by GRI to IIRF for financial stakeholders, and

(H2) GRI structured an open network in order to develop and diffuse new kinds of sustainability reporting practices.

In the next section, we conduct organizational structure analysis to test these hypotheses using social network analysis.

11.3 Organisational Structure of IIRC and GRI

11.3.1 Analytical Method and Data

In order to identify the respective network types of IIRC and GRI, this paper uses social network analysis, in particular a continuous coreness analysis. This method of analysis is an expanded version of the core/periphery analysis, to identify a set of actors who have a high density of ties amongst themselves (the core) and another set of actors who have a low density of ties amongst themselves (the periphery), by having a few events in common (Borgatti and Everett 1999). This paper uses the current or former jobs of the members of the internal bodies in IIRC and GRI as "common events." The thinking behind this is that careers of members who get involved in rule-making have a decisive influence on their preferences and needs for the rule. Therefore, organizational structure analysis based on the members' careers can reveal the kinds of actors and values that are dominant in the network.

To do so, this paper follows the following procedures. Initially, data-sets are created by personally collecting background information on the members of internal bodies of IIRC and GRI, as of December 2014, based on the curriculum vitae on the websites of both the organizations. Through this step, we generate two data-sets. One is a matrix data-set of IIRC, composed of the names of its 116 members in rows and the 111 organizations they are or were involved with, in columns. The other is a matrix data-set of GRI, with the names of its 84 members in rows and 97 organizations in columns. During the second step, each data-set is transformed to an organization-to-organization data-set, through the affiliation function in UCINET VI (Borgatti et al. 2002). Subsequently, the transformed data-sets are applied to the coreness analysis and used for creating graphs using NetDraw (Borgatti 2002).

11.3.2 Analytical Results of IIRC

The result of the coreness analysis on IIRC is shown in Table 11.1, which indicated the top 55 organizations getting high coreness scores, except for the internal bodies of IIRC

According to Table 11.1, the most influential actors were accounting professionals, including the International Federation of Accountants (IFAC; rank: #1; score: 0.096), PricewaterhouseCoopers (PwC; #4; 0.075), the ACCA (#9; 0.066), Federation of European Accountants (FEE; #10; 0.063), KPMG (#10; 0.063), Deloitte (#13; 0.062),

Table 11.1 Coreness results of IIRC

#	Organization	Coreness
1	IFAC	0.096
2	GRI	0.087
3	A4S	0.080
4	PwC	0.075
5	ICGN	0.074
5	TI	0.074
7	World Bank	0.072
8	Global Compact	0.071
9	ACCA	0.066
10	CDSB	0.063
10	FEE	0.063
10	KPMG	0.063
13	Deloitte	0.062
14	WBCSD	0.061
15	CPC	0.060
15	IOSCO	0.060
15	University of Sao Paulo	0.060
15	University of South Africa	0.060
15	WWF	0.060
20	Ernst & Young	0.059
20	Foundation for Global Compact	0.059
20	Hermes	0.059
23	PRI	0.058
23	TNT, NV	0.058
23	UNWFP	0.058
23	WEF	0.058
27	AICPA	0.057
27	IASB	0.057
27	SASB	0.057
30	BlackRock	0.056
31	APG	0.055
31	Securities Commission Malaysia	0.055
33	Global Accounting Alliance	0.054
33	ICAEW	0.054
33	UNEP-FI	0.054
36	CIMA	0.052
37	IBGC	0.051
37	Eumedion	0.051
37	Globethics.net	0.051
37	HSBC	0.051
37	Nestlé	0.051
37	Tata	0.051

(continued)

Table 11.1 (continued)

#	Organization	Coreness
43	APEI	0.050
43	Harvard Business School	0.050
43	Sovereign	0.050
46	BDO	0.049
46	CERES	0.049
46	Confederation of Indian Industry	0.049
46	Federation of Euro-Asian Stock Exchanges	0.049
46	Grant Thornton	0.049
46	Investment Leaders Group	0.049
46	Investor Network on Climate Risk	0.049
46	Istanbul Stock Exchange	0.049
46	ITC	0.049
46	Natixis Asset Management	0.049

and Ernst & Young (#20; 0.059). The following actors were international organizations, which were divided into two groups: (a) finance-related organizations, such as the World Bank (#7; 0.072) and International Organization of Securities Commissions (IOSCO; #15; 0.060); and (b) organizations related to the United Nations (UN) regarding social issues, like the Global Compact (#8; 0.071), Foundation for Global Compact (#20; 0.059), Principles for Responsible Investment (PRI; #23; 0.058), and UN Women's Empowerment Principles (UNWEP; #23; 0.058). Also included were international social NPOs/NGOs, including GRI (#2; 0.087), Transparency International (TI; #5; 0.074), and World Wide Fund for Nature (WWF; #15; 0.060), and securities-related organizations such as the A4S (#3; 0.080) and Climate Disclosure Standards Board (CDSB; #10; 0.063).

In Fig. 11.1, which shows IIRC's organizational structure, there are three kinds of nodes: square signs indicating internal bodies of IIRC; plus signs indicating organizations that have no relationship with any other organizations, except for the internal bodies of IIRC; and circle signs indicating organizations not belonging to the above two categories, which are represented at three levels, based on the strength of their relationship with other organizations.

According to Fig. 11.1, the most influential actors were accounting professionals, like the IFAC, KPMG, PwC, Ernst & Young, and Deloitte, similar to the coreness results. Other central organizations were GRI, A4S, TI, the International Corporate Governance Network (ICGN), which is an industry-led organization, the World Business Council for Sustainable Development (WBCSD), which is an investors-led organization, the World Bank and IOSCO. In addition, there are 25 plus signs, which accounts for 22.5% of all nodes.

Fig. 11.1 Network graph of IIRC

11.3.3 Analytical Results of GRI

Table 11.2 shows the coreness result for GRI. Only 49 organizations, apart from the four internal bodies of GRI, are on the list. It accounts for 52.7% of the 93 nodes. In other words, 47.3% of all nodes have no relationship with other organizations, except for the internal groups of GRI. This percentage is much higher than in the case of IIRC. Moreover, the scores that the organizations retain are the same (score: 0.015), which is lower than the scores of IIRC's top 55 organizations, as shown in Table 11.1.

In classifying these 49 organizations by attribute, the most influential group is non-financial companies, including BASF SE, Electroperu, HEAG Suedhessische energie AG, Nestlé, Solvay, Tata Chemicals, and Telefonica SA. Some industry associations are also present within these companies' groups, like the Confederation of Indian Industry (CII)-ITC Centre of Excellence for Sustainable Development, and the National Center for Sustainability Reporting (NCSR from Indonesia). Other groups, such as NPOs/NGOs, accounting professionals, consulting firms, and trade unions, are also included.

Table 11.2 Coreness results of GRI

#	Organization	Coreness
1	ACCA	0.015
1	Arabia CSR Network	0.015
1	Art of Value	0.015
1	Asian Centre for CG & S	0.015
1	AODP	0.015
1	Autogrill Group	0.015
1	BASF SE	0.015
1	BM & FBOVESPA	0.015
1	IBGC	0.015
1	BWINT	0.015
1	Campaign for Human Rights & Development	0.015
1	CECA	0.015
1	CEDHA	0.015
1	CENAC	0.015
1	Centro IDEARSE	0.015
1	CFMEU Mining & Energy	0.015
1	CII-ITC Centre of Excellence	0.015
1	CSO Partners	0.015
1	Deloitte	0.015
1	ecosense	0.015
1	EIRIS	0.015
1	Electroperu	0.015
1	Ernst & Young	0.015
1	ECODES	0.015
1	Fuji Xerox	0.015
1	GIZ	0.015
1	HEAG Suedhessische energie AG	0.015
1	IIRC	0.015
1	Integrated Horizons	0.015
1	Inter-American Development Bank	0.015
1	Kocaeli University	0.015
1	KPMG	0.015
1	KPMM	0.015
1	Liberty Group	0.015
1	NCSR	0.015
1	Nestlé	0.015
1	Net Balance Foundation	0.015
1	OECD	0.015
1	Pontificia Universidad Católica de Valparaíso	0.015
1	Rabobank	0.015
1	Solvay	0.015
1	Staples	0.015

(continued)

Table 11.2 (continued)

#	Organization	Coreness
1	Steel Authority of India	0.015
1	Syntao	0.015
1	Tata Chemicals	0.015
1	Telefonica SA	0.015
1	The Climate Institute	0.015
1	VBDO	0.015
1	Independent Gender & Media Consultant	0.015

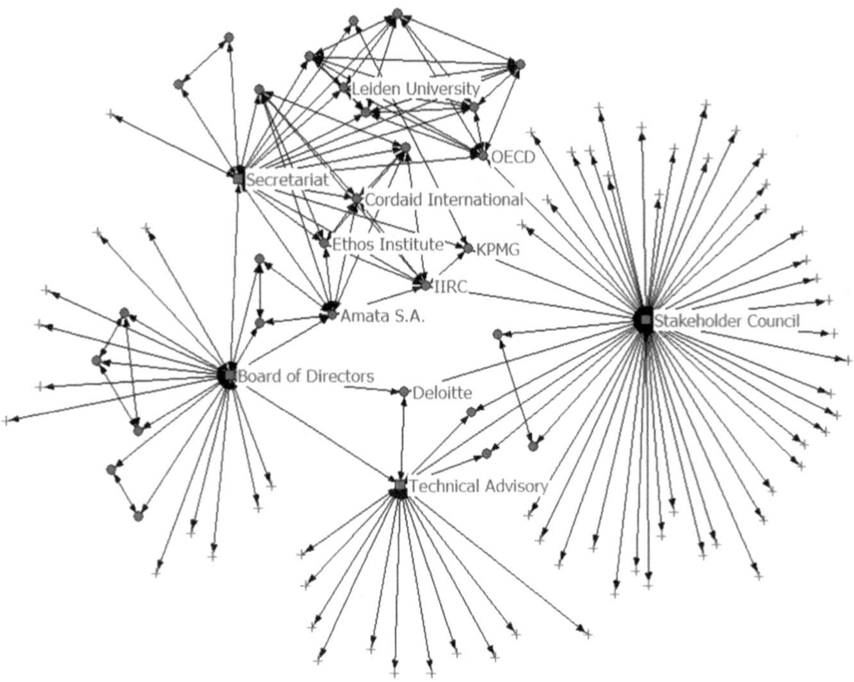

Fig. 11.2 Network graph of GRI

A network graph for GRI is shown in Fig. 11.2, similar to Fig. 11.1. However, all circle signs in Fig. 11.2 are represented in only one-staged size. In the case of GRI, a few organizations, such as the Organization for Economic Co-operation and Development (OECD), KPMG, IIRC, Amata SA, and Deloitte, work as bridges between other organizations in the network. Most organizations had no connection to other organizations, except for the internal bodies of GRI, which is equal to 66.0% of the total. It means that GRI constructed an open network for various stakeholders.

11.4 Discussion

Each organizational characteristic of IIRC and GRI is summarized below. First of all, it can be concluded that GRI was a fairly flat organization, based on the two analyses. Firstly, none of the organizations had any influential power in GRI, as evidenced by Table 11.2, in which only 50% of the organizations obtained scores, with all the scores being the same. Secondly, GRI formed a network in which most of the organizations had no connections to other organizations, except for its internal groups of GRI (as shown in Fig. 11.2), which amounts to two-thirds of the total. In summary, GRI developed a typical open network. Therefore, based on the argument of Perry-Smith (2006), GRI consolidated its position of the "developer" for creating novel sustainability reporting practices.

On the other hand, IIRC built up a network in which some limited actors, including accounting professionals, international organizations, international social NGOs/NPOs, and securities-related organizations, played central roles. Among them, the most influential actors were accounting professionals, such as IFAC, ACCA, FEE and the so-called "Big 4" international accounting firms. Fig.11.1 also indicates that these actors had many connections with other stakeholders, suggesting they were dominant in that network. The following actors were finance-related international organizations, such as World Bank and IOSCO, and UN-related organizations, as shown in Table 11.1. In accordance with the network graph, we can see that the actors interested in the securities markets matters, such as A4S, ICGN, World Bank and IOSCO, followed the accounting professionals, along with the actors interested in ESG matters, like GRI and TI.

To clarify the network feature of IIRC, we rearranged the 55 organizations shown in Table 11.1 by occupational attribute (accounting professionals, industrial-led organizations, investors-led organizations, securities-related organizations, national standard setters, UN-related organizations, international organizations, ESG-related organizations, and academics). A percentage of the total coreness scores by attribute to the total score as a whole (score: 3.213) was calculated (*see* Table 11.3).

Table 11.3 Core actors in IIRC by attributes

Attribute	Total score	Rate (%)
Acc Pro	0.849	26.4
Ind-led Org	0.689	21.4
Inv-led Org	0.233	7.3
Securities-related	0.296	9.2
NSS	0.117	3.6
UN-related	0.300	9.3
Inter'l Org	0.189	5.9
ESG-related	0.321	10.0
Academia	0.219	6.8
	3.213	100.0

According to Table 11.3, accounting professionals' group was the most influential, with the highest scores (score: 0.849; percentage: 26.4%). The second group was industry-led organizations (0.689; 21.4%), including non-financial and financial companies and CEO-led NPOs. There were no specific influential organizations in this group. The scores of the following groups were: ESG-related organizations (0.321; 10.0%), UN-related organizations (0.300; 9.3%) and securities-related organizations (0.296; 9.2%). These results indicate that IIRC was dominated by actors associated with securities markets, like accounting professionals, industry-led organizations, securities-related organizations, and investors-led organizations (0.233; 7.3%). The scores these organizations obtained account for 64.3% of the total score acquired by influential organizations. In contrast, organizations that have interests in ESG issues would never occupy central positions within IIRC.

This means, IIRC holds securities-related stakeholders in a central position, while including the stakeholders interested in ESG issues, such as GRI. In addition, 22.5% of nodes as a whole had no connections to other organizations except for the internal bodies of IIRC, as shown in Fig. 11.1. This means that about 80% of organizations as a whole in that network had some kind of connection to other organizations. In other words, the relationship among the actors in the IIRC network was very strong. Thus, it can be said that IIRC created a relatively closed network, with emphasis on the securities-market related actors, like accounting professionals. As part of this effort, IIRC would employ the ESG information produced by GRI for utilization in the securities markets.

11.5 Concluding Remark

In summary, GRI formed a network open to various stakeholders to create new sustainability reporting practices. On the other hand, IIRC developed a network that was dominated by securities-related stakeholders, such as accounting professionals, companies, industry-led organizations and investors-led organizations. IIRC applied the GRI guideline to investors-oriented guideline, in accordance with its main purpose, instead of developing new practices of sustainability reporting of its own accord. It indicates that rule-makers can potentially create a structure in order to achieve their organizational purposes and strategies. This paper illustrates that the two organizations, IIRC and GRI, which had similar purposes of presenting sustainability information to some extent, formed different organizational structures to fulfill a given role for each. It implies that defining the organizational structure of standard setter, like the kinds of organizational characteristics the setter has and the dominant actors in the organization, can reveal the direction that the rule maker takes.

Another implication of this paper is that the relationship between integrated reporting and sustainability reporting is a codependent relationship, rather than an either-or choice. This means, sustainability reports can be useful for communicating the companies' activities from an ESG perspective, while presenting them in a socially desirable format. On the other hand, integrated reports that apply ESG information to decision-making on investments can be helpful in informing investors about the value-creation ability of the companies, i.e., to evaluate the companies' ability to transform ESG-related risks to new business opportunities. With regard to increasing the interests in ESG-related problems, both reports are expected to be issued concurrently. Notably, in Asia-Pacific countries, which are making remarkable progress in their economies, even though relatively fewer companies are producing integrated reports currently, the demand for integrated reports, as well as sustainability reports, are strongly expected to intensify in the near future, similar to the success in South Africa.

Based on the situation surrounding IIRC, it can be seen that it has sought to enter into MoUs with various organizations, including the US Sustainability Accounting Standards Board (SASB), CDSB, IFAC and the International Accounting Standards Board (IASB; *see* Humphrey et al. 2017). In particular, SASB and CDSB have developed their own guidelines for sustainability reporting. It means that IIRC might be an "applied ruler" of these reporting guidelines. Recently, organizations interested in sustainability reporting have developed their own guidelines for such reporting. For example, CDSB issued its framework aimed at extending the scope of sustainability information in 2015, while SASB issued 10 Sustainability Accounting Standards in March 2016. Furthermore, GRI established an independent standard setter, the Global Sustainability Standards Board (GSSB) in 2015, which issued three original standards in October 2016. This momentum implies that leadership struggles over sustainability reporting standards have occurred, potentially causing IIRC to change its function, role, cooperative relationship with each organization, and organizational structure. Furthermore, IIRC launched the Corporate Reporting Dialogue (CRD) to address some issues regarding materiality and quantitative information in cooperation with GRI, SASB, CDSB, and IASB in June 2014. Such a collective alliance could increase IIRC's difficulty in developing a new integrated reporting framework, since it has to consider the interests of a diverse range of stakeholders. We should pay attention to the trends of IIRC in future.

References

Adams C (2015) The international integrated reporting council: a call to action. Crit Perspect Account 27:23–28

Association of Chartered Certified Accountants (ACCA) and Net Balance Foundation (2011) Adoption of Integrated Reporting by the ASX 50. [online] ACCA's website available at: http://www.accaglobal.com/content/dam/acca/global/PDF-technical/sustainability-reporting/tech-tp-air2.pdf. Accessed 2 Dec 2016

Borgatti S (2002) Netdraw: network visualization. Analytic Technologies, Harvard

Borgatti S, Everett M (1999) Models of core/periphery structures. Soc Netw 21:375–395

Borgatti S, Foster P (2003) The network paradigm in organizational research: a review and typology. J Manag 29(6):991–1013

Borgatti S, Everett M, Freeman L (2002) Ucinet for windows: software for social network analysis. Analytic Technologies, Harvard

Borgatti S, Mehra A, Brass D, Labianca G (2009) Network analysis in the social sciences. Science 323:892–895

Cheng M, Green W, Conradie P, Konishi N, Romi A (2014) The international integrated reporting framework: key issues and future research opportunities. J Int Financ Manag Account 25(1):90–119

Chiat H, Aun K, Chi W (2013) Perception of preparers and users on sustainability reporting in Singapore. J Educ Vocat Res 4(6):174–183

Defee C, Stank T (2005) Applying the strategy-structure-performance paradigm to the supply chain environment. Int J Logist Manag 16(1):28–50

Dumay J, Bernardi C, Guthrie J, Demartini P (2016) Integrated reporting: a structured literature review. Account Forum 40(3):166–185

Flower J (2015) The international integrated reporting council: a story of failure. Crit Perspect Account 27:1–17

Fried A, Holtzman M, Mest D (2014) Integrated reporting: the new annual report for the 21st century? Financ Exec 30(4):24–31

Global Reporting Initiative (GRI) (2011) Sustainability reporting guidelines, version 3.1. GRI, Amsterdam

Global Reporting Initiative (GRI) (2013) Sustainability reporting guidelines, version 4. GRI, Amsterdam

Global Reporting Initiative (GRI) (2014a) GRI's new governance structure [online] GRI's website available at: https://www.globalreporting.org/SiteCollectionDocuments/2014/GRIs-new-governance-structure.pdf. Accessed 12 Dec 2014

Global Reporting Initiative (GRI) (2014b) Forward thinking, future focus, GRI 2013–2014 [online] GRI's website available at: https://www.globalreporting.org/resourcelibrary/GRI-CombinedReport-2013-2014-forward-thinking-future-focus.pdf. Accessed 17 Dec 2014

Humphrey C, O'Dwyer B, Unerman J (2017) Re-theorizing the configuration of organizational fields: the IIRC and the pursuit of 'enlightened' corporate reporting. Account Bus Res 47(1):30–63

Institute of Management Accountants (IMA) and Association of Chartered Certified Accountants (ACCA) (2016) From share value to shared value: exploring the role of accountants in developing integrated reporting in practice. [online] ACCA's website available at: http://www.accaglobal.com/content/dam/ACCA_Global/Technical/integrate/acca-ima-report-from-share-value-to-shared-value.pdf. Accessed 1 Dec 2016

International Integrated Reporting Council (IIRC) (2012) International integrated reporting council governance. [online] IIRC's website available at: http://integratedreporting.org/wp-content/uploads/2015/03/IIRC-GOVERNANCE.pdf. Accessed 20 Oct 2016

International Integrated Reporting Council (IIRC) (2012) International Integrated Reporting Council governance. [online] IIRC's website available at: http://integratedreporting.org/wp-content/uploads/2015/03/IIRC-GOVERNANCE.pdf. Accessed 20 Oct 2016

International Integrated Reporting Council (IIRC) (2013) International integrated reporting framework. IIRC, London

International Integrated Reporting Council (IIRC) and Global Reporting Initiative (GRI) (2013) Memorandum of understanding dated 01 February 2013. [online] IIRC's website available at: http://integratedreporting.org/wp-content/uploads/2013/02/MoU-IIRC-GRI-20130201-1.pdf. Accessed 18 Dec 2014

Krzus M (2011) Integrated reporting: if not now, when? IRZ–Zeitschrift Int Rechn 6:271–276

Labrey J (2016) Integrated reporting: the view from Asia. [online] The Journal of the Hong Kong Institute of Chartered Secretaries available at: http://csj.hkics.org.hk/2016/05/integrated-reporting-the-view-from-asia/. Accessed 25 Nov 2016

Malaysian Institute of Accountants (MIA) and Association of Chartered Certified Accountants (ACCA) (2016) Integrated reporting survey. [online] ACCA's website available at: http://www.accaglobal.com/content/dam/ACCA_National/my/dis/MIA-ACCA-IR-survey-report_2016.pdf.pdf. Accessed 5 Dec 2016

Mattli W, Büthe T (2005) Accountability in accounting? The politics of private rule-making in the public interest. Gov An Int J Policy Adm Inst 18(3):399–429

Miles R, Snow C (1978) Organizational strategy, structure, and process. McGraw-Hill, New York

Milne M, Gray R (2013) W(h)ither ecology? The triple bottom line, the global reporting initiative, and corporate sustainability reporting. J Bus Ethics 118:13–29

Perry J, Nöelke A (2005) International accounting standards setting: a network approach. Bus Polit 7(3:5):1–32

Perry-Smith J (2006) Social yet creative: the role of social relationships in facilitating individual creativity. Acad Manag J 49(1):85–101

Prince's Accounting for Sustainability Project (A4S) (2015) Current activities. [online] A4S's website available at: http://www.accountingforsustainability.org/about-us/current-activities. Accessed 5 Dec 2015

Prince's Accounting for Sustainability Project (A4S) and Global Reporting Initiative (GRI) (2010) Formation of the International Integrated Reporting Committee (IIRC). [online] IIRC's website available at: http://integratedreporting.org/wp-content/uploads/2011/03/Press-Release1.pdf. Accessed 18 Dec 2014

Reuter M, Messner M (2015) Lobbying on the integrated reporting framework, an analysis of comment letters to the 2011 discussion paper of the IIRC. Account Audit Account J 28(3):365–402

Rumelt R (1974) Strategy, structure, and economic performance. Harvard University Press, Cambridge, MA

Setia N, Abhayawansa S, Joshi M, Huynh A (2015) Integrated reporting in South Africa: some initial evidence. Sustain Account Manag Policy J 6(3):397–424

Smith S (2014a) Integrated reporting, corporate governance, and the future of the accounting function. Int J Bus Soc Sci 5(10):58–63

Smith S (2014b) Strategy, sustainability, and innovative financial reporting. J Strateg Innov Sustain 10(1):19–23

Soyka P (2013) The International Integrated Reporting Council (IIRC) integrated reporting framework: toward better sustainability reporting and (way) beyond. Environ Qual Manag 23(2):1–14

Stubbs W, Higgins C (2014) Integrated reporting and internal mechanisms of change. Account Audit Account J 27:1068–1089

Thomson I (2015) But does sustainability need capitalism or an integrated report' a commentary on 'The International Integrated Reporting Council: a story of failure' by Flower, J. Crit Perspect Account 27:18–22

van Zyl A (2013) Sustainability and integrated reporting in the South African corporate sector. J of Sustain Manag 1(1):19–42

Wasserman S, Faust K (1994) Social network analysis: methods and applications. Cambridge University Press, New York

Zeff A (2005) The evolution of U. S. GAAP: the political forces behind professional standards (part II). CPA J 75(2):19–29

Chapter 12
Determinants of Voluntary Environmental Reporting by New Zealand Regional Councils

Radiah Othman, Nirmala Nath, and Fawzi Laswad

Abstract This chapter examines the determinants of regional councils' voluntary environmental reporting for the 5 years before the introduction of the Environmental Reporting Bill (ERB) in 2014. This book chapter offers a public sector perspective of the extent and manner in which environmental data is being reported. The study would bring new insights on what contributes to the understanding the factors that influence public sector organisations in voluntarily reporting on the environment. The results of the study would inform debate and discussion about whether policy interventions are needed to improve environmental outcomes through environmental reporting. The study is timely because there is an absence of pressure to comply with regulation before 2014 to legitimise regional councils' actions via environmental reporting. Our descriptive analysis shows that regional councils had reported environmental information 5 years prior to ERB. The co-relation analysis shows that size, rates income, total income, financial leverage, population size and political ideologies are statistically significant with the level of environmental reporting. These findings support the political economy theory that the managers may be in the position to decide whether to report on the environment. The consideration includes the most powerful actors, such as the ratepayers and the central government for grants and funding. It is anticipated that the new legislation would change the landscape of the accountability from voluntary to mandatory; hence the regional council managers need to reprioritise the stakeholders they want to communicate with. Due to resources constraint, they might need to strategise and refocus their service delivery.

Keywords New Zealand · Regional council · Reporting · Environmental reporting bill

---

R. Othman (✉) · N. Nath · F. Laswad
Massey University, Palmerston North, New Zealand
e-mail: r.othman@massey.ac.nz; n.nath@massey.ac.nz; f.laswad@massey.ac.nz

K.-H. Lee, S. Schaltegger (eds.), *Accounting for Sustainability: Asia Pacific Perspectives*, Eco-Efficiency in Industry and Science 33,
https://doi.org/10.1007/978-3-319-70899-7_12

12.1 Introduction

This paper examines the determinants of regional councils'[1] voluntary environmental reporting for the 5 years prior to the introduction of the Environmental Reporting Bill (ERB). The introduction of the ERB[2] to New Zealand (NZ) Parliament in 2014 was consistent with NZ's 'sense of national identity epitomised by the term "clean and green"' (Frame and Taylor 2005, p. 275).[3] The introduction of both the new Bill and an amendment to section 360 of the Resource Management Act 1991 is aimed at explicitly regulating regional councils' responsibilities for monitoring and reporting the environment. Using the political economy perspective, we hypothesise that in the period where the mandatory requirements were absent, management might use its own discretion regarding the nature and extent of environmental reporting.

Previous research has called for further examination of sustainability issues within the public sector (Ball and Grubnic 2007; Guthrie and Farneti 2008; Adams et al. 2014). Global Reporting Initiatives (GRI) (2005) emphasised that the public sector is composed of not only the largest providers and consumers of services but also a significant number of employers. As such, the State is no less complicit in environmental degradation than the private sector (Puxty 1986; Gray and Bebbington 2000). Certain scholars have stressed that the public sector exists for social and environmental purposes (Ball and Grubnic 2007; Guthrie and Farneti 2008; Adams et al. 2014) because every aspect of it shapes how people live their lives. Undeniably, the public sector is critical for the delivery of sustainable development (Birney et al. 2010, p. 3). In terms of proximity, the local councils are much closer to the community as compared to the central government and can play a more effective role in advancing the local community towards sustainability (Potts 2004; Ball et al. 2006).

To encourage public sector organisations (PSO) to report on sustainability, GRI has developed a Supplement for Public Agencies (SSPA 2005) to promote *inter alia* transparency and accountability, meet disclosure expectations, and make information available to facilitate dialogue and effective engagement with stakeholders. GRI suggests that the Applicable Sector Supplements should be used in addition to the Guidelines rather than in place of the Guidelines. In Australia, Guthrie and Farneti (2008) and Farneti and Guthrie (2009) examined the pattern of sustainability reporting in a sample of seven Australian PSOs that were using the GRI G3

[1] Local government is the system of locally elected members representing their communities and making decisions on their behalf, and a local council is an administrative body in a local government operating on the basis of an electoral mandate provided by local citizens to whom they are accountable. Currently, the local government sector consists of 78 councils.

[2] In the first reading of the Environmental Reporting Bill in Parliament (5 March 2014), the Minister for the Environment admitted that 'the environmental reporting on a national scale has been patchy and inconsistent' and 'New Zealand is one of only a few OECD countries not to currently require independent reporting on the state of the environment.'

[3] In 2003 the New Zealand government published its policy on sustainable development, and in 2006 the (then) Prime Minister reiterated the country's objective to be the first country that is truly sustainable (Clark 2006).

Sustainability Reporting Guidelines (2006) and the GRI SSPA (2005). A recent Australian study by Goswami and Lodhia (2014) showed that none of the four councils' reports were in accordance with any standardised sustainability reporting guidelines such as GRI; however, the councils reported on certain sustainability issues, which can be identified and compared with the GRI3.1 and GRI SSPA performance indicators. This therefore motivated us to use GRI to examine the nature and extent of environmental reporting disclosures by NZ regional councils.

Previous research has focussed on the extent and trend of voluntary disclosures (Ryan et al. 2002; Jones et al. 2005; Williams et al. 2011) in order to compare the underlying motivations for such reporting (Herbohn and Griffiths 2008; Farneti and Guthrie 2009; Bellringer et al. 2011). Bellringer et al. (2011) suggested that NZ provides a unique setting in which to explore the reasons why local councils prepare sustainability reports. Together, they contributed 3.6% (NZ$8.7 billion) to the total NZ Gross Domestic Product (GDP) for the year ending March 2015 (Localcouncils 2016). In the same year, they earned NZ$8.4 billion in operating income to finance the services they delivered to their communities. The communities that they serve are increasingly demanding greater and better quality services. Consequently, public relations have become an essential part of each council's agenda and, as such, there is a tendency for the information provided to the public to be 'shaped' to reflect councils' accountability as a service provider.

Barrett (2004) has contended that 'information is the lifeblood of accountability'. In NZ, the central government has in recent years introduced a variety of Bills, including the ERB. In a subtle manner, the introduction of Bills, which normally require the amendments of Acts, 'reshape' the accountability structure and require more information in the name of what Ball (2005, p. 364) refers to as 'modernisation and developments'. Regulation has been found to be effective in sealing a PSO's commitment to reporting where the information is made available which makes their performance visible (Adams et al. 2014). As such, this accountability reporting will become ritualistic and hegemonic in nature.

In NZ regional councils are responsible for managing the environment (freshwater, land, coastal waters, rivers, regional transport and emergency management (Localcouncils 2016). This study covers the period 2009–2013, and provides an opportunity to develop a discourse on the underlying motivation for the regional councils to report environmental information before the first reading of the ERB in 2014. Following Guthrie and Farneti (2008), our key research question is: What are the determinants of such reporting?

Our contributions are as follows. First, environmental issues are of local significance, with regional and global relevance. The government, including the local government, has a significant impact on the economy and the environment. This book chapter offers a public- sector perspective of the extent and manner in which environmental data is being reported. Second, Environmental Reporting Bill (ERB) is part of a broader blue-green agenda by making regional councils accountable for monitoring and reporting the environment. However, ERB is designed to sit alongside existing compliance and monitoring tools which might constrain further their resources. This study recognizes power differential of different individuals, and organisations and agencies who can exert influence on environmental decision-making by using political economy theory. Our book chapter would bring new insights on what contributes to the understanding the factors that influence public sector organisations in voluntarily reporting on the environment. Lastly, the results of the study would inform debate and discussion about whether policy interventions are needed to improve environmental outcomes through environmental reporting. Data should be meaningful to be valuable to the public thus a regulatory regime of environmental reporting is required for it to be taken seriously. Reporting is indeed not a panacea, but if the threats to the environment are not even acknowledged, they will never be addressed.

The paper is structured as follows. The next section, Sect. 12.2, reviews the literature on environmental and voluntary disclosure practices by regional councils. Section 12.3 describes the theoretical framework that informs the research, and Sect. 12.4 describes the research method. This is followed by the results and discussion in Sect. 12.5. The last section concludes this paper.

12.2 Voluntary Disclosure Practices: Local Councils' Perspectives

Previous studies that have examined the determinants of local councils' reporting are limited to financial disclosures and the incentives of public sector managers to disclose (e.g., Zimmerman 1977; Baber 1983; Evans and Patton 1987; Ingram and DeJong 1987; Laswad et al. 2005). According to Baber (1983), the elected politicians supply monitoring information to show that they, in fact, honour the pre-election promises, and their incentives to do so increase as political competition increases. In the Spanish context, the Prado-Lorenzo, García-Sánchez and Cuadrado-Ballesteros (2012) study indicates conservative parties undertake sustainability efforts in order to attract centre or left-wing ideology voters.

Several studies (Zimmerman 1977; Evans and Patton 1987; Ingram and DeJong 1987) established a significant relation between the form of local council and disclosure choice. Other studies have examined the relation between debt and size on the monitoring behaviour of local councils, with mixed and inconclusive results (Baber 1983; Baber and Sen 1984; Ingram 1984; Evans and Patton 1987; Ingram and DeJong 1987; Christiaens 1991). Within the NZ context, Laswad et al. (2005) examined the possible determinants of discretionary Internet financial reporting disclosure practices by local councils and concluded that leverage, municipal wealth, press visibility, and type of council are all associated with this practice. Their study further established that the greater the intensity of political competition, the lesser the tendency of managers of NZ local councils to use the Internet to report financial information voluntarily.

A few studies have examined determinants of non-financial disclosures such as the municipal contexts (García-Sánchez et al. 2013; Joseph et al. 2014), internal features of public entities (García-Sánchez et al. 2013; Joseph et al. 2014), and political factors (Greco et al. 2012; García-Sánchez et al. 2013; Joseph et al. 2014). Using a content analysis method, García-Sánchez et al. (2013) assessed the determinants of sustainability disclosure practices in 102 Spanish local councils. The researchers found that the disclosure practices on voluntary information were scarce and that political factors may be genuine barriers to municipal transparency. They proposed the establishment of national policies and laws to improve local councils' transparency, and suggested that accountability processes should extend beyond an economic dimension to include environmental actions undertaken. The Joseph et al. (2014) study examined the determinants of the extent of voluntary sustainability reporting on Malaysian local council websites by using a disclosure index within an institutional theory framework. The researchers reported that size, Local Agenda (LA) 21,[4] and public sector awards were all significant predictors of disclosure. The findings also revealed the presence of coercive isomorphism in explaining the extent of sustainability reporting on websites.

A number of studies have examined the environmental and sustainability issues encountered by PSOs in Australia (Gibson and Guthrie 1995; Burritt and Welch 1997; Adams and McNichols 2007; Herawaty and Hoque 2007; Guthrie and Farneti 2008; Farneti and Guthrie 2009). A few have examined sustainability reporting at the local government level (Ryan et al. 2002; Jones et al. 2005; Guthrie and Farneti 2008; Herbohn and Griffiths 2008; Farneti and Guthrie 2009; Scuilli 2009; Williams et al. 2011; Goswami and Lodhia 2014). Herbohn and Griffiths (2008) reported inherent concerns for the environment and matters of sustainability as motives for sustainability reporting by three Australian councils. The researchers interviewed three Queensland local councils who were engaging in sustainability reporting activities through the use of sustainability reporting teams. Similarly, Farneti and Guthrie (2009) focused on seven 'best-practice' Australian PSOs (three are local councils). They concluded that the environmental units within the organisations were the ones who most frequently prepared the sustainability reports and claimed that the reporting was informed by the latest GRI Guidelines' adoption, driven by key individuals in the organisations. Bellringer et al. (2011) replicated this study in the NZ local council context by conducting semi-structured exploratory interviews in each of five NZ local councils with the person responsible for preparing the sustainability report. They concluded that the reporting was mainly for internal stakeholders, and it was undertaken to demonstrate leadership, public accountability and financial responsibility.

The majority of studies on environmental reporting by local councils have examined the nature and extent of reporting; a few studies examined the motivation for such reporting (Herbohn and Griffiths 2008; Farneti and Guthrie 2009). In NZ,

---

[4]Agenda 21 is a comprehensive action plan developed at the Rio Earth Summit in 1992 to be engaged by organisations of the United Nations System at local, national and global levels. This program has been implemented to foster collaboration between local authorities, communities and the private sector to plan and manage their built and natural environments toward sustainable development (Joseph et al. 2014).

research on both areas remain in its nascence (Tregidga and Milne 2006; Bellringer et al. 2011). There is a distinct lack of comprehensive research on voluntary, disclosures including environmental reporting within the local government segment (Ball and Grubnic 2007; Gray et al. 2009; Williams et al. 2011). Research in this area would enhance the understanding of the nature of environmental accounting and accountability in social welfare and justice organisations (Ball and Grubnic 2007, p. 257).

Local government is accountable to both the central government and the local communities. In this context, the local councils are the agents expected to fulfil their obligations under various legislations, in return for a supply of funding from the principal (central government) and rates from the ratepayers (local communities). Local council managers may have the direct control over the decision-making and thus have the power to make strategic decisions and allocate resources to the group of stakeholders they would benefit from (Hill and Jones 1992, p. 134; see McMullen et al. 2016).

Within the NZ context, it is expected that a change in the Environmental Reporting legislation will impact on future environmental reporting disclosures, but the knowledge of whether the regional councils have reported on environment and the trend of environmental reporting 5 years before the ERB was introduced in Parliament is not known. Research on the state of environmental reporting by the regional councils prior to ERB would establish the extent, nature and constraints of engaging in such reporting and will also reveal whether ERB would further constrain councils who are already limited by financial and non-financial resources. This is one of the early studies that will provide evidence of regional councils' responses prior to the introduction of ERB Bill. This research contributes to the literature and fills the current research gap on NZ local councils' environmental reporting.

12.3 Theoretical Framework

The underlying motivation for voluntary reporting by organisations can be explained by a political economy theory (Okun 1970; Shapiro 1986; Clark 1991). Particularly in the public sector, managers are increasingly confronted with expectations relating to 'organisational accountability' (Gray et al. 1996; Logsdon and Lewellyn 2000). In contrast to Bellringer et al. (2011), who used public relations crisis management theory, we are inclined towards a political economy approach to examine the underlying motivation for reporting on the environment. Political economy approach concentrates on the interactions of actors within a pluralistic world (Clark 1991, p. 90). This implies that a number of different individuals, and organisations and agencies can exert influence on environmental decision-making. Our study attempts to seek answers as to what influences the regional councils to engage in environmental reporting.

As argued by Williams (1999, pp. 211–2), first, management may make environmental and social disclosures to protect their self-interests in order to foster, sustain and legitimise relationships by presenting an image of supporting society in general.

Second, management may release voluntary environmental and social accounting disclosure-related details in order to avoid possible regulatory intervention. It is therefore suggested that influential actors within the context of environmental reporting will pursue their self-interest and disclose aspects that would make them 'look good' in the absence of any environmental regulation.

12.4 Research Method

12.4.1 Sample

Local government in NZ is composed of two levels: territorial and regional councils. Data were collected via survey questionnaire from 12 regional councils. These regional councils are responsible for managing the environment, have large populations, and are expected to have greater accountability and motivations to provide environmental reporting. Large populations tend to demand more services; thus, the management is forced to address a wider variety of stakeholders by undertaking social responsibility practices and/or provide more information (García-Sánchez et al. 2013) to demonstrate leadership, public accountability and financial responsibility to the population they serve (Bellringer et al. 2011).

12.4.2 Dependent Variable: Total Environmental Score

In this study, we used GRI indicators on the environment to collect data on the nature and extent of environmental reporting disclosures by NZ regional councils. This study employed content analysis as the primary tool for analysing published environmental reporting disclosure in the annual and other publicly available reports by the regional councils from 2009 to 2013. Content analysis is used in sustainability reporting research (Krippendorff 2004; Guthrie and Farneti 2008) to determine the clear content of written or published communication by systematic, objective and quantitative analysis (Gibson and Guthrie 1995, p. 117).

Unweighted scoring is used to award regional councils with one point for disclosing an item and zero for not disclosing an item. This scoring approach is consistent with Cooke (1989, 1992), Meek et al. (1995), Inchausti (1997), Depoers (2000), and Herawaty and Hoque (2007). The unweighted scoring is the appropriate method for this study as it does not focus on the information needs of any specific group (Cooke 1989; Chau and Gray 2002; Rosair and Taylor 2000). As such, this method serves the purpose of our study, which focuses on what is and what is not being reported. The unweighted scoring method has some limitations, such as not addressing the value of information by particular user groups and not capturing the quality of reporting (Dhaliwal 1980; An et al. 2015). Earlier studies show that there are no significant differences in the results derived from the use of both scoring methods (see Beattie et al. 2004; Freedman and Jaggi 2011). Further, Garegnani et al. (2015, p. 547) emphasise that there is no one dominant scoring approach.

Two coders (the principal researcher and the research assistants) were used to score each report independently to enhance the scoring reliability. The research assistant had training in scoring reports in previous research projects. The process began with several thorough readings and discussions by both coders to familiarise with the different reports' contents, layouts, breadth and terminologies. The scoring process started with each coder assessing one report from each regional council for evidence of GRI indicators. Once the individual scores had been ascertained, the results were compared and discussed. Where discrepancies existed, those sections of the reports were reanalysed and the differences resolved. These processes were repeated again with three council reports to ensure consistency in terms of interpretation of scoring categories. When this was achieved, the research assistant continued with the scoring of all remaining reports and any problems encountered were resolved immediately with the principal researcher.

A disclosure index (DI) was then calculated to measure each regional council's relative level of disclosure. The DI is the total number of items reported by the regional council divided by the total number of relevant disclosure items in accordance with the GRI guidelines. Based on Cooke (1989), and Herawaty and Hoque (2007), the total environmental disclosure score is mathematically expressed as follows:

$$TD = \sum_{i=1}^{n} di$$

Where TED is total environmental disclosure for a regional council, d = 1 if the item i (i^{th} relevant item) is disclosed, and d = 0 if the item i (i^{th} relevant item) is not disclosed.

DI is equal to TD/n
n = the number of items required by GRI3.1 and GRI SSPA

12.4.3 Independent Variables

Table 12.1 provides a list of explanatory variables and their measurements. The data were extracted from the regional council websites, the Local Government New Zealand website and the Statistics New Zealand website.

Table 12.1 Independent variables

Variables	Definition
Total rates	Total council rates for the year
Total income	Total council income for the year
Economic development	Numerical variable that reflects the level of regional economic development measure by percentage of regional council's rates income per total income
Size	Numerical variables that reflect the size of the regional council, measured by the regional council's total assets
Financial liquidity	Numerical variable that indicates the financial liquidity of the regional council, measured by percentage of current assets per current liabilities
Leverage	Numerical variable that indicates the debt financial liquidity of the regional council, measured by percentage of total long-term liabilities per total assets
Population size	Size of the population, measured by the number of inhabitants (population)
Municipal wealth	Numerical variable that indicates the regional council's wealth, represented by total income per inhabitant (population)
Political ideologies	A binary variable that takes the value of 1 if the left-wing party is associated with the Council Chairman, and 0 for ruling party

12.5 Results and Discussion

12.5.1 Descriptive Statistics

Table 12.2 reveals that the rates and total income per year range from \$2918 to \$1,791,538 and \$9525 to \$3,139,818 respectively. In terms of total assets (size), the maximum value is largely contributed by the Auckland Council. Auckland Council was formed through the amalgamation of one regional council and seven territorial authorities on 1 November 2010. The financial liquidity ratio shows a healthy mean of 2.16. The mean for leverage (total long-term liabilities to total assets) is 8%. The populations for which the regional councils are responsible range from 31,320 people to 1,415,550 people. The mean for municipal wealth is \$0.35 of income per person. A percentage of 60% of the council chairmen was known to have an association with the ruling party, the National Party.

12.5.2 Environmental Disclosure, Rates and Total Income

García-Sánchez et al. (2013) emphasise that any innovation or reform in the public sector depends on the availability of economic and financial resources. As the major income contributors are the ratepayers, Greco et al. (2012) explain that stronger emphasis on the needs and wants of the ratepayers drives the council management's decision making, which instigated expanded reporting. In Spain, Guillamón et al. (2011) note that a local government that obtains larger amounts of financial funds shows higher levels of budgetary spending. This might include the spending on reporting regimes.

Table 12.2 Descriptive statistics of study variables

Variables	Minimum	Maximum	Mean	Std. deviation
Environmental disclosure (Scores)	10	47	25.027	7.267
Rates	2918	1,791,538	140,853	374,548
Total income	9525	3,139,818	230,023	588,115
Size	56,727	32,279,000	2,891,737	8,425,498
Financial liquidity	.02	22.10	2.16	3.62
Leverage1	.01	.22	.08	.06
Population size	31,320	1,415,550	328,000	346,311
Municipal wealth	.15	2.37	.35	.37
Political ideology	Ruling party	Other parties	Missing	
Frequencies	60%	31.7%	8.3%	
Observations (60)				

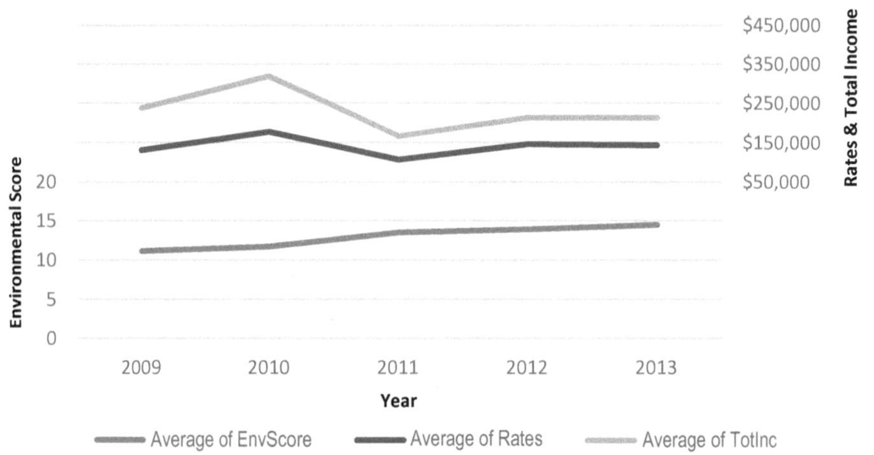

Fig. 12.1 Environmental disclosure, rates and total income

As can be seen from Fig. 12.1, rates and total incomes changed and moved in almost similar proportion. In the local government context, rates are the major contribution to regional councils' total income. Environmental reporting disclosures gradually increased from 2009 to 2013 despite the changes in both rates and total income in 2009 to 2011. Thus, it can be inferred that to a certain extent the increase in the environmental disclosures might be associated with the changes in rates and total income. This finding is consistent with the literature (Rosair and Taylor 2000; Frost and Semaer 2002; Navarro et al. 2011; Prado-Lorenzo et al. 2012; García-Sánchez et al. 2013; Alt et al. 2006). Therefore, in the NZ context, both rates and total incomes could be explanatory variables for the increase in environmental reporting.

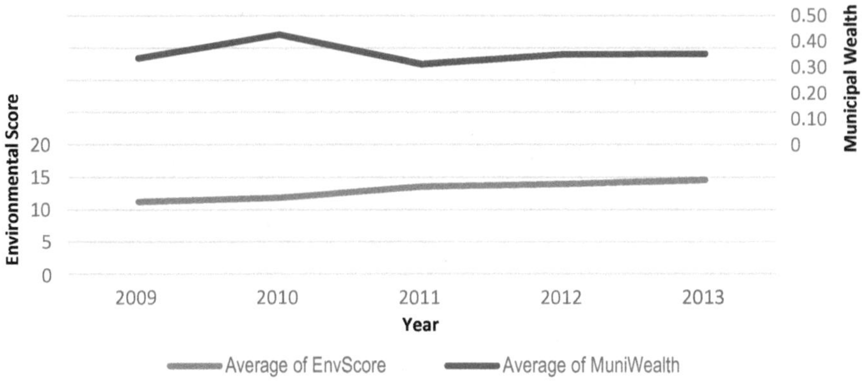

Fig. 12.2 Environmental disclosure and municipal wealth

12.5.3 Environmental Disclosure and Municipal Wealth

Literature suggests that municipal wealth is positively associated with increased social reporting disclosure. Municipal wealth is seen as a signal of management quality and thus would increase local politicians' chances for re-election (Christiaens 1999). Comparatively, management quality could be associated with regional councils' decision to report on the environment that they are responsible for.

Figure 12.2 shows a sudden increase in municipal wealth in 2010 due to the amalgamation of eight councils to form Auckland Unitary Council. This council recorded a sharp decline in rates income the following year (more than 52%). As this is the biggest and wealthiest council, the calculation of municipal wealth, which is based on both total income and population size, might have been affected by this event, thus it is more appropriate to observe the period starting 2011 when the 'aftershock' of the amalgamation was more stable. Both variables' trends were not consistent except at the start of 2011. Hence, municipal wealth might not be an indicator of environmental reporting. From the political economy perspective, the management has the potential to tell the story of their choice or refrain from doing so by weighing the benefits and the cost of doing so (Williams 1999).

12.5.4 Size and Environmental Disclosure

Previous studies show a positive effect of size and reporting disclosure (Rosair and Taylor 2000; Frost and Semaer 2002; Navarro et al. 2011; García-Sánchez et al. 2013; Joseph et al. 2014). Larger municipalities have higher degrees of political visibility, which attracts the attention of politicians, pressure groups, and the general public (Frost and Semaer 2002; see Guthrie and Parker 1990). Thus, from the political economy perspective, the management may include solely those stakeholders it wants to consider (Owen et al. 2000; Rasche and Esser 2006).

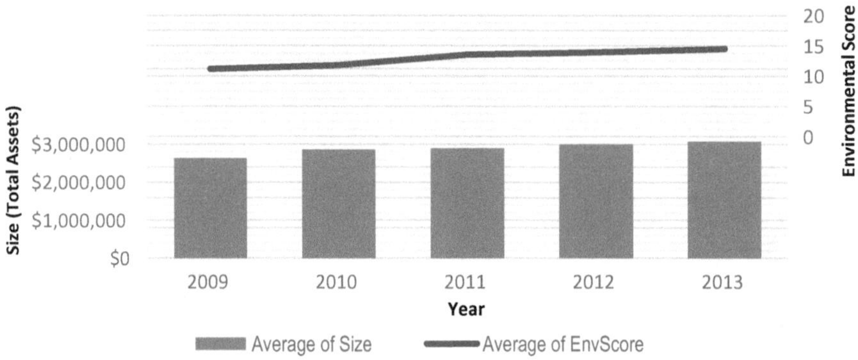

Fig. 12.3 Size and environmental disclosure

As shown in Fig. 12.3 above, the upward trend of the environmental reporting was consistent with the slow but steadily increase in the average size of the regional councils. Thus, it can be inferred that in NZ, the size of the regional councils might be able to explain the increase in environmental reporting. As explained by Navarro et al. (2010), larger municipalities tend to have more qualified staff, who may foster the voluntary disclosure. In addition, larger regional councils tend to be more responsive to pressures to report on environmental information, possibly to mitigate the incidental political costs (García-Sánchez et al. 2013).

12.5.5 Financial Liquidity and Environmental Disclosure

Organisations that operate with public funding must be socially responsible and accountable in regard to the sustainability of their operational performance (GRI 2006). Public funding provides the public with the right to require an increasing amount of information and transparency to monitor the activities undertaken by the public administration (Guillamón et al. 2011).

Except for the period 2011–2012, Fig. 12.4 seems to suggest that in NZ, despite the fluctuations trend of the average financial liquidity, the environmental reporting had incrementally increased. This seemed to suggest that financial liquidity of the regional councils might not be a factor influencing the environmental reporting. Thus, the argument by Alt et al. (2006) that the regional councils voluntarily reported environmental information regardless of their financial position and budget capacity was not supported. With management at the forefront of reporting, the political economy perspective support for pragmatism and economic rationalism fits the explanation for management's decisions.

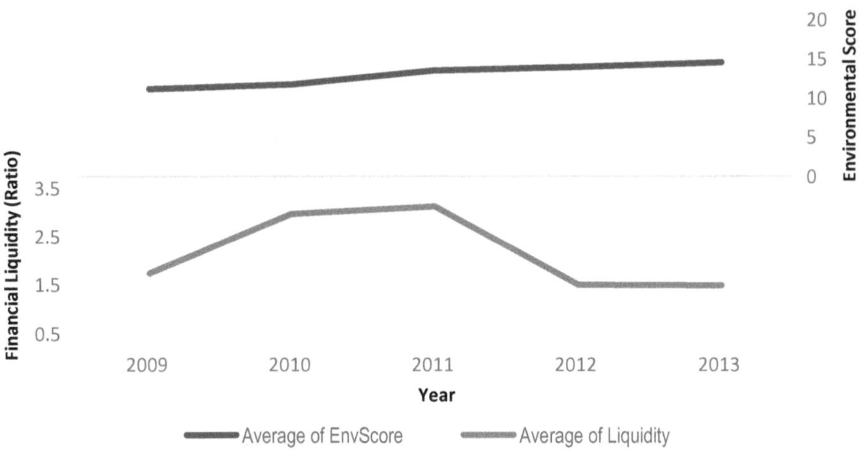

Fig. 12.4 Financial liquidity and total environmental disclosure

12.5.6 Environmental Disclosure and Leverage

It is not uncommon for local authorities to use debt to finance public activities. Burritt and Welch (1997) noted that PSOs were more likely to disclose environmental and social information due to accountability obligation to the wider community. This practice, to a certain extent, provides an incentive for public administration to reduce the cost of debt. Previous studies claim that voluntary disclosure of information facilitates monitoring by creditors (Zimmerman 1977; Baber 1983; Baber and Sen 1984; Ingram 1984; Ingram and DeJong 1987; Christiaens 1999; Gore 2004).

As can be seen in Fig. 12.5 above, the increase in environmental reporting was consistent with the increasing trend of the leverage between 2009 and 2010, thus supporting the literature (Rosair and Taylor 2000; Frost and Semaer 2002; Navarro et al. 2011; Prado-Lorenzo et al. 2012; García-Sánchez et al. 2013; Alt et al. 2006). However, the environmental reporting increased between 2012 and 2013, which was when the leverage was at a declining trend. Thus, the link between these two variables' trends was inconclusive and only partially supported.

12.5.7 Population Size and Environmental Disclosure

The literature suggests that population size is a significant variable in voluntary reporting as larger populations tend to demand more services (García-Sánchez et al. 2013). In general, the population in NZ seemed to be more concerned with the environmental issues, especially the environmental degradation and air quality, which

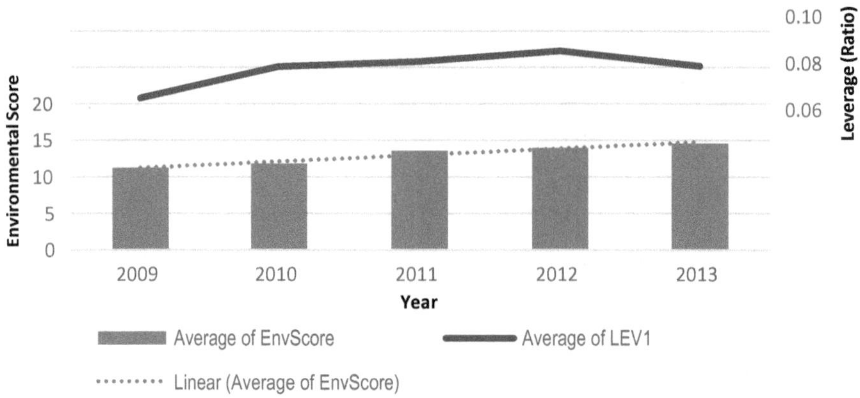

Fig. 12.5 Environmental disclosure and leverage

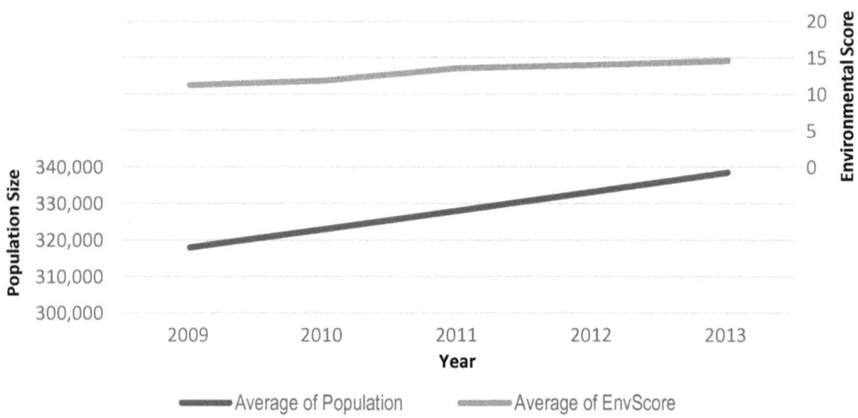

Fig. 12.6 Population size and environmental disclosure

might influence their levels of satisfaction (Howley et al. 2009). So voluntary reporting could be used as a way to demonstrate to residents their regional councils' efforts in improving the quality of life (Prado-Lorenzo et al. 2012).

Figure 12.6 above indicates that the incremental trend in environmental reporting was in parallel with the increased in the population size. This result supported earlier studies of NZ local government by Bellringer et al. (2011), which showed that voluntary sustainability reporting was being undertaken to demonstrate leadership, accountability and responsibility to the population they served.

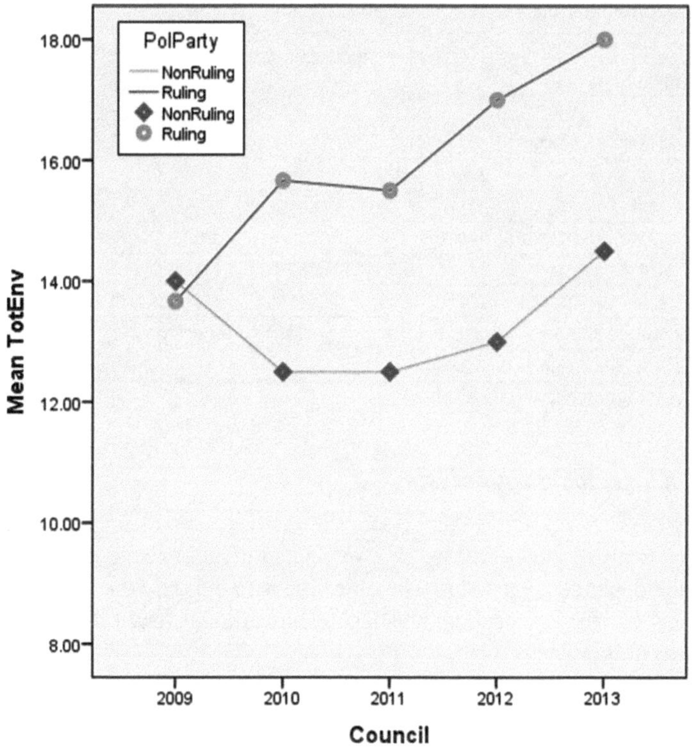

Fig. 12.7 Environmental disclosure and political ideologies

12.5.8 Environmental Disclosure and Political Ideologies

Sustainability reporting is seen as an internal initiative championed by political individuals within an arrangement between the citizens' demands and the political agendas (Greco et al. 2012, p. 701). Hence, there is a possibility that political ideologies may affect the implementation of innovations and the advancement of or a halt in the activities related to sustainability (García-Sánchez et al. 2013). A regional council might require a strong political leadership (Prado-Lorenzo et al. 2012) and adequate support from the National Party in reporting on the environment.

As indicated in Fig. 12.7, the increase in environmental reporting was markedly higher for NZ regional councils whose chairmen were associated with the National Party. This is consistent with the literature (e.g. Prado-Lorenzo et al. 2012) and contradicts with Navarro et al. (2010).

Table 12.3 Correlation analysis

	Rates	TotInc	Size	Liquidity	Lev1	PopSize	MWealth	Polid	TotEnv
Rates	1.000								
TotInc	.979**	1.000							
Size	.918**	.958**	1.000						
Liquidity	.131	.190	.258*	1.000					
Lev1	.289*	.288*	.277*	−.232	1.000				
PopSize	.970**	.976**	.941**	.174	.235	1.000			
MWealth	.489**	.535**	.521**	−.134	.587**	.433**	1.000		
Polid	.308*	.311*	.354**	.190	.022	.279*	.152	1.000	
TotEnv	.521**	.534**	.562**	.204	−.310*	.566**	.065	.338*	1.000

**Correlation is significant at 0.01 level
*Correlation is significant at 0.05 level

12.5.9 Correlation Analysis

Correlation analysis has been used to investigate the relationship between the independent and dependent variables. The objective is to measure the strengths of associations between the independent and dependent variables (environmental reporting disclosures) (Table 12.3).

The total environmental reporting disclosures were positively and highly correlated with rates, total income, size, and population size at 99% confidence level. At 90% confidence level, the environmental reporting disclosures were significantly positively correlated with regional councils whose chairmen were associated with the National Party. The environmental reporting was significantly negatively correlated with leverage, which seems to suggest that an increase or decrease in leverage has an opposite effect on the environmental reporting.

As predicted, total income, size and population size were highly positively correlated with rates. The larger the population size, the higher the rates obtained from the ratepayers, and this would increase the total income. Hence, in the light of the above correlation coefficients, a multiple regression approach to determine the influence of the independent variables on the environmental reporting disclosures was not carried out.

12.6 Summary and Conclusion

Our key objective was to determine the underlying motivation for regional councils in NZ to report on environment prior to the introduction of the ERB in Parliament. The study is timely because there is an absence of pressure to comply with regulation prior to 2014 to legitimise regional councils' actions via environmental reporting during the period studied. Our descriptive analysis shows that regional councils had reported environmental information 5 years prior to ERB. This is the opposite of the Italian society who prefers explicit laws and rules (strong uncertainty avoidance) to motivate them reporting on the environment (Greco et al. 2012).

The co-relation analysis showed that size, rates income, total income, financial leverage, population size and political ideologies are statistically significant with the level of environmental reporting. These findings support the political economy theory that the managers may be in the position to decide whether to report on the environment, depending on the context that they were in (Okun 1970; Shapiro 1986; Clark 1991; Williams 1999). This includes consideration of the most powerful stakeholders, such as the ratepayers and the central government who supplies the grants and funding. The population size also has influence over the regional councils for better environmental quality reflected in the environmental reporting. This might be undertaken to minimise the pressure from various lobby groups within the population. We also found that highly geared regional councils could be passive in reporting environmental information. They would risk public scrutiny if found to be spending on environmental reporting while having financial difficulties: in this case, avoidance of reputational risk in contradiction to an accountability perspective. In a situation in which management might be pressured by debt, the ideal choice is to determine the scope and communicate only to the stakeholders they wish to communicate with. In this case, the focus would be the financial capital (debt) provider, as part of the monitoring incentive to reduce the cost of debt. Thus, environmental information would not be their priority. The emphasis would be on information prescribed by the financial capital providers as desirable.

The support for the political ideologies variable seemed to suggest that the regional council managers could also be seen as 'embedded agents' whose social structures are subject to manipulation of the policy maker (McMullen et al. 2016). These powerful stakeholders accentuated Bellringer et al.'s (2011) claim that the voluntary reporting was undertaken in New Zealand to demonstrate leadership, public accountability and financial responsibility.

It is anticipated that the new legislation would change the landscape of the accountability from voluntary to mandatory and the focus would shift to compliance obligations instead. The juggling act of balancing the demands from the most powerful stakeholders would continue, but in the future it is expected that compliance obligations would supersede other demands and regional council managers would need to reprioritise the stakeholders they want to communicate with. This is vital as local councils are known to have constraint resources and additional reporting, if legislated, would incur most costs, thus they need to strategise and refocus their service delivery. Whether this is undertaken to the detriment of the local community is subject for future research.

With ERB, social and environmental accounting techniques are expected to form an important part of a new governance process. The process would require greater levels of accountability and transparency. Future research should examine how this shapes and reshapes the local processes and practices in regional councils and other organisations affected by a regulatory regime. Environmental accounting and reporting might take the form of working with different stakeholders. Future research should be undertaken to identify the participants, content, and context of discourse between the stakeholders. The power structures between stakeholders, such as the ratepayers, the council management, and the central government, and how these power structures are used should be examined. A longitudinal impact of the new legislation on the state of environmental reporting by NZ regional councils should be studied.

This research is not without limitations. Firstly, the data from 12 regional councils were insufficient to run regression analysis, thus descriptive statistics were used and causal-effect cannot be assumed. The conclusion made was based on the co-relation analysis. Secondly, we acknowledge that there is no standard set of factors that can explain the differences in disclosure reporting (Marcuccio and Steccolini 2009, p. 163) and certain GRI elements may not be relevant to certain councils (Goswami and Lodhia 2014).

Future studies should focus on the longitudinal impact of the new legislation on the state of environmental reporting by NZ regional councils. The longitudinal analysis can be framed into different modes, as introduced by Tilling (2004): establishing legitimacy; maintaining legitimacy; extending legitimacy; and defending legitimacy within the context of local government dependency on central government.

Acknowledgement We are grateful to Massey University for the funding of this research (MURF Grant No: 1000017839).

References

Adams CA, McNicholas P (2007) Making a difference. Sustainability reporting, accountability and organisational change. Account Audit Account J 20(3):382–402

Adams CA, Muir S, Hoque Z (2014) Measurement of sustainability performance in the public sector. Sustain Account Manag Policy J 5(1):46–67

Alt JE, Lassen DD, Rose S (2006) The causes of fiscal transparency: evidence from the American States. IMF Staff Pap 53:30–57

An Y, Davey H, Eggleton IRC, Wang Z (2015) Intellectual capital disclosure and the information gap: evidence from China. Adv Account 31(2):179–187

Baber WR (1983) Towards understanding the role of auditing in the public sector. J Account Econ 5(3):213–227

Baber WR, Sen PK (1984) The role of generally accepted reporting methods in the public sector: an empirical test. J Account Public Policy 3(2):91–106

Ball A (2005) Environmental accounting and change in UK local government. Account Audit Account J 18(3):346–373. https://doi.org/10.1108/09513570510600738

Ball A, Broadbent J, Jarvis T (2006) Waste management, the challenges of the PFI and sustainability reporting. Bus strateg environ 15(4):258–274

Ball A, Grubnic S (2007) Sustainability accounting and accountability in the public sector. In: Unerman J, Bebbington J, O'Dwyer B (eds) Sustainability accounting and accountability. Routledge, London, pp 243–265

Barrett P (2004) Financial management in the public sector – how accrual accounting and budgeting enhances governance and accountability. Paper presented at the CPA Forum, Singapore, 20–21 August

Beattie V, McInnes W, Fearnley S (2004) A methodology for analysing and evaluating narratives in annual reports: a comprehensive descriptive profile and metrics for disclosure quality attributes. Account Forum 2(3):205–236

Bellringer A, Ball A, Craig R (2011) Reasons for sustainability reporting by New Zealand local governments. Sustain Account Manag Policy J 2(1):126–138
Birney A, Clarkson H, Madden P, Porritt J, Tuxworth B (2010) Stepping up: a framework for public sector leadership on sustainability. Forum for the Future, London
Burritt RL, Welch S (1997) Annual reports of Australian commonwealth authorities: an analysis of their environmental disclosures. Abacus 23(1):69–87
Chau GK, Gray SJ (2002) Ownership structure and corporate voluntary disclosure in Hong Kong and Singapore. Int J Account 37:247–265
Christiaens J (1991) Financial accounting reform in flemish municipalities: an empirical investigation. Financ Account Manag 15(1):21–40
Christiaens J (1999) Financial accounting reform in flemish municipalities: an empirical investigation. Financ Accoun Manag 15(1):21–40
Clark B (1991) Political economy: a comparative approach. Praeger Publishers, New York
Clark H (2006) Address to NZ Labour Party annual conference. Rotorua, New Zealand
Cooke P (1992) Regional innovation systems: competitive regulation in the new Europe. Geoforum 23(3):365–382. https://doi.org/10.1016/0016-7185(92)90048-9
Cooke TE (1989) Disclosure in the corporate annual reports of Swedish companies. Account Bus Res 19(74):113–124
Depoers F (2000) A cost-benefit study of voluntary disclosure: some empirical evidence from French listed companies. Eur Account Rev 9(2):245–263
Dhaliwal DS (1980) Improving the quality of corporate financial disclosure. Account Bus Res 10(Autumn):385–391
Evans JH III, Patton JM (1987) Signalling and monitoring in public-sector accounting. J Account Res 25(suppl):130–158
Farneti F, Guthrie J (2009) Sustainability reporting by Australian public sector organisations: why they report. Account Forum 33(2):89–98
Frame R, Taylor R (2005) Partnerships for sustainability: effective practice? Local Environ 10(3):275–298
Freedman M, Jaggi B (2011) Global warming disclosures: impact of Kyoto protocol across countries. J Int Financ Manag Account 22(1):46–90
Frost GR, Seamer M (2002) Adoption of environmental reporting and management practices: an analysis of New South Wales public sector entities. Financ Account Manag 18(2):103–127
García-Sánchez I, Frías-Aceituno H, Rodríguez-Domínguez L (2013) Determinants of corporate social disclosure in Spanish local governments. J Clean Prod 39:60–72
Garegnani M, Merlotti E, Russo A (2015) 'Scoring Firms' codes of ethics: an explorative study of quality drivers'. J Bus Ethics 126(4):541–557
Gibson R, Guthrie J (1995) Recent environmental disclosures in annual reports of Australian public and private sector organisations. Account Forum 19(2/3):111–127
Global Reporting Initiative (GRI) (2005) GRI sector supplement for public agencies. GRI, Amsterdam
Global Reporting Initiative (GRI) (2006) Sustainability reporting guidelines. GRI, Amsterdam
Gore AK (2004) The effects of GAAP regulation and bond market interaction on local government disclosure. J Account Public Policy 23:23–52
Goswami K, Lodhia S (2014) Sustainability disclosure patterns of South Australian local councils: a case study. Public Money Manag 34(4):273–280
Gray R, Bebbington J (2000) Environmental accounting, managerialism and sustainability: is the planet safe in the hands of business and accounting? In: Jaggi B, Freeman M (eds) Advances in environmental accounting & management, 1. Emerald Group Publishing Limited, Bingley, pp 1–44
Gray R, Owen D, Adams CA (1996) Accounting and accountability: changes and challenges in corporate social and environmental reporting. Prentice-Hall Europe, London
Gray R, Dillard J, Spence C (2009) Social accounting research as if the world matters. Public Manag Rev 11(5):545–573

Greco G, Sciulli N, D'onza G (2012) From Tuscany to Victoria: some determinants of sustainability reporting by local councils. Local Gov Stud 38(5):681–705
Guillamón MD, Ríos AM, Vicente C (2011) Transparencia Financiera de los Municipios Españoles. Utilidad y Factores Relacionados. Auditoría Pública 55:109–116
Guthrie J, Farneti F (2008) GRI sustainability reporting by Australian public sector organizations. Public Money Manag 28(6):361–366
Guthrie JE, Parker LD (1990) Corporate social disclosure practice: a comparative international analysis. Adv Public Interes Account 3(2):159–176
Herawaty M, Hoque Z (2007) Disclosure in the annual reports of Australian government departments. A research note. J Account Organ Chang 3(2):147–168
Herbohn K, Griffiths A (2008) Sustainability reporting in local government: systems change or greenwash? Research report. CPA Australia, Melbourne. December
Hill CWL, Jones TM (1992) Stakeholder-agency theory. J Manag Stud 29(2):131–154
Howley P, Scott M, Redmond D (2009) Sustainability versus liveability: an investigation of neighbourhood satisfaction. J Environ Plan Manag 52(6):847–864
Inchausti B (1997) The influence of company characteristics and accounting regulation on information disclosed by Spanish firms. Eur Account Rev 6(1):45–68
Ingram RW (1984) Economic incentives and the choice of state government accounting practices. J Account Res 22(1):126–144
Ingram RW, DeJong DV (1987) The effect of regulation on local government disclosure practices. J Account Public Policy 6(4):245–270
Jones S, Frost G, Loftus J, Van der Laan S (2005) Sustainability reporting – practices, performance and potential. CPA Australia, Melbourne
Joseph C, Pilcher R, Taplin R (2014) Malaysian local government internet sustainability reporting. Pac Account Rev 26(1/2):75–93
Krippendorff K (2004) Content analysis. An introduction to its methodology. Sage, London
Laswad F, Fisher R, Oyelere P (2005) Determinants of voluntary internet financial reporting by local government authorities. J Account Public Policy 24:101–121
Localcouncils (2016) About local government. Available at: http://www.localcouncils.govt.nz/lgip.nsf/wpg_URL/About-Local-Government-Index?OpenDocument. Retrieve 21 July 2016
Logsdon JM, Lewellyn PG (2000) Expanding accountability to stakeholders: trends and predictions. Bus Soc Rev 105(4):19–35
Marcuccio M, Steccolini I (2009) Patterns of voluntary extended performance reporting in Italian local authorities. Int J Public Sect Manag 22(2):146–167
McMullen JS, Wood MS, Kier AS (2016) An embedded agency approach to entrepreneurship public policy: managerial position and politics in new venture location decision. Acad Manag Perspect 30(3):222–246
Meek G, Roberts C, Gray S (1995) Factor influencing voluntary annual report disclosure by US, UK and continental European multinationals. J Int Bus Stud 26(3):555–572
Navarro A, Alcaraz FJ, Zafra JL (2010) La Divulgación de Información Sobre Responsabilidad Corporativa en Administraciones Públicas: Un Estudio Empírico en Gobiernos Locales. Rev Contabilidad-Span Account Rev 13:285–314
Navarro A, Ortiz D, Alcaraz FJ, Zafra JL (2011) La Divulgación de Información Sobre Sostenibilidad en Los Gobiernos Regionales y Sus Factores Influyentes: El Caso de España'. Paper presented at 16th Congress AECA, Granada, Spain
Okun AM (1970) The political economy of prosperity. W.W. Norton, New York
Owen DL, Swift TA, Humphrey C, Bowerman M (2000) The new social audits: accountability, managerial capture or the agenda of social champions? Eur Account Rev 9(1):81–90
Potts T (2004) Triple bottom line reporting: a tool for measuring, communicating, and facilitating change in local communities. Sustainability and Social Science: Round Table Proceedings of Conference, Sydney, pp 1–26
Prado-Lorenzo JM, García-Sánchez IM, Cuadrado-Ballesteros B (2012) Sustainable cities: do political actors determine the quality of life? J Clean Prod 21:34–44

Puxty AG (1986) Social accounting as immanent legitimation: a critique of technist ideology. Adv Public Interes Acc 1:95–112

Rasche A, Esser DE (2006) From stakeholder management to stakeholder accountability. J Bus Ethics 65(3):251–267

Rosair M, Taylor DW (2000) The effects of participating parties, the public and size on government departments' accountability disclosures in annual reports. Account Account Perform 6(1):77–97

Ryan C, Dunstan K, Brown J (2002) The value of public sector annual reports and annual reporting awards in organisational legitimacy. Account Account Perform 8(1):61–76

Sciulli N (2009) Sustainability reporting by local councils in coastal regions: an Australian study. Asian J Financ Account 1(1):76–86

Shapiro I (1986) The evolution of rights in liberal theory. Cambridge University Press, New York

Tilling MV (2004) Some thoughts on legitimacy theory in social and environmental accounting. Soc Environ Account J 24(2):3–7

Tregidga H, Milne M (2006) From sustainable management to sustainable development: a longitudinal analysis of a leading New Zealand environmental reporter. Bus Strateg Environ 14:219–241

Williams SM (1999) Voluntary environmental and social accounting disclosure practices in the Asia-Pacific region: an international empirical test of political economy theory. Int J Account 34(2):209–238

Williams B, Wilmshurst T, Clift R (2011) Sustainability reporting by local government in Australia: current and future prospects. Account Forum 35:176–186

Zimmerman JL (1977) The municipal accounting maze: an analysis of political incentives. J Account Res 15(Suppl):107–144

Index

K.-H. Lee, S. Schaltegger (eds.), *Accounting for Sustainability: Asia Pacific Perspectives*, Eco-Efficiency in Industry and Science 33,
https://doi.org/10.1007/978-3-319-70899-7

Kolibri 360 GmbH
Ferdinand-Jühlke-Straße 7
99095 Erfurt, Deutschland
produktsicherheit@kolibri360.de